THEY RUN WITH SURPRISING SWIFTNESS

Peculiar Bodies: Stories and Histories

CAROLYN DAY, CHRIS MOUNSEY, AND WENDY J. TURNER, EDITORS

THEY RUN WITH SURPRISING SWIFTNESS

The Women Athletes of Early Modern Britain

PETER RADFORD

UNIVERSITY OF VIRGINIA PRESS
Charlottesville and London

UNIVERSITY OF VIRGINIA PRESS
© 2023 by the Rector and Visitors of the University of Virginia
All rights reserved
Printed in the United States of America on acid-free paper

First published 2023

1 3 5 7 9 8 6 4 2

Library of Congress Cataloging-in-Publication Data
Names: Radford, Peter, author.
Title: They run with surprising swiftness : the women athletes
of early modern Britain / Peter Radford.
Description: Charlottesville, VA : University of Virginia Press, 2023. |
Series: Peculiar bodies | Includes bibliographical references and index.
Identifiers: LCCN 2022053786 (print) | LCCN 2022053787 (ebook) | ISBN 9780813947921
(hardcover) | ISBN 9780813947938 (paperback) | ISBN 9780813947945 (ebook)
Subjects: LCSH: Women athletes—Great Britain—History—17th century. | Women athletes—
Great Britain—History—18th century. | Women athletes—Great Britain—History—
19th century. | Team sports—Great Britain—History—17th century. | Team sports—
Great Britain—History—18th century. | Team sports—Great Britain—History—19th century.
Classification: LCC GV709.18.G7 R34 2023 (print) | LCC GV709.18.G7 (ebook) |
DDC 796.092/52—dc23/eng/20221213
LC record available at https://lccn.loc.gov/2022053786
LC ebook record available at https://lccn.loc.gov/2022053787

Cover art and frontispiece:: Detail, *An Holland Smock,* John Collett, hand-colored etching
and engraving, 1770. (Collection of the author)

Like as formerly at Olympus and Lacadæmon, in more than one county of England young damsels are to be seen contending for a prize at a course. They are commonly strong robust country girls, who run with surprising swiftness.
—Jean-Bernard, Abbé le Blanc, 1747

CONTENTS

ACKNOWLEDGMENTS xi
AUTHOR'S NOTE xiii

Introduction 1

1. In Hera's Footsteps 5
2. Women Runners in Britain: The Evidence 24
3. "Of Good Conversation": From 1638 40
4. Running for Shifts and Smocks: To 1699 55
5. "A Prince's Wine and Biskets": 1700–1724 67
6. Visitors Write Home: 1725–1749 81
7. Paying the Ultimate Price: 1750–1774 96
8. Exhilaration and Athleticism: 1775–1799 104
9. The Power to Endure: 1800–1824 120
10. Moral Meddling, Cant, and Sheer Humbug: 1825 Onward 139
11. The Runners: Overview, 1638–1850 150
12. Women Tennis Players, Team Players, Fighters, and Jockeys: The Evidence 163
13. The Tennis Players 169
14. The Team Players 177
15. Cricketers of All Ages and Sizes 195

16. The Fighters 210

17. The Equestrians 227

18. Women Athletes: Summary 234

APPENDIX: Understanding Distances, Money, Wagers, and Betting 243

NOTES 247

BIBLIOGRAPHY 275

INDEX 289

ACKNOWLEDGMENTS

I am happy to acknowledge my indebtedness to the Folger Institute at the Folger Shakespeare Library in Washington, DC, for two fellowships: the first in 2018 to investigate *The Corporeal and Sporting Early Modern Woman,* and the second in 2021, to investigate the images held in galleries and collections around the world that illustrate or throw light on early modern woman athletes—*Hunting for Images of Early Modern Women Athletes.*

I am also grateful to members of the Women's Studies Group 1558–1837 in the United Kingdom for their support and encouragement and for the opportunities they have given me.

To my colleagues at *Athlos* (http://www.Athlos.co.uk), I also give my unreserved thanks for supporting the publication of the images in this book.

AUTHOR'S NOTE

Many quotations in this text come from original sources of the seventeenth, eighteenth, and early nineteenth centuries; every effort has been made to record these precisely as they were written, and only the long S has been changed. All capital letters, italics, spelling, and punctuation have been recorded as originally printed, even where there are, to our eyes, obvious errors.

THEY RUN WITH SURPRISING SWIFTNESS

INTRODUCTION

How women battled male-dominated sports in the twentieth and twenty-first centuries and overturned the apparently insurmountable obstacles placed in their way has become one of the defining stories of our age and the central story of women's sports. Of course, progress was often followed by setbacks: for example, after World War I women in Britain began to play football matches to raise money for charity, but in 1921 the governing council of the Football Association (England's governing body of football) issued a statement saying that football was "quite unsuitable for females and ought not to be encouraged" and requested that their clubs refuse women the use of their grounds.[1]

Other social critics went further: "We do say, emphatically, that it [football] should only be played by the male sex.... Women's frames are not cast in the same mould as men's, and their internal organisations are of a more delicate character.... As the mothers of our future race, they are running serious risks, which may cause them everlasting trouble and impair their life of motherhood."[2] This is only a single example from one sport in one country, but it is representative of an attitude that was international. In 1928, after the women's 800 meters in the Olympic Games at Antwerp, newspapers around the world were full of condemnation of the fact that women had been allowed to run the race and had apparently been distressed in doing it:

> Nature did not intend them [women] to participate in those exercises which call for a display of physical endurance.... In the Olympic Games girl competitors were so overcome with exhaustion that they were on the point of collapse, and it is stated that spectators protested vehemently against their being

allowed to run.... The wisdom of encouraging them in events for which they are clearly unfitted may well be doubted.... In such pastimes as football and boxing, to which it seems some of them aspire, they are only likely to become objects of ridicule.[3]

One Australian newspaper headed the story this way:

DANGEROUS STRAIN
Collapse of women at Olympic Sports
DOCTORS CONDEMN THEIR PARTICIPATION[4]

The headline was followed up with a quote from one physiologist who declared that "all women must realise that no amount of training will ever alter their physical condition." Furthermore, he wrote, "Women of this kind are not likely to become mothers." He continued, "Women are not built physically to undergo the strain of races."

Many sports organizations that had been previously indifferent to women's participation now set themselves against it. The International Amateur Athletic Federation quickly met and considered a motion to "eliminate" *all* women's athletic events from their future programs; the motion failed, but they did decide that in the future, women would not be permitted to compete in the long jump or shot put nor run any track event longer than 100 meters.[5] This decision had far-reaching consequences: women's participation in future Olympic Games was severely restricted. It also signalled that women needed to be protected from themselves—that they were physically unsuited for endurance running and for other forms of vigorous exercise, as well. Some members of the medical profession lent their support. Dr. F. Graves, who claimed the authority of being "late athletic trainer at the convalescent camps run by the British Expeditionary Force," wrote that women runners' "marked exhaustion" and their "dangerous collapse" in Antwerp would result in "serious heart strain"; if women athletes trained hard for sport they would be in "danger of a serious breakdown" and even of "mental decay." If they were to consider having children, he said, athleticism would bring three risks: "Either she will not have children (or may suffer fatally in having them) or, they, if born alive, will pay the penalty, and in what manner need not be specified here."[6] Women's participation in sports was already minimal, and in some sports virtually nonexistent, yet male governing bodies around the world set their faces determinedly against it. Those men's competitions in which women had been able to participate (e.g., road running) now banned them from doing so, and in sports where licences were needed to compete (e.g., boxing and horseracing), governing bodies would not consider issuing permits to women.

It took the determined efforts of many women who defied the rules to bring about a new future for women in sport. The names of Violet Piercy, Mildred "Babe" Didrikson, Fanny Blankers-Koen, Dale Greig, Roberta "Bobbi" Gibb, Kathrine Switzer, Gail Grandschamp, Billie Jean King, Kathy Kusner, Rachel Heyhoe Flint, and many others, deserve their place in the pantheon of those whose achievements transformed sport and society.

There is, however, another, earlier, story that tells of women in Britain in the seventeenth and eighteenth centuries who faced many of the same obstacles—and overcame them—but whose history has been largely lost. This book recovers their accomplishments. Few would expect that hundreds of years ago women played football matches specifically designed to attract spectators, were said to play cricket as well as the men, and fought professionally (including one fighter who called herself the "Championess of Europe"). A female jockey defeated the best male jockey in the country in front of thousands, and women not only defeated men at tennis, but one of them beat the "best male tennis player in England" twice in two weeks. Large numbers of women were runners, and they raced in all parts of England, Ireland, Scotland, and Wales, often over long distances. Some of them engaged in a complex racing system that required them to race up to three times in a single afternoon.

It has long been thought that women's sporting history is short and relatively recent, but *They Run with Surprising Swiftness* shows that it is as long and as rich as the men's. However, in achieving their own sporting and social landmarks, these early modern women athletes had to overcome public opinion and the barriers of their own era, many of which were ancient and deep-seated.

My main purpose has been to rediscover the women athletes of the early modern era and to place them and their achievements into historical perspective so they can take their rightful place in the history of women's sport. It is with some pleasure that I align myself with Dr. Samuel Johnson in this. In 1758 he learned about Miss Pond, who had undertaken to ride one thousand miles in one thousand hours; she completed the task in a little over two-thirds of the allotted time. So impressed was he that he wrote that a statue should be erected of her at Newmarket, "to fill kindred souls with emulation" and to "tell the grand-daughters of our grand-daughters what an English maiden has once performed."[7] Although I must add a few more *grand-daughters* to that and expand *English* to *British* and *maidens* to *women*, my intention is the same: to tell the many times great-grand-daughters of their many times great-grand-mothers what British sporting women once performed. Dr Johnson's wish is mine too.

After an initial prestory (chapter 1), the text falls into two parts. The story of the women runners is told in the most detail in chapters 2 through 11; there are regional elements to the narrative, and to set the runners into context, it is necessary to divide the story into twenty-five-year tranches so that we can see the political, social, and economic pressures that tended to shape the women athletes' activities generation by generation. There are, however, two subjects that span longer periods of time: traditions that start in the seventeenth century and endure into the nineteenth and so do not fit into the twenty-five-year structure. First is running "Kentish style," which had its roots in Sir Dudley Digges's will; second is the smockrace, which had its links in riding skimmington. These subjects are covered in chapters 3 and 4. Chapters 12 through 18 focus on cricketers and other team players, fighters, tennis players, and jockeys; their stories are more specific and more dependent on personalities, social class, and place.

Chapter 1 traces women's running back to tales told on the Indo-European plains before the advent of written history and to ancient Greece and Rome. This ancient history is not only the beginning of women's athletic history as we know it but also a history that later writers drew on and the framework through which they could see and understand the women athletes of the seventeenth and eighteenth centuries.

1

IN HERA'S FOOT-STEPS

The Earliest Runners

Women have always been runners. The myth of Atalanta—who could hunt, wrestle, and run faster than any man—is prehistoric, first told by the Indo-European peoples of the Bronze Age and then passed on by them to the ancient Greeks, who spread them around the globe (fig. 1).[1] Atalanta's became one of the world's best-known and widely traveled stories.[2] Two thousand miles from its source, and 4,000 years after it was first heard, men in England would describe a successful woman runner as Atalanta, knowing that no further explanation was needed.[3]

But if Atalanta's ability to run faster than any man was the topsy-turvy main story, there was an understory—that her attention was also easily diverted by glittering temptations. Despite her superior running ability, she was defeated by Hipponemes, who distracted her with golden apples and so won the race. Thus, Atalanta's story is double-edged.

As early as the sixth century BCE, however, real girls and *parthenoi* ran in festivals dedicated to the goddess Artemis at Brauron in eastern Greece.[4] They also raced at Olympia in festivals for the goddess Hera in three age groups, presided over and adjudicated by sixteen older women.[5] The youngest girls raced first, followed by prepubertal girls, and, finally, by the parthenoi.[6] These races could have started as early as the legendary date of the first Olympiad—776 BCE.[7] Hera is among the oldest of the Greek deities, and the first shrines to her may date back to the early Iron Age.[8]

"Parthenos(oi)" has often been translated as "virgin(s)," but its meaning is not related to sexual experience or lack thereof but rather to young women

FIGURE 1. *Running Atalanta,* Paul Manship, gilded bronze, 1958.
(Smithsonian American Art Museum)

who had reached menarche and so were marriageable. As Ken Dowden writes, "A *parthenos* is a maiden, not a virgin."[9] The races they ran were part of a transitional ritual, a prenuptial rite of passage that marked the end of their lives as young women under the protection of their fathers and opened the path to new lives under the protection of their husbands. When the parthenoi raced, briefly they were free; as married women they would not race again.[10] Why the much younger girls raced at the ceremonies has never been explained, but as they were an integral part of the same rituals as their older parthenos sisters, we must assume that their races prepared them in some way for their future roles as parthenoi.

Women and Girl Runners—as Described by Men

Pausanias visited Olympia in the second century CE and described the races of the parthenoi in the present tense, showing that the young women were still running their races to Hera as they had done for close to a thousand years. The distance they ran, he wrote, had been reduced or shortened by one-sixth in comparison to that run by the young men, who ran in honor of the god Zeus, whose Olympic festival was an exclusively male affair. Gardiner reported that the distance run by the men was a *stade*—192.27 meters (210 yds. 9.5 in.) long—and so, if Pausanias was being precise, the parthenoi would have run 160.22 meters (175 yds. 7.75 in).[11]

Herodotus, around 425 BCE, described the stade as equaling 600 Greek feet; however, the Greek foot was not a stable measure, and there may have been as many as six different versions of it.[12] Gardiner also tells us that the stade was 177.5 meters (194 yds. 4 in.) at the Pythian Games at Delphi; 181.30 meters (198 ft. 9.75 in.) at Epidaurus; and 210 meters (229 yds. 1 ft. 11.5 in.) at Pergamum. Parthenoi also ran at Delphi, Epidaurus, and Pergamum, but we do not know how far, and even Pausanias's account of the distance they ran at Olympia needs to be examined more closely.

The oldest building at Olympia was the Temple of Hera, leading Stephen Miller to write: "It is one of the greatest ironies from antiquity that the oldest large-scale monument at Olympia, a bastion of male domination, was dedicated to Hera. The Temple of Zeus, lying to the south and outside the earliest sacred area, was constructed about 150 years later. Both topographically and chronologically . . . Zeus was a later addition to Olympia."[13] It is hardly conceivable that the Temple of Hera existed at Olympia for several generations with no ceremonies or rituals to honor her taking place there; the balance of probability must be that rituals did take place and that parthenoi ran their races there and did so before the Temple of Zeus was built. Thus, the parthenoi very likely ran there before the young men began to race. The Heraian festival at Olympia took place every four years and was, of course, an all-female affair officiated by sixteen mature women who wove a robe for Hera and oversaw the festival events. Mirón described it this way: "The Heraian Games and rituals associated with them exalted feminine gender roles . . . [and] were an exclusively female ritual event."[14]

As men were excluded from this event, so were women barred from the men's events. Indeed, when the men's Olympic festival began, it closely paralleled the Heraian festival—it was officiated by the *Hellanodikai* (officials of the public games), and the young men ran a single race (the stade). The other events—longer-distance running events, wrestling, throwing, chariot races, and so on—were not added until much later. It was this larger Olympic festival that Pausanias observed in the second century CE and for which he is our primary source.[15]

Pausanias also tells us that "the [parthenoi] winners receive a crown of olive and a portion of the cow sacrificed to Hera, and they have the right to dedicate statues with their names inscribed upon them."[16] These rewards show "clear parallelism" with those the young male winners received at Olympia.[17] But by the time Pausanias arrived at Olympia, the men's Olympic festival had grown large and overshadowed the women's smaller Heraian event, so it is understandable that Pausanias, as a male, would have seen the women's race as a variant of the men's ("shortened by one-sixth"). But historically it may well have been the other way around, and the distance the men ran might more accurately have been described as a variant of the parthenoi's (i.e., "longer than" the parthenoi's event).

Describing a distance as "reduced" or "shortened" is, however, not just a description; it may also be a judgment. "Shortened" or "reduced" can imply something less than or even inferior. Mark Golden writes that the parthenoi's shorter distance would "show up female shortcomings," and Judith Swaddling comments that it reflected "the Greek male view that women were by nature inferior to men," but the young men and the parthenoi did not run at the same time or at the same festivals or, often, in the same year, and it is most likely that neither group ever saw the other race, so no direct comparison would have been made.[18] More importantly, however, the "shorter than" and "longer than" points of view may not be the only ways of looking at it. The Temple of Hera at Olympia was the oldest and second-largest temple in the sanctuary at Olympia, but it was one-sixth smaller than the Temple of Zeus, leading Golden to comment on the Heraian "shorter foot."[19] Legend holds it was Herakles who paced out the length of the Olympic stade with six hundred of his footlengths: Should we perhaps conclude that Hera had previously paced out *her* stade with six hundred of *her* foot-lengths?[20] Were Hera's feet shorter than Herakles's? The relative lengths of the feet of ancient Greek god and goddesses may seem the most arcane of academic distinctions, but it may give us insight into the position of men and women runners at Olympia and our attitudes toward them. If Herakles paced out six hundred of his feet to produce the Olympic stade, and if Hera paced out six hundred of her feet to produce the Heraian stade, then the *ritual* value of the young men's and the parthenoi's races was equal. In other words, the young men ran six hundred feet (i.e., a Heraklion stade), but the women did not run five hundred feet—they ran six hundred *Heraian* feet (i.e., a Heraian stade). In that sense, the parthenoi, in ritualistic terms, ran an *equivalent* distance.[21] The parthenoi and the young men honored their gods equally and would have derived equivalent religious, emotional, and psychological benefits from doing so. During the female-centered festival of Hera, the women, parthenoi, and girls were motivated only to honor their goddess, Hera.

The girls, parthenoi, and women of Sparta (Lakedaimonia) were the most "athletic" in the Hellenistic world. Plutarch wrote that Lycurgus, the legendary Spartan leader and lawmaker, required Spartan girls and parthenoi, as part of their education and training, to run races, wrestle, and throw the discus and javelin, as did the young men. Indeed, they even competed *with* the young men, and did so either very lightly clad or naked.[22] Plutarch thought that this made the young women modest, but this was not everyone's view; Euripides (fifth century BCE) bemoaned their lack of virtue, disliked the way they showed their naked thighs, and disapproved of their racing and wrestling with young men.[23] This disapproval was to be a recurring theme: for the next two thousand years men would raise the issue of modesty and decry what women wore to compete. We should not imagine, however, that these male concerns were always matched by the women. It is, nevertheless, an early reminder that a potential bias runs through virtually everything we know about women's sports and physical activity in the ancient world: all the contemporary reports come from men and so come to us through the prism of men's attitudes and beliefs.

Pausanias, nevertheless, is a valuable source, and he described what the parthenoi wore when they raced: "They run in the following manner: their hair hangs loose, a tunic reaches down to a little above the knee, and the right shoulder is bared as far as the breast."[24] Fortunately, we are able to confirm this account as there is a marble figure of a woman runner dressed exactly in that manner in the Vatican Museum—a Roman copy of a Greek original circa 460 BCE.[25] There is also an older, small, cast-bronze figure of a young woman runner (520–500 BCE), similarly dressed, on display at the British Museum (fig. 2).[26] It was probably made in Laconia in southern Greece but is said to have been excavated in Prizren (now Kosovo) 350 miles (560 km) away, suggesting that women runners were a more widespread phenomenon than the written record alone reveals.

For centuries the girls and parthenoi continued to run at Olympia and throughout Greece at other festivals, and their races had a ritual meaning and

FIGURE 2. *A Young Woman Runner*, bronze, 520–500 BCE. (© Trustees of the British Museum)

significance that also involved taking part in processions, making sacrifices, and singing.[27] In time, however, these rituals and festivals morphed into a mixture of tradition and sport, losing much, if not all, of their earlier religious significance, and they were copied purely as sport and spectacle in other parts of Greece. Young women also raced at pan-Hellenic games (the Pythian Games at Delphi, the Isthmian Games at Corinth, the Nemean Games in Argolis, and at other venues, too) and at Sicyon, near Corinth, and Epidaurus.

The evidence for these young women runners is fragmentary, and we can draw few conclusions from it, but at Delphi in 47 CE, Hermesianax, a citizen of Tralles and Corinth, erected a monument at Delphi that tells us that over a four-year period Tryphosa, one of his daughters, not only twice won the stade race there but also won the same event at the Isthmian Games 158 miles from Delphi, and she had traveled from Aydin, in modern-day Turkey, 294 miles away across the Aegean Sea, to do so.[28] For a young woman runner to travel so far to compete and win three major competitions over a period of four years indicates that she was a very serious competitor—an *athlete*, surely. Hermesianax's other daughters, Hedea and Dionysia, also won major stade races at Sebastea, Isthmia, Nemea, and Asclapica, and on more than occasion: an athletic family, clearly.

All may not be what it seems, however, for although the Heraian Games still continued at Olympia and can be considered as definitively Greek in spirit and tradition, when Tryphosa ran at the Isthmian Games at Corinth in 41 CE, Corinth had already become Romanized.[29] This is important because it was through the Roman reinterpretation of Greek sport that the ancient Greek sporting traditions (male and female) were spread further throughout Europe. Women ran in Rome at the Emperor Domitian's stadium toward the end of the first century CE and at Emperor Augustus' Isolympic Sebasta Games in Naples, also in the first century CE, and probably in many other places as well.[30] A mosaic in Sicily from the fourth century CE shows women running, throwing, jumping, and taking part in balancing games.[31]

We also know from vase paintings that women were physically adventurous and skilled and could stand on their hands, swim, and compete in chariot races, and there is the tantalizing image on the fresco at the Palace at Knossos in Crete from 1400 BCE of women involved in bull leaping.[32] The evidence may be sparse and difficult to interpret, but athletic women of the Greek and Roman era paved the way across a wide range of physical activities and were trailblazers for those who followed them. The origins of the modern athletic woman are to be found in the Classical world of Greece and Rome, and today the Olympic flame is still kindled ceremoniously before each Olympic Games in the Temple of Hera.

In focusing on the athletic activity of women in ancient Geek and Roman times, we should not, however, imagine that it was ever anything but a minor endeavor in comparison with the men's. Ancient Greek girls and preadolescents had the freedom to play, run around, and even be wild on occasions, but once they were married their lives were centered on the home and the indoors, which is one reason why ancient artists sometimes depicted females with lighter colored skins than males.[33] Male and female life in the ancient world was divided along clear gender lines, and, as mentioned above, our information about the athletic side of women's lives comes from men. When reading these accounts we often need to refocus and ask what biases might be skewing the descriptions and wonder how the descriptions would differ had they come from women. We can never know, of course, but this review of accounts of the athletics of ancient women teaches us not to be naive by believing all that we are told without interrogating the ancient texts further.

Physical Abilities of Ancient Women

Any attempt to understand women's activities in the ancient world requires us to shed our own twenty-first-century attitudes. We, as readers, have our own biases, often unrecognized. The late twentieth and twenty-first centuries saw women in sports creating new opportunities for themselves and setting new standards of physical performance, setting aside the centuries-old idea of women as the weaker sex, but the ancient world may have thought completely differently about the physical abilities of women. For example, take the ancient and often-repeated stories of the Amazons, told from the fourth century BCE to modern times. The warrior women of that tribe were said to be as fierce as men: they rode, waged war, and supposedly sliced off their right breasts to make it easier to draw a bow in battle, but their story is such an intertwining of myth, imagination, and history that it is difficult to make sense of. There is, nevertheless, probably a germ of truth behind the ancient tales of warrior women somewhere across the prehistoric steppes of Eurasia.[34]

The women in the preindustrial world were hardly less impressive than the myths, despite playing out their roles, predominantly, as preparers of food, homemakers, and child bearers and rearers. In 2017 a study of the skeletal structures of ancient and living women in Central Europe allowed researchers to "see how intensive, variable and laborious [womens's] behaviors were, hinting at a hidden history of women's work over thousands of years."

> It can be easy to forget that bone is a living tissue, one that responds to the rigors we put our bodies through. Physical impact and muscle activity both put strain on bone.... The bone reacts by changing in shape, curvature, thickness and density over time to accommodate repeated strain....
>
> By analyzing the bone characteristics of living people whose regular physical exertion is known, and comparing them to the characteristics of ancient bones, we can start to interpret the kinds of labour our ancestors were performing in prehistory.[35]

Using a 3D laser scanner, researchers analyzed the density 89 shinbones and 78 upper arm bones from women who lived during the Neolithic (5300–4600 BCE), Bronze Age (3200–1450 BCE), Iron Age (850 BCE–100 CE), and Medieval period (800–850 CE) in Central Europe. These results were compared with dozens of female students at Cambridge University, including elite rowers, runners, soccer players, and moderately active nonathletic women.

Results showed that the historic skeletal leg bones were unexceptional, but they identified very high levels of upper-limb loading among most prehistoric agricultural women as compared to both living female athletes and controls, suggesting not only that rigorous manual labor had been an important component of women's lives for over 5,500 years in Central Europe, but that their skeletal development exceeded that of elite modern female athletes.[36] Indeed, the arm bones of Bronze Age women were between 9 and 13 percent stronger than the modern-day elite rowers, and Neolithic women's arm bones were between 11 and 16 percent stronger. The ancient arm bones were 30 percent stronger than those of the typical, nonathletic Cambridge student, leading researchers to conclude that prehistoric women had between 5 and 10 percent more arm strength than the modern women rowers, who trained twice a day and rowed on average over 10 miles a day (75 miles [120 km] a week). The explanation for these differences, researchers believe, is to be found in the "rigorous manual labor . . . converting grain into flour" that was a woman's role in the ancient world, which not only absorbed her time and consumed her energy but changed her physical structure as well.[37]

Women and girls in the ancient world lived a life of hard physical toil that left its mark to be analyzed today. Their arm strength and endurance were greater than twenty-first-century elite competitive athletes who spend many hours in their preparation in the gym and elsewhere. This causes us to reevaluate what we previously thought about the physical capabilities of ancient women and encourages us to discard any tendency that we might have once had (perhaps unconsciously) to use contemporary women as our model for what ancient women once could do.

The story of ancient women's athletic activities, recorded and passed on to later centuries by Plutarch, Pausanias, and others, became the example that educated early modern observers used to understand and describe the women that they saw competing in races in the eighteenth century. When Voltaire saw the races at Greenwich in 1726, he looked for parallels in the ancient Olympic Games, and when Abbé le Blanc saw the "robust country girls" racing in England (between 1737 and 1744), he likened them to the to the women runners at "Olympus and Lacadæmon" (Olympia and Sparta) that he had read about from the Classical authors.[38] The examples of the mythical Atalanta, the historical parthenoi racing at Olympia, and the young Spartan women training alongside the men became the framework through which early modern observers saw women runners and athletes of the seventeenth and eighteenth centuries. We must also ask: Is it possible that this knowledge of the Classical world helped shape in some way what the girls and women in the early modern era were able—or permitted—to do?

Fun and Games in Old Europe

After the fall of the Roman Empire and throughout medieval Europe, women would continue to run and to compete in a variety of other games and sports, but references to them were still relatively sparse in comparison to the men's athletic activities. Women's sport would develop quite differently from men's: different distances run; different weights of implements thrown (shot, discus, javelin); different heights of hurdles to be cleared; different pieces of apparatus to be conquered (gymnastics); or different lengths of time that matches would take (tennis). We must learn to see women's sports for themselves and value them by appropriate measures. We lose perspective if we see them, as the male reporters and commentators often have done, in comparison to men's.

Later chapters will show that many games and sports that were once available for all to play over time were appropriated by men, who would then find reason to criticize or ridicule women for playing them and eventually prohibit them from doing so—a situation that has taken women many years of hard struggle to overcome. It is a struggle that has still not been won everywhere.

We have several examples from Europe in the Middle Ages: Walter Endrei and Lásló Zolnay list women's footraces in Florence in 1325, in Vienna in 1382, in Nördlingen, Bavaria, in 1442, in Brescia, Northern Italy, in 1444, and in Basle, Switzerland, in 1472.[39] Shepherdesses also ran races, barefooted, in Würtemberg on St. Bartholomew's Day, wearing only a petticoat and a short

FIGURE 3. Detail, *Young German Women Running for a Belt, Hat, and Shoes*, H. Sebald Beham, woodcut, 1535.

bodice.[40] They ran in Austria, too, for aprons and handkerchiefs, and in 1543 they were forbidden from undressing to their smocks when they ran (fig. 3).[41]

In Italy, however, women's racing took a different turn. From the late thirteenth to the mid-fifteenth century, the prostitutes who accompanied medieval armies when they attacked rival cities regularly ran in races. Once the attacking army had besieged the surrounded city, soldiers and camp followers enacted a kind of street theater outside the walls to taunt their trapped opponents with visions of how free and carefree their attackers were in comparison to themselves.[42] Other marginalized groups—including Jewish men—also ran races. The message seems to have been that even society's marginalized had more fun and freedom than did the besieged. Such races were held at Arezzo after years of occupation by the Purugian army; the women were required to run topless, which the Pisans repeated in Florence in 1363. Similar races were held at Verona and Sienna. Sport has many faces, and it was common for such races to become ritualized (though not run topless) centuries later in the Palio races that accompanied saints' days in many Italian cities. On the walls of Palazzo Schifanoia in Farrara we can see a woman racing in the Palio di San Giorgio in a mural painted by Francesco del Cossa 1469 and 1470 (fig. 4).[43]

Women not only ran, they also jumped. In 1263 Prince Stephen of Hungary gave Jolanta, his falconer's daughter, three bolts of velvet and a bolt of fine linen because she had beaten one of his daughters (he had four) at running and jumping.[44] Women played athletic games, too; in 1472 a young woman named Margot was said to be as good at handball as any man in Hainault in Belgium.[45] Women had raced gondolas in Venice since at least 1493 (fig. 5).[46] On holidays and at festivals and carnivals that were linked to the calendar

FIGURE 4. Detail, woman runner in *The Allegory of April*, Francesco del Cossa, 1469–70. Mural in the Palazzo Schifanoia, Farrara, Italy. (Musei di Arte di Ferrara)

FIGURE 5. Women racing gondolas in Venice, bookplate, unsigned engraving [Giacomo Franco], c. 1610. *Habiti D'Huomeni et Donne Venetiane con La Processione Della Serma. Signoria et Altri Particolari Cioè Trionfi Feste et Cerimonie Publiche della Nobilissima Città di Venetia.* (Venice: Giacomo Franco)

and the seasons, women played prisoner's base, football, stool-ball, and many more games. Such events can be traced back to the very earliest days of a community and over time became valued ways for a people to gather and have fun. They were a time for music, laughter, contests, dressing up, physical fun, and sports. People looked forward to them and attended to see and be seen; stories were told and retold about who did what, and who was going to do what, and so they became a kind of chronicle of the community's life. Stories of these festivals and events became part of a region's oral history and are difficult to verify in any objective sense; they became a blend of legend and historical record.

Games and Sport in Britain

It was in Britain, however, that women competed in sport in the greatest numbers and where women's participation involve many hundreds—perhaps thousands—of runners, cricketers, and other athletes, in every corner of the country. The practice reached its first peak in the eighteenth century, and this text tells the women athletes' story. To understand why this happened in Britain, we have to understand Britain's sporting history in the seventeenth century.

Women, of course, had always been good at horseback riding and had attended hunts at home and all over Europe. In England, Queen Elizabeth I was an enthusiastic rider and falconer, and Mary Stuart was not only an accomplished rider but also played pall-mall, golf, and tennis, which she had probably learned in France. But widespread acceptance did not come without decades of struggle.

The Antisport Polemic

In the early years of the seventeenth century, during the last years of Shakespeare's life, a strident antisport polemic developed in England. It had many strands, including the growth of religious Puritanism, which was only in part a dislike of games and sport and the fun and laughter that went with them; it also reflected the Protestant ethic that men should be sober and productive. Sport often took place on public holidays when people got drunk and lost their inhibitions and became disorderly. There was a strong Sabbatarian element to it as well—the perceived need to keep the Lord's day holy. Sport was often associated with gambling, and men (it was usually men) could lose their money and leave their families in want. Sport was also thought by its critics to have Papist undertones and was also linked by some with primitive (un-Christian) superstition. The antisport polemic grew to be very powerful, and the traditional festivals, during which sport and other frolics had taken place, began to be shut down across Britain. In 1612 Robert Dover defied what he called the "refinéd clergy" and began his Cotswold Olimpick Games.[47] In 1618 James I of England was forced to issue *The King's Majesty's Declaration to his Subjects, Concerning lawful Sports to be used*, and so sided with the common people against those who preached their antisport message. But the *Declaration* was careful to make the distinction between "lawful" and "unlawful" sports: unlawful sports and recreations were those that impinged on the peoples' duty to go to church on Sunday. His proclamation became know as *The King's Book of Sports*, and in it he decreed: "Our good people be not disturbed, letted, or discouraged from any lawfull recreation, Such as dancing, either men or women, Archery for men, leaping, or any such harmless Recreation, nor from having of May games, Whitsun Ales, and Morris-dances, and the setting up of Maypoles, and other sports therewith used so as the same be had in due and convenient time, without impediment or neglect of Divine Service."[48]

Unsurprisingly it provoked great debate that continued long after his death in 1625, and it was reissued virtually unchanged by his son Charles I in 1633. But the antisport sentiments seem to have been unaffected. In 1636 a book of poems in praise of Robert Dover and his games included a poem that declared that

> The countrie wakes and whirlings have appeared
> Of late like forraine pastimes. Carnivals,
> Palme and rush-bearing, harmless Whitson-ales
> Running at quintain, May-games, general playes,
> By some more nice than wise, of latter days,
> Have in their standings, lectures, exercises,
> Been so reproved, traduced, condemned for vices,
> Profane and heathenish, that now few dare
> Set them afoote. The hock-tide[49] pastimes are

Declined, if not deserted, so that now
All publicke merriments, I know not how,
Are questioned for their lawfulness . . .[50]

By 1643 the battle against the antisport rhetoric was lost when *The King's Book of Sport* was burned by the hangman at Cheapside. The English Civil War was now underway, and Charles I lost control of Parliament and was eventually executed. The niceties and distinctions between lawful and unlawful sports were also lost, and sport was officially banned. In many places, however, the people had lost their local festivals and sports many years before. It is true that London apprentices applied for a relaxation so that they could keep healthy and active, and that Parliament granted to them every second Tuesday of the month to recreate lawfully, but for most people in most places, sport was banned in England for twenty or more years.[51]

After the Civil War, the Interregnum, and the Cromwell years, Charles II rode into London in May 1660 to mark the return of the monarchy. Charles's accession signaled not only that sport was once again permitted—it was actively encouraged, for Charles II was himself a patron and an active participant in sport. The mood in the country was jubilant, and the people embraced their old sports with a profound enthusiasm, for they had regained something that they thought they had lost forever. Sports were taken up by the young, who had heard about them from their parents and grandparents. Members of the new Royal Society began to study them and surveyed the sports and games that were played before the ban by interviewing older people to ensure that knowledge of the traditional sports would not be lost.[52] The nation went sports-mad, taking up the old ones again and inventing new ones, and they found themselves to be very good at them.

Academics began to tell stories about the old festivals and reported how Pope Gregory had written to Melitus the Abbott in 601 CE, instructing him to embrace the old pre-Christian festivals that the Romans had found in Britain but to merge them with the new Christian ones.[53] At a stroke the church festivals at Easter, Whitsuntide, and Christmas acquired a history as old as the nation itself—indeed, older than Christianity. The sports that people played had been there before the Romans arrived; they were England itself. Poems were written in which the people's sports and recreation defined the English populace and embodied the very spirit of Englishness. So confident did people become about the importance of their sports that the Olympic Games and other sports of antiquity were said to be as good as the English ones, and not, you will note, the other way around.[54]

Women embraced the new, old sports as much as did the men, but they had barriers to face that did not exist for men. Two significant pillars of every community—the doctor and the priest—held beliefs and attitudes that were significant impediments to women taking part in sport.

The Doctors and Medicine—Women's Coldness

Medieval medicine was still dominated by the ideas of Aristotle, Hippocrates, and Galen and supported the theory of bodily fluids and the four humors, each of which had the qualities of hotness-coldness or dryness-wetness and had derived from animal dissection. From these observations Galen concluded that humankind was the most perfect of all animals and that men were more perfect than women. The balance of hotness and coldness in a man's body was deemed to be the ideal, but women were colder and wetter, and this caused their differences (i.e., defects). "The female is less perfect than the males for one, principal reason—because she is colder." From this coldness stemmed her structure as a female; her reproductive organs were the same as men's, except they were defective and had remained in her body because of her lack of heat. Her reproductive capacity was based on heat, too: if her heat increased, it reduced her femininity and compromised her ability to conceive. Women needed to be kept calm and cool, and Galen's influence remained strong until at least the late seventeenth century; in some cases it prevailed well into the eighteenth.[55]

The Priests and the Scriptures—the Weaker Vessel

For early modern women in England, church attendance on Sunday was more or less mandatory, and it was in church that their life landmarks were played out: baptism, the reading of their banns before marriage, marriage itself, the baptism of their children, the funerals of their family members, and eventually their own funerals. And it was in church that they learned from an early age about their status within the family and within society. As soon as the Holy Bible was translated into English by Tyndale in 1525, women and men learned that wives were the "weaker vessel": "Lykewyse ye men dwell with them accordinge to knowledge gevinge honoure vnto the wyfe as vnto the weaker vessell and as vnto them that are heyres also of the grace of lyfe that youre prayers be not let." This exact phrase was later adopted in the King James Bible (1611): "Likewise, ye husbands, dwell with *them* according to knowledge, giving honour unto the wife, as unto the weaker vessel, and as being heirs together of the grace of life; that your prayers be not hindered" (1 Peter 3:7). Because this was advice to husbands, it was frequently used in marriage ceremonies and so became a very well-known expression, used frequently in and outside church.

The context is important, and the advice to husbands to treat their wives as weaker vessels is said to be a way of honoring them, but the term passed into common usage and soon escaped this biblical constraint. William Shakespeare used it on several occasions—in *Romeo and Juliet, Love's Labour's Lost, As you Like It,* and *Henry IV Part II*[56]—and although he puts the words into the mouths of men in the first two plays, in *As You Like It* he puts them into Rosalind's mouth when she is dressed as a man; and in *Henry IV Part II* Mistress Quickly uses it as an insult to Doll Tearsheat, telling her that she is not only the weaker vessel but an empty one, as well. Tearsheat offers a quick reply: How can she possibly be a weak, empty vessel when she has had so much to drink, and is, apparently, not leaking? The empty vessel was such a commonplace expression it became almost a standard way to describe a woman and was part of everyday banter.

If Shakespeare was able to expand the "weaker vessel" into "weaker and emptier," we can be sure that others did as well; "weaker," after all, means less strong. It also meant weaker *than* . . . and, of course, weaker than men! And men were quick to extrapolate women's other perceived weaknesses, and sometimes under the guise of protecting them they would limit what these weaker vessels could do—only for their own good, of course. It is only a small step to the conclusion that women were weaker intellectually, spiritually, and morally. In a physical sense, men also found reason to limit what activities women were permitted to do. A weaker vessel needs protecting.

Women also needed to be protected from the gaze of other men and from any innate tendency the women themselves might have had toward immorality. If they attempted to shed any of their voluminous layers of clothing to run or play a game, they risked being described as immodest or even immoral. It was even said that taking part in vigorous physical exercise made them unattractive to men. And, of course, it would not be safe for their weaker bodies to do things that were too physically demanding. Moreover, "experts," even medical men, loudly asserted that some vigorous physical activities would harm women's child-bearing capabilities, and so it fell to men to protect women from themselves by restricting their activities.

Women's Gait

Men were not only vigilant in ensuring that women did not reveal too much of their bodies to the gaze of other men, they were also critically aware of the attractiveness of women: how women appeared and how they moved was important to them. In 1687 John Shirley gave the following advice to "Young Gentlewomen":

> Observe that you walk not carelessly or lightly, shouldering, as it were your companion, nor strutting or jutting in a proud manner; Keep (in your walk) your Head steady, your Countenance not too much elevated, nor too much dejected; Keep your Arms likewise steady and throw them not about as if you were flying; Let your Feet rather incline a little more inward than outward, lest you be censured Splay-footed. . . . Do not run or go extream fast in places of Concourse, unless great occasion require it; for in such violent motions it is not always in your power to keep your Body steady; nay by such haste you may chance to fall, and expose to view what you would conceal.[57]

The author's concern about the possibility of young gentlewoman falling was not that she might hurt herself but that she might reveal part of her body that men would see.

Such advice would hardly be encouraging to any young woman wanting to run or take part in any sport, and men's attitudes seem to have stayed much the same over the following one hundred years. Dr. Beattie expressed it this way in 1783:

> I think it is Rousseau, who observes, that, in running, a woman has nothing of that grace, which attends her on other occasions. Perhaps the jutting out of her elbows, the natural effect of endeavoring with lifted hands to secure the most delicate part of her female frame, may give her motion the appearance

of timidity and constraint. Or perhaps she may seem to fail in this exercise, merely because, according to our manners, she cannot be much accustomed to it. Ovid says, that Daphne's beauty was heightened by her running; but he accounts for it, without any contradiction to this philosophy. Virgil, in celebrating the speed of Camilla, says not a word of the gracefulness of her motion.[58]

Beattie acknowledges that women "may seem to fail" in running because they were unaccustomed to it, but an anonymous writer to the *Gentleman's Magazine* the following year expanded on Beattie's observation and came to a different conclusion: "It is observed, that the running of women is ungraceful, 'perhaps from the jetting out of their elbows.' Quere whether it may be owing to the different conformation of the joints of the hips and knees in women, to those of men, rendering the former what is vulgarly called, knock knee'd."[59] The writer thus concludes that, contrary to men, women were ungraceful when they ran because they were born that way. When women ran and played sport in the seventeenth and eighteenth centuries, they did so knowing not only that men often disapproved of what they did but also did not like what they looked like when they did it.

After the Restoration of the monarchy in 1660, women and girls took up the old sports and physical recreations and took part in new ones as soon as men, but when they did so we should not imagine that they were doing the same thing—women's participation was always enacted against the background that it was not right, or safe, or natural, or moral, or suitable, or even allowed, and that men were likely to be critical even of what they looked like. They took part nevertheless.

2

WOMEN RUNNERS IN BRITAIN
The Evidence

There is no single, reliable source about women runners in Britain in the seventeenth and eighteenth centuries, so our knowledge of them has to be accumulated from the many fragments that are to be found in ballads, posters, poems, novels, letters, diaries, handbills, images, court proceedings, and even wills. After the appearance of Britain's first daily newspaper, the *Daily Courant,* in 1702, an enormous number of other local newspapers were launched that contain advertisements and notices of women's races, and they added greatly to the mass of available information.[1]

All of the available references to women and girls running in competitive races between 1639 and 1825 have been collected in a database that records, where possible, the date, time, location, distance run, results, and the number and description of the runners, as well as their ages, names, what they wore, prizes, how the prizes were funded, officials, spectators, and other events or activities taking place at the same time. This collection of data allows patterns to emerge and consistencies, variations, and trends to be identified. They are summarized in table 1.

The data in table 1 represents nearly two thousand runners, but many more races are still to be discovered: several races are described as "annual" or as taking place "as usual," but we have no other notice of them. In 1779, for example, "young women running" were reported to have competed "for a shift decorated with crimson ribbands" at Slough Fair, "according to annual custom," but no previous report of the competition has been found. Some missing events can be inferred, however; there can be little doubt that Dover's Olimpicks took place annually in the chronological eighteenth century (1700–1799), but we have records of only fifteen of them. However, we should not doubt the existence of

TABLE 1. Footraces run by women in Britain in the long eighteenth century

	RACES IN ENGLAND	LOCATIONS IN ENGLAND	ENGLISH COUNTIES REPRESENTED	RACES IN IRELAND	RACES IN SCOTLAND	RACES IN WALES
1639–99	10	9	5		2	
1700–1724	63	33	16			
1725–49	76	48	20	3		
1750–74	65	47	20	1	2	1
1775–99	105	47	16		7	1
1800–24	183	91	26			
TOTAL	502	257*	36†	4	11	2

* Some locations hosted multiple races across the decades; the total shown takes this repetition into account.
† This counts in this column include counties that hosted races more than once (or at more than one location) across the decades; the total number of counties in which there are records of races run is 36.

the others eighty-five, although they are not included in this study. Similarly, the races at Old Wives Lees were almost certainly held every year during the eighteenth century, but records of only twelve seem to have survived. On that basis we might estimate that the current total of races in the database represents 15 percent or less of those that actually took place, but even that may be an underestimate—evidence of all eighteenth-century sport is surprisingly sparse. Take, for example, two male runners—"the famous and noted John Appleby" and "the noted Pinwherie"—who ran a ten-mile race against each other in 1733; printed reports note that the latter "has won 102 matches since 1792," but so far we have been able to document only one.[2] Thomas Trundley in 1794 wrote to the *Sporting Magazine* giving details of six races he ran in the 1730s, but there is no corroborating contemporary report of any of them.[3] It is likely that our current knowledge of eighteenth-century female and male runners only reflects a tiny percentage of those who actually took part.

In the chapters that follow I draw evidence from printed advertisements, notices, literary works, and from artists' images to create as complete a picture as possible of women runners. One thing becomes clear at once—their races were held in almost every corner of England.

Print Advertisements and a Note on Geography

Table 1 shows the number of counties in which there are records of women's footraces in England in each period studied here. County borders were not entirely stable, and in the nineteenth and twentieth centuries some county boundaries were changed, some counties were merged with others, and new counties were created; the numbers listed here reflect the counties as they were in the eighteenth century. Place-names also vary over time; where possible, I give the modern spelling in square brackets after the name that was used contemporarily. In addition, place-names were sometimes so vague that it is not always possible to pinpoint the precise location within the given area.

During the long eighteenth century, advertisements and notices were placed in newspapers to achieve two broad objectives. Some advertisements aimed to inform the public about an event—its date, time, and venue—and were clearly designed to attract crowds of spectators or customers. Others were aimed at attracting the runners and gave them information about the prizes on offer, the distance to be run, the style of racing (e.g., best-of-three), and when and where contestants should make their entries. Restrictions, such as age or where the runners lived, and any possible entry fees were also given. Many ads also specified the minimum number of runners that would be necessary for the race to go ahead and so gave a warning to the public and to the runners.

These advertisements are a significant source of our knowledge of women's eighteenth-century foot racing, but we only have results or reports of about 20 percent of the events that were advertised during the long eighteenth century. Over time this percentage increased, so by the nineteenth century 90 percent of our knowledge of events comes from newspapers that gave results or reports or races *after* they had been run but that were rarely advertised in advance.

Analysis of newspaper advertisements reveals that more than half were aimed at the public only; it is safe to suppose, then, that organizers either had other ways of contacting runners and making arrangements beforehand or they just assumed that runners would turn up. In the nineteenth century it was the practice for the women and girl runners to enter on the day of the event. Arrangements for women's footrace *wagers*, however, were quite different and also quite rare; they were private agreements between two parties who rarely welcomed a crowd, so our knowledge of them usually comes from reports of such wagers printed after the event.

In addition to the advertisements, reports, and comments about specific races, there are others references that cannot be quantified and analyzed in a database—those that appear in literature and in art, and which give us a more qualitative view.

Literature

Authors may base their work on factual events or tell stories that they think their audience will believe, but they then fashion them to suit their intention. In John Gay's *The Shepherd's Week* (1714), a poem in the Classical style about shepherds and milkmaids, the author makes passing reference to the running speed of "Deb'rah that won the smock."[4] Whether Deb'rah was based on a living person is unknown, nor do we know whether she would have fitted into his bucolic and somewhat romantic framework if she did.

In the same year the Rev. James Ward continued the rustic, pastoral theme with *The Smock-Race, at Finglas*, set in Ireland, in which Oonah, Nora, and Shevan race for a smock.[5] The sweating spectators, lured by bagpipes, leave their harvest labors and gather with the "smock high in Air display'd." The three runners "all view the waving Smock with longing Eye," and the race begins. Oonah, however, had to stop to retie the string holding up her petticoat so as not to "Expose her hidden Charms to vulgar Eyes." Weeping, she races after the other two and eventually passes them and wins "the noblest prize" to the shouts and acclamations of the crowd. Felim, however, had been watching Oonah throughout:

> Stript for the Race how bright did she appear!
> No Cov'ring hid her Feet, her Bosom bare
> And to the Wind she gave her flowing Hair.
> A thousand Charms he saw, conceal'd before
> Those, yet conceal'd, he fancy'd still were more.

And the poem finishes with the memorable couplet:

> Oonah e'er Morn the Sweets of Wedlock try'd
> The Smock she won a Virgin, wore a Bride.

As an imaginative narrative it is effective enough: Oonah pursues the smock while Felim pursues Oonah, and both are successful. A happy-ever-after story. But can we rely on the details as historical truth? We can believe that such a race took place in the late summer or early autumn and that crowds gathered, briefly taking a break from their harvesting chores; were it not so, readers would not believe the story at all. There is also no reason to disbelieve that there were three runners, as it is consistent with what we know from other sources; we can believe, too, that the runners ran barefooted, but are we to believe that her "bosom" was "bare," or is that just a convenient rhyme for "flowing hair"? Within the context of the whole, "bare" seems to be an overstatement and inconsistent with the rest of the poem, in which Oonah struggled to conceal her "hidden charms" while Felim imagined them. We might expect the poet to explore the hidden thoughts of Oonah, who is striving to win the smock, and of Felim, who strives to win Oonah, but he adds nothing reliable to our factual knowledge of women's foot racing.

William Somervile's long, mock-heroic poem *Hobbinol, or the Rural Games* tells much the same story, and we know that he must have been familiar with Ward's poem, for he reuses two of his lines, slightly changing them to "To win a Virgin, and to wear a Bride."[6] Published in 1740, it was based on an earlier work, *The Wicker Chair*, written in 1708, closer to the date of the race he describes. Canto III gives an account of a race between Ganderetta, Fusca (a Roma girl), and Tabitha for a "rich laced smock," probably based on events at Dover's Olimpick Games, which were held less than twenty miles from Somervile's home; the lines have the feel of an eyewitness account. As in *The Smock-Race, at Finglas,* there is a large, rowdy crowd and three runners, and once again one of the runners, Ganderetta, wins not only the race but the love of Hobbinol, who, at the games' beginning had been chosen King of May, while Ganderetta was chosen queen. This is not a happy-ever-after story, but the story carries many of Ward's themes: fate intervenes, one runner drops out, and, to the crowd's delight, Fusca slips and falls, leaving Ganderetta to win the smock and Hobbinol's heart. And here, also, a runner's "hidden charms" are on show:

> Her Looks assure Success, now strip'd of all
> Her cumb'rous Vestments, Beauty's vain Disguise,

She shines unclouded in her native Charms.

. . . .

Her heaving Breast, thro' the thin Cov'ring view'd,
Fix'd each Beholder's Eye; her taper Thighs,
And Lineaments exact, wou'd mock the Skill
Of Phidias . . .

So, once again, it is not just the runners' athletic ability that was being closely watched. Unlike Ward's poem, this event was part of a larger occasion that included dancing, cudgeling, and much more and was perhaps similar to the events that were described in a letter about a supposed "country wake" that appeared in September 1711 in the *Spectator*.[7] It told of cudgel players, a football match, wrestlers, and women pitching the bar and explained that the underlying purpose of such wakes was that both the young men and maids "strived to recommend theselves to each other, by making it appear that they were all in a perfect state of health, and fit to undergo any fatigues of bodily labour."

In reply, the *Spectator* (in this case Eustace Budgell) informed the readers that such "bodily exercises or games were formerly encouraged in all the commonwealths of Greece, from which the Romans afterwards borrowed their Pentathlum." He went on to say that "love and marriage are the natural effects of these anniversary assemblies" and that "nothing seems more likely to promise a healthy offspring or a happy cohabitation." He concluded with some historical context from White Kennet, who wrote in 1695 "that this laudable Custom of Wakes prevailed for many Ages, till the nice Puritans began to exclaim against it as a Remnant of Popery."[8] It is tempting to accept many of the small details that Somervile gives, such as the Master of the Ring establishing the course by pacing it out and the description of Tabitha as a successful runner who was the pride of Tewkesbury and had won "many a Prize" there, but the tale as a whole is an entertaining fable that does little to enrich the historical record.

On a much more domestic level, the vicar's wife in Oliver Goldsmith's *Vicar of Wakefield* (1766) complains that smock running was not in keeping with the decorum and gentility that was expected of young women: "You know the church is two miles off, and I protest I don't like to see my daughters trudging up to their pew all blowzed and red with walking, and looking for all the world as if they had been winners at a smock race."[9] She reminds us that women and girls who raced could not always expect approval, even at home.

In 1773, under the pseudonym Geoffry Wildgoose, the Rev. Richard Graves published a "comic romance" in three volumes entitled *The Spiritual Quixote*.[10] In it he takes us to Dover's Olimpicks, which he must have known well, for it was held only three miles from his home at Mikelton. In volume 1 Geoffry Wildgoose, a travelling Methodist preacher, approaches six "young women" who were preparing to run for a "holland smock" and lectures them that they are "making provision for the lusts of the flesh" and that instead of wanting such smocks with their pink ribbons, they should "labour after the celestial robes, the spiritual decorations and saint-like ornaments of piety, meekness, and chastity."[11] Unconvinced, the young women continue with their race "in a dress hardly reconcilable to the rules of decency." The minister's message had clearly fallen on deaf ears, and he is driven away by orange peel, horse dung, and clods of earth thrown at him by the crowd, as had happened to Hudibras a century earlier (see chapter 4).

The context of Graves's novel makes his observations difficult to interpret. The text was supposed to have been written "some years ago" about events that had taken place at an even earlier unspecified time by an author (i.e., Wildgoose) who had been inspired by the writings of those who opposed "the regular clergy and the established church." However, Graves, an ordained minister in the Church of England, created a narrator who was a sort of itinerant, self-appointed Methodist; thus, he was expressing through Geoffry Wildgoose the attitudes that he thought a Methodist minister would have had perhaps two or three generations earlier. Who these opinions really belong to is lost in the telling and adds little that is reliable to the historical record.

Women in a footrace next appear in literature in 1778 in Frances Burney's epistolary novel *Evelina*.[12] Volume 3, letters 64–68, tell the story of two men, Mr. Coverley and Lord Merton, who, to settle a wager of £1,000 between them, arrange a footrace between two eighty-year-old women. All the other members of their party were encouraged to take sides and lay bets. In the race, the two women collide and fall on a gravel path, bruising themselves badly; the race, however, was resumed. When one woman slipped and fell again, spectators who rushed to help were greeted with cries of "no foul play!" Any help given her would have interfered with the outcome of the wager.

The fallen woman was too hurt to move and so lost the race, and the man for whom she was running swore at her with "unmanly rage, and seemed scarce able to refrain from striking her."

It is an extraordinary episode that sticks in the mind. In 1994 Margaret Anne Doody edited *Evelina* for Penguin Books and added an explanatory note that this episode "(including its setting and arrangements) is not incredible given the rage of the time for staging races and other events on which wagers could be laid."[13] Later, Betty Rizzo also described it as "perfectly typical of the time" and on that basis concluded that literary descriptions of women's foot racing "animalized the contestants."[14] These are curious conclusions as there is nothing in the historical record that supports the idea that Burney drew her story from life. No confirmation of two old women racing against each other has been discovered in the eighteenth-century record, nor any record of women being coerced into racing as surrogates for two men, and no record has been found of any race, for men or women, over such an extraordinarily short distance (twenty yards). Burney seems not to have any knowledge whatsoever of foot racing. Curiously, however, Doody supports her contention by referring to a 1980 essay by Earl Anderson in which he attempts to unravel this mystery but in doing so admits that "the earliest evidence which I have been able to find for a woman participating seriously in pedestrianism occurs in May 1820."[15]

Clearly, Earl Anderson knew nothing about women's foot racing in the eighteenth century, either, and produced no evidence to support Doody's assertions that Burney's race was "not incredible" or was "perfectly typical." The race described by Burney is, nevertheless, very striking in its brutality and callousness and seems to demand an explanation. Six months after Anderson's "Footnotes More Pedestrian than Sublime," Arthur Sherbo offered his own addenda to the footnotes, but he does not mention women at all, so the assertions of the credibility and typicality of Burney's race remain unsupported by either Anderson, Sherbo, or Doody.[16] In the years since then, my database, on which this monograph is based, contains nothing even remotely like Burney's account, and so we must conclude that the event was an invention, a product of Burney's fertile imagination, and we can only guess at her purpose: was she telling her readers that the behavior of some men toward women could be cruel, uncaring, and brutal and that *nothing* would be beyond them?

However, is it likely that Burney would have included an episode that her readers would not have believed? No doubt, this was an age possessed by a kind of gambling mania, and men and women would bet on almost anything. One story that everyone seemed to know on "good authority" reached the status of an urban myth: two men wagered one another that each would outlive the other. One day one of them collapsed in the street, and the other would not help him and would not allow anyone else to help, either, because to do so would interfere with the terms of the wager. Other, similar, wagers followed, with people betting on which two people that they knew would die first. Tobias Smollett took aim at that practice in his novel *The Adventures of Ferdinand Count of Fathom* (1753). In chapter 50 he wrote: "The whole mystery of the art was reduced to a simple exercise of tossing up a guinea, and the lust of laying wagers, which they indulged into a surprising pitch of ridiculous intemperance. In one corner of the room might be heard a pair of lordlings running their grandmothers against each other, that is, betting sums on the longest liver."[17]

The image of "a pair of lordlings running their grandmothers against each other" is so close to Burney's scene that it could even be the source of it. Was Frances Burney's creative imagination sparked by Smollett's words? Did she imagine what it would be like to actually race grandmothers against each other? Or did she read so quickly that she missed the clarification that the bet really concerned which woman would live longer and was not about running at all? Creative writing and eighteenth-century literature benefitted from Burney's story of old women running and falling, but it adds nothing factual to our historical understanding of women's foot racing.

Images

Images can be misleading, too. In 1811 Thomas Rowlandson published a series of etchings entitled *Rural Sports*, which included an image called *Smock Racing* that shows four young women competing, one of whom has been tripped by a dog.[18] Accepting the image as an accurate historical record, Allen Guttmann observes that it "offers another glimpse into the carnival mood. Bare-breasted, long-skirted girls race while uninhibited male and female bumpkins cavort and brawl."[19] All is not what it seems, however. Rowlandson borrowed this image from John Collett, who created it in 1770 (figs. 6 and 7).[20] Rowlandson's two

FIGURE 6. Detail, *An Holland Smock*, John Collett, 1770.

central runners are so like Collett's that they must have been traced, and Rowlandson also adds many other elements from the Collett image: the fat lady being pushed into a wagon in which a man holds a flag over the runners, and the horse and cart that are being driven into the runners from behind. Rowlandson then gives it all a burlesque treatment, turning into a kind of farce, but, more crucially, he also eroticizes the runners. No bare breasts are shown in Collett's original. Thus, Rowlandson's image, produced forty-one years after the original, distorts not only the details but also the mood of the event and cannot be taken as a historically accurate representation of a women's smock race in 1811.

Smock (or shift) races were very common in the long eighteenth century, and popular themes for artists include moments before, during, and after the race, and even the smock itself. Some works were anonymous, but some provide considerable information: among these John Collett (1725–80) is the most important.[21] Others were Joseph Parry (1744–1826), Thomas Rowlandson (1757–1827), Henry Thomas Alken (1785–1851), Philip Francis Stephanoff (1787/88–1860), and Robert Cruikshank (1789–1856). Several artists illustrated the various editions of William Somervile's *Hobbinol*, to which a smock is central: Anthony Walker (1726–65), John Thurston (1744–1822), Thomas

FIGURE 7. Detail, *Smock Racing*, Thomas Rowlandson, hand-colored engraving, 1811. (Collection of the author)

Bewick (1753–1824), John Bewick (1760–95), and Charlton Nesbitt (1775–1838). The latter's images were works of imagination in which they attempt to illustrate Somervile's text, which was also a work of the imagination, so the events portrayed have passed through two levels of creative imagination before we see them; we might assume that both writer and artists drew on things they had seen or knew, but to what extent is impossible to say. Nevertheless, the imaginations and their audience were of the eighteenth century, so the images may contain useful information. In Walker's engraving of Ganderetta being presented with the smock by Hobbinol, Walker seems to show Ganderatta as bare-legged, most unusual for an eighteenth-century woman in public, but we do not know whether this a faithful representation of something he had seen or if he had drawn from his imagination.[22]

Other artists show wider scenes, with a smock flying overhead or held aloft on a pole, advertising that a smock race would soon be held there, even though there may have been other competitions at the event. The smock race was commonly the last competition, but the smock flew overhead throughout the other sports. See, for example, William Hogarth's *Southwark Fair* (1733), an anonymous image of *Fairlock Fair* (1815), and William Redmore Bigg's *A Village Fair* (1820s).[23]

Images are, of course, genuine sources for the historian, but we should not expect them to be faithful recordings of historical fact, and sometimes they contain obvious mistakes. Rowlandson, for example, apart from copying and then distorting Collett's earlier image, commits the sin of placing the wrong arm forward for two of his women runners (ones that he did not copy from Collett). In Rowlandson's version, these runners have their arms and legs out of sequence (i.e., right leg and right arm forward); if an artist's powers of observation cannot be trusted on such a simple matter, how can he be trusted on anything else! Cruikshank was not much better than Rowlandson on the matter of arm and leg synchrony.

There is another question regarding authenticity and historical accuracy of images: Was falling down a common experience for the runners? One of Collett's runners has tripped and fallen; Rowlandson copies this. Henry Alken produced an image of a smock race that shows a woman runner spread-eagled on the floor and another looking as if she has fallen and is being helped to her feet.[24] Charlton Nesbitt and John Thurston, who produced the images for an 1813 edition of *Hobbinol*, turn the falling figure of Fusca into something monstrous about to strike down the runner in front of her (Ganderetta).[25] The anonymous artist who created an image of a *Smock Race at Tottenham Court Fair* (1738) shows one of the runners falling over someone who appears to be trying to recover an escaped litter of piglets.[26] Another anonymous artist shows three women racing for the garland with another who has fallen just before the end.[27] Should we believe that all runners were so accident prone? Did so many women runners fall? Somervile's poem famously tells of Fusca falling, but the reports in newspapers and elsewhere tell us that while the events could be full of incident, nothing suggests that women fell over on the scale that the images would suggest. Perhaps we can conclude that artists and poets favored falling women because they created dramatic interest and tension. There is also no evidence that eighteenth-century artists went to sporting events to draw from life; they seem to have drawn from their imaginations or to use a story or a recent event about which they knew but had not seen themselves.

"The Best Woman in Three Heats"

Images must not be undervalued, however; they can, if produced by the right hands, provide us with information not readily available elsewhere. An engraving by John Collett, published in 1770, had the following caption: "An

FIGURE 8. John Collet, *An Holland Smock to be run for*, hand-colored etching and engraving, 1770.

HOLLAND SMOCK to be run for, by any Woman born in this COUNTY: The best Woman in three Heats. NB. The Runners all to be enter'd by the Clerk of the Course before starting, and after the Race; Cocking as usual" (fig. 8).[28] It is the best image we have of a women's footrace in the eighteenth century, but although it can be enjoyed for its decorative qualities and, in the spirit of Hogarth, is full of detail and incident, it is almost entirely unintelligible to twenty-first-century audiences. To fully understand women runners of the eighteenth century, this image needs deciphering.

The caption tells us that the event is well organized; a Clerk of the Course is responsible for the arrangements and is the person to whom the runners had to report before and after a race. The reference to "cocking as usual" tells us that other entertainments (i.e., cockfighting) went alongside it, so this race was part of a country sporting festival or fair. That is reinforced by the notice pinned to the tree (left, under the man on the branch) that tells of men running in sacks (i.e., a sack race), and the two youths who are engaged in a single-stick[29] match inside a ring of women spectators (right, just behind the horse).

The system of racing—"The best Woman in three Heats" (here referred to as best-of-three)—was not that old, however, and women probably first ran it around 1730. The number of best-of-three races grew throughout the century until it became the most common system of racing for women; it had one major advantage for the organizers—breathing space between each race allowed the competition to entertain the crowd for a considerably longer time than a one-off race. It had originally come from horseracing a century earlier, when Charles II initiated a "new Round-heate" horserace at Newmarket that he declared would go on annually "for ever."[30] The best-of-three system was, of course, much tougher on the runners.

There are three runners in Collett's image; the center figure is the composed runner. Another, behind her, has been tripped up by a dog (see detail in fig. 7), and another is in front, just partly visible through the trunks of two trees on the left. The smock, the prize for which they are running, flutters overhead, hanging in the branches of a tree. Before we get down to detail, however, we can see that this image is dominated by women and girls, and not just the three runners. This is a smock race, and we have to ask whether women taking control was an essential part of the competition. (This will be explored further in chapter 4.) A girl (bottom left) is drawing beer to get a man drunk so that another girl can pick his pocket. She relieves him of a copy of the *Compleat Peace Officer*, showing him to be the local justice of the peace. A young, well-dressed girl standing just to the left of the central runner has been brought by attendants (including a black boy with silver buckles on his shoes) to see the races. Women hang out of windows to watch (upper right); a woman (center right) needs two men and a helping hand to heave her onto a cart; and a woman (far right, whip in hand) drives a horse and carriage along the very road the women are running and so threatening to drive over the fallen runner.

There are men there, too, but they are in the main either silly, passive, or just part of the supporting cast. The man in the branches of the tree upskirting the smock is silly, surely, in anyone's eyes. Isn't the man allowing himself to get so drunk that he opens himself up to having his pocket picked silly, too? The young man (bottom left) is so ardent in his admiration of the young woman with whom he is nose-to-nose that he is as oblivious of what anyone thinks of the public display as he is of the race unfolding behind him; just as oblivious are the chimney-sweep boys fighting over a ginger biscuit crown (bottom right), and the official-looking gentleman reading the notice on the tree while the runners pass by unnoticed. A male passenger sits passively in the carriage while the woman driver whips the horse. The man in the center with his hand protectively on the shoulder of the expensively dressed young girl seems to tell a more caring story, however, as does the one-legged man who has come to the aid of the tripped-up girl: Is he a veteran of the Seven Years' War? Yet they are still but members of the supporting cast.

In the best-of-three system, all participants run in the first race, and the winner is noted. After a designated breathing space, or rest period, they all run for a second time. If the same runner wins again, she wins the competition outright, as she has won two of the three races. She would then just walk or run over the course a final time alone. However, if a different runner wins the second race, a third race is required to decide the overall winner. But there was another important rule that was of great significance, for it affected the strategy of the runners—the distance rule. Just right of center we can see a man in a cart holding a flag. What is the flag for? It isn't the finishing line because two runners have already passed it, but it clearly has some importance. The answer is that it is the distance flag.

The distance flag was set up some lengths before the finish. This idea had come from horseracing, too, where in a four-mile race a distance flag or post would be positioned about 240 yards from the finish, and that distance would be lined and kept clear.[31] If a runner had not reached the distance flag by the time the winner crossed the finishing line, they did not qualify to run again. A runner might try to outpace the others and win the first heat before her competitors had reached the distance flag in the hope that they would be eliminated from the rest of the competition, leaving the winner to run alone thereafter. There was a risk, of course, in attempting such a strategy; a runner could expend so much of her strength that if the others weren't eliminated, the winner might not be competitive in the next races(s). Other runners, knowing that they could not catch the runner in front, would concentrate on getting to the distance flag before the runner in the lead finished and so give themselves a chance in the next race. It was important for an official to be posted at the distance flag who was able to also see the finishing post, and the position was an appointed one. When the distance flag was adopted for foot racing, the distance to the flag had to be approximated, and we might expect the distance flag or post for a one-mile race to be set about sixty yards (i.e., about one-thirtieth of the total distance) from the finish.

Collett's image captures a critical moment around the distance flag. One runner has been tripped right under it: Will she be able to get up and make her distance before the winner reaches the finishing post? Who will decide? That person is having difficulty getting into position on the cart and so cannot see the finishing line. The man holding the flag is simply furniture—he has no authority and so looks passively ahead. It is a critical moment, and this, the main subject of Collett's image, would have been recognized by eighteenth-century viewers. The person responsible for setting the distance flag and officiating during the race was usually an experienced former runner: Is this an extra layer of the story, that an ex-runner could in her later years has declined physically as to need help performing her officiating duties?

A runner who knew she had failed to make her distance would not usually continue, for she would be eliminated. In the official record she would be described as having been "distanced." A winner in such a race would be described as "winning by a distance," even though the defeated runner may not have finished.

The above explanation shows that Collett's image is an invaluable source of information on women's running in the eighteenth century, and particularly of the best-of-three system, a practice that will be expanded on in later chapters.

3

"OF GOOD CONVERSATION"

From 1638

In the spring of 1638 Sir Dudley Digges (1583–1639; fig. 9), the Lord of Chilham in Kent, was unwell and anxious to add a codicil to his will to distribute more of his wealth to the needy and deserving. Being already too weak to write, he dictated it to John Wyborne, his servant. By the terms of that codicil, a "a young maiden of good conversation between the ages of 16 and 24" would be nominated by the Lord of Faversham (who was based in Sheldwich Lees, five miles away) and his advisors; another young maiden would be nominated by the Lord of Chilham (i.e., himself or his successor) and *his* advisors, and these two maidens would then run against each other, head-to-head, for £10 each year on the anniversary of his birthday, 19 May. The codicil also specified the same arrangements for two young men similarly described.

In the same codicil he gave twenty pounds annually for the repair of St Mary's church in Chilham and to provide a dinner for the young men who had rung a peal of bells in his memory there (twenty shillings [one pound] was set aside for that); whatever was left of the twenty pounds was to be "distributed between twenty Poor Men twenty poor Women and twenty poor Children of the Parish of Chilham such as take no Alms or Allowance from the Common Purse." Sir Dudley Digges died in March of the following year, and his oldest son, Thomas, was charged with the responsibility of enacting the terms of the will.[1] Thus did 19 May became a local festive day each year, with footraces, bell-ringing, dining, and the distribution of charity to the poor, all in celebration of the memory of Sir Dudley Digges.

There are several striking features of this will, including Sir Dudley's specification that the candidates should run against each other for his bequest.

FIGURE 9. *Sir Dudley Digges*, Charles Turner after Cornelius Johnson, mezzotint, 1813. (National Portrait Gallery, London)

This seems to be a unique provision in a will, so why did he do it? Was he attracted by the idea of self-help, believing that potential recipients of the charity should be rewarded for their ability and effort rather than merely accepting it passively? Or was there already a local tradition of running races on festive days? There was a local field known as the Running Field Mead, at Olders [also Older's, Oulders, or Oldwood] Lees, a hamlet about a mile due north of Chilham; in time it came to be known as Old Wives Lees, and it is here that the races for the two ten-pound prizes were always run. When the Running Field Mead got its name has been lost. Chilham, however, was a well-established old community with its own castle, church, festivities, and traditions going back to 1086, when the *Domesday Book* listed it as Cilleham and named its tax burden at "five sulings." Several centuries later, as the Lord of Chilham, Sir Dudley rebuilt the castle. He was not only the richest, most successful, and most powerful man in the neighborhood, he was also Master of the Rolls and a prominent member of Charles I's Third Parliament in Westminster, although he had a troubled relationship with the king, who dissolved Parliament, an act that eventually led to his execution.

An equally striking feature of the codicil to Sir Dudley's will was the inclusion of young women in his bequest and the specification that they were to receive the same sum as the young men. Such an egalitarian provision was certainly unusual and came with all sorts of complications. For example, under English law could a sixteen-year-old girl own ten pounds in her own right, or did it legally belong to her father? The runners had to be unmarried (Digges referred to them as "maidens" and not "women")—the complications, had they been married, would have been even greater. By specifying that the candidates for the prize had to be "of good conversation," he disqualified some of the most needy—vagabonds, tinkers, and itinerant peddlers, for example; those wishing to race for the prize had to be respectable as well as needy. But where did he get the idea for young men and women to race for a prize on the annual celebration of his birth? Sir Dudley was well educated and well read: Had he read Pausanias?[2] Did he know of the young men and women who ran at Olympia and elsewhere in the Greek and Roman world? In the 1690s James Brome, who had been vicar of Newington and later rector of Cheriton (both in Kent), wrote about the races at Old Wives Lees, which by then had become one of the sights of Kent.[3] He describes the length of the races as being "a certain *Stadium* of Forty Rods" (italics in the original), thus making a direct comparison with the stadia of the ancient world.[4] At that time the word *stadium* was virtually unknown and unused in Britain except in the context of ancient Greek or Roman sport. Indeed, it remained unused outside that context until deep into the eighteenth century and is not listed in Dr Johnson's *A Dictionary of the English Language*. Forty rod is tantalizingly close to the distance run at ancient Olympia; a rod was 5.5 yards, so 40 rod was 220 yards, and the stade at Olympia was 210 yards and 9.5 inches. Was this mere coincidence, or were these races for young and unmarried men and maids between the ages of sixteen and twenty-four at Old Wives Lees *designed* to capture something of the history and spirit of the young men and parthenoi at ancient Olympia? Did the races at Old Wives Lees make Brome merely *think* of the ancient Olympic Games, or were the ancient Olympic Games Sir Dudley Digges's inspiration? We may never know, but in 1612 the Olympic Games had already become the inspiration for another new sporting event in England: Robert Dover's Cotswold-based Olimpick Games at Chipping Campden, a dozen miles south of Stratford-upon-Avon, which continued annually for the next 239 years.[5] These Olimpick Games had already been celebrated twenty-six times by the time Sir Dudley Digges added the codicil to his will, and they were well known throughout the country. In addition, in 1636 there was yet another source of information about these games; Mathewe Walbancke published *Annalia Dubrensia*, a collection of thirty-four poems in praise of Robert Dover and his games.[6] The anthology included poems by such luminaries as Ben Jonson and Michael Drayton, both of whom Sir Dudley may have known personally.[7] By 1641 the Olimpick Games were so well known around the country that the event had even slipped into the dialogue in a popular play on the London stage, in which it was listed as one of the sights in England that one should see.[8]

A striking feature of Sir Dudley Digges's codicil is that he thought that bellringing, feasting, and footraces for young men and women would be the best way for him to be remembered after his death. To understand how this codicil came about, we need to understand the context in which it was made. Robert Dover's Olimpick Games was a deliberately anti-Puritan annual event and a valiant attempt to counteract the continuing rise of the antisport polemic; many of the poets in *Annalia Dubrensia* lamented the influence of the puritanically minded and powerful clergy. One of the poets, John Trussell, put it this way:

> The countrie Wakes, and whirlings have appeer'd
> Of late, like forraine pastimes: *Carnivalls,*
> *Palme* and Rush-bearing, harmlesse Whitson-ales,
> Running at Quintain, May-games, generall Playes,
> By some more nice, then wise, of latter dayes,
> Have in their Standings, Lectures, Exercises,
> Been so reprov'd, traduc'd, condemn'd for vices
> Profane and heathenish, that now few dare
> Set them afoote; The Hocktide pastimes, are
> Declin'd, if not deserted; so that now
> All Publike merriments, I know not how,
> Are question'd for their lawfulnesse.[9]

Others wrote of the "Zealous Brother[s]," those "Who thinke there is no mirth but what is Sin," while others bemoaned "these dull yron Times" or the "Iron-dayes" in which they lived.[10] It would have been quite impossible for anyone to propose footraces, bell-ringing, and celebratory dining in 1638 without being aware of how they would be perceived; thus, the races Sir Dudley launched at Old Wives Lees were as deliberate an anti-Puritan statement as were Robert Dover's Olimpick Games in the Cotswolds 165 miles away.

Although Sir Dudley Digges died in 1639, we cannot be certain when the commemorative events began. Their funding depended on the conversion, after her death, of the property in which Lady Cleeve lived, so that the income from a new let could be used for charitable purposes. It seems likely, however, that they began before 1642 and the start of the English Civil War; otherwise, they would not have begun until 1661 at the earliest, when Charles II was crowned, and twenty-two years after Sir Dudley's death. It is easy to envisage the resumption in 1661 of an old tradition, as was the case with May Day and dancing round the Maypole, but difficult to imagine the beginning of a new tradition or one that had been dormant for over twenty years. However, after the Civil War and the Cromwell years (and probably before), the races were held annually on or near 19 May, just as Sir Dudley Digges had planned, and continued through the next four generations of the Digges family.[11] By that time the races had become part of the local fabric, even though by then there was no one alive who could remember Sir Dudley Digges.

Ten pounds was an enormous sum of money in 1638 and remained the largest sum of money that women would regularly compete for during the next three hundred years; Brome called it a "pension." There are many alternative ways of calculating what that amount would mean in today's currency. If we were to calculate it in terms of what it would *buy* today (c. 2022), we might estimate it as equivalent to £1,651. If we were to calculate its worth in terms of *earnings* today, we might estimate it as equivalent to £28,160, and if we were to calculate its worth in terms of its *relative value,* or the relative "prestige value" it had compared to other values, we might estimate it as equivalent to £47,250 today. But if we were to calculate its worth in terms of the total value of the national economy (using GDP), we might estimate it as equivalent to £487,000.[12] Winning it would change the lives of its recipients, and for that reason, new regulations emerged over time, one of which was that a person may win it only once in their lifetime.

Sir Dudley Digges's codicil carries all the marks of a document hastily drawn up in which the intent and principles are clear but which offers very little detail. How far should they run? Where? How was "good conversation" to be determined? How often could the same person or family benefit?

How limited were those who selected the runners? Could they select anyone, or was it expected that they select someone from their own area? This last question seems to be answered by Brome, who wrote that the annual races at Old Wives Lees were a "Trial of Skill" between those from "adjoining Hundreds." A hundred was an ancient grouping of parishes for legal and administrative purposes, and so it seems that the runners were selected to represent two neighboring hundreds. The Lords of Chilham and the Lords of Faversham and their advisors, therefore, chose a representative from their own hundreds, and the races would have seen a degree of local rivalry between the two hundreds as well as personal rivalries between the individual runners. They may even have come to be seen as representative races, or Chilham versus Sheldwich Lees.

As a local event there was no need to advertise it, and no one seems to have seen the need to report or record the races, either, but they did continue, year after year and generation after generation, but we have only indirect evidence of them. Nevertheless, 19 May became a popular festive day featuring foot racing, bell ringing, and feasting and was well known beyond the boundaries of Old Wives Lees, Chilham, and Sheldwich Lees. Year after year runners committed themselves to run for the big prize, supported by their families, all of whom would have benefited in some way from a victory.

The success of the event triggered imitators, and as years passed other nearby communities began to organize their own festive days with foot racing and other attractions. By 1726 footraces were organized at Brabourne Lees as part of a horserace meeting in July; three "maids" ran—one each from the parishes of Mersham, Smeeth, and Brabourne—which took the idea of races between maids from adjoining hundreds and expanded it to a match between maids from three adjoining parishes.[13] At Brabourne, however, unlike at Old Wives Lees, there were no races for men. The maids of Mersham, Smeeth, and Brabourne were clearly not running for themselves alone but for their parishes, a clear example of young women involved in representative sport, which would have generated much partisan support from the crowd. The Brabourne organizers, however, did not have the resources of Sir Dudley Digges's bequest, so the maids ran for a smock of unknown value, donated by Richard Watts, a local dignitary who was later mayor of Rochester. They also reduced the distance the maids ran to 30 rod (165 yards). The shadow of Old Wives Lees, nevertheless, hung over the Brabourne race, for the organizers included the following in their regulations: "None to compete who have won it before, or that have won the £10 at Oulders Lees."

Such a regulation makes it clear that without the restriction, the winning maids from Old Wives Lees would have wanted to run at Brabourne, too, which shows that the runners were willing to travel to compete. Brabourne was eleven and a half miles from Old Wives Lees, Mersham twelve miles, and Smeeth thirteen, and with travel among the rural poor being no faster than six miles an hour, the running maids were clearly willing to travel for a couple of hours to run in an event and repeat it to go home at the end of the day.

In 1731 footraces were also organized at Sandwich Salts [probably Gazen Salts], nineteen and a half miles east of Old Wives Lees, and they were held on Whit Monday. The races were advertised for "Women or Maids" and for "Married Men and Batchelors," too. The sixteen to twenty-four age range imposed at Old Wives Lees had been discarded, but the organizers at Sandwich Salts also adopted a now-familiar regulation: the race was closed to any "man or Woman . . . that hath ever won the money the 19th of May at Olders-Lees, or that hath ever won a Shirt or a Smock at Sandwich or Waldershare."[14] By 1731 races at nearby Sandwich and at Waldershare had been added to the race calendar around Old Wives Lees, but winning at Old Wives Lees led to an almost blanket ban on entering any other race in Kent.

In 1751 on Lynsted Park there was a "match of running," which was a popular team game. Women played it as well as men, and it drew large crowds, though in this instance the match was between two teams of men. In addition, however, there was a race for maids for a "Holland Shift," but once again, the regulations stated that it was "to be run for by Maids, that never won the Ten Pounds, or Half a Guinea Value, to run in the same manner as they do at Oldwives Lees."[15] And in 1756 races for men and maids were organized at Sandgate Castle, twenty-one miles southeast of Old Wives Lees. Again, the regulations specified that "No Man or Maid that has won the ten Pounds, or that ever won the Shirt or Shift at the Place are to start."[16] By the 1750s more than fourteen different venues in Kent featured women's races, particularly for young women, a number that was significantly higher than events for men. Kent had become a hotbed of women's running, and women were willing to travel to compete despite the regulations that were in place to prevent it.

The races at Old Wives Lees, had, however, undergone some significant changes in the way the runners were selected and in the number of runners who could take part. In 1798 Edward Hasted described a system of "tyes" through which runners had to qualify to get to the final at Old Wives Lees.[17] One tye was held at Sheldwich Lees on 1 May, followed on the next Monday by another tye at Old Wives Lees, with the winner of each progressing to the final on 19 May. A unique style of racing had evolved that became known as the "Kentish manner," in which races were run head-to-head by two runners. Lots were drawn to establish the pairings and also perhaps to determine who ran to the left or right of the other. In 1751 it was described this way in a race for a silver cup: "No less than eight to start, to run 40 Rod after the Kentish Manner, viz. two and two, which makes four Races; then the two Winners to run for the Cup."[18]

Even that description is incomplete though, for the eight initial runners would have been reduced to four after the first four races; then these four winners would have to race each other in two more races before getting to the final two, who would then run against each other in the final (i.e., a total of seven races in which the winner would have to run three times). Therefore, at Old Wives Lees there were now two qualifying races culminating in the final, and their popularity had probably never been higher; they were not merely local events attracting the country folk but drew a "great concourse" that typically gathered there to see them. The crowd was described by Hasted as made up of "the neighbouring gentry" as well as the locals.[19]

In addition, because of the popularity of footraces in this part of Kent, new events, on Midsummer Day, were added to the athletic calendar, such as in 1743 at Old Wives Lees, when the runners took part in a best-of-three system of 40-rod races for a shift, an entirely different system of running from the traditional head-to-head system; men ran 80 rod (quarter of a mile) for a shirt.[20] The old head-to-head races still continued, however, but even this wasn't the limit of the racing opportunities for the young women of eastern Kent.

As early as the 1690s Brome had described Stroke-Biass (an earlier name for a match of running) which was a unique running game between two parishes.[21] It was one of England's first team games, and it later became known as goal running,[22] or, more simply, a "running," which was a highly complex "touch" game with similarities to prison bars or prisoner's base, played on summer afternoons and evenings with anywhere from twelve to twenty-four persons to a side.[23] Big matches attracted crowds of thousands. The playing area was marked out a day or two before the match by the players and match officials who met for that purpose. Players then submitted their names, agreed on an alternative date in case the match was disrupted by rain, and agreed on the position of the buoys on the field and on the position and size of the goals. The game had its own technical language, not all of which is now clear, there were "courses," "traverses," and "Wing Boughs" as well as buoys and goals, but what precisely these items were is unknown.

After drawing lots, one team sent out a runner who attempted to make the goal, but the opposing side would match her with one of their own, who attempted to stop her by touching her. Such a touch was called a "stroke," and it eliminated the stroked player. Once the first runner had begun running and evading her opponent, a second runner went quickly out to make the goal, and she, too, was matched by a runner from the opposite side, determined to stroke her. This continued until all the players were on the field, and the playing area would be filled with runners trying to run to their goal while being pursued by their opposite number determined to stroke them. Each pair was fixed—no runner could stroke anyone other than the opponent they were paired with—so, much of the skill and strategy would have involved matching players with their opposite number. The team that first made seven strokes won the game. The size of the playing area was variable and was agreed upon between the teams beforehand, but there are records of buoys being set at 15 or 20 rod (88.5 and 110 yds., respectively). The length of games was variable, too, but they were not short. There are records of a match having to be stopped because it was too dark to carry on, but the details of the match were agreed upon in articles of agreement, and the matches were officiated by anything from two to four independent umpires.

Stroke-Biass, or a match of running, was a popular spectator sport as well as a popular participation one; Blome wrote in 1697 that "the Country resort in great Numbers to behold the Match," and they continued to do so for at least the next seventy years; "much company,"[24] a "vast concourse,"[25] and a "great concourse" were among the terms used to describe the spectators.[26] It was played by men and by women, but they played separately, and Brome noted that the women were "as Vigorous and Active to obtain a Victory" as were the men. In 1768 a maids' match was advertised on Barham Downs for 18 July—and advertised two weeks in advance—with the prize of a smock for all the winners. But even before that match was played, another match was advertised to take place two weeks later; the maids' running matches were obviously popular. There can be no doubt that there was in east Kent a running culture for women stemming from the races at Old Wives Lees and bolstered with races at many other Kent venues as well as the matches of running—but not everyone approved.

Two days before the 1769 match, a letter appeared in the *Kentish Gazette* expressing the pleasure of the writer at hearing that orders had been given for the constables to "apprehend and take up" the maids who were planning to run, describing them as "loose, idle, and disorderly persons."[27] They were also called "lewd." The names of those who could not be "taken up" should be given to the justices of the peace so that they would all be committed. The writer, who went by the initials R.F. and was surely a man, adopted a tone of moral superiority and claimed to be speaking on behalf of "all orderly and well-behaved persons" who had been "highly offended" the last time the young women had run. The scene, he wrote, had been "indecent" and the young women "impudent"; they had "scandalized" anyone with any sense of "modesty," and he complained that the young women had "expose[d] themselves in so shameless a manner." This, therefore, was an attack not so much on their sport, or even on their supposed disorderliness, but on their dress and supposed lack of modesty.

One of the customs of the game was for the players to "strip" at the start as a sign that the game was about to get underway, just as a later age would use the expression "kick off" to describe the time when a football match would start (see fig. 10). In 1770, for example, a match of running was advertised for men who were instructed to meet at "Four o'Clock—and strip exactly at Five o'Clock."[28] In 1773 the advertisement for a match of running at Badlesmere Lees carried the following: "To Strip at Six in the Evening."[29] Similarly, the advertisement for the Maid's Match in 1769 contained the words "To Strip at Five o'Clock."[30] Stripping was necessary, not merely because these were summer evenings or because the runners needed greater freedom of movement, but because they needed to shed any voluminous clothing that would have helped the opposition achieve a stroke. The teams ritually stripped in their own goal, and thus were visible to all, and no one seems to have objected to the men stepping out of their breeches on the goal line and then running in their "shirt and drawers," but when the young women similarly stripped, it was different. Weren't young women expected to be modest? This public stripping certainly wasn't that.

FIGURE 10. Advertisement from the *Kentish Gazette*, 19–22 July 1769. (© British Library Board, all rights reserved; with thanks to the British Newspaper Archive)

There must have been considerable tension at the stripping time at five o'clock on that Monday afternoon, and it must have taken considerable bravery for the maids to go ahead with the match after the public attack on them and their morals and the call to have them committed, but the match did take place and did so to "the great satisfaction of a vast concourse of people." We do not know whether the constables failed to act or whether they were biding their time, but the letter, nevertheless, in the longer term achieved its objective—there are no more reports of women playing a match of running after this. Perhaps they were eventually stopped by the constables or perhaps it was thought unwise to advertise or report them, while they went on quietly without publicity as they had for generations.

There is, nevertheless, something curious about the advertisements for these matches, for unlike similar advertisements for men's matches that were advertised as being, for example, between the Gentlemen of the Hills and the Gentlemen of the Dales (1751),[31] the Gentlemen of Canterbury and the Gentlemen of the Isle of Thanet (1768),[32] the Gentlemen of St. Peter's Parish in Sandwich and the Gentlemen of Deal with adjoining Parishes (1769),[33] and many more, the maids' races did not mention that the teams came from anywhere in particular (see fig. 10). It does not appear that the "vast concourse of people" went to see the rivalry between two teams or to support one team against another; apart from family and friends, the crowd seems to have gone to watch because they were young women.

After R.F.'s letter to the *Kentish Gazette,* the maids of Bridge Hill can have had no doubt that when they ran and played sport, the public perception of them was quite different from that enjoyed by the young men who did the same thing. The men were never called immodest, impudent, indecent, loose, disorderly, or lewd for doing so. When the men played, the crowd watched the match; when the women played, the crowd watched the women. Perhaps this is an overstatement: loving mothers and fathers, brothers and sisters, would have watched, too. There may have been as many different reasons for watching as there were people in the crowd, although it is tempting to turn the tables on R.F., maybe it was in the minds of some of the male spectators that we would have found immodesty, impudence, indecency, looseness, and lewdness, rather than with the runners.

This is a central theme in eighteenth-century sport: women might participate in sport as soon as the men, and play it as enthusiastically and competitively and even as well as men, but they had to brave public and private censure in doing so. That so many did is testament to their spirit, to their unwillingness to be restricted. Men had to be "manly" in their sport, of course, but the women also had to be physically prepared, skillful, and competitive. But there was always an extra dimension to their public performances—they were being watched, and often judged, as women. It took an extra element of courage for women to enter the sporting arena in the long eighteenth century; they carried with them their womanhood and all the public attitudes about their necessary modesty and decorum, as well as the perceptions of their incipient weakness, frailness, and all-round unsuitableness for the task.

But social forces are powerful. There must have been many young women who were inhibited or prevented from taking part, but it was largely from within the ranks of the urban and rural poor that we find our competitors, for they were less limited by social constraints than those higher on the social ladder. Economic forces are powerful, too, and some women were driven by sheer need; they competed for the prize or for the money, as many probably did under the terms of Sir Dudley Digges's will in 1638.

At about the same time that R.F. was making the public case to identify and "apprehend and take up" the women runners at Bridge Hill, an attempt was made to stop *all* the races at Old Wives Lees, men's and women's. Sir

Dudley Digges's lands had long slipped out of the family's hands, and from 1774 were owned by Robert Heron, who had no wish to celebrate the birthday of a man born nearly two hundred years earlier; nor did he wish to find the money every year to pay for the prizes. However, he eventually found that he didn't have the power to stop them, and they continued annually as before.[34]

The newspaper notices of these many events and locations in eastern Kent give us insights into how these races were run and financed. The races at Old Wives Lees, with their own finance stream from Sir Dudley Digges's will, remained unique; those who organized events elsewhere, however, had significant financial and organizational problems to overcome. The cost of prizes (usually smocks for the women and shirts for the men) was met by a local dignitary donating a garment, such as Richard Watts at Brabourne Lees in 1726,[35] Capt. Smith at Sandwich in 1730,[36] and James Boxer at Sandgate Castle in 1756,[37] even though the smock was probably made locally and the costs met by the benefactor. Local taverns and their landlords also played important roles: runners often had to enter their names at a local tavern or inn. For example, at Sandwich in 1730 the runners had to go to the Sign of the Rose at one o'clock on the day of the race to enter, and the race was held later in the afternoon. A year later, entries had to be made at the Flower-de-luce by twelve o'clock.

Finances were always an issue for the organizers, and at Sandwich in 1731 the runners were required to pay an entrance fee—sixpence for the women and one shilling for the men, which was to be the prize for second place. We don't know what the value of the smock was, nor how many ran for it in 1731, but we do know that the previous year the smock was valued at one guinea and six women competed for it. On that basis, the smock was worth forty-two times more than the entrance fee, and six runners would provide a purse of three shillings for the runner-up. So, before entering, the runners would have had to assess their own form and that of the others and then calculate the odds. Sixpence was also the entrance fee at Lysted in 1751 and at Sandgate Castle in 1756 and seems to have been the going rate.

The distance women ran at Old Wives Lees on the 19 May was 40 rod (220 yds.), and they continued with the same distance in 1743 when the Midsummer Day races began. The men ran 80 rod (440 yds. or a quarter mile). In 1726 at Brabourne Lees the maids ran 30 rod (165 yds.), as they did in 1743 at

New Romney Warren. But at Sandwich in 1749 and 1750 they ran a quarter mile (the men ran a half mile), so the women's running culture in Kent seems to have been for sprinters (165–440 yds.). These extended sprint distances are never easily run by novices, as they rely on a combination of speed and endurance rather than pure native speed. Any novice who decided to run flat out from the start would pay the price long before the finish. Indeed, at New Romney Warren in 1743, the maids had to run the best-of-three (i.e., compete in up to three races against each other, each of 30 rod); the first maid to win twice was the overall winner. Despite the breathing space in between the races, this would have been a challenge to all but the very well prepared.

There were other challenges, too, not least of which was the presence of dogs at matches. Dogs could, and did, spoil horseraces and cricket matches, sometimes out of exuberance. But there was always suspicion that they could be trained to disrupt a race or a match; they could spoil footraces, too. In 1749 the newspaper announcement of the races at Sandwich for a shirt and a smock ended with the words: "N.B. All persons are desir'd to leave their Dogs at Home, or they will be shot."[38] The notice was repeated the following year and again in 1751 by the organizers at Lynsted Park.[39] John Collett's image from 1770 of women running a footrace (fig. 8) illustrates clearly the problem that dogs could cause. These were, nevertheless, days of entertainment at Sandwich, designed to attract a crowd, with other events arranged around the footraces: a pig hunt for six boys and "several other diversions." There were also cudgeling for a hat and a sack-race for a wig at New Romney Warren in 1743, and at Lynsted in 1751 the landlord of the Black Lyon apologized for having run out of "liquor" the previous year and promised "all gentlemen, ladies and others" that it would not happen again.

The races at Old Wives Lees on or around 19 May continued throughout the eighteenth century, although the records of them are intermittent, but by the 1770s we begin to get our first reports of the winner's names. In 1774 Jane Izzard (from Boughton-under-Blean) beat Mary Taffenden (from Boughton Corner) in front of "a greater concourse of people than has been known to attend on the like occasion for many years."[40] In 1776 a young woman from Selling beat one from Ashford, though their names were not given.[41] In 1788 we get the first details of the tyes too: at Old Wives Lees, Mary Parker (from Chartham) beat Susan Kemp (from Lower Hardres)[42] and then went on to win the final race on 19 May against the winner of the other tye at Sheldwich Lees.[43] Other winning maids at Old Wives Lees are listed below, along with the years of their victories and their places of origin when known.

1778	Anne Hawkes	
1787	a maid	Selling
1789	a maid	Willtborough [Willesborough]
1790	— Ford	Brook
1796	— Stubbles	Adisham
1802	— Walker	
1803	— Howland	Sheldwich
1804	a young woman	Sheldwich
1805	a young woman	Beaksbourne [Bekesbourne]
1806	a maid	Faversham
1807	— Blake	Faversham
1808	— Finn	Chilham
1812	— Wraight	Canterbury
1816	Hannah Amos	

Sir Dudley Digges's codicil made Kent a center for women's running for two hundred years and prompted many other competitions in Kent, where women's running became established alongside men's. In Kent many hundreds, perhaps thousands, of eighteenth-century women ran for money and prizes in races and in running team games. This running culture was, however, unique to the locale; elsewhere in Britain women young and old also ran, but they ran in different types of competitions, over longer distances, and rarely alongside men, and rarely if ever in such numbers, and certainly not for as much money as at Old Wives Lees. Throughout the eighteenth century the women's running culture in Kent remained distinct from the rest of Britain.

4

RUNNING FOR SHIFTS AND SMOCKS

To 1699

In February 1659/60 a mood of uncertainty hung in the air over London.[1] Oliver Cromwell had died on 3 October 1658, and his thirty-two-year-old son Richard had taken over as Lord Protector, but things never went well. The Third Protectorate Parliament (27 January–22 April 1659) had been convened amidst talk of divisions everywhere and the army agitating about their backpay. Was it possible that the Commonwealth for which the nation had struggled (for and against) for years, over which so much blood had been spilled, could unravel? Amidst this turmoil Samuel Pepys recorded in his diary that on a Friday evening, just as it was getting dark, he and his young wife Elizabeth had gone out for a stroll in St. James's Park while their dinner was being prepared. When it was ready, Theoph was sent out to tell them so, but she arrived just as a poor woman was offering to run against Elizabeth for a pot of ale. Theoph joined in and beat both; Elizabeth was eighteen and Theoph seven or eight.[2] In these uncertain times a poor woman had to live by her wits . . . and, so it seems, by her running ability. Pepys leaves us wondering, however, whether the poor woman got her pot of ale.

But in less than four months Charles II would ride into London to resume the monarchy that had effectively ended twenty years earlier in 1642 when civil war broke out, which led to the execution of his father, Charles I, in 1649. These were extraordinary times; the results of the English Civil War were reversed, and the about-face had major political, social, religious, and economic repercussions. Puritanism lost steam, and those who had bemoaned the loss of the traditional sports and recreations were jubilant as the repressions and restrictions imposed by the puritanically minded were instantly cast aside. Dover's Olimpicks resumed in the Cotswolds, Maypoles were again erected all over the country, and young men and maids began racing again at Old Wives Lees.

In Edinburgh the *Caledonian Mercury* reported that "six brewster wives, great with childe, are to run from the Thicket Burn to the top of Arthur Seat, for a groaning cheese of one hundred pounds weight, and a budgell of Dunkel aquavitæ, and a rumpkine of Brumsweek mum for the second, set down by a Dutch midwife."[3] Roughly reinterpreted, this tells us that six heavily pregnant brewers' wives were to run the mile from the Figgate Burn to the top of Arthur's Seat in Edinburgh, a climb of 820 feet, for a huge cheese, a bottle of Dunkeld whisky, and a quantity of German beer given by a Dutch midwife for the runner-up.[4] A most unusual race, there is nothing similar, before or since, with which we can compare it. Robert Chambers made reference to it in 1859 when he compiled his *Domestic Annals of Scotland* and pointed out that the runners were all "in condition which makes violent exertion unsuitable to the female form," but that was almost certainly the point, for the race was all about pregnancy and childbirth.[5] The women were "great with childe," a Dutch midwife provided at least one of the prizes, and the main prize was a large "groaning cheese" (almost certainly Dutch). There was an old English tradition in which the father of a newborn baby brought a very large, flat, round cheese to the baby's christening. The cheese would be cut into slices from the center, making a large hole, and the slices were handed out to those in attendance (fig. 11). The baby would then be passed through the hole for luck. "Groaning" was said to be a reference to the noises that the mother made during delivery.[6] This race was not one of those activities devised by publicans to attract a crowd to which they would sell ale, for it was held some distance away from the populous area and its wealth of taverns. It may have been a promotional event to advertise a shipment of Dutch cheese and German beer that had recently arrived at Leith, Edinburgh's docks.

The next day, sixteen fishwives from Musselburgh planned to run to Canongate, Edinburgh, just over six miles away, for "twelve pair of lambs harrigals."[7] The prize was probably offal, the intestines of sheep (i.e., "lungs and lichts"—lungs and gastrointestinal tract), the constituents of haggis, and a much more modest prize than those offered the day before.[8] The prize of twelve pairs of lamb's harrigals for sixteen runners does not sound like much of an incentive to race for, but maybe they were made up into twelve portions, and the winner got to chose the one she wanted, and so on for each of the finishers.

FIGURE 11. Baby passing through a *Groaning Cheese* at its christening, bookplate, artist unknown. From John Brand, *Observation on Popular Antiquities*, vol. 2, 1841.

On the other hand, maybe they did not need much of an incentive, as it would have been a "fun day at the office" for them: the fishwives ran the same route with a heavy creel of fish on their backs four days a week.[9] Musselburgh fishwives came from Fisherrow, Musselburgh's fishing village on the Firth of Forth, and in the words of the Rev. Alexander Carlyle, they had carried loads of fish on their back from Fisherrow into Edinburgh "ever since Edinburgh became a considerable city."[10] Three women were responsible for a creel; one would carry it on her back for a hundred yards or so and then transfer it to another, who would then repeat the process. By trial and error over the generations, they had worked out the most efficient system—each runner would carry the load for a half-minute or so and then have a minute's respite (but still running with the others) before repeating the sequence. In this unique method, they passed the load swiftly to each other on the run ninety times between Musselburgh and Edinburgh. It was calculated that this method let them carry the heavy creel five miles in less than forty-five minutes, and so the Fisherrow to Edinburgh journey would be completed well inside an hour. The creels they carried were said to be never weigh less than two hundred pounds, and they could carry them twenty-seven miles in five hours. It was also believed that individually they could carry loads of up to 250 pounds in their creels. The fish wives were very remarkable women, and Carlyle wrote that they were "educated to it from their infancy, [and] . . . to which they must have been bred."[11]

Fisherrow fishwives must also have been the prime candidates for the pregnant runners' race the day before. Carlyle wrote: "Some of them have been brought to bed [given birth], and have gone to Edinburgh on foot with their baskets within the week. It is perfectly well ascertained, that one, who was delivered on Wednesday morning, went to town with her creel on the Saturday forenoon following."[12] We must be cautious about thinking of the Fisherrow fishwives as poor, downtrodden women, for they ran a steady and consistent business dealing with individual Edinburgh merchants with whom they had agreements, maybe even contracts, and their businesses lasted for many generations. One eminent Edinburgh merchant, with whom they did £600 of business a year, said that he had "never lost a farthing" when dealing with them. They also took great responsibility within their own families and took "so great a share in the maintenance of the family, they have no small sway in it . . . and their strength and activity is equal to their work."[13]

Carlyle referred to them as an "inferior class" and wrote that their manners were peculiar, loud, and rude, and he noted that they went everywhere barefoot (except on Sundays) which disgusted "strangers from the south." Nevertheless, his tone in describing them is celebratory; he praises their "untainted morals" and their scrupulous honesty. He admired their irrepressible spirit and knew of "no employment, that conduces more to health and good spirits than theirs."[14]

It was almost inevitable that the explosion of interest in sport and recreation in Britain after Charles II's return would go too far, particularly as it was so often associated with wagering. Within four years of his return, Charles II had to pass a law against "deceitfull, disorderly and excessive gaming" in an attempt to curb the excesses at "cards, dice, tables, tennis, bowles, kittles, shovelboard, cocking, horse-racing, dog matches, and foot-races." Anyone who got caught gambling had to forfeit three times their winnings.[15]

Some wagers, however, were just fun and games within the family, such as a Sunday morning in the spring of 1667 that Pepys described. Only six months had passed since the Great Fire had swept through London; together with the houses that were blown up to stop the fire spreading, the catastrophe had made seventy thousand people homeless. The new, stone-built city was beginning to move from the drawing boards to the new layouts on the ground, but it was time to take a break away from the noise and confusion. Pepys and his wife went across the River Thames to Jamaica House for the first time, and they took with them Mary and Anne Mercer, Barker, and Jayne, all young maids or companions to Elizabeth. The Jamaica House had a tearoom, gardens, and a bowling green, and for fun the young women ran races against each other on the green: "The girls did run for wagers over the bowling-green; and there, with much pleasure, spent little, and so home, and they home."[16]

Although they were few in number, one aspect of the races run by girls and women in Britain in the seventeenth century was that, unlike the men's competitions, serious, big-money betting was not a feature. Almost all of men's sport at that time seems to have been associated with—indeed, driven by—wagers and betting, and in this women's sport took a different path. Small, domestic wagers had, nevertheless, always been part of people's fun. Long before the Civil War, William Blundell wrote a song about an evening when men and women in Lancashire danced till dawn, trying to keep going after the others had given in to exhaustion, and even trying to outlast the musicians. The women, of course, danced as long and as hard as the men:

> But Gilbert and Thomas and Harry
> whose sweethearts were Nell Nann and Marie
> Tooke sides against Gyles James and Richard
> whose wentches weare Jeane Jane and Bridgett
> The wager was for a wheate Cake
> They daunst till thire bones did ake
> That Gilbert and Nannie and Nellie
> Did swett themselves into a Jelly.[17]

Dancing till their bones ached was fun in itself, but the wager of a wheatcake made it more so. It is a reminder that in an age before electrical or steam power and the internal combustion engine, physical fun was an important part of life and was one of the ways that people entertained themselves and each other. Everyone then was more physically involved in life than would be true in later ages. For those not of the affluent classes, a woman's life was full of labor: carrying water from the well, working around the home, washing, cleaning, carrying the children, were all hard and continuous. In the song above, the young maids have to leave at cockcrow to get the fires started to warm the house before anyone else gets up. The Fisherrow fishwives were said to play golf and football for recreation. Men and women turned to physical activity for fun even when their lives were already full of physical toil.

In the early 1680s a ballad was published that described a two-mile race between four "supposed Virgins" on Temple-Newsham [Temple Newsam] Green, near Leeds, Yorkshire; one of the runners was Ann Clayton (a.k.a. bonny Nan), who was already a well-traveled and successful racer, having beaten a man named Luke on Bassing Hall [Basinghall] Street in the City of London; she won this race on Temple Newsam Green, too. The ballad's tone is celebratory, even excitable, and has two main themes: one is an account of the runners and the prizes, and the other praises Yorkshire girls in general, for whom the balladeer would "freely dye."[18] There were three prizes for the four runners: a silver spoon, a silver bodkin, and a silver thimble. "Such a race was never seen" between "four Virgins that supposed were," but the ballad describes neither the runners nor the race, though we are told of the order in which they finished, and we are also told that they all ran in "half-shirts and Drawers," with Ann Clayton clad in red drawers, Pegg Hall in blue, Alice Hall in white, while the fourth runner goes unnamed and her clothes unknown. The Yorkshire maids had already established a suitable way of dressing to race and had even agreed colors to help with identification.

At almost the same time, but on the other side of the Pennine Hills, the description of another race was far from celebratory. The Rev. Oliver Heywood, a Presbyterian minister, was told about a women's race and was shocked and offended by it. He described it in his diary as "a strange unheard of race on Karsy [Kersal] Moor, near Manchester. . . . It was run by 3 or 4 women stark naked only their privitys covered with a rag. . . . Oh unparaleled impudence! . . . this horrid shameless spectacle . . . Lord awake." He was almost certainly not there in person, since he did not know whether there were three or four runners, and we cannot rely on any of his details, particularly as he is hostile to the very idea of the event. But he did record how the women wore next to nothing, that thousands went to see it, and that "many loads of bottles of ale" were taken there to keep everybody lubricated. Elsewhere in his diary he described horse races as "sad, dreadful" and thought that God was dishonored by them, and he also recorded how "hell is broke loose" when "a great number of persons of the poor and baser sort" put up a Maypole.[19] The puritanical classes had not been silenced with the return of the monarchy and the demise of Cromwell's Commonwealth.

The Reverend Heywood does, however, give us one valuable piece of information—he tells us that the runners' prize was a "holland shift." A Holland shift, known in some parts of England as a Holland smock, became by far the most common prize for women to run for over the next 150 years and virtually became the symbol of women's races. Within a few years, races for Holland smocks were being run for in other places, too. In July 1696, thirty-five miles from Kersal Moor at the horse races on Martin Mere, near Ormskirk, women ran for a smock plus a guinea in gold; men ran for a tumbler worth five pounds.[20]

Smock racing spread quickly to the south of England; at Abingdon, Berkshire, a smock valued at "near 50s" (fifty shillings) was run for in 1697 at a horserace meeting there.[21] In 1698 young women ran about a mile and a half for "a fine Holland Smock" on the road from Isleworth to Brentford, west of London.[22] Smock racing had quickly taken hold all over England.

As in the example of the Reverend Heywood, smocks were sometimes called "shifts" and were the same garment. In and around London—in Middlesex, Surrey, Essex, Berkshire, Hertfordshire, and Buckinghamshire—they were always known as smocks. In the West Country—Cornwall, Devon, Somerset, and Dorset—they were known as shifts. In the Midlands and in the north of England, "smock" dominated, as it did in Ireland. In Kent, however, "smock" and "shift" were used almost interchangeably, and as the century progressed, "shift" came into more common use generally. Very occasionally, when they were offered as a prize for runners they were referred to as an "under garment" or "petticoat" or even elevated to a "gown," and in the early nineteenth century, a "chemise." Nevertheless, more than 80 percent of usage referred to a "smock." To avoid confusion, I will refer to them as smocks and the races run for them as smock races.

Holland was a fine, plain-woven linen with a dull finish that made it more or less opaque and had been used in Britain since the fifteenth century. The fabric was so called because it originated from Holland. Women and girls wore smocks or shifts under their outdoor clothes and often wore them around the house when they weren't expecting visitors. They even wore them to bed, and they were very much a woman's personal item.

It might have been expected that after the collapse of Cromwell's Commonwealth and the return of Charles II, that women would begin racing in village fairs, festivals, and wakes again, but there is no evidence that they did.

Absence of evidence is not, of course, evidence of absence, and we cannot doubt that fairs, festivals, and sports went on as they had for centuries, but we have very few details of what was done at them or by whom. However, Shakespeare, in *The Winter's Tale*, uses the character of Polexenes, King of Bohemia, to tell us about Perdita, a shepherd's daughter:

> This is the prettiest low-born lass that ever
> Ran on the green-sward; nothing she does or seems
> But smacks of something greater than herself,
> Too noble for this place. (act 4, scene 4, lines 185–88)

The Winter's Tale was first performed at the Globe Theatre on Wednesday, 11 May 1611. Thus, it had been well-known for a long time that women were runners and that they could be ennobled by running, despite being of lowly birth.

There is, nevertheless, little evidence that women ran races to any great degree *before* the Civil War; the evidence that men ran races at that time is surprisingly sparse as well. In John Stow's *Survey of London* (1598), he lists "leaping, dancing, shooting, wrestling, and casting the stone" as the summer sporting activities of youths, but he does not mention running.[23] In *The King's Majesty's Declaration to his Subjects Concerning Lawful Sports to be Used* (1618), specific mention is made of "dancing, either men or women, Archery for men, leaping, or any such harmless Recreation," but there is no mention of running races.[24] Shack Marmyon's poem in *Annalia Dubrensia* in praise of Robert Dover and his Olimpick Games does refer to "running, Leaping, and throwing of the barre," but of the thirty-two or thirty-three poets in that collection, only two mentioned running at all.[25] So perhaps running as a sport was not a major one for men at that time either. The database shows, however, that seventeenth-century women did run in stand-alone races on the roads and public areas in and around towns—the fields, greens, marshes, and moors—and they also raced at horserace meetings. The evidence is sparse, but apart from the maidens of Kent who ran sprint distances, the women runners elsewhere in England ran longer distances: one mile up a steep hill, five miles, two miles, and one and a half miles. The smock had already become the most common prize. However, the smocks weren't just prizes for the winners; they were important items in their own right—carefully made, elaborate, and expensive—and they acquired an important symbolic value. To explain why, we need to look at a rural custom—riding skimmington.

Riding skimmington was the English equivalent of *charivari,* a folk custom also found in Europe and North America under several names. In England it was a way of humiliating those in the village whose marriages were breaking social norms. Most commonly, this was a woman assuming the so-called man's role in the family and dominating her spouse verbally and even physically. The village would gather and form a noisy procession with drums, pipes, fiddles, and whatever was available to make raucous music. A surrogate man and wife, or stuffed effigies of them, were placed on a horse but with the man sitting backwards; he held a distaff while the woman beat him with a ladle.[26] We should not get too focused on its name, however. Samuel Pepys came across one in Greenwich in June 1667, arranged because the constable of Greenwich's wife "beat him"; Pepys simply called it "a great riding."[27] Henri Misson saw one on the streets of London before 1698 and said it was because "a Woman had given her Husband a sound beating;" but he too failed to give it a title but told his story of it under the heading of *Cornes* [Horns].[28] Such rides, named and unnamed, had begun in the sixteenth century, lasted through the eighteenth century and continued well into the nineteenth; under the guidance of William Combe and Thomas Rowlandson, Dr. Syntax met a skimmington ride in 1820:

> Tis a procession us'd of course,
> When the grey mare's the better horse;
> When a wild wife doth play the game
> Of wearing what I must not name,
> Though I must own that my tongue itches
> To say, when she doth wear the breeches;
> And the poor fool dare not resist
> The terrors of her threat'ning fist.[29]

Such "ridings" continued in rural communities well into the nineteenth century—in 1886 Thomas Hardy described a "Skimmity Ride" in *The Mayor of Casterbridge.*[30]

Central to our knowledge of the skimmington ride, however, is *Hudibras,* a very popular, rambunctious, mock-heroic poem that came out in three parts, in 1663, 1664, and 1678, respectively, and remained in print for several generations. It was not until 1678 that the skimmington ride came into the story, and even then not by name.³¹ *Hudibras,* written by Samuel Butler, was a satire against Cromwell and his supporters. The eponymous hero, Sir Hudibras, and his squire, Ralpho, get caught up in events Don Quixote–style. Afterward they discuss their adventures, each taking an opposing view. Sir Hudibras often takes the puritanical, pedantic, Presbyterian side, while Ralpho voices the independent or anti-Puritan side, though not consistently. Each part of *Hudibras* has three cantos, and in part 2, canto 2, a noisy skimmington comes into view led by drums, pipes, horns, and dogs and boys. Butler, too, called it "a Riding."

> A Smock display'd did proudly wave:
> . . . .
> Next after, on a raw bon'd Steed,
> The Conqu'ror's *Standard-bearer* rid,
> And bore aloft before the *Champion*
> A *Petticoat* display'd, and rampant;
> Near whom the *Amazon* triumphant
> Bestrid her *Beast,* and on the *Rump* on't
> Sat *Face* to *Tail,* and *Bum* to *Bum,*
> The *Warrior* whilom overcome;
> Arm'd with a *Spindle* and a *Distaff,*
> Which as he rode she made him twist off:
> And when he loiter'd, o'er her Shoulder
> Chastis'd the *Reformado* Soldier.

This was humiliation for the man—exposed to public ridicule by being dominated by a woman.

> When Wives their Sexes shift, like *Hares,*
> And ride their Husbands, like *Night-Mares,*
> And they in mortal *Battle* vanquish'd,
> Are of the *Charter* dis-enfranchis'd
> And by the right of War, like *Gills,*
> Condemned by *Distaff, Horns* and *Wheels,*
> For when Men by their Wives are cow'd,
> Their *Horns* of course are understood.

But the spectacle was also intended as humiliation for the woman—shaming her for her unacceptably dominant behavior. Hudibras and Ralpho, of course, see it from different points of view; Ralpho talks disparagingly of

> Breeches greedy *Women* [who]
> Fight, to extend their vast *Dominion* . . .

Then Hudibras reminds him that during the Civil War, women had not only fed their husbands to give them strength to fight but also used their own strength directly for the cause. In London had they not

> March'd Rank and File, with *Drum* and *Ensign*, Rais'd
> T'intrench the City for Defence in?
> Raide'd *Rampiers* with their own soft Hands,
> To put the Enemy to Stands;
> From *Ladies* down to *Oyster-Wenches*
> Labour'd like *Pioneers* in *Trenches*,
> Fell to their *Pick-Axes* and *Tools*,
> And help'd the Men to dig like *Moles*?

The symbolism of the skimmington ride, therefore, had two faces: one the horns, denoting (perhaps unexpectedly) the man's weakness; and the other the smock and petticoat, which symbolized women's dominance. But the process of the skimmington ride seems to have created a kind of alchemy and transformed what began as the public humiliation of a man and a woman into a statement about women's strength. Butler tells us that the smock, held aloft, "did proudly wave," and he writes of "the *Amazon* triumphant," the "*Female* brave," and "this proud *Dame*."

These examples show that by 1699, noisy skimmington rides could be found in almost any corner of England, with the symbolic smocks and horns carried overhead like banners—the horns denoting the husband's weakness, and the smock announcing his wife's unacceptable power over him. Butler writes of women wanting to wear the breeches, but, begrudgingly perhaps, he also acknowledges their strength. Simultaneously, across England, women began running footraces for smocks that were not simply prizes for winning but came to symbolize something greater, something that later ages might have called "petticoat power," or even "girl power." But perhaps this spirit had already been present in England for a very long time. In Queen

Elizabeth I's reign, in 1599, a Swiss visitor to England named Thomas Platter described how "the women-folk of England ... have far more liberty than in other lands, and know just how to make good use of it, for they often stroll out or drive by coach in very gorgeous clothes, and the men must put up with such ways, and may not punish them for it, indeed the good wives often beat their men."[32]

5

"A PRINCE'S WINE AND BISKETS"

1700–1724

As the clock turned, the seventeenth century slipped into memory and the eighteenth became the new reality. By this era some women were proud of their athleticism and wanted to test it publicly, not least Susan Butterfield, also known as Dame (or Lady) Butterfield, who kept a turn-of-the-century roadhouse for eating and entertainment at Nightingale Hall, also known as Mob's Hole, near Wanstead in Essex.

> TO ALL GENTLEMEN AND LADIES.
> If Rare Good young Beans and Pease can Tempt Ye,
> Pray pass not by my Hall with Bellies Empty;
> For Kind Good Usage every one can tell,
> My Lady Butterfield does all excel;
> At Wanstead Town, a Mile of the Green Man,
> Come if you dare and stay away if you can.[1]

Susan Butterfield was not just a restaurateur with a penchant for bold advertising; in 1699 she was fifty-six years old and described herself as "an old Hunter."[2] She knew that in that entertainment-hungry age she could turn her athletic prowess to her advantage and use it to drum up more business. Two years later she advertised as follows:

> To all Gentlemen and Ladies that are disposed to recreate themselves in the country, this is to give notice, That Dame Butterfeild's [sic] Feast [i.e., her birthday] will be kept, at mob's Hole near Wanstead, in the County of Essex, a mile beyond the Green Man, and it has been kept 2 years, on the 30th of April, 1701; where will be a very good entertainment all the year afterwards. I give

a challenge to leap a horse, or ride a horse, or run on foot, or hollow with any woman in England of my age: I will not under-value my self with any that is older than my self; but if they be one or two years younger, I will engage when, and as soon as you please;

> So I remain your humble Servant,
> Susan Butterfield.[3]

Although the challenge remained much the same, year after year, Susan Butterfield became something of an institution as she repeated her challenge annually with only slight variations. In 1717 her challenge read:

This is to give notice to all my honoured masters and their ladies, and the rest of my loving friends, that my Lady Butterfield gives a challenge to ride a horse, to leap a horse, or run on foot, or halloo, with any woman in England, seven years younger, but not a day older, because I would not undervalue myself, being now 74 years of age. My feast will be on the last day of this month, April, when there will be good entertainment for that day, and all the year after, at Wanstead, in Essex.[4]

The following year she repeated the advertisement again, but without giving her age.[5] There is no record of who, if anyone, took up her challenge, or for what activity or for what stakes they agreed to compete, but even if no one ever dared challenge her, her challenges were a testament to her confidence, particularly when she was in her seventies, and particularly for running. For all the other named activities, horses might have to take some of the credit.

In March 1702 Queen Anne came to the English throne; she was thirty-seven years old and a sports enthusiast. Before becoming queen, she had ventured inquisitively into that male preserve, the cockpit, before being summarily dismissed from it. She liked horseracing and established racing at Royal Ascot; she also loved Newmarket and not only patronized the races there but rebuilt the royal residence and supported the town as well, giving a thousand pounds to pave its streets and endowing two schools, one for twenty boys and another for twenty girls, with each school receiving an annuity of fifty pounds.[6] After the Act of Union in 1707, Anne became Queen of Great Britain, and she reigned until her death in August 1714. Under the rule of Queen Anne, women runners thrived.

Susan Butterfield wasn't the only woman to issue challenges: young women did so as well. The following appeared in 1712: "This is to give Notice, That there is a young Woman, born within 30 Miles of London, will run, for Fifty or a Hundred Pounds, a Mile and an half, with any other Woman that has liv'd a Year within the same Distance; upon any good Ground, as the Parties concern'd shall agree to."[7] The prize amounts suggested—fifty or one hundred pounds—were enormous sums then, and the "young Woman" must have been an exceptional runner with very confident backers, but other women ran for more modest sums. Also in 1712, two women ran on Hounslow Heath for a wager of five pounds a side; the runners were the Flying Milk Woman of Ormond-Street and the Mad Bess of Southwark.[8] The women must have been well known to have gone by their nicknames; there is no record of the result. Was the Pig-Pok Girl another exceptional runner? She was specifically named as the one person who could not enter and run for a smock valued at "one guinea or thereabouts" on Wantage Down, south of Oxford, in 1720.[9] Was she so good that it would have spoiled the race? There is no evidence of betting on women's racing at this period, though it would be very strange if none took place.

This example shows, however, that smock racing had taken hold in England and very quickly came to dominate women's running. On Easter Monday 1700, after a cricket match on Clapham Common, south of London, maids were invited to run for "a Lac'd Smock, Value 4l [£4]" and to start precisely "at three o'clock from the Watch-House."[10] This was the most valuable smock ever raced for up to that date (that we can document), but that distinction would not last long. Smock races began to appear at a bewildering number of festive occasions and seemed to become an almost required part of them. The horse race meeting at Woodstock Park is an example: it lasted two or three days, and the women ran in the morning of the last day for a smock valued at two guineas. These sports were advertised every year from 1702 to 1707 and took place in late August or September. Woodstock Park adjoins Blenheim Palace, which was constructed to commemorate the Duke of Marlborough's victory at Blenheim in 1704. Work did not begin on the palace until the winter of 1704–5, so the smock races were a part of Woodstock life before Blenheim Palace was even thought of, and they continued during the early stages of its construction, attracting, no doubt, many Blenheim Palace laborers, masons, and their wives.

Traditions can be adopted and used for another purposes, and by 1706 "festivities for the honour of the battle of Blenheim" were held in Woodstock Park and were celebrated on the traditional date, and at the same venue, where the annual horse race meeting had taken place. The women now raced for the smock as part of the Battle of Blenheim celebration.[11]

Horse race meets were good places to see smock races,[12] each of which had its own character, but smock races were also arranged after cricket matches (see above), cudgeling,[13] and prison bars matches.[14] They were also held to top off afternoons of eating, drinking, music, and dancing. In 1710, at Lambeth Wells, across the River Thames by horse ferry from Westminster, there was music, dancing, and "very good entertainment" every Monday, Thursday, and Saturday afternoon starting at four or five o'clock, for seven weeks. Lasting from August until Old Michaelmas Day, top billing for the festivities always went to a Holland smock race between "three maids."[15] They always ran "5 times round the Walks at Lambeth Wells" near Harpur's Walk, a distance of one and a half miles or so. Lambeth Wells was a kind of mini spa where people went to drink the "purging waters" and perambulate around the walks, and it became a favorite watering hole, but in its early years the entertainment was weather-dependent and only went on if "fair."[16] Later, the accommodation seems to have allowed the music and dancing to go on in any weather. The advertisements were always addressed to "all Ladies and Gentlemen and others," and the events were obviously successful, for they went on unchanged for several years.[17] So successful were they that in 1712 the season was started in May, thus extending it by three months, and the starting time crept forward to one o'clock. Whatever the time of year, however, the maids' smock race was always the top attraction, and there seems to have been one every day—not, presumably, involving the same runners, three days a week, for months! There must have been an almost endless supply of smocks and maids to run for them at Lambeth Wells during Queen Anne's reign, and we can imagine the runners coming from all over Surrey, while others caught the horse ferry from the Westminster side of the Thames. Between 1710 and 1716 there may have been as many as two hundred smock races at Lambeth Wells, with an unknown number of young women taking part. Were some of the runners old favorites who ran every week and every year? The historical record is regrettably silent on this. It was clearly a commercial operation, and there was no suggestion that the young women had to apply to enter or that there might be more (or fewer) than three runners. It was all organized in advance, as were the musicians and the supplies of food and drink.

A smock race was sure to draw a crowd, and there seems to have been no shortage of runners, but organizers took pains to make their prizes as attractive and tempting as possible. The laced smock that maids ran for on Clapham Common in 1700 was valuable, but the prizes on offer in Epping Forest were valuable, too. Epping Forest was an ancient woodland with some equally ancient clearings and lay about seven miles north of the City of London. A smock race was organized there in 1704 with a first prize of "a very fine Lac'd Smock" plus two guineas, and entries from young women had to be made to John Staton at the Green Man a week in advance; he began to advertise it three weeks beforehand.[18] The runners had to work for the smock, though; the race involved two laps of a one-mile course marked out near the Green Man. Stanton described the two guineas on top of the "very fine Lac'd Smock" as "encouragement," but the encouragement did not stop with the winner. The runner-up also received two guineas, and the third-placed runner received one guinea—a very substantial outlay of prize money and significant because prizes for second and third place had been added to the all-important smock. In 1713 the smock to be run for on Wanstead Heath (also in Epping Forest) was even more valuable. The contest was advertised as a race between five women with a first prize of a "Lace Smock of 4 Guineas Value."[19] This may well have been a smock *made* of lace, for (by the evidence we have) it was the most valuable smock ever run for up to that date. However, the other prizes were unusually valuable, too: a petticoat valued at two guineas for second place and a gold ring valued at one guinea for third place. Runners had to register their names at the George Inn at Woodford at least two days before the race. This sort of investment required that the organizers got their money's worth, and to ensure this they required the women to run twice. The first race was simply to establish who were the fastest three of the five; after a breathing space, those three ran against each other a second time for the prizes. Perhaps this was the reason for advertising for "women" runners and not "maidens," as they might be more able to race hard twice. (Although the distance is not mentioned, it was likely to be one and a half to two miles.)

The number of smock races and their popularity gave women runners a profile that they could use to make money, and it is clear that many of the women who ran in these races had joined the commercial world. They ran for the money and other prizes, as well as for the smock, and the best of them were well rewarded. This was possible because their presence drew a crowd that enabled organizers or landlords to turn a profit. This business flourished in the first quarter of the eighteenth century, and the women runners had made a step toward the "middling sort," or those who traded or sold their skills for money. Just as the winners at Old Wives Lees had lifted themselves out of the group in need of charity by winning ten pounds in the seventeenth century, the eighteenth-century smock racers improved their economic lot.

The smock races in this period fell into two broad categories. In the first, the smock race was the sole or main attraction, and expensive prizes were offered to attract the best runners. These events were most likely to capture the spirit of skimmington. By some people's standards, they may have seemed rough and disorderly, but the smock races were well organized with the runners knowing when and where to enter, and at what time.

> To enter betwixt 9 and 10 at the Market Cross on the said Day, and to be on the Course between 12 and 1.[20]

> At Two of the Clock in the Afternoon . . . to enter their Names any time before Ten a-Clock that Day with Mr Davies at the Castle and Three Tuns at Highgate.[21]

> At three a-Clock in the Afternoon . . . to be enter'd at the King's Head before 12 a-Clock in the Forenoon.[22]

The second category consisted of bigger sporting occasions comprising two or more events of which the smock race was only one, and on these occasions the prizes were usually more modest. These events resembled the traditional country fairs that were often considered a good day out for the whole family and were designed for local participation; however, the smock races were still high-profile and often the highpoint of the day. An example was the annual sports event held at Acton in west London. In 1719 a full day of sport was advertised starting at ten o'clock in the morning, with *three* women's smock races, men's wrestling, and backsword playing.[23] The first smock race was for a "lac'd Holland Smock" worth one guinea; the second race was for a "Holland Smock" worth fifteen shillings; and the third race, between six women, was for a "muslin apron" worth ten shillings, a second prize of "a pair of scarlet stockings with clocks" worth seven shillings, and the third prize of "a pair of silver laced shoes" worth six shillings.[24] Despite the relatively low-value prizes, there seems to have been no shortage of runners wanting to take part in the races, even though the women had to run over three miles—from the Crown and Half Moon in Acton to the middle of Ealing Common (one and a half miles) and back. By 1720 the three races at Acton had been reduced to two and remained at two for several years, always with modest prizes. By 1724 there were only prizes for the winners and runners up.[25] The events were always advertised for women rather than maids or maidens. The relatively poor prizes suggest that it was sometimes difficult for organizers to finance the prizes. In some cases this problem was solved by having patrons donate the smocks so that the events could go on; this happened in 1712 at Newcastle where the first prize of a silk hood was "given."[26] Similarly, in 1721 at the race between six "young women" at Jeremy's Ferry, Hackney, the fine Holland smock, valued very precisely at £1.1.5d, was given "by a set of Gentlemen."[27] A fine hat and ribbon valued at a half guinea was given to the runner-up, presumably donated by the same gentlemen; they were on display in advance at Jeremy's Ferry House.

A smock race could also occur in the most unexpected places. In 1721 John Hinton arranged fundraising events at Hammersmith "at the New Square formerly called Pingarfield," which included a "Raizing Dinner" and "Several Sorts of Diversions," including music, backsword and wrestling competitions, and a race for a Holland smock between "four young Women"; this gives us further evidence that the young women runners had become part of the entertainment business.[28]

The public appetite for smock races seems to have been almost insatiable, and there must have been as many reasons for the public wanting to see the women run as there were people who went to watch them. Some went for the sport and to see the competition, some to be part of the occasion, and some will have been like Zacharias Conrad von Uffenbach, a German visitor to Oxford in 1710, who did not go to Port Meadow to see "the womenfolk run for a prize in petticoats and low-necked shifts" but wished that he had.[29] This observation cannot be used as a description of what the runners wore, as we know that he didn't see them, but it does tell us what people were saying about them. Men liked to see women wearing less than usual. There is at least a hint of this attitude in the notice for a race for a smock worth three pounds at Windsor in 1721 "to be run for by Young Women, not exceeding thirty Years of Age."³⁰ The appeal was more explicit the following year in the advertisement for the horse races at Arundel, Sussex: there was to be a race "by pretty Sussex Spinsters."³¹ Such references stand out, however, because they are unusual, but there can be little doubt that some people went to the races to watch the women rather than to watch the race. Whatever the motives of the organizers and the crowd, the smock races provided opportunities for the women to compete, gain recognition, and win costly prizes or money.

In this period there were references to women racing for smocks at Guildford (Surrey), Woodstock (Oxfordshire), Lambeth (Surrey), Oxford, Elswick (Newcastle-upon-Tyne), Finglas (Ireland), Bourne (Lincolnshire), Acton (Middlesex), Odsey (Hertfordshire), March Common (Isle of Ely), Wantage (Oxfordshire), Hurstpierpoint (Sussex), Windsor (Berkshire), Gawsworth Park (Cheshire), Arundel (Sussex), Sleaford (Lincolnshire), Enfield (Middlesex), Yaxley (Cambridgeshire), Lilley Hoo (Hertfordshire), and Sunderland (County Durham). Women could also be seen racing on common ground all around London—Clapham Common, Ealing Common, Finchley Common, Epsom Downs, Wanstead Heath, Epping Forest, Hackney Marsh, and Wimbledon Common—as well as on the roads and in town squares. However, an event that demonstrates the interest in, and the status of, the women's smock race and shows how the racers were perceived took place in the Little Park at Hampton Court in September 1716. A race had been organized there for "young Women" for a smock, "a quilted Petticoat," and "a Sarcenet Hood" (the latter two probably for second and third places).³² The thirty-three-year-old Prince of Wales (George Augustus, later King George II) was present, and he initiated something unique: "Those who lost had 10s. a-piece, and a pair of Scarlet Stockings; and besides, were all treated with Wine and Biskets, by his Royal Highness's Order. The Country People seem extreamly well pleas'd with the Generosity and affability of the Prince, who shews himself with a great deal of Condescension at these Rural Diversions."³³

Everyone, it seems, was a winner; the runners were all well rewarded, even the losers, and they all received royal recognition. The crowd was pleased with the prince's treatment of the runners, and the prince's reputation rose because of it. The significance of this event was even greater than it seems now, however: two months earlier King George I had returned to Hanover for six months and had left his son, the Prince of Wales, in charge of Britain as Guardian and Lieutenant of the Realm. At the time he ordered wine and biscuits for the runners, he had all the authority of the king and was the most influential and important person in the land—the women smock racers had received true royal recognition.

The smock race phenomenon, however, could not have taken place had there not an underlying predisposition among women to showoff their physical skills and to be free, even temporarily, of the social restrictions that normally inhibited them. Susan Butterfield—who issued tough physical challenges to other women all her life—and the young woman who wagered fifty or one hundred pounds against any other local woman to run one and a half miles are just two examples.

The rapid rise of smock races, and the value and care taken to ornament the smock prizes, requires some explanation, however. Smock races were unlike the races run by men at the time and were unlike all other forms of early eighteenth-century sport. Smock racing became a unique craze, but its popularity was not the product of wagers nor was the practice dominated by betting. For an explanation, we need to return to the processions and "rides" that occurred around the county—the skimmington rides. In 1724 William Hogarth contributed plates for a new edition of *Hudibras*; one of them captures the double-edged iconography of horns, smocks, and petticoats (fig. 12). In this image the cowed "husband" is just left of center, facing backwards on the horse and behind his wife, who sits forward and holds the reins but is looking back at him and holding a ladle threateningly. Hogarth places a witch (in a pointed, tall hat) and cauldron in the central foreground, perhaps as a symbol of women's often frightening and unsettling power. Horns are clearly on show and a smock is carried on a pole like a banner.

As noted in chapter 4, Henri Misson, a French visitor to England, described such a riding as a *charivari* under the heading "Corns" (i.e., horns) because, he wrote, the surrogate version of the man being beaten by his wife was "crown'd with very ample Horns," presumably because he had lost his own.[34] It is not surprising that these rowdy processions with their hangers-on and raucous music would end up as an event of some kind, and it may have been one of those "Horn Fairs" that Daniel Defoe encountered at Charlton, not far from Greenwich, in 1724. Such an event could hardly celebrate a man's weakness, but it could certainly celebrate a woman's strength, and in this instance women had taken control and used the occasion to conduct

FIGURE 12. *Hudibras Encounters the Skimmington*, William Hogarth, drawing with color wash, 1724. (Royal Collection, RCIN 913465)

a fair that they conducted by *their* rules and their rules only. Defoe wrote: "The Women are especially impudent for that Day; as if it was a day that justify'd the giving themselves a Loose to all manner of Indecency and Immodesty, without any Reproach, or without suffering the Censure which such Behaviour would deserve at any other time." Such events, he wrote, ought to be suppressed: "Indeed in a civiliz'd well govern'd Nation, it may well be said to be unsufferable."[35]

But the idea that a woman's strength, even if socially unacceptable, could still be celebrated became an established idea. A hundred years after Defoe's observations, William Combe used one of his Dr. Syntax stories to explain the thinking behind it:

> . . . when in matrimonial strife
> A husband's cudgell'd by his wife
> In country-place, 'tis rather common
> Thus to complement the woman[36]

Identifying a skimmington ride as a "complement" to the woman gives the event quite a different character; it becomes an occasion in which women are celebrated for being strong and dominant and so not constrained by the usual forces that require them to be well-mannered and modest; it produces a kind

FIGURE 13. *Eccles Wake Fair,* Joseph Parry, oil on canvas, 1822. (Salford Museum and Art Gallery, UK)

of topsy-turvy occasion in which the normal rules of society are suspended. Around the same time, under the heading "Riding Skimmington," Francis Grose explained that "a smock displayed on a staff is carried before them as an emblematic standard, denoting females' superiority."[37] The smock, boldly displayed, had become the symbol of female "superiority," which came to be expressed in smock races that entered their golden age in the first quarter of the eighteenth century. The smock's display was always part of the ritual. In *The smock-race, at Finglas,* James Ward wrote of the "waving Smock . . . high in Air display'd," and for the next hundred years writers, reporters, and artists highlighted the prize smock being paraded to the race grounds on a pole, hanging high on a tree's branches or some other elevated position and blowing overhead. At Eccles Wake the smock was carried on a pole to the race grounds like a banner (fig. 13).

We can see that in the intervening years between Butler's text of *Hudibras* (1678) and Thomas Rowlandson's image *Dr Syntax with the Skimmington Riders* (1812; fig. 14), the skimmington ride had become a celebration by women for women, for by the early nineteenth century it was the women who carried

FIGURE 14. *Dr. Syntax and the Skimmington Riders*, Thomas Rowlandson, pen and ink drawing, undated [1812?]. (Huntington Art Museum, San Marino, California)

the banners, beat the drums, and formed the largest part of the skimmington procession. The smock as a symbol of woman's dominance was not limited to the smock race, however. In 1816 Francis Philip Stephanoff showed a smock being carried in front of a man and a woman sitting on a horse, skimmington-style, and he labeled his drawing *The Shrew* (fig. 15). Dominant women could be too dominant for many men's tastes. Nevertheless, dominant women who had no intention of being subservient to their husbands had a long history in England; in 1599, Platter drew attention to an English proverb that began, "England is a women's paradise..."[38]

The smock, therefore, was never just an item of clothing given as a prize; when it was displayed, it became a symbol of women's "superiority," marking a time when they could publicly demonstrate their strength, endurance, and resilience. Smock races in the seventeenth and eighteenth centuries were not trivial or simple events run purely for fun and laughter. In this upside-down world, the girls and women who ran in smock races could assume a boldness that might be censured at other times but in which they reveled all the more because they knew it was temporary. Smock races in Britain in the seventeenth and eighteenth centuries were a social as well as a sporting

FIGURE 15. *The Shrew*, Francis Philip Stephanoff, bookplate, 1816. From Edward Wedlake Brayley and Francis Philip Stephanoff, *Popular Pastimes, Being a Selection of Picturesque Representations of the Customs & Amusements of Great Britain, in Ancient and Modern Times*, 1816.

FIGURE 16. Women running for smocks at a horn fair, Henry Alken, c. 1820s, hand-colored engraving. (Collection of the author)

phenomenon. Men never experienced anything like this, so the smock races are unique in the history of sport as well as in women's history.

The smock races of the nineteenth century never completely escaped the legacy of the horn fair and the skimmington ride. Henry Alken's image from the 1820s of women running for a smock has at the bottom right, next to the white horse, a man carrying a stick crowned with horns and bells, while two smocks flutter overhead like flags—a reminder of the smock race's heritage and one that everyone in the first quarter of the nineteenth century, even princes, would have understood (fig. 16).

6

VISITORS WRITE HOME

1725-1749

Smock runners were such a familiar sight in England that they became a must-see feature for overseas visitors. In 1726 Voltaire saw them at Greenwich and wrote home about them, saying that the sports, of which they were a part, made him think he was at the Olympic Games. He also thought that the spectators were "exceedingly beautiful, all of them were well-made; there was such neatness, vivacity and pleased contentedness about them that it made them all look pretty."[1]

Later, after he had been told that they were just students, apprentices, maidservants, and country girls, he regretted the comment. However, Jean-Bernard, Abbé le Blanc, who visited England in 1737, rather liked maidservants and country girls and saw them very positively. He stayed in England for seven years, and when he saw the young women race he also saw in them a reflection of ancient Greece, and wrote: "Like as formerly at Olympus and Lacadæmon, in more than one county of England young damsels are to be seen contending for a prize at a course [race]. They are commonly strong robust country girls, who run with surprising swiftness."[2] He also saw them somewhat romantically: "A young country girl, in other countries, is a mere peasant; here, by the neatness of her dress, and genteelness of her person, you would take her for a shepherdess in one of our romances."[3] Earlier, César de Saussure, a Swiss traveler, had written home in 1728 remarking that the women and girls who ran races on Kew Green were "scantily clothed."[4] But rather like von Uffenbach eighteen years earlier, Saussure passed on the information despite not seeing the races for himself. Again, as with von Uffenbach's account, it does tell us what people were saying about them.

There was, however, an unexpected twist to the story of what the women wore to race. It began with the report of a wager in October 1725, and was widely reported in the newspapers:

> On Tuesday last a notable Foot-Race of a four Mile Course, was run on Barnet-Common, by two young Damsels, for five Guineas of a Side; but several hundred Pounds of Bets, alias Bites: The one was a London Lass, and the more delicate, tho' weak; the other a Barnet Breed, and more robust: Vast numbers of the lower Class of Gentry attended on that Occasion, expecting they would have run *in puris naturalibus;* but that was over-ruled, and they were clad in white Waistcoats and Drawers, but without Shoes and Stockings. They perform'd it in 39 minutes; but the London Girl falling down, was run over by an Horse, much hurt, and thereby distanc'd, and the other won the Wager.[5]

Several striking features mark this report. This is the first known notice of a serious wager involving a women's race that included heavy betting. The race was unusually long, and it was also unusual to record the time of the winner (which was quite slow), but it seems to have been an unruly event. The runner from Barnet had no reason to run hard once her opponent had been knocked down and was out of the race. Most striking, perhaps, is the fact that they were to run *in puris naturalibus,* literally, stark naked. In this period, however, there were other examples of this practice. One took place in August 1735, when "six Women ran, not incommoded by Cloaths or Modesty, three Times round the upper Quarters in Moorfields [c. one and a half miles], for a Holland Shift and half a Guinea, and gave abundance of Sport to a numerous Company of Spectators."[6] Also in August 1735, the *Caledonian Mercury* reported that "2 naked Women ran in Stepney-Fields for a Guinea, a Holland Shift, an Apron and a pair of Stockings, which afforded much Diversion to the Gentlemen and Ladies present; but 'tis said for Decency's [sake] they will hereafter run with Draws on."[7] The race had been run annually since 1730 "for Girls under 20."

In September 1740 an "impudent Serving Maid" ran a solo race "quite naked" at Great Haywood, in Staffordshire.[8] Solo races, in which the runner tried to run a stipulated distance in a specified time, were very common among men but virtually unknown for women. Finally, on Walworth Common in June 1748, "the noted Mary Weaver of the Borough" and "Sarah Lucas from Rotherhide [Rotherhithe]," ran "stark naked" for a Holland Smock after a cricket match between High Kent and the Black Swan Club. This report is unusual as well, as it is the first recorded instance of two women runners being identified by their own names rather than by aliases.[9]

It might be expected that women ran stark naked from pressure by race organizers who wanted to attract a crowd, but in at least one instance, the reverse was true—in July 1748 the organizers of the Newcastle-upon-Tyne races at Croft placed a note in their advertisement to inform the runners that running naked would not be allowed.[10] In that instance, at least, it wasn't the organizers who were responsible, and so the impetus to run naked must have come from somewhere else. A clue to understanding this phenomenon may come from the fact that the organizers at Croft (above) were addressing themselves to women and *men*. Of the thirty-four known events in which runners were reported to have competed stark naked in England in the seventeenth and eighteenth centuries, thirty were run by men. It should also be noted that three of the four races in which the women ran naked were for wagers, the way that men's races were organized, rather than smock races common among women and girls.

Sometime in the 1660s Francis Willughby, an original member of the Royal Society, collected notes for a *Book of Playes*.[11] His intention was to collect information on the sports that might have been lost during the period of the Puritanical suppression. When describing running races, he wrote: "Running of Races is when 2 or more run for a prise or wager which they agree upon.... They run often naked or in their shirts, & if it bee a great wager they use to exercise themselves & run the ground over before in their cloths."[12] At about the same time, Philip Kinder collected notes on his tour of Derbyshire's Peak District and wrote of the locals: "Theire exercise for a greate part is ye Gymnopaidia or naked boy, an ould recreation among ye Greeks, and this in foote-races. You shall have in a winter's day, ye earth crusted over wth ice, two Antagonists starke naked runn a foote-race for 2 or 3 miles, wth many hundred spectators, and ye betts very smale."[13]

Here we have two consistent accounts; both describe naked runners, both describe males, and both refer to the betting. Willughby's is a simple description of footraces in general, while Kinder's has the feel of an eyewitness account of a specific event and carries much more local detail. In 1660 Willughby had toured Yorkshire, Cumberland, and Lancashire, and in 1662 he toured Staffordshire, Cheshire, and Wales. Both descriptions are matter-of-fact in tone, and neither of them expresses surprise or shock by the nakedness they report. Kinder even seems impressed and sees echoes of the Greek Classical past in them, for later in the passage he extends the comparison and describes the locals as being like "Lakedaimonians."

Men continued to run naked all over England, particularly when large sums of money were involved. Thomas Hearne recorded in his diary for 20 September 1670 that at Newmarket Lord Digby walked "stark naked & barefoot" for fifty pounds in the presence of Charles II and his court, and men continued to compete naked for the next fifty years.[14] In September 1720, a few years before the young damsels were stopped from running naked on Barnet Common, two running footman raced in Woodstock Park. It was a race

> for 1400 libs [£1,400], between a running footman of the duke of Wharton's, and a running footman of Mr. Diston's, of Woodstock, round the four mile course. Mr. Diston's man being about 25 years of age, (and the duke's about 45,) got it with ease, out distancing the duke's near half a mile. They both ran naked, there being not the least scrap of any thing to cover them, not so much as shoes and pumps, which was looked upon deservedly as the height of impudence, and the greatest affront to the ladies, of which there was a very great number.[15]

Erasmus Philipps, an Oxford undergraduate, was also there and recorded even more details of the event in his diary, but he made no mention of their nakedness, indicating that it was so commonplace it didn't need mentioning.[16] This attitude prevailed throughout the eighteenth century when elite male runners took off all their clothes to run. Some reports even failed to mention the fact. Another example occurred in September 1790—Abraham Wood from Lancashire and Harper from Cheshire ran a one-mile wager on the New Road to Islington in London for one thousand guineas. It attracted a "great concourse of people" and was widely reported in newspapers all over Britain, but the readers of the *Craftsman* and *Adams's Weekly Courant* would not know that they ran naked because the publications failed to report the fact, perhaps assuming that their readers would know it anyway.[17]

Big-money racing and nakedness seem to have gone together with men's sport; in December 1787 Powell ran a trial as preparation for a one-thousand-guinea wager that he could not run a mile in four minutes and "performed it within three seconds of the time. He ran entirely naked."[18] There can be no certainty about why some of the best male athletes took off their clothes to run. Was the Olympic tradition of men running naked behind it, as Kinder suggested? Was there a lost folk custom in which nakedness symbolized purity? Was there a religious source for it? (The Adamites [see below] who ran naked in Hyde Park seem to suggest a reference to humankind's naked origins in the Garden of Eden.) Were clothes eschewed for purely athletic reasons? Was nakedness and barefootedness a way of ensuring that no runner could claim that the other had unfair advantage?

Some men continued to run naked in their wagers until well into the nineteenth century, and it seems to have been so commonplace that people thought it was the "normal" way of doing it. A corresponded to *Notes and Queries* reported that in 1824 on Whitworth Moor in Lancashire he saw six naked men run a seven-mile race: "There were hundreds, perhaps thousands, of spectators, men and women, and it did not appear to shock them, as being anything out of the ordinary course of things."[19]

Taking off one's clothes in public can never be a straightforward thing, and neither can the reaction of the members of the public. Men seemed to find it quite acceptable in front of other men, but men running naked in front of women made some men feel uncomfortable: they thought that women would be offended, embarrassed, or shocked. In May 1733 Baron de Pollnitz, another overseas visitor to London, saw a naked man run "thro' an infinite Concourse of People" in St James's Park and the Mall: "The ladies astonish'd at such a Sight, knew not how to keep their Countenances; Some turned their heads aside, others hid their Faces with their Fans, but they all made a Row, as well as the Men, to let him pass by."[20] In 1792, however, the stark naked men ran "to the amusement of a great number of spectators and the delicate nymphs of the Horse Guards."[21]

As early as 1641, however, there is a reference to a woman's reaction to seeing men run naked. It comes in *A Jovial Crew,* a comic play written by Richard Brome and first produced on stage in 1641 at the Cock-Pit Theatre, Drury Lane, London. In act 2 Vincent tries to tempt Meriel and Rachel with the prospect of some fun and freedom by offering them various entertainments in London: "Shall we make a fling to London, and see how the Spring appears there in the Spring-Garden; and in Hide-park, to see the Races, Horse and Foot; to hear the Jockies crack; and see the Adamites run naked afore the Ladies?"[22] Rachel replies: "We have seen all already there, as well as they, last year."

The question and its lackluster response indicate that in 1641 the naked runners in Hyde Park were simply sights to be seen, but the above example is still a man's view of what he *thinks* women would think. The only women's view that we have is from Henrietta Howard, Countess of Suffolk, who in 1722 reported on a race "for young wenches" at Gosworth [Gawsworth] Hall in Cheshire; she added: "The pleasure of the day ended with a prison base; all the swains from the neighbouring towns performed feats of activity and ran against one another with little more than a fig leaf for their clothing, and we, being in a state of innocence, were not ashamed to show our faces."[23]

Henrietta makes this sound more like a religious experience than one of shock and embarrassment that many men might have supposed. Even for the men we do not know what the range of opinions and attitudes would have been. It is not hard to imagine that there was an element of voyeurism when men watched the women run naked, but just how erotic it was, or even how erotic it was meant to be, must be open to question. Had the people who arranged the race for the young "lasses" on Barnet Common wanted to stage it as an erotic experience for the male spectators, they could surely have thought of something better that a four-mile race in the chill of October.

In puris naturalibus was only a very minor theme in the story of women's foot racing—unlike the men's, in which it plays a significant role—but it reminds us not to make assumptions too readily. Perhaps the events in the eighteenth century that women ran naked signaled that the women wanted to be treated as serious runners and not an indication that they were being exploited as mere titillating entertainment arranged by men, for men. Nevertheless, the practice lingered on until the nineteenth century, but in very small numbers.[24]

We should not doubt that some women runners took racing very seriously and that smock racing continued to attract a lot of runners in the eighteenth century—indeed, more than ever before—and this despite a new form of racing being introduced that made racing harder. In 1730 the first best-of-three competition appears in the database. As described in chapter 2, this system required the runners to race twice or three times instead of once. It grew in popularity with organizers because it provided more sport and more entertainment for spectators; it was at the same time much more challenging for the runners.

The first example for which we have evidence is also the most extreme in terms of distance and was advertised in the *Daily Post* in September 1730.

On Monday next, being the 21st of this Instant, will be given, by Mr. JOHN FIG, a Holland Smock to be run for, three Heats, by six young Women or Maidens, one of them a black Girl.

N.B. They are to start at Two o'clock from Mr. Fig's House at the Sign of the View of Oxford near Buckingham Gate, and run to the New Bridge at Chelsea, and back to his House, which is one Heat; and to rest or rub one Hour before every Heat. Note, no less than four can start for the Smock.[25]

John Figg (or Fig) was one of the six brothers of James Figg, the famous prizefighter who ran his own amphitheater and who was said to have fought 271 undefeated matches in the prize ring when he retired in 1729.[26] James Figg had arrived in London in 1718 at the age of twenty-six and at first made his living by fighting; later he taught his techniques of attack and defense and promoted events in his own house, or tavern, with its adjoining great room, or amphitheater. When he arrived in London the tavern was known as the Boarded House, which he changed to the Sign of the City of Oxford to reflect not only the fact that it was on Oxford Road in Marylebone but that he was an Oxfordshire man.[27] He would present himself, when making or receiving a challenge, as "I James Figg, from Thame in Oxfordshire, Master of the said Science." Or, on one occasion, "I James Figg, Oxonian, Professor of the said science."[28] In his amphitheater James Figg promoted various sporting events—wrestling, fencing, smallsword, backsword, and boxing—to sold-out audiences, but he was well known for promoting women's events, too. The *Annual Register* described it this way: "He was for many years proprietor of the boarded house in Marylebone-fields, near Oxford-road. Here he frequently exhibited his own skill, and at other times made matches between the most celebrated masters or *mistresses* of the art, for the noble science of defence was not confined to the male sex; we find Mrs. Stokes, the famous city championess, challenging the Hibernian heroines to meet her at Mr. Figg's."[29]

Even more immediately, only a few weeks previous to the footrace described above, women fighters had drawn good crowds at a series of fights at Figg's as well as at Stokes's amphitheater. James Figg did brisk business: events began at three o'clock in the afternoon, the main performers came on at six, and the matches lasted late into the evening. When his brother John arrived in London, he took over his own house at Buckingham Gate, a couple of miles south of James's establishment, hoping to attract a share of this business. He began by establishing his connection with his famous brother by naming his house the Sign of the View of Oxford. He, too, was a man of Thame in Oxfordshire. John Figg's house, however, had a major drawback; it didn't have the seating capacity of Figg's Amphitheater and so could not accommodate crowds to watch indoor bouts, but he *could* attract other mistresses of sport—the runners who competed outdoors.

The event he advertised in September 1730 was arranged to give anything from five to eight hours of entertainment and so boost the sale of ale and gin, but it was a very tough event for the runners. The advertisement shows that John Fig had already made agreements with the runners—one of them "a black girl"—but there was also a recognition that one or more might not show up at the start, so it was also a warning that if fewer than four turned up, the event would not take place. Buckingham Gate was situated at the southeast corner of the Buckingham House grounds (now Buckingham Palace), where the two branches of the road now called Buckingham Gate make a right-angle turn. The "New Bridge at Chelsea," the midpoint, was indeed a new bridge and had yet to open to traffic. It was timber-built, and construction had begun six months earlier. It would be opened two months later when Frederick Louis, the Prince of Wales, would be the first person to cross. In fact, its name was misleading, for it would more correctly be described as the "New Bridge at Fulham," for it connected Fulham (north of the River Thames) to Putney (south of the river).

No report of the race has been discovered, but the runners would have begun with Buckingham House on their right and then run down the road to Chelsea and joined the King's Road, notorious for footpads and highwaymen. They would then follow its almost straight course to the new bridge, about four and a quarter miles total. The runners were required to touch the staff of an official stationed there for that purpose, then turn and retrace their steps back to the Sign of the View of Oxford—a total of eight and a half miles. After an hour's rest, they would have set out and done the same thing all over again. Even if one runner had out-distanced the rest, and so eliminated them, she would have been expected to run the course a second time—a total of seventeen miles. All of the runners would have arrived at the initial starting line at two o'clock knowing that they might have to run the course *three* times—a total of twenty-five and a half miles! This was the longest distance ever recorded for a best-of-three competition, and none, surely was ever tougher than this.

Smock races of more modest distances continued to attract good crowds all over England. Voltaire had remarked on "an immense number of comely young people" at Greenwich in 1726.[30] Two months later there was "a great Concourse of People of all Ranks" on Durdham Downs outside Bristol to see "several modest females" run a one-off race for a Holland smock.[31] Women runners attracted crowds in London, too. In October 1733 four women ran a best-of-three competition for a Holland smock from the King's Arms on Pall Mall, London, to the Gloucester Tavern in St. James's Street, at the bottom of Pall Mall—about one and a quarter miles. "The Windows and Balconies of all the Houses in Pall-Mall were crowded with Spectators, and the Streets were never seen fuller of People on any Occasion whatever."[32]

In this event, two of the four runners were distanced in the first heat, leaving two to run against each other in the second. The same runner won both heats and so won the smock; accounts differ as to the winner: some gave victory to Hannah Williams and some to Anne Laurence.[33] In a gossipy letter from Thomas Hill to the Duke of Richmond, Hill elaborated and said she (presumably the winner) was John Russell's sister (probably a married sister) and a servant to a butcher in Hungerford Market, but Hill then confusingly adds that she was forced by her employer to sell her "prize smock to buy two of coarse thread," the first evidence we have of someone selling their prize smock.[34] It was her second win that year, having already won a race along the Mall. How her employer had the power to require her to sell the smock, which surely was her own property, was not explained. Hill, incidentally, calls her "a lady." There were other prizes, too: a cap, clocked stockings, and laced shoes. The shoes went to a runner who was distanced in the first heat.

One week later another smock race was held in the same vicinity, this time for a "Smock with Orange colour'd Ribbands and Cambrick Tucker."[35] The second-place runner would receive a pair of worsted stockings with orange-colored clocks, and once again it was a best-of three competition; all the runners were under twenty years old.[36] The course ran from the King's Head south across Piccadilly, across Pall Mall, across the Mall and St James's Park, before turning into Whitehall to the Banqueting House (from one to one and a half miles).

The descriptions of the races from the King's Arms and the King's Head pose logistical problems, for after the first heat the runners would need breathing space, maybe a timed half-hour, before the next heat. During that time they needed to rest, have something to drink, and prepare for the next race. Some runners might need, or expect, a massage. These were serious athletic events, and the runners were treated like athletes and so given time for recovery and a "rub" between heats.[37] But this would have left the runners at the wrong end of the course at the end of heat one. The greatest likelihood is that they were out-and-back races, thus doubling the distance to two or three miles

Racing in front of large crowds was almost commonplace for women; they did it on the streets of London and at horserace meetings all over the country. In 1749, at the races on Durdham Downs, near Bristol, the five women who ran for "a Holland smock and one guinea" did so in front of "a great number of booths and scaffolds . . . for the accommodation of spectators, who were vastly more numerous than has ever been seen there on any other occasion."[38] Also in 1749, an eighteen-month-old girl was the center of attention for "Thousands of Spectators" in St James's Park, London, when she walked the length of the Mall (half a mile) in twenty-three minutes, having been given half an hour to do it "for a considerable Sum of Money." It was described as "very extraordinary" at the time, and it seems no less so more than 274 years later.[39]

In general, the value of the winners' smocks had dropped from their height of four guineas or four pounds in the early part of the century, but they were still attractive prizes and worth winning: three guineas on Datchet Common, Berkshire, in 1729; and two guineas on the Carrs, outside Stockton in County Durham, in 1735.[40] But one exceptional smock stands out. In July 1748 at the Newcastle races at Carthorpe, the Holland smock was of an unusually high value at five guineas. Four "ladies" competed for it, and it was won by Miss Molly Shepard against the odds; she was not the favorite in the prerace betting.[41] But prize smocks could vary greatly in value; a year earlier a smock was advertised at nearby Broughton [Boughton] Green Fair, Northamptonshire, for ten shillings and sixpence, one-tenth of the value of that won by Molly Shepherd.[42] In 1746 an even less valuable smock was offered as a prize in the Hall Garth, near Winlaton in County Durham; it was worth only eight shillings, the least valuable smock prize ever recorded. (Both Hall Garth and

Boughton Green were in the northeast of England.) The variations in prize amounts are a reminder that almost no generalizations can be made about smock races; every community and every promoter or organizer did things differently. The event at Hall Garth, Winlaton, was also unusual in other ways: men's races were included, and they were only open to the "workmen belonging to the Factory of Ambrose and John Crowley," and workwomen too![43]

The Winlaton factory was a major center for the manufacture, storage, and distribution of iron products nationally—particularly nails that were supplied to the Royal Navy. Ambrose Crowley, a Quaker industrialist and politician, had set it up in the 1680s, and it was continued after his death in 1713 by his son John, by which time it was probably the largest ironworks in Britain. John died in 1728 but the factory continued under another Ambrose Crowley, a grandson of the original.[44]

The original Ambrose Crowley, however, was as well-known for the way he treated his workforce as he was for the success of his ironworks.[45] He expected hard work over very long hours (five a.m. to eight p.m.) from his workers, but he built living quarters for them in a locked, gated compound. It included a chapel and a minister, compulsory schooling for the workers' children, a court to settle disputes, a health fund, debt relief, and a pension scheme, all paid for out of deductions from the workers' wages. This was not meanness on the part of Crowley but was meant to encourage a spirit of self-help and responsibility. Committees ran the community and appointed officers, constables, and so on, but its organization was laid out originally in 97 laws that governed virtually every aspect of the workers lives. Over time the number of laws grew to 127, but within this, the workers themselves had a degree of influence. It was undoubtedly a patriarchal, authoritarian system, but it was designed to keep the workforce sober, hard-working, safe, and sociable. They were a self-contained, almost insulated, community and became known as Crowley's Crew. They may have been fined for swearing, betting, and fighting, but they organized their own social life, of which a smock race was a part. The workmen had a footrace, too, with a prize of one guinea. The low value of the prizes was because the money had to be raised by the workers themselves. Nevertheless, they also raised the money for "a Purse of Three Guineas" for a footrace between "Reputed Footmen" (i.e., athletes) on the same day as the smock race. The runners had to pay a three-shilling entrance fee, which went to the second-place runner.

In earlier years Crowley's Crew had subscribed to a ten-pound prize for a horse race at what was called the Winlaton Races; Ambrose Crowley donated an eighteen-pound prize, and Theodosia, John Crowley's widow, donated one at twenty pounds. After Theodosia's death, the innkeepers of Winlaton stepped in but could only manage to finance a twelve-guinea prize. To attract good horses, the workmen increased the value of their prize, but eventually the Winlaton Races ceased.

The initiative to start footraces had two clear advantages: they would be cheaper to underwrite than horseraces, and they could involve Crowley's Crew in their own races. The arrangement gave them what must have been one of the earliest examples of a works' sports. They were held on a Thursday, with the big race scheduled for five o'clock. Were the workers given a half-holiday to attend?

The financing of the smocks was always an issue for a race promoter, and the solution was often found by locating a patron to donate them or to at least pay for them, for the garments were almost always made and decorated by local women. In 1725 the smock and velvet cap, valued at two guineas, at Stockton Races was "given by a Gentleman."[46] At Long Marston in Yorkshire in 1726, the smock was "given by Colonel Ligonier."[47] The event was a major celebration of Prince of Wales's birthday, organized by Edward Thomson, MP for York, but there was an inevitable political edge to the festivities—the differences between prince and his father were very well known. In addition to the smock race, the event featured a foxhunt, a cudgeling competition, and dancing. "When this was over, all that could bear Arms formed into a Battalion, fired three Rounds, drinking his R. Highnesses Health, with a Huzza after each Fire; several Ladies bore Arms on this happy Occasion." This salute was followed by a ball, a bonfire, ringing of church bells, and a variety of toasts; it was a very full day of birthday celebrations. John Ligonier had entered Britain as a Huguenot exile, joined the army, and was a colonel in Lord Cavendish's Regiment of Horse. By 1758 he had risen to be commander-in-chief of the British Army. Some very influential people supported smock races.

By 1727 George Augustus, the Prince of Wales, had become king, and in 1733 a smock was raced for by five young women in House Park, adjoining Hampton Court Palace.[48] The smock had been given by a Captain Little of the First Regiment of Foot (Grenadier) Guards.[49] The race was attended by the new king, George II, who was so pleased he "order'd two Guineas to her that won it," a local woman. This smock race was not part of a larger multisport event or horse race—it was the *only* event, just as it had been seventeen years earlier, when, as Prince of Wales, the king ordered prizes and "wine and biskets" to the runners. We have to conclude that George II wanted, specifically, to see the young women race. Royal recognition and approval were becoming a habit.

Smock racing was a necessary part of almost any celebratory event. In addition to a royal birthday or a factory sports event, a smock race could be arranged as part of a treat for tenants, as it was in Ireland in 1731,[50] or as part of the celebrations to mark the completion of a new road,[51] and, of course, at Easter, Whitsuntide, Midsummer Day, and various saints' days. The average distance that the women ran (with the exception of Kent) was about two miles, but with the best-of-three system this distance had to be run more than once by those who were successful in the first heat, and on some occasions they had to run much further. Women in Kent, however, still ran extended sprints of 165 yards to 440 yards.

The women who ran did so under numerous descriptors: girls, maids, maidens, milkmaids, virgins, young women, wenches, jolly wenches, lasses, modest females, women, married women, women-kind, and ladies; even older women ran. Black girls and Roma girls ran, and even men dressed as women tried to get in on the action. In 1728 a two-mile race for "young Women" at Hackney Marshes, northwest of London, drew a good crowd. Three runners were dressed and ready to start when it was discovered that one was a man. He had arrived on a horse, riding sidesaddle to add to the deception, but it turned out that he was a "Running Footman to a Person of Quality." "The Mob understanding the matter pursued him in order to duck him in the River, but to make the more speed, he dismounted, rid himself of his Petticoats, took to his Heels and got clear of them, after much more Diversion than the Race, which was afterwards run by the other two."[52]

As years went by and organizers became more experienced, it is not surprising that entry regulations became tighter. In 1729 the women who wanted to run in the one-mile race for "a Fine Holland Smock, of three Guineas Value" had to "enter their names and places of abode" at the White Hart in Windsor,[53] and in 1737 the women who wanted to run in the four-mile race for a smock had to pay a one-shilling entrance fee by ten o'clock at the Windmill on Finchley Common, on the morning of the race. If they failed to do so and still wanted to run, they had to pay double.[54]

A new kind of running event appeared in Kent in 1748: "At the Halfway-House between Dover and Canterbury... will be given to be run for, by three Maids against three Married Women, either party winning, each to have half a pound of tea, and half a pound of sugar."[55] Kent had already seen women's running matches between parishes,[56] and the women were familiar with Stroke-Biass (a match of running) and so knew all about women competing in teams, but this was a new venture.[57] A generation of women runners in Kent had now grown up not wanting to concede superiority to their daughters. In the years ahead, the "married vs. single" format would become very popular in cricket and stool-ball, and various running games would give future generations of older women many outlets for the cooperative and competitive among them, enabling them to continue to develop their skills and find fun in sports. Already, however, the married vs. single format had taken hold in the southwest of Scotland in curling matches. There is also a suggestion that those who ran in all races were somewhat older than had been the case in earlier generations, for more of them are described simply as women, rather than as maids or maidens.

The second quarter of the eighteenth century saw foot racing for women expand into many more corners of British life, and some competitors acquired nicknames by which they were known: the Flying Milk-woman of Ormonde Street, Mad Bess of Southwark, a Basket-woman of St James's Market, Brentford Moll, the Little Bit of Blue (a.k.a. the Handsome Broom Girl), Black Bess of the Mint, and a Kingswood Girl. In a few cases we even learn their proper names to add to the rollcall of successful early women runners—Hannah Williams/Anne Laurence and Molly Shepard.

After several generations of women runners, it was no longer surprising to see women athletes on the road, and those who were motivated by their health and the sense of freedom that sport gave them wanted the acclaim that went to the women athletes. In July 1746 Elizabeth Carter wrote to Catherine Talbot, a friend, about how she spent her time in Kent; she had been on one of her long walks:

> Towards the conclusion of our walk, we make such deplorable ragged figures, that I wonder some prudent country justice does not take us up for vagrants, and cramp our rambling genius in the stocks. An apprehension that does not half so much fright me, as when some civil swains pull off their hats, and I hear

them signifying to one another, with a note of admiration, that *I am Parson Carter's daughter*. I had much rather be accosted with "good morrow, sweetheart," or "are you walking for a wager."[58]

Everyone in the country knew about women athletes, but Elizabeth Carter was much more than just Parson Carter's daughter: she was a translator, Classical scholar, and poet, as well as being a prodigious and persistent walker. She also placed health centerstage; in 1744 she wrote: "I am at present engaged in a very eager, and I may add a violent pursuit of health. I get up at four, read for an hour, then set forth a walking, and without vanity I may pretend to be one of the best walkers of the age."[59]

But it wasn't just pretense; during her lifetime she walked thousands of miles in the Kent countryside and believed that through physical effort she was able to understand herself and relate more completely to the world around her.[60] By the middle of the eighteenth century, women of all classes, including one of the country's finest brains, were challenging the old social norms.

7

PAYING THE ULTIMATE PRICE
1750–1774

By the mid-eighteenth century women runners were known all over Britain and ran in smock races in more places and more often than ever before. Women runners were in demand, the races were appealing and satisfying for the women, and they were exciting to watch. Thus, promoters found them attractive, but for the runners it could be a very tough business. Best-of-three competitions were now commonplace, but they did present particular challenges. One can imagine a well-conditioned runner finding a one-off race relatively "easy," and perhaps the first or second races of the best-of-three—but not the third! The third race always featured at least two runners who had each won an earlier race and had also been beaten in them, plus others who had been beaten twice (but not by much). The third race was the decider, one in which the winner had to beat runners who had themselves already defeated others that day—a major physical, psychological, and emotional test. And all performed in public—triumph or defeat would be there for all to see.

Take, for example, the "Handsome Smock" that was advertised to be run on Chelsea Common in August 1755. It was advertised as a best-of-three, one-and-a-half-mile competition, with no fewer than four to run, and was to start at the Cow and Calf at four o'clock in the afternoon. This, however, was not just a local event: "Two note[d] Welch Girls" had arrived to take on the "Earl's Court Girls." Both groups had a reputation to uphold, and both would have been well prepared.[1] It was a tense, needle match with three races of one and a half miles each in a single afternoon—a serious athletic challenge. Purely local events could bring their own tensions, though, such as the half-mile best-of-three event at Castle Carey in Somerset in 1769, when Nan Francis and her sister Pegg raced it out, winning a "shift" and "ribbands," respectively. Parson Woodforde wrote in his diary that he had never seen the park so full of people in his life.² Spectators enjoyed a relaxing day out, but the three half-mile heats that the Francis sisters had to run in the afternoon would have been hard work. Nan Francis ran one of them in three minutes, in all probability with bare feet and on an indifferent surface.

A particularly grueling event was held in July 1766 when three young women ran a best-of-three competition for a Holland smock from Bethnal Green to Hackney (anything from one and a half to three and a half miles); this competition went to the third race, too, which "was with difficulty won by a girl belonging to the brickmakers."³ "Girl" was commonly used to describe young, unmarried women and did not mean a child.

Even one-off and apparently one-sided races could end up in a hard tussle. In 1753 a married woman of thirty took on two fifteen-year-olds over two laps of the Bray Commons in Dublin (about a mile and a half per lap). The older woman was a hardened competitor and had already gone thirty miles to Dublin and back *before* the race. One of the fifteen-year-olds was said to be "pretty fat" and was soon distanced, but the other led the married woman at the end of the first lap and continued to race hard for the next lap; she "push'd the Woman very hard to the last."⁴

Pushing hard, whether you are fifteen or thirty, is part of racing, but it can take its toll. In 1765 at Alconbury in Huntingdon, five women (also called "girls") ran in a best-of-three competition for a smock over an unrecorded distance; in the first heat, two runners ran so hard that they distanced the other three, so the second heat was between the two remaining runners only. The runner-up in the first race needed to win the second or the competition would be over for her, so she ran hard to win it. The report of the race tells a grim story: "The girl that won the second heat was so dead run, that by straining she burst one of her blood-vessels, and died soon after."⁵ This event marks the first known fatality among the women runners, but hard running was known to be risky. Racehorses, dogs, and racing men were all known to have died by overexerting themselves. In 1723 a racehorse named Molly, which belonged to a Mr. Panton, "died in great agony" in the first heat of a race against Badger at Newmarket, after having beaten Snip and Witty Gelding two hours earlier.⁶ Spanking Roger died after running a trial in 1741,⁷ and in 1743 The Old Montague Mare came second in the first two heats at Carlisle against Teazer but died soon after.⁸ The list could go on. In 1788 Parson

Woodforde wrote in his diary that his greyhound, Hector, had been "running about the Cover all the Morning before breakfast . . . and broke (by some furious running) some Vessel near his Heart, as he never got up after he laid down—very soon dead indeed."[9]

Men fared no better, and even if death was not instant, a severe effort might so weaken them that death came later, or so it was thought.[10] In 1733 the "famous and noted" John Appleby ran a ten-mile race in fifty-two minutes in Sherwood Forest against Pinwherie. Appleby "died 4 hours after, and it is thought that Pinwherie cannot live."[11] In 1737 Griffith Morgan (a.k.a. Guto Nythbran), the extraordinary Welsh runner, won a twelve-mile race against an English runner by the name of Prince, but on reaching the finish his patron and supporter clapped him on the back by way of congratulation, and he died on the spot because his heart was "displaced" from beating so fast. He was thirty-seven years old.[12]

In 1754 Stephen Morris, a "noted" runner, was engaged to run forty miles in seven hours at Hampton Court for a "considerable sum"; after six hours he had completed thirty-eight miles but then "fell down and expired soon after."[13] In 1771 John Simpson ran about two and a half miles on Greenwich Park in fourteen and a half minutes, but it "cost him dear, for overheating himself he died the next day of a violent Fever."[14] In 1793, when the famous Foster Powell died unexpectedly at home, one report attributed his death to "the great exertions of his last journey to York" (taken in response to a wager to walk five hundred miles in seven days), an opinion also supported by "the Faculty," even though he had completed the journey more than nine months earlier.[15]

There seems to have been no escape from the consequences of strenuous physical effort, great exertions, or excessive labor. The famous Swiss physician Samuel Tissot began his text on health by citing the consequences of "Excessive Labour."[16] Chapter 1, section 1, began: "The most frequent Causes of Diseases commonly incident to Country People are, 1. Excessive Labour continued for a very considerable Time. Sometimes they sink down at once in a State of Exhaustion and faintness, from which they seldom recover: but they are oftner attacked with some inflammatory Disease, as Quinsey, a Pleurisy, or an Inflammation of the Breast." If this was the lot of the "country people," kings could not escape it either. In 1724 the King of Spain died;[17] after the autopsy his physicians declared that he had overheated his body while hunting and had died from the "violent exercise," which led to the speculation that the French king (Louis XV) must be taking a similar risk because he was often "no less violent in the same exercise."[18]

With running horses, dogs, laboring men, and even kings at risk from the adverse effects of strenuous or prolonged exercise, there was a kind of fascination about those who did expose themselves to the risks voluntarily. This is one reason the famous runners and long-distance walkers of the age drew such big crowds. One way to help prepare for hard racing was to take a series of "sweats." Earlier in the century, John Hall of Beverley, Yorkshire, a well-known trainer, had replied to Sir John Sinclair's questionnaire on training methods, saying: "The utility of the sweating process is to remove the obesity; and is produced by running exercise; increased by feather-beds and warm diluents. Three sweats in two days, well rubbed with flannel, and kept within doors till cool."[19] On further questioning, he expanded on his methods: "They must be put between feather beds, as often as good sense and judgment dictates, under the circumstances presenting themselves in the act of training. The necessary diluents are warm mountain wine, to cause sweating."[20]

A tongue-in-cheek advertisement for a smock race at Saltmoor Wells, near Ludford in Shropshire, made fun of this process.[21] Saltmoor Wells was a small rural community with entertainments in keeping with its size (hence the value of the smock was only fifteen shillings), but the organizers advertised it as if it was the biggest and best in the land, knowing that the locals would understand and smile. In addition to the smock race there was to be a cricket match, and a Mr. Birch challenged any man in England at tennis on their "extraordinarily good tennis court." But no-one believed that the tennis court was extraordinarily good, or that Mr. Birch would have to play anyone other than the local men, and everyone knew that although it would be good fun, the Gentlemen of Shropshire and the Gentlemen of Herefordshire hardly knew how to play cricket at all—it was all an extended joke as if they were the Gentlemen of Sussex and the Gentlemen of Surrey who played at the Artillery Ground in London in front of the Prince of Wales and sundry noblemen.[22] Cricket had barely established itself in Shropshire or Herefordshire, and Buckley's survey of eighteenth-century cricket lists no games of any note being played there at all.[23] In similar vein, the advertisement advised that "no girl to run for the smock that was in training last season as a racer, nor been in sweats before the 1st of April last, to be attested by her mother at the time of entering, which is to be at the starting post. There are already three girls that intend to run for the said prize. The knowing ones now lay 5 to 4 on the Clayland lass ag[ain]st the field, but 'tis thought the bets will be higher before starting."

Likening the local girl runners to racehorses in training was part of the joke, as was the idea that "knowing ones" would be laying odds on them, but it was well known that unless officials were watchful something very similar might happen at local horserace meetings; for example, the Reading Races in 1746 advertised a race for hunters

> that never started for Match or Plate, but have been actually used as Hunters last Season, not such as were only hunted a few Times on Purpose to be called so, nor such as have been in Sweats with an Intention to run . . . since last Lady Day. . . . The Master of every Hunter shall be obliged to make an Affidavit . . . to certify that his Hunter is qualified in every Respect . . . which Affidavit shall be produced at the Time of Entering, or before Running.[24]

Advertisements were, of course, local affairs, meant to engage with local audiences, and advertisements in different parts of the country could serve quite different purposes. Although they might all refer to an upcoming smock race, those races, too, would take on their own local character. But advertisers could often reach for a joke similar to the one used at Saltmoor Wells. In 1773 a handbill advertised a jackass race and a smock race at the White Hart at Battle-Bridge in St. Pancras, Middlesex—"No Ass to enter that has won a King's Plate this Season"—a knowing wink to readers that the King's Plates were open only to the very best racehorses in the land.[25] But this event shows how the smock racers got caught up in all the local events; in this case John Wilkes supporters and the Friends of Liberty were expected to show up to turn this into a rallying event. After the extraordinary events of 1769, when John Wilkes had been expelled from the House of Commons three times and was then reelected each time by his constituents in Middlesex, his popularity with his followers never faltered; one of his supporters was elected mayor of London, and on 1 October 1773 a medal was issued to honor Wilkes, inscribed "To whose spirited Conduct the Nation is indebted for the small Vestiges of Liberty now remaining."[26] It may sound like a simple festive day out with an ass race and a smock race, but the women who ran for the smock at Battle Bridge that day were at the heart of a very significant political movement.

Within a year John Wilkes was once again elected to Parliament by the people of Middlesex.

Those who ran in the smock race at Bushy-Heath [Bushey] in August 1767 were taking part in a very different event. It was part of a cudgeling match between the Men of Harrow and the Men of Stanmore as an element of a vast entertainment organized by Tommy Lowe, a well-known singer.[27] This event was his fourth within six weeks, and for good reason: ten thousand people were said to be there. On the day of the match, the Men of Harrow were victorious, and Susan Lovit won the smock after some disagreement over how many heats should be run. However, it was the women runners en masse who seem to have stolen the show. After it, one correspondent wrote: "We expect this Race of Girls will produce a Running among the Men—such is the Power of Love—for there is not a Youth in Watford, Harrow, and Stanmore, that is not all on fire with the Love of these four fair Damsels. And as it was the Custom among the Enamorators of old the shew their Love for their Mistresses, by their Prowess in Tilts and Turnaments, our modern Swains will prove the Ardour of their Flame by running."[28]

Not everyone felt as positively about fair damsel runners and how they set the young men on fire with love for them. In 1752, as in other times, there was an element who objected to women runners. Three women ran for a smock on Barnet Common, and one of them so out-ran the others in the first heat that they could not make their distance; the winner ran alone in the second heat, but one observer did not concentrate on the running: "They were all stripped to their Shifts and Under Petticoats, and exposed themselves very indecently."[29]

Annoyance turned into action to put a stop to a women's race at Finchley, Middlesex, in 1774. A men's sack race and a women's race for a Holland smock were organized along with gingerbread and toy stalls, but a local gentleman complained beforehand to the justice of the peace, who sent thirty constables to suppress it, which they did with heavy hands, "knocking down the Gingerbread stalls and taking some old Women into Custody."[30] The women were later released after they pleading their "extreme Poverty," but there can be little doubt that they were arrested because they were the organizers, which is consistent with the idea that not only did women run in smock races, they also organized them.

Whether the smock races were organized by women or men, or both, their content and style continued to be highly individual, location by location: the distances, numbers who ran, and the ages of those permitted to race all varied greatly. There is evidence, for example, that women in some places wanted to continue racing well past the time when they might be called maids or maidens, and some organizers tried to accommodate them; as younger women still wanted to race, some promoters and organizers tried to satisfy both groups. The race at Bray in 1753, described above, is an obvious example, with one thirty-year-old married woman running against two fifteen-year-olds, but this was not unusual. In 1773, at Yattendon, Berkshire, the organizers of the annual revel tried to be inclusive and set age limits of fifteen to forty for those wanting to race for their "fine Holland Smock."[31] That regulation must not have satisfied everyone, for the following year the age limit was tweaked to seventeen to forty.[32] In both cases, the event was a best-of-three.

The problem of age limitations was a common one; at the sports on Gray's Meadow, Oxford, in 1774, the age limits were set at sixteen to thirty. The main concern seems to have been to keep numbers down to a manageable level while still having enough runners to make the race viable, but it is not clear why there were age limits at all—in many cases the advertisements for the races simply specified that they were open to "women." It seems likely that the crowds wanted to see younger women run rather than older ones. Were the regulations at Yattendon (above) in place because women *over* forty wanted to run and the promoter rather wanted younger ones?

One promoter in 1756 found a solution by putting on two races for women: one for "young Women" who would run for a Holland smock at three o'clock and the other for "married Women" who would run at four o'clock for a pig. This was a commercial event alongside a cattle fair in a field at Edgware, London, which was "a very convenient Place for Hawkers and Pedlars in an Orchard adjoining the aforesaid Field, for their Stalls, gratis."[33] The two-day Belmont Fete, held at Warnford Park, Hampshire, in 1774—for which John Smith de Burgh (the 11th Earl of Clanricade) provided two smocks, one on each day—probably solved most problems, for the races were open for women of any age, apparently.[34]

Although there were great variation and individuality surrounding women's smock races in the third quarter of the eighteenth century, there was at least one general trend, and that related to the smock itself. The value of smocks after the middle of eighteenth century never reached the dizzy heights of four or five guineas on offer earlier, perhaps because of the economic state of the nation; during this period money was devalued. The races went on with undiminished enthusiasm, it seems, which suggests, perhaps, that the value of the smock had not been the main point in the first place.

It should not be surprising that during this period some women produced outstanding performances; one young woman was reported in 1765 to have walked seventy-two miles from Blencogo, Cumbria, to within two or three miles of Newcastle—a journey that took her virtually from the west coast to the east coast of England all "in one day."[35] Her performance was deemed so outstanding that it was reported again in the *Monthly Miscellany* twelve years later and was still the only female performance listed thirty years later, in 1804, among "Pedestrian Feats."[36]

Women could be such good and dependable walkers that men would set wagers for them; it was unusual, but it did happen in March 1761 when a farmer wagered twenty pounds against a gardener that four Welsh women could walk from Westminster Bridge to the Boot & Crown over Deptford Bridge and back again (about ten miles) in two and a half hours. They did it with three-quarters of an hour to spare. How much of the twenty pounds each of the four women won is unknown; the winnings went to the farmer who wagered on them. But the women would have agreed on their cut beforehand, and it must have been enough to motivate them to succeed. These Welsh women were obviously seasoned walkers and probably did such distances daily carrying farm produce into London. It shows that women were not deterred by long distances and were sometimes motivated by what look to us to have been quite small sums.

8

EXHILARATION AND ATHLETICISM
1775-1799

There are significant differences between the culture and practice of women running for smocks in the first quarter of the eighteenth century and the last. Sometimes changes can appear so slowly they are hard to detect, but there are hints in the last quarter of the eighteenth century that in some places women's smock races had become more unabashedly entertaining than athletic. Paradoxically, the proportion of smock races that were run as best-of-three events was higher than ever before, but the distances are seldom given, and the athletically challenging races held earlier in the century virtually died out. Moreover, no values were given for the smocks the women ran for; this is a major change, as great pride was taken in the early part of the century in declaring publicly the value of the smock.

The most obvious example is not a smock race in the traditional sense but a sack race for a Holland shift. Its significance is that it did not take place during a fair, revel, or fete but onstage at the Leeds Theatre in 1781.[1] Mr. and Miss West were appearing in "Positively the Last Night" of their engagement there and had devised a program that was close to what we would later call "music hall" (or variety). The advertisements told the good people of Leeds that they were about to see acts that had come straight from London, "perform'd at the Theatre Royal, Drury Lane." The program included plays, dances, comedy, and Morris dancing, much of it performed to make the audience laugh. But Leeds was a strongly Methodist town with its own chapel at which John Wesley himself had preached, and it must have been a hard task to make a success of such a show.

The bill also included "a race by Holbeck Girls, in Sacks, for a Holland Shift." Holbeck was in the center of Leeds, so this was a strategy to get the girls' friends and family to attend the show. The girls who "ran" in the sack race knew without doubt that they were part of the entertainment business. This was not sport at all, but for it to work it had to have the appearance of an old-fashioned country fair or bullbaiting. In urban Leeds the old country sports were now a fit topic to parody.

There was also an element if not of parody, then of deliberate and self-conscious imitation of the traditional country fair in the sports that were advertised at Brighton in August 1789. Only one poster for them is known to have survived, but it tells us what activities were used to tempt the local people. The poster is about one foot by six inches and printed on course, thick paper rather like that used in many eighteenth-century newspapers (see below), but it does not tell the whole story.

Jackass racing was always a big draw and thus was a headline event, and at rural fairs it often was paired with smock racing. But this was not a country fair; it was a royal celebration, and the clue to its significance comes at the bottom of the poster, which describes three sailing matches in honor of the Prince of Wales's twenty-seventh birthday (fig. 17). George Augustus Frederick (who would reign as George IV) had arranged the celebration personally, and Prince William (the Sailor Prince, Wales's second brother and three years younger) was back in England to take part in the celebrations.

In his biography of George IV, Christopher Hibbert describes the event as "various ludicrous sports," but they were not.[2] Rather, they were highly significant in their timing, in the people who attended (and who did not), and in the political message they conveyed.

Only six months had passed since King George III's almost miraculous recovery from his now-famous bout of "madness" that had provoked a constitutional crisis. William Pitt, the prime minister, had played every political card possible (some of which were unconstitutional) to keep the Prince of Wales from assuming power. Pitt and the Tories acted to save their political necks during the crisis, for they knew that their careers would be over if the Prince of Wales, next in line of succession and a Whig, took control. When the king recovered, Pitt briefed the queen, falsely, about the behavior of the princes during the crisis, and she believed him. She was so annoyed, and the princes so annoyed at the way they had been misrepresented, that a major rift developed within the royal family. The king and queen and the other children went to Weymouth, a seaside town in Dorset, as part of the king's

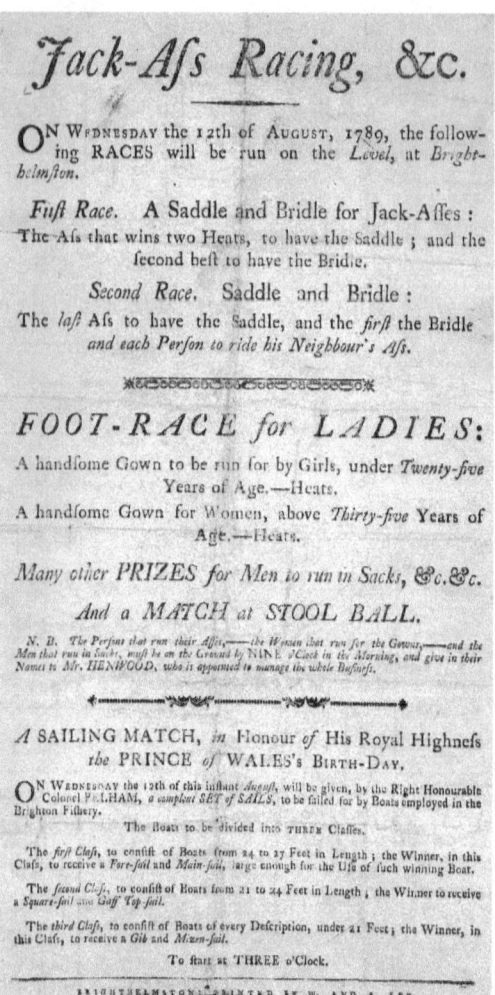

FIGURE 17. Poster for the Prince of Wales's birthday celebrations, 1789. (Collection of the author)

recovery, while the Prince of Wales and his two oldest brothers celebrated their birthdays at Brighton, 125 miles away.

As part of the prince's celebration, buildings in Brighton were "splendidly illuminated" and were hung with "transparencies very grand"—the predominant themes being the Prince of Wales's feathers, army and navy flags, and the motto "United for ever"—a reference to the inseparable closeness of the three oldest royal brothers. One eyewitness guessed that the crowd was twenty thousand strong; this was a colossal sporting, social, and political event.[3] So many prominent Whigs went to support the Prince of Wales that the event had something of the mood of a Whig rally. Blue-and-buff ribbons waved everywhere; band members wore blue-and-buff uniforms; blue-and-buff cockades adorned hats; horses sported blue-and-buff girths and headdresses; and blue-and-buff ribbons were tied to the prizes that the competitors won. The Whigs, of course, were the party of opposition to Pitt's Tories. The "handsome gowns" that the women ran for would have been decorated with blue-and-buff ribbons, too. Most significantly, the Prince of Wales had chosen as a format for his birthday celebration an old country fair, so loved by the common people and open to all—men, women, and children, rich and poor.

Within the context of the king's malady, the split within the royal family, and the political ramifications of both, this was a highly significant moment in the nation's history, but it was made immeasurably more so by the events just a few miles across the English Channel. Less than a month earlier, the Bastille had been stormed by the people of Paris, and the French had slipped into the grip of the Great Fear. King Louis XVI had lost control of his army, the clergy and nobles had been forced to renounce their traditional privileges, and the white flag of the Bourbon royal family had been replaced by the tricolour. The Prince of Wales was well aware of the political and social consequences of the historic events in France and had already personally gone to the coast to receive some French families who had been forced to flee. "France" it was said, was "on the eve of a civil war."[4] Louis XVI was only two weeks away from losing the centuries-old recognition of his divine right to rule when the National Assembly issued the Declaration of the Rights of Man on the 26 August.

None of the princes, politicians, or friends thereof thought that the Prince of Wales's birthday celebrations at Brighton, just eighty miles as the crow flies from the French coast, was merely about jackass racing and various ludicrous sports. In analyzing the program, the prominence of women's events stands out—two best-of-three races and a stool-ball match. The provision of two races for women (with one for the over thirty-fives and one for the under twenty-fives) is unique, but it is also seems odd that there should be no race for those between twenty-five and thirty-five; the explanation, however, is probably because many of the key runners of that age were already committed to playing in the stool-ball match. The poster describes the races for women rather grandly, as "Foot-Races for Ladies," and the prizes to be "handsome gowns," but one newspaper promptly brought the events down to earth, calling the women "wenches" and their prizes, "Holland Smocks."[5] In addition to the first prizes, runners-up won hats, and caps were also awarded. As the races were best-of-threes, there would have been at least two races for each age group, and perhaps three, so there were anywhere from four to six "ladies" races spaced throughout the day, more than any other activity. They were the framework around which the other events fitted. Sadly, there is no description of them and no report of the results.

Prince Frederick (the Duke of York) and Prince William (the Duke of Clarence) had birthdays within days of the Prince of Wales's, but Wales's celebration was different from his brothers': he alone included women's events and advertised them prominently. William Henwood from the New Inn in Brighton was given the job of running the sporting events on the day, but he took no part in their planning: that alone belonged to the Prince of Wales. His attitude toward women taking part in sport was shaped by his childhood. The royal family was large: George III and Queen Charlotte had six girls and seven surviving boys (two boys died young). The children were brought up in a strange sort of seclusion, relying on each other but with no outside friends. From an early age they played sports together, and the older boys depended on the older girls to play cricket, hockey, football, skittles, and every other kind of game. The princes had every opportunity to be grateful for the ability and willingness of their sisters to play various sports with them. Princess Charlotte (the Princess Royal) was particularly proud of her cricketing skills.[6] So, too, was her sister Princess Augusta, who, when she was over seventy years old, remembered playing cricket, hockey, and even football with her brothers, and recalled that she had been quite a good cricketer[7] The princesses often rode with their brothers, as well. Princess Charlotte was an exceptionally good rider, and when she was only fourteen, newspapers reported: "The Princess Royal attended His Majesty, the Prince of Wales, and the Bishop of Osnaburgh [Prince Frederick], at the hunt on Saturday last, mounted on a beautiful Roan; Her Royal Highness was dressed in blue and Gold, with a plain black hat, and never lost sight of the King during the whole Chase."[8]

Whether the Prince of Wales encouraged women to take part in sport or whether he just accepted that they could and should be able to is a distinction that is now hard to make, but when he became involved in a sport, women's participation in it soon followed. In 1788, for example, he accepted the position of patron to the Royal Toxophilite [archery] Society and the Royal British Bowmen, and in 1789, the Royal Kentish Bowmen.[9] Almost at once women became conspicuously involved in archery; in 1788 Miss Byng was proposed as a member of the Royal British Bowmen, and in 1789 Lady Jane James accepted the office of Lady Patroness of the Royal Toxopholite Society and presented an honorary badge, which was shot for on a day called the Lady Patroness's Target Day. Winners of the Royal British Bowmen's ladies' prize became "Lady Presidents," and women became prominent archers. In 1791 the results of the Royal British Bowmen competition show that special distances were arranged for women to shoot for the "Prince's Prizes." In time these distances became known as the "Prince's Lengths," and this innovation played a major part in attracting women into the sport.[10]

At the Brighton festivities in 1789, those who arrived at the Level in response to the poster found that there were other events, too: a cricket match (Brighton vs. the Adjoining Parishes), a jingling match, boxing, and wrestling, with prizes presented by the princes.[11] "But the most manly, the most elegant amusement in which skill and dexterity were manifested as are seldom witnessed, was a fencing scene between the celebrated Chevalier DE ST. GEORGE, and other adepts in that science. The contest was exceedingly interesting, and terminated, as might be expected, to the honour of M. DE ST. GEORGE; to whom his Royal Highness made a present, in token of his approbation, of a most elegant sword, adorned with knot of blue and buff ribbons."[12] He also presented swords to two French fencing masters who had been part of the display. The Chevalier de Saint-Georges was one of the finest fencers in Europe as well as a gifted violinist and composer. He was a French Creole: his mother, Nanon, had been a slave in Guadeloupe. The Prince of Wales invited him to the birthday festivities because of the friendship that had developed between them when the chevalier had fenced the Chevalière d'Eon (whose gender fluidity was the talk of Europe) at Carlton House in 1787, again at the Prince of Wales's invitation. On that occasion, the Chevalier de Saint-Georges and the Prince of Wales had also fenced against each other.

Attention at the Level then turned to the sea, between a half-mile and a mile distant; the Prince of Wales took to the water and led a "marine procession" in a boat named after his sister, the *Princess Charlotte*, to watch the local fishermen race for sails in three categories, and he not only presented the prizes to the winners but also handed out "a new jacket and trowsers" to each of the winning crew.

The events on land and sea lasted all day, from the time the participants handed their names in to Mr. Henwood at the New Inn at nine o'clock in the morning. During the day the crowd and VIPs moved back and forth between the Level and the coast. The crowd steadily grew throughout the morning, and the *Public Advertiser* reported that "the number of persons from the neighbouring villages was prodigious," with a "prodigious number of Nobility and Gentry," all rubbing shoulders amicably with each other.[13]

Soon after dawn the Prince of Wales had arranged for workmen to start erecting "pavilions and marquees" on the Level, a park about a half mile outside of Brighton in the valley leading to Lewes. There was a marquee for the Prince of Wales's party, one for the Corporation of Lewes, and several others for private parties. He also arranged for the workmen to erect "a temporary kitchen" where soup was warmed up and "an ox roasted whole" was turned slowly on its spit. (Some accounts said there were two.) Mr. Mercer, the Prince of Wales's butcher, carved the meat with a huge broadsword and then handed it out to the crowd on the prongs of an enormous fork, deadly looking enough to stop people getting too close or too eager.[14] Twenty hogsheads of strong beer was also provided for the crowd, and an undisclosed amount of wine was available in the tents for the nobility and guests. Deep into the evening people picnicked and partied on the grass.[15]

When the sports and prize-giving were over by late afternoon, the Duke of York's band entertained everyone as they ate and relaxed. Surrounded by the throng, Charles James Fox toasted "the Prince of Wales and the Constitution" with "three by three" rousing cheers, and the Prince of Wales, in return, stood and provocatively proposed "Charles Fox and the liberty of the subjects." These were followed by toasts to the Duke of York and the army, the Duke of Clarence and "the wooden walls of old England" (i.e., the navy), the high sheriff of Suffolk, "the Whig interest throughout the kingdom," and "many great and popular Members of both Houses of Parliament."

All this was followed by a "superb and magnificent ball and supper" for up to five hundred people at the Castle Tavern, given by the Duke of York and Duke of Clarence in honor of their brother, and when the late summer light faded, a large bonfire and a fireworks display lit up the cricket field. After this the band, preceded by the Queen's Light Dragoons, paraded along the Steine and around the streets of Brighton and did so for half the night. A mood of warm self-congratulation engulfed Brighton as everyone there told everyone else what a great day it had been and how glad they all were to have been part of it. It was a huge success and accompanied, said the *Public Advertiser*, by "every demonstration of joy."

> The heavens smiled on the scene; a more beautiful day could not have been wished for: the heat was not excessive, and, besides, tempered by fine cooling breezes....
>
> No man ever witness more real joy and happiness than was diffused among all ranks of persons, on this auspicious day.—Happy Britons! Smile on your favourite son, and receive, with transports, the acclamation of millions, encouraged by hope, firmly founded, and approved by Heaven![16]

No women runners had ever raced, nor stool-ball players ever played, in front of such a large, heterogeneous, and distinguished crowd. In addition to the Prince of Wales, the Duke of York, and the Duke of Clarence, they could look around them and seen the Duchess of Rutland, Mrs. Fitzherbert, the Duke of Queensberry, the Earl of Clermont, Lord Robert Spencer, Lord North, Lord Pelham, Lord Foley, Lord Gage, Lord Sheffield, Lord Seymour-Conway, the Chevalier de Saint-Georges, the Rt. Hon. Charles James Fox, the Hon. Mr Fitzroy, Sir Harry Inglefield, Mons. de Colonne, William Windham, Richard Brinsley Sheridan, General Smith, General Dalrymple, Mr. Harvey Aston, and Colonel St Leger. Many celebrants, such as Lords North and Seymour-Conway, brought their families along.

Two years later the Duke of York was tempted to adopt but modify his older brother's arrangements for his own birthday celebrations on the Level at Brighton, but it came to nothing. Nevertheless, his plans show how the royal brothers were willing to experiment with new rules. The jackass race and ox-roasting were to remain as before, and he, too, wanted to include smock races, but with a difference. There were to be three quite short ones (300 yds.) to be run as follows: race one, ten runners would run for the smock, with the runner-up getting a half-crown; race two was to be the same but with ten different runners; race three, however, known as the Ultimate Prize, was open to everyone, including those who had run in the first two races. These arrangements meant having at least twenty women runners; the age limit for entry was as follows: "No girl under 15, nor above *seventy-five years of age*, to be permitted to enter."[17] This has to be just about the most inclusive age grouping!

The footraces that the Prince of Wales had arranged divided the women into two categories, those under twenty-five and those over thirty-five, but in 1792 the people of Darlington, County Durham, had gone further and arranged races in *three* categories: one for "any old women"; another for girls fifteen and under; and finally, "any women that choose to start." The old women ran for "a Dozen of Pipes of the best Tobacco under the sun," which suggest that there was a prize for winning as well as prizes for taking part. The winner in the fifteen-and-under group won "a fine muslin Apron and Ribbon," but the main prize, open to "any women," was for "a new full trimmed Holland Smock."[18] This fun-and-games holiday on Whit Tuesday included the almost obligatory jackass race but also a race with Shetland ponies and one for "any number of boys," too.

Increasingly, smock races were part of the lusty, bucolic fun for the masses. This had always been an element in women's smock races but now, as the distances of the races grew shorter and less demanding and the values of the smock went undeclared, fun and games increasingly became their *raison d'être*. The idea of comparing untrained girl runners with horses that were not in training, which had appeared in Ludford in the middle of the century, now took hold. In 1778 a parish clerk made an announcement from the pulpit that the justices had renewed Joseph Dodd's license to put on a smock race for "Fillies, that were never in training," but he didn't mean horses.[19] In 1796, at the Exlade Street Revel in Oxfordshire, a Holland smock was on offer for "fillies that never won a prize."[20] They were again called "fillies" in 1794 at Stockwell Green in Surrey, and the runners had to be twenty-one-years or younger.[21] Greater emphasis was placed on what the women looked like and on their supposed morals; at Pinkneys Green Jubilee in 1796, the women running for the Holland smock had to be twenty years old, "handsome in person and chaste in principle.—Neither bandy legs or hump backs will be permitted to start."[22] And the following year at the same jubilee, the restrictions went even further: "*A Holland Chemise, or linen convenience (vulgarly called a Smock) of large dimensions, to be Run for,* By Young Ladies, poetically described as Nymphs, whose characters are unsullied, and persons will be impregnable. To prevent disputes no lady will be permitted to start who has ever been detected in an improper situation."[23] This last stipulation seems pointedly personal, as if it was directed to someone well known around Pinkneys Green. It was clear though—if she did appear she would not have been permitted to start.

Not permitting someone to run in a smock race, for whatever reasons, could have repercussions, though. A report from the Bow Street Public Office in April 1791 tells of a number of men who were brought into the office "for making a dangerous Riot . . . in Tottenham Court Road" the previous evening.

> The Dispute was occasioned by a Nymph of St. Giles's, who desired to shew her Agility in running for a Smock, which, as Holiday Sport, was held out to the Victor. But whether the Umpires thought her unworthy the noble Contest, or that she took Offence at their Conduct, she suddenly retreated to her own Neighbourhood, and brought to her Assistance about a dozen daring Fellows with Bludgeons, who immediately began to belabour all around them. The real Objects of the Heroine's Resentment took Refuge in a Bricklayer's House, which, with another adjoining, had all the Windows broken, and the Insides were otherwise much damaged. The Mob being very numerous by this Time, took an active Part on behalf of the Fugitives, and the Battle became general.—Bludgeons, Brick Bats, and various missile Weapons did so much Mischief, that several were carried to St. George's Hospital, one of whom, it was reported, died.[24]

History has not otherwise remembered the Tottenham Court Road Smock Battle but denying access to a runner for a Holland smock was not a minor act, and this response indicates that women thought that organizing a smock race gave them a right to compete. In 1799, on the Heights of Shorn Cliff [Shorncliffe], near Sandgate, Kent, five runners went to the starting line to run for the first heat of a best-of-three competition for a Holland smock: "But a dispute arising about a Mary Britt, she was at length declared disqualified."[25] This left Folkestone Bess to win the first two heats easily and so win the smock but leaves us with no information about why Mary Britt was not permitted to run. The dispute at Shorncliffe and the riot on the Tottenham Court Road seem to have been the result of the women's response to an official's decision that they were disqualified from competing—or unworthy to take part—rather than any action on the day by the women themselves. We can imagine that had she turned up at Pinkneys Green Jubilee, the "lady" referred to in their regulations would have also been at the center of a heated dispute. Organizers and officials were becoming much more judgmental and authoritarian about women runners, but the women were responding. No community wanted disputes, and rules were put in place to prevent them, such as at the Peppard [Rotherfield Peppard] Revel in Oxfordshire in 1780, where a notice was put up stating quite clearly that "if any disputes arise, to be settled by the umpires."[26] It was signed by Henry Biddle, the chief constable, and Thomas Alaway, the petty constable, but such an authoritarian approach could actually *cause* disputes, as there seems to have been no mechanism to resolve them and no attempt to hear other views.

Not surprisingly, other venues stressed how respectable they were, such as at Keswick Regatta in 1788 at which "well-made country lasses" ran, and it was reported that it was "by much the greatest and most brilliant concourse of ladies and gentlemen ... ever remembred [sic] there on any former occasion."[27] At Aberystwyth, Wales, where three women ran for "a shawl, and three yards of ribbon" and men ran for a hat, the report boasted that "there was a very genteel company of ladies and gentlemen; and no accidents happened."[28]

Accidents were not always the fault of the competitors or even the officials. For example, at Battersea in 1776 "a number of women ran a race for a Holland Smock."[29] A second report explained that "just before the girls started for the smock, a temporary stage fell down, by which Mr. Stanhope, of Greek-Street, Soho, had his leg broke, and several others were bruised in a terrible manner."[30]

Perhaps it is unsurprising that the events in which women ran provoked quite startlingly different responses. In August 1791 the *World* reported on the Aldenham Races, north of Watford, Hertfordshire. The races were augmented with all the events of a country fair: jumping in sacks, jackass racing, grinning through a horse's collar, fire eating, and women running for a Holland smock. The report concluded: "Never surely was the interference of the Magistracy more necessary to the peace of a quiet neighbourhood than on the present occasion."[31] This judgment immediately provoked a response from the *Morning Post:* "The late sports at this place [Aldenham] have been grossly, and malignantly misrepresented, we must observe that they were not only conducted with the greatest propriety, and afforded a fund of innocent entertainment to the inhabitants, who expressed great desire that they might be annually repeated, which now probably will be the case."[32] The opinion that the games gave a good reason for the magistrates to intervene seems to have carried the greater weight, as there is no record that the sports at Aldenham were ever repeated.

The enforcement of rules to exclude people was not just about their morals or any other supposed criterion. The correspondent for the *World* gave the game away when he opened his report with the words: "On Monday, in imitation of their betters, several tradesmen were successful in kicking up the dust on this Common, by the very fashionable amusements ... [etc.]." "In imitation of their betters" reveals attitudes of the new middle class toward those they considered lower on the social scale; concern for the "lower sort's" morals was supported in part by the spirit of Methodism that had swept the country, even among those who were not Methodists. It also prefigures attitudes that would grow stronger over the next several generations. The old world in which the smock race had been born was coming to an end.

A glimpse into the future comes in a handbill for sports on Bishopgate-Heath, near Windsor Great Park in 1781. The two evenings of horseracing were conducted in a country-fair spirit, accompanied by races between asses, ponies, and "Maidens of all ages, of Berks and Surrey." The "maidens" ran for "a fine Holland Smock, tied in the newest taste, with true Rodney ribbons, and a genteel Hat properly mounted. ... The Smock for the first, and the Hat for the Second in this race; to run the best of three Heats."[33] The races were to be "conducted agreeable to the general rules of racing," but the organizers were striving for something different: "These Races are framed on the model of the antient Olympic Games, and are intended to exhilirate [sic] the Spirits, more than fill the pockets." This captured the fun-and-games spirit of the old country fairs but suggested the additional idea that the prizes should not be the main point—the exhilaration of the runners was more important. This notion looked forward one hundred years to the "Great Amateur Age" during the reign of Queen Victoria.

Almost exactly one hundred years later (1880), the Amateur Athletic Association was formed in Oxford, and it took as its motto $\tau\alpha\chi\upsilon\tau\grave{\alpha}\varsigma\ \pi o\delta\tilde{\omega}\nu\ \grave{\alpha}\kappa\mu\alpha\acute{\iota}\ \tau'\ \grave{\iota}\sigma\chi\acute{\upsilon}o\varsigma$ (the speed of the feet and the acme of physical strength) from one of Pindar's Olympian odes. By 1948, when the Olympic Games were revived after World War II in London, the organizers adopted Discobolus, the Roman copy of a Greek discus thrower, as their emblem to advertise the games to the world. The idea and ideal of the Olympic Games breathed through the endeavors of runners in Britain generation after generation.

The idea that the "lasses" of Bishopgate Heath should run for the exhilaration of it rather than for the prize was a novel one in 1781, but it had probably been bubbling on covertly for a long time; as the value of the smocks dropped, the women seem to have been motivated by something other than the value of the prize. A smock, no matter how lavishly it was decorated, was not anything you could wear to impress friends or wear to church, and so attaining it was somewhat symbolic, as it always had been.

As we have seen, those who wrote about women's races and the sporting events into which they were sometimes subsumed had for generations reached for the Olympic Games as a way of describing them, and they had the example of Robert Dover's Olimpick Games that were still held every year in the Cotswolds, as they had been since 1612. In 1786 the sports at Hendon, Middlesex, were also described as a "burlesque imitation of the Olympic Games."[34] Nan Peacock won the "laced shift" there against three others. "A prodigious concourse of people attended," including "the Tripoline Ambassador, and several foreigners of distinction." The Tripoline ambassador was Sidi Haji Abdrahaman, who was in London negotiating with Thomas Jefferson and John Adams over a substantial payment he deemed was necessary to ensure peace between Tripoli and America.[35] What Ambassador Abdrahaman thought of Nan Peacock's victory seems not to have been recorded.

Despite the emergence of new ideas and new attitudes, the old ways continued. Women still ran for smocks at Easter, Whitsun, May Day, and on Midsummer Day, and they took part in the sports that were organized to celebrate marriages and for special events such as the Scouring of the White Horse at Uffington, but there were new sorts of events, too.[36] In 1798, when tension was high in England because of the revolutionary events in France, various militias, infantry, and cavalry regiments were on maneuvers on Horsham Common at the time of the King George III's birthday, and officers decided to hold various sports to mark it. They held manly contests: running and shooting matches, a match of prison bars between two Welsh militias, and the almost obligatory jackass race, sack race, and grinning through a horse's collar. The men's running events included "noted" runners, and it seems likely that the "barrack ladies" who ran for a Holland smock would have been tough competitors, too. Nancy Francis won first prize; Miss Sukey Ives was runner-up and received a pair of cotton stockings and scarlet garters.[37]

Despite changing attitudes among society's moral watchdogs, women still took pride in their athleticism. Women still ran hard in tough competitive races, such as that at the Mill Green Sports in Essex in 1799, when twelve "sporting ladies" ran such "an excellent race" that the judges were only able to place the first three.[38] There was still local pride in the ability of local runners to beat the opposition, as at Keswick, where they thought the "the Fell-bred Lasses" would beat "those of the Plains" for the Holland smock.[39]

It is a fifteen-year-old runner from Wrotham (pronounced "Root'm") in Kent, however, who provides us with the most outstanding example of women's athleticism in the whole of the eighteenth century. The event occurred on Saturday 11 July 1795 and arose from a wager, which in itself was an unusual undertaking for women. The wager was for two guineas that she could or could not run a mile in 5 minutes 30 seconds; she completed it in 5 minutes 28 seconds. The *Lincoln, Rutland, and Stamford Mercury* reported that she ran with "apparent ease" and published the report under the heading "Strange Occurrences," as it certainly was. No report uncovered to date records any women running such a time prior to this, and it would not be improved on for another 137 years. It is necessary, of course, to consider the accuracy of the measurements of time and distance, but there is no way that either of these can now be verified. Nevertheless, the accuracy of time and distance measurements in *men's* wagers in the eighteenth century was very good, and of the hundreds of wagers that men ran, a remarkably small number were ever disputed at the time. A wager consisted of two sides, each of which stood to win or lose money, so prior to the race each side had to agree that the distance was correct; during and after the event they had to agree that the time had been recorded accurately; and the person holding their respective stakes would not release them unless all involved were satisfied that all particulars of the wager had been complied with. As the wager stipulated 5 minutes 30 seconds or under, an official (or more than one) stood at the finish line with watch in hand and called out "Time" at that mark. In this instance it was estimated that the runner had crossed the line two seconds earlier. In this way, men's times were recorded in seconds as early as 1733, when it was reported that John Appleby ran ten miles against Pinwhire in Sherwood Forest. Appleby won it in

52 minutes; Pinwhire ran the course in 52 minutes 3 seconds.[40] "Time" would have been called at 52 minutes, when it was estimated that Pinwhire was still three seconds from the finish.

Although time in seconds may often have been estimated, it could also be measured accurately. John Harrison's H-4 watch, which he perfected in 1759, was accurate to five seconds in eighty-one days—and not on a workbench but aboard a ship that pitched and swayed its way from Portsmouth to Jamaica and back. This is a timing error of less than one-thousandth of a second; easily good enough to measure a five-and-a-half-minute mile.[41] Harrison's H-4 watch was not available to everyone, of course, but watches were high-status, finely crafted objects in the eighteenth century, and they recorded time very accurately; cheap and unreliable watches were still sometime in the future. Similarly, by 1795 distances were routinely measured using agricultural chains that were accurate to a quarter of an inch, and we should not doubt their ability to measure the distance of a mile accurately. Nevertheless, because they *could* measure both a mile and five and a half minutes accurately, it does not necessarily mean that they *did*.

In 2003, to improve our understanding of eighteenth-century running races, I conducted a study with John Ward-Smith using 536 eighteenth-century men's footraces. We compared the best of them with the best in the nineteenth and the twentieth centuries.[42] To aid comparison, all distances were converted to yards, all times were converted to seconds, and times were plotted against distances. A. E. Kennelly showed as early as 1906 that many racing records, including the men's world running records, could be successfully represented by simple power-law relationships.[43] Results of our analysis of the eighteenth-, nineteenth-, and twentieth-century curve-fits revealed an internal consistency (root-mean-square errors) for each century of 3.750, 2.587, and 2.910, respectively, all within a very similar range.

Men ran so many wagers in the long eighteenth century that it is possible to plot as many as twenty performances by a single athlete and so plot the internal consistency *within* an athlete's reported times as well as *across* the population as a whole; these show performances that are athletically and statistically consistent and so produce robust data.[44] The chances that the internal consistency of the eighteenth-century performances was so similar to that of the twentieth century simply because measurement errors of time and distance cancel each other out are virtually nil, so we have to accept a high level of reliability for both sets of data. Further analysis of men's eighteenth-century running performances revealed performances of very high quality even judged by the standards of 100–150 years later.[45] The rare wagers involving women would have been conducted under very similar conditions to the men's, so it seems as reasonable to accept the performance of the anonymous young woman from Wrotham in 1795 as it does to accept the men's results. Her one-mile time of 5 minutes 28 seconds was not beaten in Britain until 20 August 1932, when twenty-seven-year-old Ruth Christmas ran a mile in 5 minutes 27.5 seconds.[46]

9

THE POWER TO ENDURE

1800-1824

The air of apprehension that hung over Britain after the French Revolution in 1789 hardened when the French National Assembly declared war on England in 1793, on the very day that London heard of the execution of Louis XVI. It hardened yet again when Napoleon took control of the French Army. The mood fell short of fear because of Britons' self-confidence and buoyancy, but there was a sense of foreboding, of waiting for something to happen. Rumors of invasions abounded, and there had even been attempts at them; to be prepared, the nation became militarized. Men in uniform were seen everywhere. This affected everything, even the nation's sports. We see it in October 1801 when sports were held at Bodmin, Cornwall, to celebrate peace. Looking back now, we know that it was not to be a long-lasting peace and the worst was yet to come, but on 30 September the Treaty of London was signed as a preliminary to the Treaty of Amiens (1802), and there was such a feeling of relief that war with France had ended that Bodmin celebrated in style. The day after the news arrived, ale was distributed to the "poorer ranks," the local volunteer force fired celebratory *feu de joie*, and "according to the custom of the place on joyous occasions, the women raced for a shift, which was given by the late Mayor."[1]

No other sporting event took place that day, so women running for shifts had, it seems, become the symbol of celebration at Bodmin: "I never remember to have seen such ecstatic joy depicted in every countenance as on the present occasion; and we look forward with pleasure to the extension of our wool trade, which the war, for some time past, has rendered dull," wrote one reporter.[2] England had been at war with France for eight years already, and it was having its toll. New taxes to pay for the military effort hurt everyone;

because the taxes supported the Prussian army as well as paying for fortifications and the greater mobilization of British troops, they had little noticeable domestic benefit.

The Treaty of Amiens produced a year of peace, but during that time Britain continued to invest heavily in military preparation because in a short while Britain would again be at war with the French. Despite Britain's naval supremacy, Napoleon's blockade of Britain in 1806 added to the misery, and increased food prices hurt everyone. Taxes were raised again. Would there be no end?

Such external pressures revealed many internal fault lines as tensions rose. In July 1802 the "respectable inhabitants" of Mortlake, west of London and south of the River Thames, decided to take "active measures" to stop strangers from arriving, setting up stalls, and holding a fair on Barnes Common. They had been trying to stop the practice for three or four years, but this time they brought in London's Bow Street Runners (the city's first professional police force) to end it. They did end it, and the Mortlake Fair did not take place. However, the Bow Street Runners did permit a number of rural sporting events to take place, of which the centerpiece was a race for a Holland smock: "Three girls ran for a Holland shift round a large pond about a quarter of a mile round, which was won by a Shropshire girl, about 18 years of age: the prize shift was ornamented with a cockade of Mr. Byng's on one side, and one of Sir Francis Burdett's on the other."[3]

George Byng and Sir Francis Burdett were in the midst of campaigning in a hard-fought Middlesex election. Byng was the sitting MP and a Whig; Burdett was running as an Independent Radical, but he was also a Whig of the Fox variety, a faction that had many influential supporters, including Georgiana, Duchess of Devonshire, who campaigned for him. Even in rural sports the organizers, and even the runners, had to tread a fine line to avoid offending someone, and Mortlake wasn't even in Middlesex! Though they did risk annoying Mortlake's sitting MP, William Mainwaring, whose colors seem not to have appeared anywhere.

In 1802 the "respectable inhabitants" of Mortlake may well have been influenced by other social and religious forces—the Evangelical revival with John Wesley at its heart. In the words of Richard Turnbull, it "had a profound and lasting effect on English culture and society."[4] We can see it at work in an event in 1809, when the women's race for a smock at the Plaistow Fair ended up in court. Plaistow, a hamlet about five or six miles east of London, was in

Essex and so the case was heard at the Lent Assizes at Chelmsford the following year. It must be one of the strangest cases ever to appear in an English court; one element of its strangeness was that although a charge was brought against the plaintiffs alleging conspiracy and riot, the main arguments by the prosecution were not about conspiracy and barely about riot. Rather, they argued about what women wore when they ran and what others did to them as they ran. To add to the strangeness of the case, those who prosecuted had not even seen the events they objected to. The prosecution case was that "a certain number of women" were invited as part of rural sports "to run in their chemises."[5] Later, the counsel for the defense said that the prosecution implied that they ran naked.[6] The prosecution, however, claimed that "three miserable women, of the lowest order, lost to every sense of sex and decency, regardless of female propriety, and abandoned to the most loathsome degradation, exhibited themselves on the race course in the manner I have already described, followed by a fellow lashing them with a whip to urge them on. This is a practice, I am persuaded, my learned friend, the King's Serjeant, would neither sanction by his voice nor approve of by his example."[7]

No evidence was ever produced to support the charge that the women ran naked or that they were lashed with a whip to urge them on. It seems that the prosecution dropped this latter point of attack when the facts were explained to them, and their subsequent cross-questioning was limited to whether the women had been struck by the constables. They had not. The whipping that the prosecutor had heard about was the practice of whipping ahead of the runners to clear the way of pedestrians. We can see this in the drawing of George Wilson in 1815 (fig. 18). The competitors were never whipped. Whippers were also employed at prize fights to keep the area around the ring clear, not to the whip the boxers.

The defense witnesses were all clear: the women ran "in their natural and ordinary dress" (Mr. Ward), and in the summing up for the defense, Mr. Serjeant Best described them this way:

> The women were not naked, but attired as they are used to be, when engaged in the labours of the field. I hope the *saints* of Plaistow are not so hot-blooded that the appearance of women so habited can excite their passions, or so shame-faced that it can shock their modesty. If they are, they must lock themselves up during the harvest months, or their virtue might be exposed to such continued

FIGURE 18. George Wilson, the pedestrian, making his way through a crowd of onlookers on Blackheath Common, J. T. Smith, etching, 1815. (Collection of the author)

attacks as all their sanctity will not enable them to withstand. But this sort of half-dress, so unseemly in the eyes of the *men of grace,* has been sung of by the poets, and extolled by philosophers, for its simplicity and decency.[8]

While the prosecution's arguments seemed to be about decency and respectability, is hard not to see them as equally driven by class. In addition to being described as "miserable women, of the lowest order," the women were also described as "not the most respectable" and "common low women."[9] In their defense they were described as "common hard working women." "I hope, therefore, they are not the less entitled to consideration," observed Mr. Common Sergeant. Would the case have been brought if those involved had been less "common"? The counsel for the defense certainly thought that prejudice against the working classes was behind the prosecution. In his summation, he said: "Let no man suppose that I am contending for drunkenness and debauchery. If these occur, let them be punished; but I cannot perceive that these are more connected with the merriment of the lower classes of the community when assembled at these wakes, than with the jovial meetings of persons of superior station."

He also thought religious tensions might have played a part: "I have to complain in the instructions given to my learned friend . . . that my clients *'threatened to pull down the Methodist Meeting-houses.'* . . . It has been further said, that the defendants will not allow these Methodists to worship God in their own way." The jury unanimously found the defendants not guilty on all counts. At this time of national stress, the runners had to steer clear of any number of sensitivities.

A nation suffering blockade is changed by it. Britons were proud of their resolution and portrayed their struggle as one between the sturdy and reliable "John Bull" and the untrustworthy "Boney" (Napoleon), but their resolution was tested. It was in this period that the nation began to notice the men and women with powers of endurance, who showed publicly that they would not give in. Older women were particularly noteworthy; they were deemed to be frail on two counts: their gender and their age. Now their robustness was seen in a new light, though in truth it had always been there. In 1808 an eighty-nine-year-old woman, surname Patrick, was reported to have walked seven miles in East Sussex, "through fields, intercepted by stiles, bars, &c. and performed her journey with a degree of ease and alertness that would have given pedestrian fame to many of our dashing damsels of eighteen."[10]

Men and women, young and old, tramping long distances on the roads were such a familiar sight they were almost invisible. During this time before railroads, traveling on foot was the cheapest means to get around. In 1773 Foster Powell had been the first to attract public attention by doing it; he worked for an attorney delivering documents but became so notorious for his long-distance walks that he laid wagers on them, wagers that were particularly conspicuous because they were so small. The point seems to have been that the challenge, the achievement, and the eventual notoriety were the reward rather than money. He is remembered for his walk in 1773 from Hicks Hall, a courthouse in Clerkenwell, London, to York (394 miles) in 5 days and 18 hours. He repeated versions of it in 1788, 1790, and 1792, when he was fifty-eight.[11] After this final walk, "on his return home he was saluted with the loud huzzas of the astonished and anxious spectators." Most people walking roads were poor and had no other option if they wanted to travel, but a few did it for other reasons, not all of them obvious. Take, for example, Robert Barclay-Allardice, the Great Master of Ury, who in 1788 was elected as MP for his local Kincardineshire constituency on the east coast of Scotland and chose to take up his seat at Westminster by walking there—it was over five hundred miles. He remained their MP for nine years and was said to have often walked to Westminster. By the end of the eighteenth century, feats of long-distance walking were taking center stage—quite literally in Foster Powell's case, for such was his fame he appeared at Astley's Amphitheater on Westminster Bridge in September 1790, "where he was crowned with Laurels. He wore the dress he wore on the York road and gave a specimen of the pace he commonly kept."[12] The show was scheduled for two days but the run (no pun intended) had to be extended. Walking, and even watching people walking, became a new craze.

In 1815 newspapers reported that Mary Wilkinson, a Yorkshire woman who lived to be 109, had walked several times to London from Yorkshire (a distance of 290 miles) in four days when she was young, and when she was ninety she was said to have done it in five days and three hours with "a keg of gin, and a quantity of provisions on her back." No-one saw fit to record these feats when she was a young woman or when she was ninety, but they did so in 1815 when she was 109, and within twelve days her story was repeated in newspapers across the length and breadth of England.[13] The story of the young woman who in one day walked the seventy-two miles from Blencogo, Cumberland, to two miles short of Newcastle-upon-Tyne in 1765 was also not reported at the time, and the story only appeared in the enthusiasm that followed Foster Powell's first walk to York nine years later.[14]

It was in this mood that Ellen Weeton from Up Holland, Lancashire, walked. She "had a scheme to walk the length of Wales unaccompanied (about 150 miles), but abandoned the idea when she reflected on the many insults a female is liable to, if alone."[15] She did walk in London, however, and calculated that in one month she walked more than 538 miles while sight-seeing; she even managed ascents of Snowdonia in North Wales and Snaefell on the Isle of Man, surely more hazardous undertakings. It was, of course, just about this time that Dorothy Wordsworth went rambling in the mountains in the Lake District with William, finding at least one climb to the summit "very easy."[16]

These long-distance walks and climbs were not all for pleasure or out of necessity; for some, they were an athletic challenge. At the end of January 1807, Martha Mahoney, "an Hiburnian lass," wagered one pound that she could run eight miles in an hour on a mile-long out-and-back course on the New Road from Tottenham Court to Battle Bridge in North London. She began much too quickly, as almost all runners did at that time did, and ran the first mile in six minutes.[17] It would be a hundred years before Arthur Kennelly's studies demonstrated that the best results were achieved by running at an evenpace.[18] In the eighteenth and nineteenth centuries, runners set off at the pace they thought they could maintain and then slowed as they found they couldn't. Martha Mahoney's first mile was extremely ambitious; her second mile slowed to seven minutes (so two miles in thirteen minutes), but an eyewitness wrote that "she did not appear in the least fatigued." The next four miles were covered even more slowly, but she still ran them "without apparent distress." Over the last two miles, however, she paid the price for her overambitious start when she "seemed to labour much." Still, she managed to keep going and won the wager by half a minute. The first two miles, at least, were an outstanding example of running quality in the early nineteenth century. She certainly impressed the assembled crowd who "made a collection for her."[19]

For a while, running was eclipsed in the public imagination by walking, and the nation's craze for walking competitions probably reached its pinnacle in the summer of 1809 when Captain Barclay, the son of the Great Master of Ury (mentioned above), concluded a wager to go on foot one thousand miles in one thousand successive hours for one thousand guineas.[20] The wager required him to walk a measured mile on Newmarket Heath in *every* hour for just under six weeks. Those who could went to Newmarket to watch him; those who could not followed his progress daily in the newspapers as he dragged himself through the dark hours before dawn but rallied during the days. This was not about speed but about tenacity and the grim business of doggedly carrying on. It was unspectacular, but his resilience and determination seemed to capture the spirit of the age. He succeeded on 12 July having had not a single continuous night's sleep (or even a continuous two-hour sleep) for nearly six weeks. During the event he had lost thirty-two pounds, and yet only eight days later he joined a huge force on the south coast of

England and sailed to Walcheren at the mouth of the River Scheldt to take on Napoleon's forces.

At this time the words "pedestrian" and "pedestrianism" came into common use. Being a pedestrian, running or walking, was now something that anyone could be—even a woman. In 1811 a woman wagered ten pounds that she could walk forty miles in ten successive hours on the Uxbridge Road in London. She was aged thirty and the wife of a painter, and she won by forty minutes, attracting "a vast concourse of people, and a great number of bets."[21]

Britain was changing in many ways; when the unnamed woman described above walked her forty miles on the Uxbridge Road, she was doing so in Regency Britain, for the Regency Act had been passed by Parliament in February 1811. It was an odd time: celebrating was not quite in tune with the fact that the George III was still alive, but he was old and physically and mentally unwell. The population was increasing rapidly and was approaching ten million (52 percent of whom were females). More than a million people lived in London, and for the first time, more families in Britain were engaged in trade and manufacture than in agriculture. The war continued to depress trade, and new technologies syphoned jobs from the ordinary people just when they needed them most. Captain Ludd was on the march, breaking up spinning frames, and a fear of civil unrest troubled the towns and cities. The number of men in military uniform was at an all-time high, and young men and women were growing up knowing nothing but war with the French. In May 1812 Spencer Percival, the prime minister, was shot through the heart in the lobby of the House of Commons. Rays of hope emerged, however, when the Duke of Wellington and his fellow generals forced the French out of Portugal, then blockaded and eventually took control of Ciudad Rodrigo, stormed Badajoz, and entered Madrid.

Lady Bessborough described the prevailing mood in the country as one of "military mania"; even the women adopted epaulettes and short, military-style jackets.[22] Everyone knew that although their future lay in the hands of the Duke of Wellington and the Admiralty, they would be powerless without the strength, courage, and fortitude of the fighting British men, qualities that the British public admired as they had seldom done before.

In 1812 two boxing histories were published anonymously, one entitled *Pancratia*[23] and the other *Boxiana*.[24] Within a year a history of runners and walkers followed, entitled *Pedestrianism*.[25] Each of these works extolled the particular qualities of British men and advocated better military training for them, but their authors repeatedly stressed that they were the men they were because of their involvement in the old country fairs and in the old British sports. Pierce Egan, the author of *Boxiana*, wrote on page 1 of his dedication of "THOSE SPORTS that tend to invigorate the human frame, and inculcate those principles of generosity and true courage, by which the inhabitants of the English Nation are so eminently distinguished above every other country."[26] If that seems excessively jingoistic, it should be noted that Egan was an Irishman. It should also be noted that his comments about inhabitants of the English nation only referenced 48 percent of them.

Britons were proud of their unique sporting record. Egan described it this way:

> That athletic exercises have not been performed in foreign countries at various times, by particular individuals, is not our intention to deny; but in speaking generally, as a national trait, we feel no hesitation in declaring, that it is wholly—BRITISH.
>
> And, were it materially necessary, the curious OLD ENGLISH SPORTS might be traced through the succeeding reigns with every degree of certainty, except in some few instances, where the conquerors introduced *effeminate refinements*, of which Leland, and several other historians speak, as tending towards creating a degeneracy of spirit among the natives of the island.

Perhaps it is understandable that amid all the change, unrest, and uncertainly, a nostalgia would develop among the people for the Britain that they believed they had lost—the old innocence, the old ways, the old sports— when people strove honestly and laughed without fear. The Olde Englande. A writer in the *Sportsman's Magazine*, who signed himself as "T from Huntington," wrote *On English Fairs and Feasts:*

> The festivities of England, in a great degree, claim attention. It is there and there only, that the true English character is to be found. Devoid of all affectation (how unlike our neighbours, the French, in this respect), a real joy paints every countenance with smiles, and with a peculiar warmth they receive with open arms every friend, every new comer; and should even an enemy appear, he too is welcome. This praiseworthy disposition is almost indigenous to our own *isles*. The festivities of other countries, such as Italy and France, are

conducted with more shew, yet they fall far short of us in that most necessary of all ingredients to harmony—heartfelt hilarity. After the conclusion of one feast, our villagers count the weeks to the next; . . .

Life in London may, and does, display a great variety of character; but Life in the Country, in my opinion, alone exhibits the true character of our countryman.[27]

Such expressions of English exceptionalism and the naked nostalgia for a bucolic, happy sporting past may seem too extreme to be representative of the common view, but when Napoleon abdicated unconditionally on 11 April 1814 after a string of defeats by Marshal Blucher's Prussian troops and the Duke of Wellington and allies, communities large and small all over England looked for a suitable way to celebrate, and they turned to their own, local versions of a country fair.

Between June and August 1814 country fairs under various names were organized across England to celebrate peace, and in them women ran races for smocks, shifts, shawls, gowns, gown pieces, chemises, and ribbons. The database contains over thirty such events, but there were many others simply described as "footraces" without specifying whether women or girls took part. Many other events were not considered newsworthy—there were just so many of them. Every town, and every village, it seems, put on an event to celebrate the peace, and they almost always included the old English sports as well as dancing, bonfires, and a community feast. Over that three-month period in 1814 more women ran in more races and in more places in England than had ever done so before or would again for at least a hundred years. Not one was a best-of-three competition, and none would test the athletic abilities of the runners; they were more like the frolics on the village green that they imagined were typical of "Olde Englande." Nevertheless, women ran because they wanted to and because others wanted them to; women running for various items of clothing seemed to represent in the public mind the 52 percent's version of cudgeling and wrestling that had made it possible for the people of England to be eventually victorious. Women running represented freedom, energy, and high spirits.

It was not, of course, the ultimate peace that everyone had imagined. Napoleon escaped from his imprisonment on Elba in 1815 and so began his famous (or infamous) Hundred Days campaign, which culminated in the Battle of Waterloo in June 1815 that finally sealed his fate. A lasting peace with France was finally secured. In 1815, however, the people of Britain did not repeat the celebrations of the previous year.

The smock races held at the 1814 peace festivals were unlike those of earlier times; Edward Brayley wrote that "an hundred and fifty, or two hundred yards, and back again, is commonly the appointed distance."[28] If he is to be trusted, this is a very great change from, say, one hundred years earlier. In the eighteenth century women only ran sprint races in Kent. Perhaps this was why so many of the peace celebration smock races were described as being run by "girls." Brayley, however, was not known to be an authority on women's smock racing or of any other kind of sport. He had made his reputation with *The Beauties of England and Wales,* a multivolume work describing the counties and districts of England and Wales, in which he collaborated with John Britton and wrote much of the text. Brayley's *Popular Pastimes* follows the same approach but describes British customs and pastimes, and he collaborated with Francis Stephanoff, who supplied the illustrations (fig. 19). Brayley has a flowery, pompous style and describes smock racing as if he is describing an activity in the remotest corner of the globe of which none of his readers could have any knowledge, even though smock races had been run in every corner of England within the past couple of years and in greater numbers than ever before. He writes of those who ran the races as if they were members of a distant tribe. Note his attempt to describe what a woman runner felt before she ran: "Though, perhaps, backward, at first, the feelings of timidity and shame, yet the desire of wearing so attractive an object, conjoined with the hope of victory, generally proves sufficiently powerful to induce many a blushing maiden to enter the lists, and like a new Atalanta, exert her utmost speed to conquer in the race."

Here is Atalanta again, but for Brayley the main interest seems to lie in the possibility that that one or more of the runners might fall:

> This pastime affords considerable amusement to its roguish patrons, who usually promote the race for the sake of participating in "the rustic's loud laugh" (to employ the words of the old song), should either of the contending wenches expose, by tripping in the course, those charms which her modesty would conceal....
>
> The encumbrance of the female dress frequently occasions a false step, and the career of expected conquest is checked by a sudden fall; but this instead of

FIGURE 19. *A Smock Race*, Francis Philip Stephanoff, bookplate, 1816. From Brayley and Stephanoff, *Popular Pastimes*, 1816.

exciting commiseration for the disappointed damsel, is commonly the signal for shouting and laughter on the part of the spectators, and the poor girl for the remainder of the day, becomes subject to be quizzed by her compeers.[29]

Conversely, we might imagine that the women runners took part because of the fun and excitement involved, and because it gave them the opportunity to be centerstage, to be involved in something rather than being a mere spectator looking on. Of course they ran for the prize. Brayley's male perspective was that if the women tripped and fell, they would reveal "those charms which her modesty would conceal," thus reminding us of just what the women and girls had to endure, and had endured for generations, whenever they ran.

This attitude is reminiscent of the Rev. James Ward's poem written in 1714 (see chapter 3), which spoke of the "thousand Charms he saw, conceal'd before." Artists, too, seemed particularly drawn to women runners falling, but the prevalence of this in actual races isn't supported by the eyewitness accounts. Eyewitnesses give us a huge variety of details of women racers:

how many there were, what they wore, how old they were, how many got eliminated in the heats, and even when one died—but *not* of them falling over. There seems to be a gulf between what in fact happened and what male poets, writers, and artists imagined might, or could, happen.

One anomaly, however, seems to belong to three generations earlier and seems out of tune with 1814. The Staffordshire villages of Brocton, Milford, and Baswich combined to celebrate the peace in July 1814, and there was a "dinner, consisting of excellent roast beef, a sheep roasted whole, plum pudding, &c.," followed by "rural sports, such as prison bars, bag and barrow races, and foot-races." According to the *Staffordshire Advertiser,* "An excellent foot race by women excited much merriment; all were satisfied with their speed except the women engaged, who declared that they could have run much faster in a state of *nudity*."[30] It may well have been said in jest, but it is interesting that the idea came from the runners themselves and not from the organizers, perhaps as it had in the 1730s and 1740s when the runners themselves decided to run naked. Dancing on Milford Green followed and brought to an end "one of the best regulated and convivial scenes that has been witnessed in this neighbourhood." Men might have watched the women runners and imagined what they might reveal if they lost control and fell, but some women outdid them and imagined *themselves* running stark naked.

Postwar euphoria seldom lasts long, and the difficulties facing the British people became worse after victory. Thousands of discharged soldiers and sailors came home looking for work, but manufacturers who had flourished on government war contracts now failed, and by 1816 the British economy was on the brink of collapse. Strong, resourceful men and women turned to their physical abilities to make a living. One such was George Wilson, a poor man from Newcastle-upon-Tyne who had spent much of his life in various debtors' prisons. Inspired by Captain Barclay's thousand-mile walk six years earlier, he devised a plan to walk one thousand miles at the rate of fifty miles a day for twenty consecutive days. He was fifty years old and walked with a slight limp, the legacy of an injury he sustained some years earlier when he was attacked with a red-hot poker in a family dispute. The walk began in September 1815 on Blackheath Common in Surrey and produced so much interest and public attention that the bailiffs took him into custody to preserve public law and order after he had completed 751 and a quarter miles. Unlike Captain Barclay's effort, little or no money was involved in George Wilson's, primarily because he didn't have any. He hoped, nevertheless, that by attempting to complete the wager he would lift himself out of obscurity. He put it this way: he hoped "it would open my road to celebrity and emolument. It was the *spark*, perhaps a mere *ignis fatus* [sic], that cheared me by day and lighted me by night in many a tedious journey, gave new spring to my sinews, and encouraged, perhaps, my vanity, to perseverance."[31]

Much attention has been paid to the gambling culture of the eighteenth and early nineteenth centuries and to the high-rolling lords and gentlemen at White's, Brooks's, and Almacks.[32] We must not assume that the poor—and that included all but the highest-ranked women—had an access to this world, too; for the most part they had no money with which to make extravagant wagers, no matter what their talents were. Wilson is again an example of this; in 1805 he was engaged to walk from Bristol to London by a man named Nelson, a London publican.

> I walked down [from London], by Nelson's desire, to Bristol on that occasion, in order that he might, if possible, set a walking match on foot for me there. On my arrival, he gave out that I was to walk to London in 36 hours [114 miles via Marshfield], it being the month of January, and the ground covered with snow. I accordingly started, having first received two guineas; and it being understood, if bets were to be made against me, I was to receive a fair proportion of the winnings. I accomplished my task in the time stipulated, but no bets being made, I received no further reward, and as no other match could be made, I returned to Newcastle [another 282 miles on foot].[33]

The rewards of long-distance walking performances were uncertain, but they at least offered hope of something. About the same time that George Wilson was stopped by the bailiffs in his thousand-mile attempt, one of his daughters tried her luck, too: "It is said that his daughter, a young woman turned of twenty, is to succeed her father in another exploit. She is to walk two hundred miles in three days."[34] George Wilson went further and offered to match her "to go 60-miles [on foot] with any man." His other two other daughters were also both said to be "celebrated walkers."[35]

Women began to sense that they could do as well as anyone; indeed, many already supported their families by carrying various goods to sell from town to town, door to door, when no other work was available. In December 1815 Mary Frith agreed a wager of thirty guineas that she could go six hundred miles at thirty miles a day for twenty successive days at Maidstone, Kent. She was a poor woman, thirty-six-years old, with six children, and for years she had travelled twenty to twenty-five miles a day on foot to support her family "with different articles for sale, returning every night to her family."[36] No results of the wager have been found.

After the peace of 1815, unrest among the poor grew to such a pitch that Parliament suspended Habeas Corpus in 1817, partly in response to riotous activities after the public meeting in Spa Fields, London, in December 1816. Radical sentiments were not squashed, however, and fear of disorder and organized confrontation ran rampant. It was in this world, in August 1817, that Hester Crozar (aka Esther Crozier) first came to the public's notice when she walked from St Andrew's Church in Holborn, London, to Chelmsford and back on the same day, a total of fifty-eight miles. She agreed to attempt seventy miles in a day when the weather was more settled.[37] In October 1817 she undertook to walk a thousand miles at fifty miles a day for twenty days. She was thirty-eight years old, 5 feet 4 inches tall, and never married, and had traveled the country on foot selling pocketbooks.[38] The event took place on the Croydon Road in Brixton, South London, but after 350 miles she gave up "in consequence of some dispute." In September 1823 another woman, "nearly Fifty Years of Age," engaged to walk forty miles in eight hours on the Wellington Cricket Ground, near Sloane Square in London.[39]

In May 1820 "a female, apparently about seventeen years of age," probably from Birmingham, attempted to go 240 miles on foot at the rate of forty miles a day for six days on the Warwick to Leamington Road. She started from the Punch-Bowl Inn, on the Butts in Warwick, on a five-mile course that she had to complete eight times each day. No one could be found to provide a wager, so she set out without one, hoping for "remuneration as a generous public might bestow." Sadly, it seems, the public was not generous, and "she acquired little beyond the fame of her exploit." This harsh tale is backed by an even harsher observation: "The public wisely discouraging an abandonment of useful labour for the vagabondizing habits of a female pedestrian."[40]

This attitude did not just reflect a dislike of poor women who tried to create lives for themselves outside the one deemed to be their "proper" place (which meant being diligent, hard-working, and obedient members of the workforce). It also indicated a growing fear among the more affluent middle class of working-class people who were clamoring for a fairer system of work and fairer rewards for it, a clamor that was becoming more visible and more strident. Lord William Lennox disagreed with the newspaper author's tone, which he thought ungallant, and made an observation that would not have been out of place a century later: "We do not mean to say that pedestrianism forms part of a woman's destiny; but as men often leave theirs, to stand behind the counter, as measurers of tape, silks, and satins, we ought not to be too hard on the feminine gender who wish to emulate the deeds of Barclay (of Ury), and other pedestrians."[41]

Indeed, we ought not, but even he saw the issue from the middle-class point of view of shops and shopkeepers—not a common opinion in 1820, particularly when speaking of poor, working-class women. The public's attitude to women performing physical tasks in public has always been more openly critical than it has been toward equivalent men. Women pedestrians have always had to develop thick skins, just as did the smock racers.

Of course, old, poor women were still on the roads traveling on foot as they always had done, and they usually were not drawing attention to themselves. In September 1822, for example, Mrs. Wilson, a seventy-eight-year-old widow, traveled 180 miles in five days from a small village in Westmorland to visit her son in Mansfield, Nottingham; it was remarked as "an instance of strength rarely to be met with in a person so far advanced in years."[42] But it was not so rare. Ann Sim, who was seventy and lived in the poorhouse in Sandbed, Dumfriesshire, was often known to walk to Dumfries and back again (50 miles) by midday. She would also walk to Edinburgh and back in forty hours (174 miles).[43]

Age, however, was no limit. Perhaps the most striking example of how long-distance walking could be used to support a family came in July 1823 when Emma Matilda Freeman set out to walk thirty miles in eight and a half hours on Penenden Heath near Maidstone, Kent. She was "scarcely eight years old" and came from Strood, so she was only about ten miles from home.[44] A 440-yard circuit had been marked out that she would have to complete 120 times. Rain came down heavily for most of the day, but she completed the task in 7 hours and 57 minutes—thirty-three minutes inside her schedule. A month later, on 11 August, she appeared in London on the Chelsea Cricket Ground; this time she took part in a wager to go thirty miles in eight hours. She accomplished this, too, in 7 hours and 49 minutes, and so was eleven minutes within the allotted time. The laps had been shortened to one-sixth of a mile, requiring 180 circuits: "She occasionally took a little refreshment of wine and water, and appeared in excellent spirits to the last."[45] She finished the wager "with perfect ease," and her last mile was the fastest of the day.

Two weeks later she appears again, this time at the Green Dragon Gardens in Stepney, East London. Once again, she was faced with going thirty miles on foot in eight hours and was given a lap of one-fifth of a mile to complete (i.e., 150 laps). Six hundred people turned out to watch, and she made her appearance with her father at 12:30 in the afternoon. She completed the task in 7 hours and 52 minutes, "without any apparent fatigue." The *Morning Advertiser* announced that "a collection was subsequently made for the child by the persons in the gardens, and the subscription was most liberal."[46]

Our final glimpse of Emma Freeman comes three weeks later, on Monday 16 September at the Bayswater Tea-Gardens. After three successful attempts at thirty miles, all completed "with ease," a sterner test was needed, and so she attempted forty miles. If the report is correct, she walked it in 7 hours and 50 minutes, but there can be no certainty about what the target time was or her actual time. The track was 220-yards long, and she would have needed to complete 320 laps! It was said that there was a wager of one hundred pounds aside, but there is no certainty about that either: "But as to her having done the distance *faithfully,* or that a hundred pounds a-side were laid upon the performance, we have good reason for doubting; yet, allowing that *the scorer* might (as he did) *get on* a little too fast occasionally, the space gone over by her was great indeed for *such a child.*"[47]

It is worth giving the additional details of Emma Matilda Freeman, her parents, and how the event was setup, as it gives us a unique glimpse into this new foot racing world that they invented and in which they had to improvise as they went along. "She is an interesting little girl, very confident of her powers for *going along,* and her parents (out of Suffolk) were present; they took payment at the door for the *entrée,* for which they got abused, by a knot of bargemen's ladies, through the railings, and that kind of payment is all they would receive for the undertaking."

Driven by hardship and need, we should not imagine that these women (and girls) were crushed and downtrodden by their poverty. If Emma Matilda Freeman is any example, they may have been confident of their powers and in excellent spirits, bravely setting themselves challenges while knowing that others would disapprove. Perhaps, like George Wilson, they hoped that they too might find celebrity and emolument in their efforts, a hope that gave new spring to *their* sinews and encouraged a little well-deserved pride in their achievements.

Some women and girls had become so sure of their abilities that they even took on men. In January 1823 a young woman from Queensferry, Scotland, issued a challenge to race fifteen miles against "any Lanarkshireman." The race took place near Westcraigs [West Craigs], near Edinburgh, on the road between Edinburgh and Glasgow. A youth from the Lanarkshire hamlet of Dalserf took up the challenge. Both had backers (from Glasgow) for unknown sums. The young woman led for the first eight miles inside the hour, at which point the youth shot past her. She made a big effort to get back in contact and took the lead again, but when she was passed again, she collapsed, exhausted. On winning, the youth said he would never have been able to go home again if he had been beaten by a woman. Nevertheless, despite her defeat, she deserves credit for being the first known example of a woman challenging a man in a footrace and following it up by actually racing.[48]

Perhaps the best example of a woman running not out of need—or for profit or even for reputation—but for the sheer satisfaction doing it (and having to overcome obstacles that no man would face) came at the end of 1823 at Castle Douglas, Kirkcudbrightshire, in southeast Scotland. This event featured an eleven-year-old girl. A young itinerant (male) pedestrian had arrived in town, and one morning in January announced through the town crier that at two o'clock that afternoon he would attempt to walk eleven miles in two hours. Markers were set out a half-mile apart on the highway at the end of the town. He would walk out and back between them, hoping for "whatever the spectators were pleased to give him." It was, however, "a little girl, about 11 years of age, from the town," who stole the show.

> She started with him and kept up with him for two rounds [two miles], in her clogs; but at the end of the second round, ran home with them, by which one round [one mile] was lost, but she again started with him at the commencement of the fourth, and kept by his side till he finished, though often encumbered by a crowd of boys; one of whom was so troublesome, that she was obliged to stop and give them battle; but she quickly put him to flight, and notwithstanding the interruption, soon made up her ground.[49]

Despite the very considerable political and social changes that had taken place during and immediately after the Napoleonic Wars, and the emergence of so many endurance-based performances, some things proved to be remarkably resilient: one was that the hard-run smock races reemerged after the fun-and-games events of the celebratory country-fair-style races for girls in 1814 (table 2).

TABLE 2. A sampling of smock races in the early 1820s

DATE	LOCATION	NOTES
October 1820	Hungerford R	Twenty to thirty old women running for one pound of tea; "Astonishing to see with what agility the old dames run in order to get their favourite."
January 1821	Houston	Mary Mulford (chemise); half-mile heats.
May 1821	Chaple Heath	Miss Jones (chemise); half mile, beating five others; Welsh milkmaid won.
July 1821	Fordenbridge	One-mile heats (chemise); Miss Drew won two heats each in under six minutes.
December 1821	Fordenbridge	One mile (chemise); Miss Mills won in seven minutes; Miss Jolly, second. Judges placed them.
March 1822	Chapel Row	Seven runners (chemise); half mile; Miss Dearlove won, less than three minutes.
April 1822	Gray's Inn Rd.	Committee of Molls (smock); three-well contested heats (chemise); three Cinderellas, Sall Chapman of running notoriety.
July 1822	Wandsworth Fair	Circa half mile, one heat (smock); Bet Beasley, Sal Humphries, complained to the stewards of unfair play, dismissed.
July 1823	Belmore, Hants	Half mile, three heats, six ran; Miss Betsy Shum won in two heats, Miss Pewsey, second.

10

MORAL MEDDLING, CANT, AND SHEER HUMBUG

1825 Onward

In the years of economic hardship leading up to the mid-nineteenth century, radical voices became more strident, and an aggressive national labor protest movement known as Chartism gave voice to the problems and frustrations of working people who wanted their labor to be recognized and properly rewarded. The great Reform Bill was passed by one vote in 1832 and changed Britain forever. The reform-minded Charles Dickens rose to fame, and Queen Victoria came to the throne. Yet somehow the nostalgia for "Olde Englande" still persisted: William Cobbett (of the *Political Register* fame), Samuel Coleridge, and others wrote of a benign, kindlier time, now lost. The essayist William Hazlitt actually gave it a name—Merrie England. It was a fantasy, of course, but one that people were happy to indulge during holidays when they could put on a pastiche of the sports of old and imagine that they were part of a living past.

But there developed in the country an ugly mood of "us versus them." Sometimes it seemed to be town versus country, but more often it appeared as the working class versus the rest. "The rest" complained that the working class was not sufficiently educated or sufficiently cultured or sufficiently moral. Their entertainments were too raucous, too rowdy, and they drank too much, all of which led them into poverty and unproductiveness. For the first time in British history a nationwide police force was created, and in every family in the land, male authoritarianism grew taller and taller, as eventually did their top hats.

How this affected sports is best described by a writer to the *Morning Advertiser* in 1828, who wrote regarding proposed rural sport sat Hendon in north London.

The Rural Sports of Hendon Wake

With the growth of the city the distance expands that separates the native from a casual snatch of enjoyment, in witnessing the occasional exhibition of the rural sports that once constituted the great annual village holiday: amusements of which the by gone was wont to furnish fire side conversation for at least one half of the succeeding year, and the other half was much deficient to admit of all that was to be anticipated from what was to arise. Having this situation of affairs in view, great pains were taken to propagate the variety of fun that might be expected at Hendon, by advertisements in the journals, placards on the walls, and numerous little snuffy-nosed men parading the streets, bedecked with boards resembling millboard monuments, stuck full of bills of fare, purporting that the "Rural Sports of Hendon" were to be a non-such kind of a treat. There was promised "Wrestling—Walking Backwards—Quoit Playing—Jumping in Sacks—Running a match—Women Running—Climbing a Greasy Pole—Grinning through a Horse collar—and other things too tedious to mention." For all of which a fair provision was made, and every thing going on promisingly until the expected morning; and then just as the rustic circles had wound up their minds for a nice day's enjoyment, the cup of pleasure was dashed from their lips by the interference of Magistracy. For what cause? It may be asked. Why, for the sake of morality, it must be answered. At least said the Magistrate.

... For an authority undeniable, early in the day, put his veto on the items of merry-making that had been concocted, and said that such things should not be, because of their *immoral tendency*—and so the whole affair was strangled at birth.

Whatever reason, however, conscientious magistrates may have for interfering with a certain description of public exhibitions, designated "Olde English sports," it is certainly a matter questionable wherein they could attach a pretext for the suppression of such amusements as were premeditated at this village wake, unless it is to be understood that the province of the labouring classes now is to labour only, and that to enjoy themselves is henceforth to be held as criminal and immoral. . . .

The company was certainly thinner in consequence of the visitation of the beak . . . and thought of exceeding in spiritual matters, they had only to turn round and the stocks and whipping-post stared them broad in the face, to remind them of carnal humility and corporal punishment. No booths were allowed for profane dancing; but Harry did his best to make the people comfortable within doors, and Sir Richard Birnie[1] had not neglected good order; for a detachment of "Robin Redbreasts"[2] were on the ground pacing about to check the operations of the "lifting operatives."[3]

The most prominent feature of the scene was the greasy pole that rose to a towering height, and on its topmost pinnacle did swing a prime leg of mutton, which was to be the prize to any one who could aspire to cut it down. At a quarter to six the first feat of interest commenced by Jem MacCarthy, the pugilist, walking backwards one mile for 10*l.* [ten pounds] in thirteen minutes. Time was backed at starting 6 to 4; but Time was floored.—Jem did it; he did it, but that was all. If he had had three strides more to make, Time had pocketed the odds.

The match of quoits, for 10*l.* a-side, was played by Messrs. Marsh and Marbeth, and the latter was the winning man.

In the running match for the carter's whip, Joe Burgess, carter to Mr. Bignell of Hendon, carried off the prize.

No lady could be found to start for the female race, so that was quashed.[4]

Smock racing never completely died out, but there are fewer and fewer references to them, and the events in which the women ran seem to become less and less significant as the years passed. Pierce Egan uses one in his hugely popular *Tom and Jerry—Life in London* series. In his final version (published in 1828), Tom, Jerry, and Logic went to Tenterden (only twenty miles from Old Wives Lees) in Kent, and saw the Tenterden Races, an event based on fact but cast into a kind of extended in-joke.[5] Five young women ran for a smock, and each was given a name (after some well-known gents in the college) and colors by which to identify them. The whole event was described in the language of horseracing: "Racing Calendar," "Ascot," "Doncaster," "fillies," "outsiders," and so on.

Robert Cruikshank illustrated Egan's text and produced a telling image of the Tenterden Races (fig. 20). The men in the foreground are solid and have their feet on the ground. They are real people. The buildings on the far side of the road are only lightly sketched in, but the spectators hanging out of the windows have some substance. The women runners, however, are treated as ephemeral, wispy creatures, as if they are being blown along by the wind.

FIGURE 20. *Running Race for Young Ladies at Tenterden,* Robert Cruikshank, bookplate, c. 1828. From Pierce Egan, *The Finish to the Adventures of Tom, Jerry, and Logic, in Their Pursuits through Life In and Out of London,* c. 1828.

Unlike Collett, Cruikshank did not concern himself with the niceties of trying to portray the runners' balance and effort, nor did he worry himself, as Rowlandson did, about which arm and leg should be forward (a detail that Rowlandson eventually got wrong). Neither did he choose to show the exertion and exuberance of racing, as did Stephanoff. Here Cruikshank depersonalizes the runners, who resemble colorful fairies on the top of a Christmas tree. Their arms seem to float neither forward nor backward, for they are merely frail symbols; in this image, only the men are real.

Outside the pages of Egan and the pencil and paint of Cruikshank, the women walking and running on the roads were real enough. There were many of them, mainly poor women running for whatever money they could collect from the passers-by, and their races were lone efforts without the support of any external organization, patron, or supporter. As I noted earlier, we should not imagine downtrodden women who shuffled along looking for sympathy as well as a donation; rather, we should imagine tough self-starters who achieved at least two minor—or perhaps not so minor—landmarks. The first was perhaps the earliest praise of a woman's athletic powers ever to be printed in the press, and the other, a physical performance by a woman that inspired a man to try to match it. The two women were Mary Butler and Mary McMullen, respectively.

In April 1826, "a woman" at St. Thomas's Fair, Exeter, undertook to walk fifty miles in ten and a half hours, but she completed the distance "with ease" in eight and a half, a time that was on par with what the best men at the time could accomplish.[6] She did it on a 440-yard "piece of ground" between the Lamb and Lion and the Dunsford Turnpike Gate, but no wager was involved—her prize money was contributed by the spectators. It seems very likely that she was Mary Butler. If so, she was later described as getting up next morning "with the lark" and working through the day unaffected by her previous day's walking.[7]

On 1 May 1826, also in Exeter, Mary Butler undertook to walk fifty miles in ten hours, which she successfully completed in eight and three-quarters hours, also done with "the greatest ease." The following day she engaged to walk twenty miles in four hours while carrying fourteen pounds on her back, which she also completed "without the least inconvenience" in about three and three-quarters hours; one report gave it as three and one-quarter hours.[8] These very impressive performances were recognized as such in the press: "The facility that this female walks, renders it probable that neither is she, or the public, aware of the extent of her athletic powers. She seems to walk with so little exertion, that if met on the road, her speed would pass unnoticed; but those who accompany her, give us the best proof of her celerity; most are obliged to trot, while others, whose pedestrian powers are tolerable, require great exertion to keep her pace but for a short time."[9] Mary Butler was the widow of a soldier of the 32nd Regiment of Foot; she had four children and earned her living by washing clothes. Two of her other performances are also recorded: one from the Guard House, at the entrance to Devonport, to the Eagle Inn; and the other on "the old road by the Naval Hospital," but one (or both) may be versions of the first two.[10]

The woman with the most extensive record of performances done over the longest distances was Mary McMullen. Records exist of over a dozen of her performances between September 1826 and May 1830. Known as Mrs. McMullen or the "Female Pedestrian," she may have been born in 1763/4 and was believed to be of Irish origin but lived in Yorkshire and may have later moved to Scotland. She was probably the mother of William, Bernard (Barney), Patrick, and Edward McMullen, all pedestrians, who traveled the country—often together or in twos and threes—performing pedestrian feats. But their mother was the most outstanding and the most durable walker. Uncertainties abound in the accounts of her performances, for itinerant pedestrians leave few permanent traces. She seldom competed in wagers but set herself time-targets and announced her attempts in advance, thereby earning money by collecting it from passers-by or from those who stopped to watch.

We get our first sight of her in September 1826 when she undertook to walk forty miles in ten successive hours at York, an exercise that was proclaimed by the bellman the day before. She was described as being "sixty years of age," and she started at 8:30 a.m.

> The *fair heroine* appeared at the starting place, where a box affixed to a chair, was placed, having a label soliciting the pecuniary aid of the spectators to the *pedestrianess.* From the chair, half a mile was measured along the high road, and in this course the *lady* performed her task. She is a tall woman, and was attired in a dark coloured skirt, a white cotton waist, over which was pinned a colourful neckerchief; a white muslin cap completed the upper part of her costume, whilst a pair of black stockings finished her attire; she wore no hat or shoes.[11]

She finished the task "exhibiting no sign of fatigue" with "an hour to spare" and was not disappointed with the money that was collected.

One week later, also in York, she engaged to walk ninety miles in twenty-four hours.[12] She began at four p.m. from the Asylum Gates, having again a half-mile course measured out on the North Road. Because she was well known from the previous week, "the concourse of spectators was particularly numerous" and greatly increased into the evening and to such an extent they caused her "some little interruption." She was hindered by several droves of cattle, but, most seriously, "by young men who had made bets against her, and attempted by every means to induce her to relinquish her undertaking, or to render her incapable of persevering in it. Notwithstanding this brutal conduct, she kept on her way," and she still completed her task with fifty-three minutes to spare. The *Annals of Sporting* wrote: "There is no doubt, but had she undertaken 100 miles, as many men have done, in the same time, she would have completed it, allowed fair play."[13]

Mary McMullen had not had fair play, but toward the end of the performance "several elegantly dressed ladies" went to watch her, "many of whom were liberal in their *doucers* to the poor old woman." "In performing her last mile, she stopped at the door of a house at Clifton, the mistress of which, placed upon her head a new white muslin cap, profusely trimmed with light blue ribbon; she was also presented with a new white apron, and in these she walked in triumph to the goal, preceded by a fiddle and a tambourine. Hearty cheers announced the conclusion of the task, to witness which there would not be less than six thousand persons assembled." This was the pinnacle for women pedestrians; a laboring man named Askew from nearby Layerthorpe wagered five pounds that he could repeat Mary McMullen's task and did so with forty-five minutes to spare. The correspondent to the *Annals of Sporting*, however, wrote that doing what a woman had previously done "was nothing to brag about."[14] It is nothing to be modest about, either: ninety miles walked in twenty-four hours is a significant achievement, particularly when you have young men doing their best to stop you. Did the man from Layerthorpe have the same obstacles to overcome as did Mary McMullen—and was he received at the end with the same enthusiasm?

We cannot be sure of Mary McMullen's other performances because many reports of women pedestrians give no names, but table 3 shows the most likely. The event at Sneinton, Nottingham, was stopped because her presence was said to have caused "complete commotion." "The crowd continued increasing till nearly ten, at which time she had more than completed a fourth of the distance, when the nuisance was become so intolerable, that the parish authorities interfered, and compelled the old lass to desist."[15] Were the crowds so large that public order was threatened? Or were there other unspoken motives behind the parish authorities' actions?

Was she also the center of the crowd three years later in Scotland? The unnamed pedestrian had set herself to go ninety-six miles in twenty-four hours, the sort of event that seems to have been Mary McMullen's trademark. She would have been sixty-nine or seventy years old at the time.

> A female, said to be about seventy years of age, who had undertaken to walk ninety-six miles in the space of twenty-four hours, commenced the feat on Wednesday evening last, at six o'clock, on the road leading from Paisley to Renfrew. The vast assemblage of people soon collected spectators, and by nine o'clock the road, for half-a-mile beyond the toll-bar, the space chosen for the performance of the exploit, was entirely obstructed by the crowd. About four in the morning the heroine, who had walked forty-miles, and seemed in a fair way of accomplishing her undertaking, was apprehended by a warrant from the Sheriff of the county, and lodged in durance; and so the affair terminated.[16]

TABLE 3. Other likely performances by Mary McMullen

DATE	DISTANCE	VENUE	TARGET	RESULT	SOURCE
5 Dec.1826	20 miles	Nr Godmanchester	4.5h	Within time	*Annals of Sporting*, Dec. 1826, 49
4/5 Dec. 1826	92 miles	Wisbech	24h	23h 42min	*Belfast Commercial Chronicle*, 13 Dec. 1826
7 Dec. 1826	92 miles	Spilsby	24h	24h 8min (obstructed)	*Annals of Sporting*, Jan. 1827, 49
23 Jan. 1827	20 miles	Mansfield	4.5h	4h 10min	*The Sun*, 27 Jan. 1827
March 1827	10 miles	Knutsford	2h	1h 55min 30s	*Tipperary Free Press*, 28 March 1827
24 May 1827	92 miles	Carlisle	24h	23h 29min	*Bristol Mercury*, 28 May 1827
4/5 June 1827	100 miles	York	24h	Stopped after 65miles in 17h	*Annals of Sporting*, July 1827, 44–45
1 Nov. 1827	20 miles	Kingsbury	4h	3h 59min	*London Packet*, 5–7 Nov. 1827
19 Nov. 1827	15 miles	Windsor	3h	2h 15min	*Morning Post*, 26 Nov. 1827
18 Sept. 1828	92 miles	Newcastle	24h	23h 37min	*Newcastle Courant*, 20 Sept. 1828
12 Oct.1829	96 miles	Ranelagh Gardens	24h	23h 49min[?]	*Norfolk Chronicle and Norwich Gazette*, 17 Oct. 1829
Nov. 1829	95miles	Carlisle	24h	23h 30min[?]	*Sussex Advertiser*, 16 Nov. 1829; *The Atlas*, 22 Nov. 1829
14 Dec. 1829	96miles	Winchester	24h	23h 40min	*Hampshire Chronicle & Southampton Courier*, 14 Dec. 1829
18 May 1830	96miles	New Snenton [Sneinton]	24h	Stopped after 24 miles in 5h	*Nottingham Review and General Advertiser*, 21 May 1830

It is puzzling that the crowds gathered to watch her were seen to be such a threat that someone saw fit to seek a warrant and then to secure her arrest and imprisonment. Why did the sheriff not simply clear the road? Was there some deep-seated antipathy to seeing a woman on the road, and an old woman at that?

Perhaps we can begin to see the answer to these questions in the case of Mrs. Harrison, who in 1843 set out to repeat Captain Barclay's famous performance of a thousand miles in a thousand successive hours. She established her base at Leeds, and the newspapers reported on her progress, but one newspaper added an opinion: "It is a pity that the husband of this woman can't find her some employment more befitting her sex. Such exhibitions are a disgrace to society."[17] In Victorian Britain the authorities expected women to be less visible and, of course, to be under their husbands' control. But perhaps that isn't the full story either. In 1830, only a week or so after Mary McMullen was prevented from walking at Sneinton, Nottingham, by the parish authorities, a woman at Basford, also in Nottingham, who was said to be sixty-two, undertook to walk five miles in an hour. It is unlikely to have been Mary McMullen; she was never involved in such a short event, and the speed matched that she employed over considerably longer distances. However, "She . . . would easily have accomplished it, but that the women of the parish . . . interfered, and prevented her from finishing her task."[18] Some women were as opposed to women performing as were the men.

Such challenges may seem to modern observers a long way from sport, but Captain Barclay's thousand-mile event was always considered sport—one man, unaided, against the clock—and Mary McMullen's walks were no different. On that basis, perhaps we should consider her to be a forerunner of professional women athletes. Many other women had made excursions into that territory, but Mary McMullen lived by the success of her physical challenges and the willingness of the public to support them. Unfortunately, the opposition to them did not come from the men alone.

The comment about Mrs. Harrison—that her husband should find her "some employment more befitting her sex"—is also revealing. Engaging in versions of Captain Barclay's challenge was still a popular activity thirty-four years after he first performed it. In October 1843, just two months before Mrs. Harrison began her attempt, James Searle was performing it at Holbeck, near Chesterfield.[19] While Mrs. Harrison's attempt was underway, Benjamin Ryding (a.k.a.

the Morning Star) completed 1,500 miles in 1,500 successive hours,[20] and John Perry, "a man of colour," was attempting 1,250 miles in 1,250 successive-hours.[21] It was almost commonplace for walkers to be engaging in one version or another of the so-called Barclay match, but they were all men. Mrs. Harrison's challenge was the first attempt by a woman, and it was met with disapproval because it was seen as not "befitting for her sex." Men did not want women inside their masculine worlds, and some women agreed with them. The forces lined up against the women were perhaps greater than ever before.

The old, more traditional sports pitting runner against runner, such as the races at Old Wives Lees and Dover's Olimpicks, were also slipping away. In 1830 at Old Wives Lees: "The female who was the winner last year has had several journies to Chilham Castle to obtain the money, and was at last told that the prizes for running would be discontinued in future; she however had £1 given her as recompence for her lost journies."[22] "Humbug," shouted a writer a week later to the same paper. "Another attempt is making to crush the few remaining sports of the poor. . . . This is an age of moral meddling and cant, and sheer humbug."[23]

There was talk of an event being held after this, and the date of the final race at Old Wives Lees was still listed in the *Kentish Gazette* until 1865, but the event that Sir Dudley Digges had initiated in his will of 1638 had died.[24] After World War II an event was held there again to celebrate victory, and it was said that "the Diggs' bequest was put to a use more in keeping with the times—the provision of coal for the aged poor."[25]

In the Cotswolds, Dover's Olimpicks had been in decline ever since the Dover family lost its influence over them and their organization fell into the hands of various publicans and committees.[26] In 1846 the Rev. G. D. Bourne arrived to become rector at Weston-sub-Edge, the parish in which Dover's Hill was situated, and he described Dover's Olimpicks as "a meeting place of the lowest classes merely for debauchery—no longer to witness or take part in manly games and true English sport, but simply for the indulgence of the grossest wickedness—the most sensual crimes. . . . I have seen as many as 30,000 there, but I am told that many more were assembled."[27] There was much talk of "lawlessness," the "vagrants and criminals," the "armed bands of Birmingham yahoos," the "turmoil," "disorder," and "disturbances," and they all came from Bourne and those whom he informed and influenced.[28] The reverend was "determined if possible to stop this evil."

The mechanism he used was land enclosure. Unenclosed land (i.e., public land, to which all had free access) had the precedent of ancient history behind it, but it was unpopular with Victorian landowners, who thought such common grounds should be enclosed (privatized). The local villagers would traditionally graze a cow on public land or even have a small-holding in a corner of it, and there were common rights for a multitude of purposes. The Reverend Bourne worked with a few influential local men, and they applied to have the land enclosed on which Dover's Olimpicks were held. In June 1850 it was announced that royal assent had been granted. After 238 years, Dover's Olimpicks were over.

In 1996 C. J. Bearman investigated the nature of the mechanism by which Bourne secured the enclosure and the nature of the disorder that made it necessary.[29] He searched all contemporary newspaper reports, letters, and even the duty diary of the police superintendent for the years leading up to the application for enclosure, looking for reports or evidence of disorder and debauchery. Bearman determined that "there is not a single piece of evidence to justify any of these allegations." He concluded that perhaps the Reverend Bourne was "suffering from moral panic: not the genuine alarm arising from injury or outrage but a fearful horror at any assembly of the lower orders, and was willing to repeat gross exaggerations amounting to deliberate lies to convince others of the dangers he felt."[30] The historical record sometimes moves in a series of uncomfortable loops: Were Robert Dover's Olimpick Games eventually closed by a puritanically minded clergyman and his supporters, rather like the "refinèd clergy" who had originally inspired Robert Dover to create his Olimpick Games to confront?

Bearman also concluded that the Reverend Bourne would only have needed the support of nine other persons to secure the enclosure, and that when the enclose was complete the land was distributed among local landowners. In that process, Rev. G. D. Bourne secured for himself 63 acres, 1 rood (a quarter-acre), and 1 perch (thirty and a quarter square yards).

11

THE RUNNERS

Overview, 1638-1850

Two Cultures

Looking across the two-hundred-year history of women's running summarized in the preceding chapters it is possible to see which elements were stable throughout this period and which underwent significant change. The database shows that women's running culture in Britain in the seventeenth and eighteenth centuries was quite unlike the men's, but there were regional variations. In Kent it grew out of a codicil to Sir Dudley Digges's will of 1638 by means of which two "maidens" raced head-to-head annually for a very significant sum of money. The young women of Kent ran extended sprints from 165 to 220 yards, but this had increased to 440 yards by the mid-eighteenth century. So successful were these races that other communities in Kent copied them, and this style of race—two runners racing head-to-head—became known as racing Kentish style and continued for over 150 years, but it was not copied anywhere else in Britain.

In the rest of England, Ireland, Scotland, and Wales women usually ran in races of three or more competitors and over distances ranging from one to four miles. Occasionally longer or shorter races were held, but they were never as short as those in Kent. The database shows that more than 80 percent of these races were for smocks. Racing for smocks also appeared in Kent in 1726, but the distances run in Kent and the way the races were run separated them from the rest of Britain. If we were forced to categorize them, we might say that the women runners in Kent had to rely on their speed endurance, whereas in the rest of Britain they ran longer distances and relied on their aerobic endurance.

The Historical Record

It is inescapable that the evidence for this study is biased at source, for almost all the data, in all its forms, comes from men, and that fact always needs to be borne in mind. Many of those who ran, played cricket, fought, and so on were country girls and women and those too low on the social ladder to tell their own stories—or even to attract much attention—so their stories have to be interpreted from many small fragments from which "meaning" has to be teased. The letters of foreign visitors are a rich source, for they wrote home about the things they saw, especially things that struck them as unusual or noteworthy, while those who lived here seem not to have noticed them, or they thought them too commonplace or inconsequential to comment on. When seeing women and girls engaging seriously in sports, observers who had no other frame of reference often thought of ancient Greece, Olympia, the Olympic Games, the Spartans, and mythic characters such as Atalanta. These perspectives in some cases may even have helped to legitimize, and shape, what they saw.

The Smock Race

Most women in the seventeenth and eighteenth centuries were certainly aware of the label men attached to them—the "weaker vessel." The creation of the smock race gave them a kind of haven: a place and a space not otherwise available to them. The database shows that they used that freedom to run long, hard races against each other for a smock that had been carried ceremoniously on a pole to the race ground and that fluttered bravely overhead until it was won. The women who exercised that freedom to run numbered in the hundreds, perhaps thousands, in every corner of England and in Ireland, Scotland, and Wales. The races were often boisterous, noisy occasions held alongside a jackass race or men's cudgeling matches; they happened in conjunction with a men's cricket match or a horse race, or on almost any celebratory occasion and on any piece of accessible land or road. And those who raced could be of any age and included married women and older women as well as many maids and maidens. The records also show Roma and Black girls racing. Many women also raced for notoriety as well as for money and prizes, and some built reputations as successful racers and traveled many miles to take on the opposition.

Beginning in the seventeenth century, the popularity of the smock race spread quickly and, unlike many sports, was attached to no special day or season. When Britain was predominantly rural, country smock races fitted easily into local festivals, holidays, and special birthday celebrations.

Status

Despite its origins in the old rural traditions of skimmington and horn fairs, which aimed to shame over-dominant women and weak men, the public display of a smock mysteriously metamorphosed into a topsy-turvy celebration of women's power, and racing for the smock became a time of celebration, when the restrictions normally placed on women and girls were set aside (fig. 21). Horns and smocks were part of the iconography of the skimmington ride, but over time the horns were discarded, and the smocks that had been carried as an ironic symbol of women's dominance became assertions of their physical power.[1] Grose's description of a skimmington ride contains the following: "A smock displayed on a staff is carried before them as an emblematic standard, denoting female superiority."[2]

Smock races attracted women, young and old, for over 150 years and were sometimes organized, overseen, and officiated by women, for whom these events must have had a carnivalesque quality. Other observers, however, thought the behavior and dress of the women on these occasions were unacceptable and unsuitable, even for those lower on the social scale. Nevertheless, for most people, in most places, and for most of the time, smock races were accepted, even welcomed, perhaps because the freedoms they gave women were only fleeting. Alessandro Arcangeli has commented that "one should never forget that a carnivalesque reversal of convention can barely be regarded as a threat to the status quo unless contextual information suggests that it was performed with subversive intentions."[3] As Britain became urbanized in the late eighteenth and early nineteenth centuries, smock races were to be found in the towns, and factories included them in their sports days; the old, rural roots in the skimmington rides became blurred and were eventually lost.

The many hundreds of accounts of smock races make clear that in the main they were empowering events for women and girls of all ages. If anyone

FIGURE 21. *Eccles Wakes*, Joseph Parry, oil on canvas, 1808. Detail showing women gathering under the smock before the race. (Manchester Art Gallery)

denied them the opportunity to run, things could quickly become disorderly,[4] and if they thought they had been unfairly treated they could respond angrily.[5] Many women were emboldened not only by racing for a smock but by the environment that was created by the smock displayed on a pole or hanging overhead from a tree.

The Smock

When organizers and promoters of smock races placed their advertisements, they tried to make their prizes sound attractive, and the description "a fine Holland Smock" became very common. Some promoters wanted to emphasize that *their* smock was something special: "a lac'd Holland Smock";[6] "a Fine Lac'd Holland Smock";[7] "an exceedingly good HOLLAND SMOCK."[8] Or perhaps they might stress the garment's monetary value or the prizes for runners-up. After 1775 the smocks' values were seldom given, and the descriptions became even more florid: "a Holland Smock highly ornamented with pink and blue ribbands";[9] "a new fully-trimmed Holland Smock, with a fashionable Cap";[10] "a fine Holland Smock, tied in the newest taste, with true Rodney ribbons, and a genteel Hat properly mounted."[11]

After 1800 the data show that smocks and shifts were also less likely to be made of Holland, so the traditional expression, "Holland smock," began to fall out of use. Of the thirty-three footraces in the database for the summer of 1814, when women and girls ran to celebrate the peace, not one smock prize was described as being made of Holland. The days of racing for a Holland smock were over. Holland smocks did not disappear, though, and were on sale in Britain well into the twentieth century, though largely as children's wear. But the world in which women and girls ran for them in almost every county in England had passed into memory.

In the early nineteenth century the "smock" became a "chemise," perhaps with a view to elevating it from its humble past. New descriptions were used that rather spurned the idea of the common smock. "A new Holland Chemise [for] *young* Ladies (under 60)" was advertised at Margate in 1808 but attracted only one competitor, even after repeated announcements on the ground that "the prize (then elevated on a stand) was equal, in *substance,* to a fashionable gown and petticoat."[12] At Margate they had begun calling their prize smock a "chemise" as early as 1802,[13] and at Pinkneys Green they had done so since 1797.[14] Others followed: Tothill Fields, Middlesex (1805),[15] Datchet, Berkshire (1806),[16] Greenwich, Kent (1807),[17] Uffingdon, Berkshire (1808),[18] for example, in what seems to have been an attempt to aggrandize or even gentrify the humble smock. In 1789 the Prince of Wales had even called his prize smocks "Handsome Gowns." It is hardly surprising that the symbolic value of the smock described by Grose as "denoting female superiority" was lost as its very name faded into history.[19]

Distances and Venues

Because of their history and status, smock races were always tough, physical challenges—their toughness was the point, at least in part, and so the women ran races that revealed their physical strength and endurance (typically from one to four miles). But with the introduction in 1730 of best-of-three races, the women had to run a given distance up to three times in a single afternoon or evening; the most extreme example was advertised in 1730, from Buckingham Gate to the new bridge at Putney and back (eight and a half miles).

By 1750, however, we learn less about the distances that the women ran, and best-of-three competitions became the norm, an obvious additional athletic challenge. Although referring to women runners during this time as "athletes" is an anachronism, it seems an appropriate way to describe those who raced hard, and repeatedly, and did so successfully.

In the nineteenth century smock racing changed its character. Best-of-three competitions become rare and distances were reduced. In 1814, for the celebrations of victory over Napoleon, shorter races were organized, and the runners were often called "girls." These were the days when the events they ran were often attempts to recreate the spirit of Merrie England: deliberate attempts at cultural nostalgia, of remembering the days before the crowded cities became commonplace, before the new industrialized societies took root. They attempted to evoke memories of the days when the old, rural, agrarian societies had unbroken links with the past. It was a fiction, of course, but nostalgia drove a move for events that were fun and raised the spirits rather than events that were athletically challenging. The number of races that were held, however, showed no sign of declining, and women of all ages continued to race in tough half-mile events for chemises. The shorter distances that the girls ran in 1814, however, were never as short as those deemed the "safe" maximum for women by the International Athletic Federation in 1928. Attitudes toward the physical capabilities of women were clearly very different in the seventeenth, eighteenth, and early nineteenth centuries.

Publicly accessible places such as commons, greens, heaths, moors, and the public roads were usually the venues chosen to stage races. They also took place alongside fairs, festivals, and multisports events, and horse race meetings up to 1740, after which legislation reduced the number of small horse race meetings.

Money, Wagers, and Betting

Significant historical events and social changes took place in Britain during the period covered in this study, and it is inevitable that sports would reflect these. In particular, the value of the pound varied greatly and affected the worth of the prizes on offer and their desirability. The fluctuation in the value of the pound affected the lives of women runners in other ways, too, of course. For example, figure 22 shows the purchasing power in 1638 of the ten-pound prize at Old Wives Lees and in the two hundred years that followed.

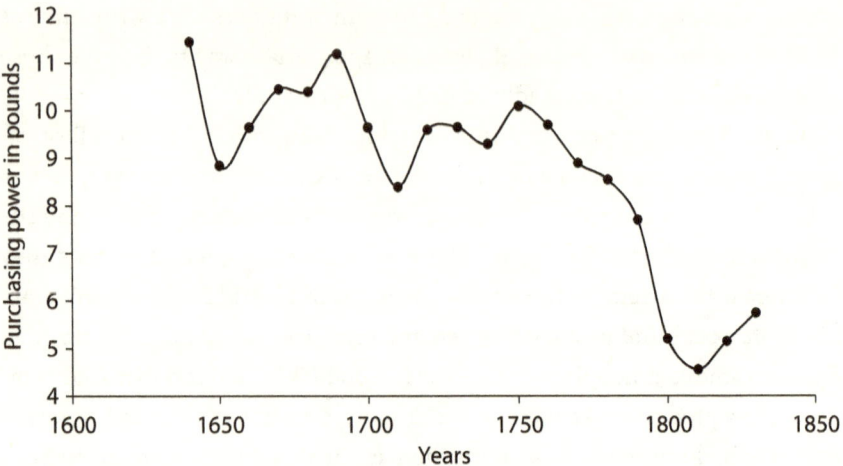

FIGURE 22. Purchasing power of the ten-pound prize at Old Wives Lees, 1640–1840.

In the second half of the eighteenth century, the purchasing power of the pound began a steady decline; by the end of that century and the beginning of the nineteenth, the winner's prize at Old Wives Lees had less than half of the purchasing power that Sir Dudley Diggs had originally envisaged. In such times of economic hardship, however, the ten pounds would nevertheless have been very welcome.

Figure 22 also reflects the general economic conditions in Britain, and graphically shows that in the second half of the eighteenth century, money purchased much less than previously. The devaluation created inevitable hardship among the less well-off, but its impact fell on everyone, including the organizers of events who had to find money for the prizes.

Figure 23 shows the distribution of first-prize values, which varied greatly from one venue to another, although after 1720 most venues tried to produce a smock valued at one guinea. The mean trendline shows the first-prize values declining throughout the eighteenth century, and this, combined with the decline in the value of money, caused the monetary value of prizes to cease being the main motivating factor. The smocks became perhaps even more symbolic. After 1775 organizers rarely declared the prize values at all.

While men's footraces during this period were driven by wagers and bets, it was unusual for women's matches, perhaps because of the smock races' own unique culture and history. We cannot rule out the possibility of small

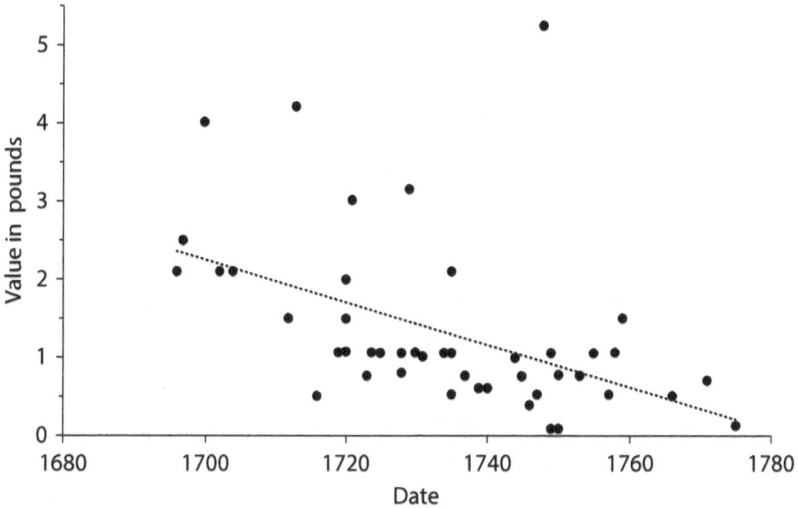

FIGURE 23. Drop in value of first prizes in smock races, 1696–1775.

wagers adding to the excitement, but money and betting were not the driving force.[20] Nevertheless, women running for wagers was not unknown, and they sometimes led to outstanding performances, such as the fifteen-year-old girl who ran a mile in five minutes and twenty-eight seconds for a two-guinea wager in Kent in 1795.

Celebrations

In addition to the opportunities they gave to the women runners and their role as public entertainment, smock races in the long eighteenth century became a familiar part of local festivities and of celebrations to mark Whitsun, Easter, Midsummer's Day, saints' days, and other special occasions. In this way the women runners found themselves at the heart of celebrations in which they were significant actors. The numerous peace celebrations in 1814 were part of a surge in patriotism in which communities gathered to honor the end of nearly two decades of war, and women's and girls' races were a very common element of them. But even as early as October 1801, when notice of the signing of the Treaty of London arrived at Bodmin, Cornwall, the town was illuminated, and the chief magistrate ordered two hogsheads of ale to be distributed to the poor. The local volunteer militia fired a *feu de joie* (a celebratory rifle salute), and "instead of boys letting off fireworks (a thing unknown here), according to the custom of the place on joyous occasions, the women ran for a shift, which was given by our late Mayor."[21]

Thus, the women runners of Bodmin became the heralds of peace. But elsewhere they found themselves at the heart of politics and other major local and national events. On 20 July 1802 at the rural sports event at Barnes, south of the River Thames, the Holland smock on offer as first prize was "ornamented with a cockade of Mr. Byng's on one side, and one of Sir Francis Burdett's on the other."[22] A fiercely contested parliamentary election campaign was in full flow, and voting had started one week earlier and would go on for another week. There was great animosity between the candidates, and the smock race organizers were hedging their bets even though the voting was taking place at Brentford, on the other side of the river and in another county. It might be imagined that the election would have been a matter only for those men who could vote (i.e., those who owned land with a rental value of at least forty shillings per annum), but that was not so. Everyone was involved and took sides and wore the colors, or ribbons, of one side or another to show their allegiance. In this case, however, there were three candidates in the election, and the race organizers had decided not to tie the colors of the third candidate (William Mainwaring) to the smock. Mainwaring was the sitting Tory MP; he was unpopular, and the Radical Tory, Sir Francis Burdett, had whipped considerable animosity against him. The race organizers must have decided that support for either of the other two contestants was better than continuing with the status quo. The eighteen-year-old runner from Shropshire who eventually won the carefully beribboned prize would have been well steeped in Middlesex and national politics before she eventually went home with her smock ornamented with two (not three) rival colors.

Smock race organizers were not shy about showing their allegiances and drawing the runners to enter; in 1781, at Windsor, the maidens from Berkshire and Surrey ran for a Holland smock adorned "with true Rodney ribbons,"[23] showing the organizers' support for Admiral George Brydges Rodney, who was not only the sitting MP for Westminster but also a successful admiral who had just captured St. Eustatius (a small but vital trading island in the Caribbean to the east of Puerto Rico) from the Dutch. Admiral Rodney was a controversial figure but popular with the king and court. He had won his seat for Westminster in absentia against a vigorously battling Charles James Fox. Rodney was an establishment figure, and those at Windsor who chose to sew his colors to the Holland smock must have made a strategic as well as a political decision. Reports from Rodney, and about him, were regular features in the newspapers, and letters from him were in the newspapers the day before the smock race was held, so neither the runners nor the crowd could have been unaware of the significance of the Rodney ribbons.

The ladies who ran for the "handsome Gowns" at Brighton in August 1789 cannot have been unaware of the political significance of the Whig's blue-and-bluff ribbons attached to all the prizes, nor can they have been ignorant of the fact that their king was recovering from a bout of madness. A major rift split the royal family, with the Prince of Wales and the oldest royal princes on one side and the king and the rest of the family on the other. Crowds were drawn to sporting events because of the fun and entertainment, but these events could also be a magnet for all sorts of people: the women runners could as easily find themselves racing in front of John Wilkes's Friends of Liberty, as they did at Battle-Bridge, St. Pancras, in October 1773,[24] or for the enjoyment of Abdrahaman, the Tripoline ambassador and "several foreigners of distinction" in June 1786.[25]

The women runners, therefore, often took part in events that assumed a sociopolitical significance far beyond the mere running of a footrace, and the races offer a rare insight into the roles that ordinary local women played in major national and international dramas. Royal birthdays were also occasions for local rejoicing and well-attended celebrations. In 1726 sports were held at Long Marston, Yorkshire, when eight maidens ran for a smock. The race was followed by toasts to the king, the Prince of Wales, the royal family, and to "Prosperity to the Trade and Navigation if the City of York, and the Manufactures of the County."[26] The sports to mark a later Prince of Wales's birthday have been noted above, but the celebration of royal birthdays can be surprising. At the end of September 1798, Duchess Maria of Württemberg's thirty-second birthday was celebrated with a fête at Maiden Castle, near Weymouth, Dorset, and she was accompanied by Queen Charlotte, the Duke of York, and many of the royal princesses.[27] The duchess was visiting George III and the royal family, who were staying at Gloucester Lodge, where they had spent part of each year since 1788 when the king went there recuperate from his bout of "madness." The duchess was the sister of Frederick, Prince of Wurttemberg, who had married Princess Charlotte, the Princess Royal, the previous year, so the Duke of York and the royal princesses were escorting their new sister-in-law. Elizabeth Ham went to see it all and wrote in her diary about "women racing for *under* garments," one of the rare instances in which we have a woman as the source of information.[28] Four months earlier, the king's birthday had been celebrated at Horsham with sports and races. "Barrack ladies" ran for "a Holland smock ornamented with blue ribbons.[29] In 1821 sports were held all over Britain to celebrate George IV's coronation, and at Brighton there were "foot races for prize-favours,"[30] while at Wisbech, on the Isle of Ely, the women "forty years and upward" raced for a "coronation bonnet and a cap."[31] Smocks were increasingly out of favor by 1821, but women runners of all ages were at the heart of local events and celebrations.

Men's Attitudes to the Women Racers

Throughout the whole of the period under study in which women ran competitive races, men commented on what they wore. Many thought they wore too little or revealed too much, which was an additional obstacle for women to overcome; men were never criticized in that way. In addition, the women runners' morals were suspected because of it. But men often went to see women run *because* of their reputation for wearing too little and revealing too much, and men's imaginations went even further. Some fantasized about women falling over in a race; in losing control they would reveal even more. Artists and poets were particularly prone to this. The contemporary record, however, contains very few reports of it; it seems to have been a fantasy of the male creative mind, perhaps as a counterbalance to the whole idea of the smock race, which was an assertion of women's power. By showing the women runners falling, by showing them losing control, did the male artists hope to draw attention to the paradox of their weakness at the very time they were demonstrating their strength? It wasn't only the men, though; Fanny Burney created a scene in which an old woman falls heavily during a race—an episode that is not supported by the historical record.

Women runners needed a thick skin and had to learn to ignore many of the male attitudes toward them, but society can be a harsh judge, and women runners were criticized for not behaving according to various social, religious, and moral standards. They were even opposed by other women, leading to calls for runners to be prevented from competing by law-enforcement officers. A complex mix of attitudes often lined up against women runners and pedestrians, but they continued to race in the face of them all. As nearly all the contemporary information about women runners in the early modern period comes from men—as reporters, poets, balladeers, or artists—it is one of the challenges of this study to recognize the biases that this inevitably creates.

Dress

We learn surprisingly little about what the women racers wore, but it seems that they almost always ran barefooted and wore their everyday clothes while shedding a layer or two, sometimes down to their own smocks. We do read of some, however, who wore drawers and waistcoats to race, a clothing choice designed to give them freedom of movement and to provide some support. This was innovatory and two centuries ahead of the "bloomers" that women adopted in the mid-nineteenth century. We also read of occasions when they ran naked, which seems to have been an imitation of the elite male runners and may have been more an expression of their aspiration to be considered serious runners than pandering to the wishes of some of the male spectators.

The Runners

To understand the early modern women runners, it is important to recognize that they were not runners in the sense that many in twenty-first century are—they were racers. When they ran, they did so in contests with rivals hoping and trying to defeat them. This is a particularly challenging form of running, but women raced at almost any age and in every corner of England, and in Ireland, Scotland, and Wales, too. Some were very successful, became very well-known, and traveled considerable distances to race. "Two noted Welch [Welsh] Girls" traveled to London to race against "the Earl's Court Girls" in 1755, and, as mentioned above, in 1795 one fifteen-year-old from Kent ran a mile in time that would remain unbeaten 137 years. Although the latter was run in a wager, there are very few reports of women running thus and few mentions of any betting involved in their races.

Pedestrians

Independent of the smock races or those in Kent inspired by Sir Dudley Digges's bequest, women also traveled long distances on foot for the sake of economy and were employed to deliver messages.[32] With the passing of the age of the Holland smock, emphasis moved to the pedestrians (or pedestriennes) who performed long distances on the road, often motivated by poverty and need in the hope of making money. Such challenges revealed that women were particularly good endurance athletes, a fact that the world at large would not catch up with for another 150 years, by which time the efforts of the early pedestrians had been almost completely forgotten. Let them now take their place in the rich history of women's athleticism.

12

WOMEN TENNIS PLAYERS, TEAM PLAYERS, FIGHTERS, AND JOCKEYS

The Evidence

Contemporary sources for early modern women team players, games players, prizefighters, and equestrians are extremely varied: the primary sources include newspapers, posters (handbills), challenges, and local surveys such as the Statistical Account of Scotland, as well as literary collections, drawings, and other images. Secondary sources, such as highly sport-specific biographies and histories, also supply us with information.

The activities of the cricketers and fighters have already attracted the attention of other writers and academics. Works on cricket include Alfred Bedford, "Women at Cricket" (1927); Nancy Joy, *Maiden Over: A Short History of Women's Cricket and a Diary of the 1948–49 Test Tour to Australia* (1950); Rachel Heyhoe Flint and Netta Rheinberg, *Fair Play: The Story of Women's Cricket* (1976); Kathleen McCrone, *Playing the Game: Sport and the Physical Emancipation of English Women, 1870–1914* (1988); Catriona M. Parratt, *More than Mere Amusement: Working-Class Women's Leisure in England, 1750–1914* (2001); Betty Rizzo, "Equivocations of Gender and Rank: Eighteenth-Century Sporting Women" (2002); Isabelle Duncan, *Skirting the Boundary. A History of Women's Cricket* (2013); and Rafaelle Nicholson, *Ladies and Lords: A History of Women's Cricket in Britain* (2019).[1] Joy's *Maiden Over* and Flint and Rheinberg's *Fair Play* are particularly noteworthy because they comment on fifteen and twelve (respectively) women's cricket matches up to 1825—remarkable feats of detection in an age before computers, online databases, and word-searches. Joy and Flint were also outstanding international cricketers. The present study is based on an examination of reports of thirty-one matches during this period; this is a considerable advance on what was available to previous analysts, for *all* the previous studies make reference to a total of only seventeen matches between them, and this number includes one match that did not take place.

Interest in documenting the histories of women's fighting sports started much later. Works include Malissa Smith, *A History of Women's Boxing* (2014), and L. A. Jennings, *She's a Knockout: A History of Women's Fighting Sports* (2015).[2] There is, however, another minor genre: fictionalized histories of women fighters. Works include Paul Creswick, *Bruising Peg: Pages from the Journal of Margaret Molloy, 1768–9* (1898); and Anna Freeman, *The Fair Fight* (2014).[3] These works set their action in the days of the prizefighters, and Creswick's Peg is so successful that she is given three and a half pages in a history of the sport.[4]

My analyses in the next chapters examine all known cricket matches and women's fights in the long eighteenth century, but the evidence I present likely falls far short of the actual number of cricket matches played and fights fought and represents but a tiny percentage of what in fact took place. This is not because women's sports in particular were poorly reported but rather that *all* sports were poorly reported. For example, in August 1742 the *Daily Advertiser* reported that "the above Parish [Slindon] has play'd forty-three Matches and lost but one."[5] These were men's matches, but records of only five have been found and not one was reported in the newspapers.[6] Accounts from contemporary sources claim the prizefighter John Parkes fought 350 bouts in the ring up to 1733, but evidence of fewer than ten has survived.[7] In 1730, when Sarah Barret challenged Elizabeth Stokes, she described herself as "Mistress of the Science of Defence, who in above 40 Battles, have distinguished the Power of my Sex," but no record of any of the forty fights has yet come to light.[8] This may be true of all eighteenth-century sports, with the possible exception of horse racing, giving plenty of scope for future historians.

Sources of information about women's sports in the long eighteenth century tend to be sport-specific. For example, the sources for cricket are almost exclusively newspaper reports of matches that had already been played; they list venues, teams, results, and often prizes, although some of these reports mention challenges for future matches. Our knowledge of prizefighting, however, is the opposite and relies almost exclusively on challenges for future fights that were printed in newspapers; aggravatingly, the results of these fights were not reported, although sometimes a result can be inferred from future challenges.

Advertisements and Notices

How advertisements were used by different sports tells us not only the details of the advertisements themselves but may also give us clues about the relationships between the organizers, the public, and the athletes. Attitudes of newspaper editors and owners, and their readers, have an impact, too.

For footraces, advertisements in newspapers were used to attract a crowd and (sometimes, but not always) to attract the runners; the pattern of advertising for other sports was often quite different. For example, the advertisements for a match of running at Bridge Hill in East Kent seem straightforward enough; it was aimed at the public, telling them when and where the match would take place, but it also communicated directly to the runners, telling them to attend a pre-event (in effect a run-through for the sake of the officials) and giving them a precise date and time to be there. It was a well-constructed advertisement with a heading in several fonts, an illustration, and the necessary content. It seems reasonable to assume placing such an advertisement twice within a week would have been costly: But who would have done so, and why? No one seemed to benefit by attracting a crowd to Bridge Hill. It was public land, and asking spectators to pay an entry fee to sporting events was very rare and could only be enforced if the ground was enclosed; in this case, it was not. There is no suggestion that there were stalls or booths selling drink and food, so there would have been no obvious way of making money out of the event. In other words, no one would have benefitted financially by attracting a crowd. Was the advertisement in effect a public service announcement, informing the public of an event in their neighborhood and informing the runners of what was expected of them? If so, did the editor waive any costs involved?

For cricket, however, no similar newspaper advertisement has been found for any of the thirty-one women's matches in the long eighteenth century (up to 1825); we know of twenty-nine of these matches only from reports of them afterward. The first exception was the match at the Artillery Ground in London in 1747, which did provoke newspaper comments before it took place; this was the only women's cricket match in this period (as yet discovered) that was played on an enclosed ground where spectators had to pay to enter. Comments in the press noted that the match would go ahead, and the date and venue were given. These seem to be addressed to potential spectators and were followed by the match organizer, George Smith, talking directly to the public in the columns of the newspapers: "It is to be hop'd, that the paying Sixpence for Admittance to this Match will not be taken amiss, the Charges thereof amounting to upwards of Fourscore Pound. Tickets for the Rooms and Gallery fronting the Ground to be had of Mr. Smith."[9] A few days later: "[George Smith is] hoping the Company [spectators] will be so kind as to indulge them [the players] in not walking within the Ring; which will not only be a great Pleasure to them, but: a general Satisfaction to the whole."[10] This was an active use of the newspapers to talk to potential spectators, but they were hardly advertisements in the traditional sense. The second exception of information offered prior to a cricket match was the single poster for an intercounty match in 1811.

There is one other reference in a newspaper to a "women's" cricket match before it was played.[11] In 1772 there was an item about a proposed "whimsical" match of eleven women against twenty-two men, for a five-hundred-pound prize. There is no evidence that the match was ever played or even seriously considered, and the item seems to have been inserted as a light-hearted thing to make readers smile.

There are many reports of large crowds attending women's cricket matches, so the apparent absence of advertisements for them is something of a mystery. Were posters commonplace but are now lost? Was it done by word of mouth? Could the organizers not afford to advertise? Did they not want to advertise for fear of attracting too great a crowd of drawing one of the wrong sort?

Conversely, virtually all the information that we have about women's prizefights comes from advertisements, but we know very little about their results. Challenges were very complex affairs. One of the conventions of issuing a challenge was that it had to be made publicly; this was true of all sports, and we can see that in 1793 when newspapers reported that the women cricketers of Bury St. Edmunds in Suffolk had challenged "any eleven in their own county,"[12] or even "their own country."[13] The *Times* wrote that "so famous are the Bury women at this game, that they have challenged all England."[14] In 1822 the *Annals of Sporting* reported that "the damsels of Cheriton [in Hampshire] have thrown down the gauntlet to any eleven in all Hampshire."[15]

In the prize ring, however, they did things more formally; the match was more gladiatorial—and so more personal—and challengers began by announcing themselves by name in newspaper advertisements and declaring where they were from. For example: "I, Mary Welch, from the Kingdom of Ireland";[16] "I, Ann Field, of Stoke Newington";[17] "I, Sarah Barret, from Whitehaven in the County of Cumberland."[18] They present their credentials, too. In the order, above:

> ... being taught, and knowing the noble science of defence, and thought to be the only female of this kind in Europe ...

> ... well known for my abilities in boxing in my own defence wherever it happens in my way ...

> ... Mistress of the Science of Defence, who, in above 40 Battles, have distinguished the Power of my Sex, and shone like a Star of the first Magnitude in the Opinion of the Publick; having defeated the famous Mrs. Mary Barker ...

Such declarations provide invaluable information for the historian. The somewhat stylized formula continued with the challenger acknowledging the status and ability of their opponent. The acceptance of the challenge usually followed, and fighters gave further details. They were simultaneously challenges and advertisements, and they were placed in the newspapers and paid for not by the fighters but by the amphitheaters in which the events were to take place. Once the challenge/advertisement had achieved its objective of attracting spectators, no further money was spent reporting the fight or even giving the result, and no independent reports were published. Thus, for historians of women's prize fighting, the challenges and advertisements are our primary source, in contrast to cricket, for which the reverse applies.

Images

The archives offer us a number of images of a women's cricket match or of women cricketers. For example, John Collett, *Miss Wicket and Miss Trigger*, printed for Carrington Bowles (1 January 1778); T.H., *Cricket Match Played by the Countess of Derby and Other Ladies at the Oaks, Surrey*, watercolor; Thomas Rowlandson, *Rural Sports or a Cricket Match Extraordinary*, published by Thos. Tegg (10 October 1811); and Anon., *The Grand Female Cricket Match*, published by J. Pitts (30 October 1811). The images are not as historically informative as we would wish, however. The watercolor by T.H. seems to rely heavily on John Collett's earlier image, and the artist was almost certainly not at the match he drew (see chapter 14). Rowlandson and the anonymous artist who each created images of the women's intercounty match in 1811 were probably not at the match, either. Their works do not match the eyewitness accounts in the contemporary newspapers of what the women wore. In addition, these two images disagree with each other: Rowlandson's women wear shorter skirts, and their hair hangs loose; the anonymous artist portrays the players wearing caps or headscarves. The eyewitness accounts describe the women as having ribbons in their hair. As with his portrayal of runners, John Collett is the contemporary artist who gives the most trustworthy image of eighteenth-century women cricketers.

There are no known contemporary images of women prizefighters, but the search goes on. Collett provides us with an image of a woman's fight (*The Female Bruisers,* oil on canvas, 1768), but this seems to portray a street fight rather than a sporting event. An image by Charles Williams, *The Boxing Baroness* (1819) later became the subject of a Staffordshire pottery figure.[19] The "Boxing Baroness," however, was neither a baroness nor a boxer; she was Mary Ann Pearce, whose story more properly belongs in a study of drunk and disorderly public figures.[20]

For tennis we have neither advertisements nor public challenges, and the sources are almost entirely from contemporary newspapers reporting results, with a little gossip, and from French contemporary commentators.

13

THE TENNIS PLAYERS

Women were not tennis players in early modern Britain, although there are stories of Mary Stuart playing tennis on the court at Falkland Palace; however, she had lived in France until the age of eighteen and had learned the game there, and there is no evidence of widespread or even minor centers of women's tennis in Britain at that time. In France and Belgium, however, tennis and other associated games had been popular with women for centuries. In 1427 Margot, a young woman in her late twenties or early thirties, arrived in Paris from Hainaut and "played better at hand-ball than any man had seen; and with that she played both fore-handed and back-handed very powerfully, very cunningly, and very cleverly, as any man could, and there were but few men whom she did not beat, except the very best players, and it was the Court in Paris where the best play was."[1]

In the final third of the eighteenth century, however, two French women tennis players visited London and produced some landmarks in British sporting history. The story of French women tennis players in England may seem out of place in a study of British women in sports, but their presence in England—and their stature and performances while they were there—was an important part of British women's sporting history inasmuch as it helped redefine what sportswomen could achieve and even helped British women reexamine the accepted status quo regarding men's and women's respective physical abilities.

It began in May 1767 when English newspapers reported that a "French Lady" was practicing every morning from five to seven a.m. at the tennis courts in St. James's Street, London, in readiness to play "the best Player in England, for a considerable Sum of Money."[2] This daily, two-hour, very early

FIGURE 24. The Royal Tennis Court, St. James's Street, Leicester Square, by Thomas Hosmer Shepherd, hand-colored engraving, 1850. (Trustees of the British Museum)

morning training is the first we have found in the record of such activity by a sportswoman. The French lady was Mme Bunel, but for reasons unknown the match did not take place for nine months.[3] Five in the morning is a very early start, and in the days before 21 May, sunrise in London occurs two or three minutes on either side of five, so Mme Bunel practiced at first light.[4] The tennis courts in St. James's Street dated back to 1637 and comprised one of London's largest indoor spaces. The building was described as "old" as early as 1752 (fig. 24).[5] It was also known as "the King's," "His Majesty's," and "the Royal Tennis Court"; it was said to be a favorite haunt of Charles II; and its royal connections were revived when Frederick, Prince of Wales, started to play there in April 1730. It was also sometimes described as being in Leicester Square, Whitehall, or the Haymarket—all nearby. It was large enough to house two tennis courts with a keeper's house in between,[6] and because of its size it sometimes acted as a playhouse[7] and hosted prizefights[8] and animal fights[9] as well as tennis matches. This was "real" or "royal" tennis, of course. Lawn tennis was still a century in the future. Large windows in the walls allowed light for play, but at five a.m. that light was still likely to be indifferent, at best. This was almost certainly the least favorable time for practice, so Mme Bunel may have had it at a reduced rate or perhaps no-one else wanted it at such an unfavorable time.

In April 1767 a "celebrated" tennis match had taken place there when Mr. Tompkins from Oxford, said to be "the greatest player in England," played Monsieur Masson, who was "Marker to the King of France" (Louis XV).[10] Tickets to see the match cost a guinea each but were still hard to come by.[11]

Total bets placed on the match were variously estimated at between £50,000 and £60,000.[12] Masson was the clear prematch favorite but with odds ranging from to 3 to 2 to 12 to 1.[13] He won by four sets to three.[14] Two weeks later they met again in another seven-set match, and again Masson won, this time, 6–1.[15] In the second match Tompkins was playing for five hundred guineas,[16] which must have been a significant incentive, but Masson was reported to have "cleared near a thousand pounds"[17] in the month he was in London.

It was just after Masson's return to Paris that Mme Bunel was seen practicing in the early morning. The match for which Mme Bunel was preparing eventually took place on Friday 19 February 1768 at the Royal Tennis Court in St. James's Street. "The best player in England" was the same Mr. Tompkins who had just been beaten by M. Masson.

Mme Bunel was a professional tennis player; thus when the match with Mr. Tompkins could not be finalized, she arranged other matches and demonstrations to earn a living and played various noblemen and gentlemen who were drawn, no doubt, to the novelty of the situation.[18] Sport was a man's world, and women were not usually even spectators at tennis matches, let alone playing in them, but in July 1767, when she was arranging matches, Mme Bunel also arranged that "ladies might observe unseen from a private apartment"—a secret window onto an unseen male world.[19] No record has been located telling us of how many women took up the offer or what the charge was.

People were uncertain of Mme Bunel's name, which suggests that she was more talked about than read about; they had heard her name but had not seen it in print or writing. The *St. James's Chronicle* called her "Mme Bunnel,"[20] *Jackson's Oxford Journal* called her "Mme Bunell,"[21] and the *Caledonian Mercury* called her "Mme Brunell."[22]

Mr. Tompkins had much the same problem, so inaccuracies in spelling were not just because of unfamiliarity with the French language. The *Derby Mercury* could not decide whether to call him "Mr. Tomkins," "Mr. Tomkyns," or "Mr. Tompkyns," and at various times called him all three.[23] *Jackson's Oxford Journal* (Tompkins's home town newspaper) called him "Mr. Tompkins."[24]

He was Edmund Tompkins, who held the lease of the Merton Street Tennis Court in Oxford and who also managed a court in Windmill Street in London. If ever there was a thoroughbred tennis player, it was Edmund Tompkins; his father, also Edmund Tompkins, had been "esteemed the best tennis player in England" but had drowned four years earlier in the River Isis.²⁵ On his father's death the son inherited his father's court on Merton Street, his name, and his title—the best tennis player in England—and moved to London to make best use of them.²⁶

Mme Bunel was almost certainly Louise-Bonne Bunel, a member of a famous French tennis playing family, several of whom had been Paumier du Roi.²⁷ She was "thin with quite long limbs" and was about forty years old in 1768.²⁸ On court, she was described as wearing "a short skirt and an easy jacket, which placed no restraint upon the activity with which she flew from side to side of the Court."²⁹ In 1763 Louise-Bonne Bunel had played a match against "Monseigneur le Prince de Condé" (Louis François de Bourbon, Prince of Conti), when she "threw herself into the game like a grasshopper," suggesting that she was very active on the court and that her long, strong legs gave her unusual leaping ability.³⁰

The match between Mme Bunel and Edmund Tompkins, which had been delayed by nine months, was described as a "great Match"³¹ on which "considerable Bets were depending."³² It was eventually played on 19 February 1768, and Mme Bunel won it by two sets to one. The record offers us no information on those "considerable Bets."³³ Those who lost money (mainly the English) were not satisfied by the result and wanted a rematch to recoup their losses. Confidence in Edmund Tompkins was obviously still high; he was a strong hitter of the ball and could chase down a ball as well as anyone.

The news of Mme Bunel's victory was reported in London newspapers, although not as quickly as might be expected.³⁴ Nevertheless, before the end of the month it was reported in the Oxford papers,³⁵ and then in Scotland,³⁶ and eventually even in Williamsburg, Virginia.³⁷ Mme Bunel's victory over Edmund Tompkins had become international news.

Eleven days later (1 March 1768) they played again at the same venue for "a considerable sum," and once again Mme Bunel won, this time by four sets to two—there is, again, no mention of the odds. It seems likely that she defeated Tompkins by the accuracy and precision of her strokes.

The matches involving Edmund Tompkins, M. Masson, and Mme Bunel in 1767 and 1768 attracted the attention and the interest of the French, not only in London but in Paris as well. In April 1767 the *Public Advertiser* wrote of the interest in the Tompkins-Masson match: "The arrival of many of the French Nobility here lately is in great Measure, attributed to the Desire of being a

Spectator at this Tennis Match."[38] The French bet heavily on the event, too.[39] In 1768 French interest was piqued again, this time by the Tompkins-Bunel match. "His Excellency the Count de Chatelet [Compte de Châtelet], the French Ambassador, several of the Nobility, and other persons of distinction, were present on the occasion."[40] These matches were clearly significant social and political events that attracted high-profile English and French spectators and helped transfer a lot of money from English pockets into those of the French and from London to Paris—and a French women was at the center of it. The betting would have been along national lines: the English mostly betting on Tompkins and the French betting on Masson and Mme Bunel.

In terms of athletic competitions, it was unprecedented. My searches of the records have produced no previous reports of a woman defeating the "best" man in an athletic activity in which the man was skilled and in which he was doing his utmost to win. We do not know how her victories were received. Was she regarded as a mere novelty? After eleven days Mme Bunel repeated her first victory, so the result can hardly have been regarded as a freak or a fluke. Did it help redefine what women could do?

Mme Bunel was clearly an exceptional tennis player and competitor, but she was not the only one; Mme Masson was also an outstanding, combative player, though physically shorter than Mme Bunel, and "kept the Court in the Rue Grenelle St. Honoré" in Paris.[41] Reviewing the lives of Mme Bunel and Mme Masson in 1783, when Mme Masson was twenty-eight, Louis-Claude de Manevieux wrote:

> There are women with enough strength of constitution & courage to play tennis, and who might succeed better than the best men. . . . But if a woman, determined to play tennis, embraces the activity that is required in this game, and with the right character & the right physique, we cannot doubt that she would make her fortune . . . having more strength & courage than people think. Do we not now see women, as men, with prodigious talent, dancing on the tightrope, twisting their bodies into amazing positions that require as much strength as application? Don't we see others running as well as horses & employing in these activities grace and composure?[42]

The idea that a woman could make her living at tennis, that she could be a professional, must have been as challenging to an Englishman in 1767 as it was to Manevieux when he wrote of it sixteen years later. Manevieux also wrote about suitable clothing for women tennis players: "Wearing a simple corset & soubrevest with breeches that go to mid-calf, they would be suitably dressed to take on anything."[43]

A soubrevest was a loose, sleeveless covering for the upper body worn over other clothing rather like a two-sided bib, tied at the shoulders and around the waist. Although I have translated "des pantalons qui iroient à mi-jambe" as "trousers of mid-calf length," perhaps "breeches" would be a better word, or even "drawers," which were worn in England by women runners and prize-fighters.[44] Manevieux even describes a suitable hairstyle for the elite women tennis players: "Their hair would be only held by a comb."[45]

There is no suggestion in Manevieux's text that women were not equipped physically, strategically, or commercially to be successful tennis players, and Mme Bunel must have played a significant part in dispelling any previous doubts, for dispelled they were. In 1784 the Communautés d'arts et métiers changed their rules to allow women to join, and Louise-Bonne Bunel was admitted to the guild shortly afterwards; she would have been fifty-six. We do not know how commercially successful Mme Bunel was, but she had considerable athletic longevity and was still playing tennis at the age of sixty.[46]

In 1768 the performances of Mme Bunel would have been striking on several levels. By taking on a man in a public tennis court and being the subject of considerable betting, Mme Bunel was demonstrating qualities of independence, assertion, and confrontation that would have run counter to the expectation of her as a woman. Demonstrating her *physical* superiority over a dominant male was unprecedented. Her audience would have assumed that men were the stronger sex, more courageous and determined, and that in a tight situation men would be more able to keep a level head and think more clearly. Mme Bunel turned all those expectations on their heads.

Twelve years later, in March 1790, Mme Masson decided to follow in Mme Bunel's footsteps. In the aftermath of the French Revolution, France was in turmoil; the old provinces were disbanded, and monks and nuns were ordered out into civil life. No one knew what major changes lay ahead. Now thirty-five years old, Mme Masson decided to make the journey from Paris to London to see how she would be received there and to see if she could make money playing tennis. A newspaper ad announced that she would "play any person in Europe for 1,000 guineas."[47] Mme Masson knew that in placing such a value on herself, she would not be playing other women. What is surprising, perhaps, is that so many men wanted to play her. Her fame went ahead of her, of course, and the men who took up the challenge must have known that there was a distinct chance that they would be defeated—beaten by a woman. Even if they did manage to beat her, they would not be able to boast very loudly about it. After all, wasn't it given that men should defeat women? It was a defining moment in the perception, even assumption, of male physical superiority.

On her arrival, Mme Masson was quickly able to secure an early audience with the Duke of York, who agreed to play a match with her. He was to be her first opponent, and she would play "in her female attire, *a la Greque,* with short petticoats and drawers."[48] An audience with the Duke of York was a great social coup; Prince Frederick Augustus was second in line of succession to the British crown (after his brother the Prince of Wales). He was twenty-seven years old and at his physical peak and had fought a duel just a few months before. In 1795 he would become the head of the British Army. Regrettably, no evidence has been found that indicates his tennis match against Mme Masson was ever played.

One week later, however, Mme Masson did play Banastre Tarleton, and she beat him. He was thirty-six years old and MP for Liverpool; he was also a villain or a hero of the American War of Independence, depending on which side one views it from. He had friends in high places and was as well-known in Britain as anyone. In fact, he was infamous for having accepted a large wager that he could "win" actress and writer Mary Robinson; he then escalated the bet by adding that having done so, he would then jilt her. He then won both wagers.[49]

Both men were obvious alpha males, and one must wonder at their motives in wanting to play a tennis match against Mme Masson. At almost the same time as the Tarleton match—maybe even on the same day—she also played George Bisset, a young Irishman who had been an undergraduate at Christ College, Oxford, from 1783 to 1787 and was twenty-one years old.[50] Almost nothing is known about George Bisset, but he must have been an outstanding tennis player, and he had the advantage of youth. He beat Mme Masson.

In April 1790 Mme Masson also played Richard Barry, 7th Earl of Barrymore, known as Hellgate. One of the notorious Barrymore family, his brothers were known as Newgate and Cripplegate; a sister was known as Billingsgate.[51] He too was twenty-one, but his youth did not help him. The newspapers printed the bald facts: "The lady beat the noble Earl."[52]

We should not assume that these matches were played for one thousand guineas, Mme Masson's original challenge. They were probably played for much more manageable sums; otherwise the newspaper editors would have passed on the details. Mme Masson seems to have stayed in London for only a month or so, but in that time she played three tennis matches against men and won two of them and had an audience with the Duke of York, who agreed to play her. Her reputation and status were so elevated that men were unabashed by the prospect of being beaten by her; was she the last woman to ever be in that category?

These two visits to London by French women produced at least two landmarks: Mme Bunel defeated the reputed best male player in England twice and drew international attention to the fact. Mme Masson, whose skill and standing were such that she visited London with the intention of *only* playing men, succeeded in attracting high-profile personalities who must have expected to lose even before they started. Both women would have been acutely aware of the gender issues that surrounded them. Mme Bunel even arranged for women to watch her play while remaining unseen themselves. She knew that her performances posed searching questions about men's assumption of physical superiority—and not just in tennis.

14

THE TEAM PLAYERS

Traditional life in England held to the rhythms of the seasons and the church calendar, and that included the games that people played. In March 1633 Thomas Crosfield noted in his diary that women were playing stool-ball in Oxford, while men played football.[1] It was Shrovetide, the three days before Lent, and so marked the last chance for fun and games for several weeks. In May 1715 Nicholas Blundell recorded in his diary that the young women of Little Crosby in Lancashire had treated the men to a Tandsey [or Tansey or Tansy] because the young women had just lost to them at stool-ball.[2] It was Easter week, and a tansy cake or tansy pudding was a common, if slightly bitter, treat at Easter time.

Both men and women played stool-ball, and whether played at Shrovetide or in Easter week, it was all a matter of local traditions. Stool-ball was also a women's Easter sport in Swansea in South Wales, and in 1733 the *London Magazine* published a 252-line poem entitled "Stool-ball, or the *Easter* Diversion," which defended the women who played it—only necessary because not everyone approved of it:

> Where does the shame or crime appear,
> Of harmless romping once a year?
> No rule of virtue it offends;
> And health on exercise attends.
> Such motion brings delightful rest,
> Nor kindles passions in your breast;
> Quickens the fluids in their pace,
> And spoils no charm of woman's face . . .[3]

It was the fun that counted—a harmless romping once a year.

These games were played by the locals and may have had a variable, and flexible, number of players on each side. Some games escaped calendar constraints and became so popular they could be played at almost any time, although some needed the dry, thick grass of summer and others needed to be vigorous enough to keep the players warm in the winter. Football was an example of the latter, and there were so many versions of football that it was more a concept than a defined game. Versions of it were played by men and women, with any size of team and on almost any surface of almost any dimensions. When football games were linked to the calendar, they tended to be Shrovetide games, but matches could be played whenever there were players and time to kill. There could even be an element of spontaneity about them, as captured by Sir Philip Sidney around 1580:

> *Will:* A tyme there is for all,
> My mother often says
> when she, with skirts tuck'd very hy
> with girls at football playes . . . [4]

Early Organized Games

In the enthusiasm for sports after the return of the monarchy in 1660, other games were developed, adapted, or invented that weren't attached to any date on the calendar. Cricket is an example of this, though it did need the dry grass and long days of summer. Once free of their calendar associations, sports had many new possibilities. In 1726 newspapers reported that young women had been playing six-a-side football matches at Bath for the "Diversion of our polite Gentry." This was an entirely new idea—a game (in this case football) adapted and modified not for the players but for the spectators. Richard "Beau" Nash (master of ceremonies at Bath) must have been behind it. Note that it wasn't a *game;* it was a *match.* It was formal. Matches have winners and losers, often with money or prizes at stake, whereas the winning or losing of a game is forgotten almost as soon as it finishes. These six-a-side football matches were played on a bowling green and arranged in advance. The team rosters had to be deep enough to let players be selected while others were held in reserve; it required a whole new level of organisation that was unnecessary for spontaneous games. This is the first example of a football match played on grass, with teams of a fixed number, and played for the benefit and amusement of a crowd. This setup is very familiar now, but it was not in 1726.

Each team would have been keen to pick a fast runner, because one feature of the game—lost when rules the football rules were codified in 1863—was how the game started. Frances Willughby tells us that the earlier rules required the players of each team to line up on their respective goal lines facing each other, with the ball on the center spot.[5] On the signal, the runners set off, each running to her designated position on the pitch: right, left, or in defense. The fastest runners from each side would race to reach the ball first—a very exciting start for the spectators.

Team games could be adapted for such a variety of purposes that they became very popular all over Britain. They could help to express local pride (rival communities challenging one another) or to develop community spirit (intra-community play). In Tynron, a small village in Dumfries, southwest Scotland, a curling match was played in 1740 between the local married women and the unmarried girls: "A famous Curling Match was lately play'd on the Water of Skarr [Scour Water] in Nithsdale, between the married Wives and the young Girls of the Parish of Tinron [Tynron]; the Maids shew'd a good deal of Dexterity in handling the Stones, and will, no doubt, be very expert in Time; but they were defeated by the more experienced Wives, after a Trial of a great many Hours."[6]

Even such a tantalizing fragment as this can contain a lot of information. It is obvious that women had been curling in Tynron for years, perhaps generations, before this. Obvious too is the expectation that daughters would learn the skills from their mothers and that a significant amount of time could, and would, be set aside to play. It is also obvious that players were expected to hone their skills for years to come, and that such skills would become a matter of personal pride. This is a very early date for mention of a "married vs. single" match, a concept that later became a feature of other games in other communities. Its growth shows how sports were adapted as local entertainments that gave focus to special days when big matches were anticipated, prepared for, and afterwards remembered and savoured.

Team games posed the eighteenth-century women players many more difficulties than those faced by the runners. To arrange a team game, organizers had to convince multiple women to agree to a time and a venue, and each of those women had to persuade others to permit them to play. A team needs an opposition, who must also be organized. Decisions about officials and rules (such as how to distinguish one team from another) were further considerations.

In addition, participating in team sports requires specific skills that no one possesses naturally; they must be learned and practiced. All this takes time and requires others to be helpful, and maybe even encouraging. Organizers and participants have to think ahead and possess a degree of certainty when the plans are being made. For example, is the venue you want available? Will your other team members turn up on time and stay till the end? Will the opposition's do so as well?

It is important to note here that these games as they developed did not belong to either girls or boys, women or men—they were just games. The idea that a particular sport was a male pursuit or a female one emerged later. Team sports could be played by anyone; women or men might prefer one or another or be better suited to one or another, but the games belonged to all. Still, teams of women and men seldom played against each other. The idea that specific sports belonged to men came much later, after the creation of governing bodies that controlled the games, defined membership, and regulated who would be permitted to play and where.

In 1745 a cricket match satisfied all the necessary criteria, and "the greatest Cricket Match that was ever played in the South Part of England" was played by women on Gosden Common, near Guildford. To provide some historical context, on the day before that match (25 July), Charles Stuart (Bonnie Prince Charlie) landed on Eriksay in the Hebrides and so began the Jacobite Campaign of 1745, but no one on Gosden Common had any notion of that.

Cricket

The report of this 1745 match in the *St James's Evening Post* for 8–10 August 1745 is the most frequently quoted in the history of women's cricket and is perhaps the most important single source in the history of all of women's sport, for it makes several extraordinary claims. First, that it was the "greatest Cricket Match that was ever played in the South Part of England"—not the greatest women's match, but *any* match.

> The greatest Cricket Match that ever was played in the South of England, was on Friday the 26th of last Month, on Gosden Common near Guildford in Surrey, between eleven Maids of Bramley, and eleven Maids of Hambleton, dressed all in White, the Bramley Maids had blue Ribbons, and the Hambleton Maids red Ribbons on their Heads; the Bramley Girls got 119 Notches, and the Hambleton Girls 127; there was of both Sexes the greatest Number that ever was seen on such an Occasion, the Girls bowled, batted, ran and catched, as well as any Men could do in that Game.

All the great cricket matches had taken place in the south of England, so this writer's meaning is clear: this was the greatest cricket match played anywhere, ever. This would be a bold statement at any time, but some of the recent men's matches had been so praised and celebrated they had become almost legendary. The (men's) Kent vs. All-England match played on the Artillery Ground in London on 18 June 1744 had been described as "the greatest cricket-match ever known"[7] and was followed up within twelve days by the publication of "An Heroic Poem," which extolled the manly qualities of the game and the heroic qualities of the players.[8] James Love, its author, not only wrote and published "An Heroic Poem" but also performed it as an actor. We do not know how often, or where, but we do know that after he performed the piece in Dublin in 1770 he republished it. It was in three "books" with a total of 310 lines: book 1 praises cricket above all other games, while books 2 and 3 tell the story of the Kent vs. England match.

The unknown 1745 newspaper correspondent responds to the major elements of Love's poem in such detail that there can be little doubt that it was deliberate, and any reader knowing anything about cricket at that time would have read it that way. The anonymous newspaper author wrote that the match that James Love immortalized was not the greatest after all. Love's "wondrous throng" and "exalting thousands" weren't the biggest and best crowd, and the players, likened by Love to "Hercules" and "Mercury," were outdone, or at the very least equaled, by the maids of Bramley and Hambledon. This was a very bold report. Neville Cardus, the most celebrated and respected of twentieth-century cricket writers, would later write: "The main point of women's cricket is that none of its exponents wishes to compare it with men's"[9] But the anonymous writer of the 1745 report could not resist it, not because the comparison reinforced the idea of men's superiority but because it did not. It was a factual piece, with apparently no personal bias and no hint of condescension that, for example, the players were very good considering they were only maids. The match is reported and the result given. But who would make such a comparison with the men, and state so clearly that the game on Gosden Common was the best ever, that the crowd was the best ever, and that the players were as good as the celebrated men? At first, the writer might be assumed to be a man. But on reflection, is it not more likely to have been written by a woman? One who wrote to newspapers?

The positive terms used to describe the cricketing skills of these Surrey maids tell us that this was by no means the first time they had played, despite the popular belief that this was the first women's game ever. Many women's cricket matches must have preceded this. Indeed, sixteen-year-old Anne Lennard, Countess of Sussex, was said to be growing tired of cricket in East Sussex three generation earlier.[10]

The report of the match on Gosden Common in 1745 was reprinted in newspapers all over England and traveled to parts of the country where women's cricket was unknown. It was reprinted even where there is no record of cricket being played at all: Derby,[11] Newcastle-upon-Tyne,[12] and Stamford.[13] Local newspaper editors must have been intrigued by the story even though they knew that their readers knew little or nothing about cricket. Their motive may have been the piece's claims about the women's abilities relative to men's.

My speculation above—about the gender of the reporter of the Bramley vs. Hambledon match—and the observation about Anne Lennard raise a new idea in the history of women's sports in the early modern world: the possibility that women of a higher social class, even aristocratic ladies, supported or even helped women lower on the social scale to develop their skills to play and to compete. The first firm evidence of it is comes from 1747 with a newspaper comment about a "long talk'd of" match between "the Women of Charlton and Singleton" and "the Women of West Dean and Chalgrove [Chilgrove]," all in West Sussex: "Twenty two Women are coming to Town from Sussex, to play a Match at Cricket in the Artillery Ground, eleven on a Side; it is said they play very well, being encouraged to improve themselves in that Game, by a Lady of very high rank in their Neighbourhood, who likes the Diversion."[14]

The Lady was Sarah Lennox (née Cadogan), Duchess of Richmond, who had been Lady of the Bedchamber to Queen Charlotte and who lived at

FIGURE 25. Sarah (Cadogan) Lennox, Duchess of Richmond, unknown artist, oil on canvas, c. 1720.

Goodwood House with her husband Charles Lennox, 2nd Duke of Richmond, to whom she had been married when she was thirteen years old (fig. 25).[15] They did not live together until she was sixteen, and theirs became one of the great love stories of the age and remained so. In 1745, nine months after giving birth to their eleventh child, Sarah, by then forty-five years old, set out from Goodwood to be near her husband, who had left to go north to take charge of the cavalry to confront Charles Stuart on his march south. The duke and duchess were highly accomplished people and relied on each other; in 1730, for example, the duke wrote to Peter Labbé, his secretary: "As for this money I sent you, you will consult my wife, or send her a list of what people ought to be pay'd with it."[16] The couple were engaged in local, national, and international politics, matters of state, their family, building, and sports. The duchess knew the maids from these four Sussex villages from foxhunting and probably knew their families as well.

In 1729, "after divers and important Consultations," the Duke of Richmond and the Earl of Tankerville had created the Charlton Congress, in essence a foxhunting club. It had formal aims and objectives, criteria for membership, codes of behavior, and a formal understanding of how the finances would be handled.[17] Its rules on behavior even specified who could talk, and when, during a hunt and set out a clear and formal structure to everything they did. This is significant because in becoming a member of the Charlton Congress, other dukes, earls, and even overseas princes relinquished their social and aristocratic status and followed the rules. For example: "The Huntsman only to speak to the Hounds, and the less the better."[18] For the first time, a sport and its rules took precedence over aristocratic rank. The Charlton Hunt was based in Charlton, three miles north of Goodwood House, and it became the most famous hunt in Britain and even further afield.

> The fame of Charlton had now reached other countries. St. Victor came from France to return his friend's visit, and both that country and Germany sent admirers of the sport to Charlton, with probably half the aristocracy of England.... The hunt in their hands assumed an importance and regularity scarce before known: every morning a hundred horses were led out, each with his attendant groom in the Charlton livery of blue, with gold cord and tassels to their caps.[19]

This was wonderful theatre, but the Charlton hunts were not mere bouts of well-dressed enjoyment. They were the focus of the winter's entertainment, with forty-five days each year allocated to them. However, the hunts brought with them a logistical problem: Where were all these noble people, each with their own entourage, to stay? Charlton was a small village; it had no hotel, and they couldn't all stay at Goodwood House. Indeed, even the Duke and Duchess of Richmond did not stay at Goodwood House. In order to be at Charlton each morning, ready for the start at sunrise, eight a.m., club members built a small Palladian hunting lodge, which became known as Fox Hall. The other aristocratic visitors, their families, guests, grooms, and servants had to find accommodation in Charlton and the adjoining villages: Singleton, West Dean, East Dean, and Chilgrove. The farms and cottages were turned over to the influx of visitors for the duration of each hunt. Who managed to stay where was a matter of local knowledge and recommendation, but it was an important source of income for the villagers and drove a small local economy. The villagers' accommodation was essential for the Duke and Duchess of Richmond, for without it their hunt would not have flourished the way it did.

Consequently, the Duke and Duchess of Richmond and the villagers at Charlton and the surrounding villages knew each other well and became mutually dependent, and the social activities after each hunt also became entertainment and a source of employment for the villagers. Two packs of hounds were kept at Charlton all year, which provided year-round employment, plus fees earned for stabling horses.

Women played an important part in this hunting scene. Many of the club members' wives and daughters rode, but at their head was Sarah, Duchess of Richmond. On one famous day—Friday, 26 January 1738—a hunt from Charlton lasted ten hours and the last hour and a quarter was ridden in the dark. It was regarded as the greatest hunt ever and became known as "The Grand Chase." It was later commemorated with a detailed description of every person there, every horse, and in particular every dog. Every fall was described, every twist and turn, Of the twenty-two riders who started, only the Duke of Richmond and Billy Ives, and perhaps General Hawley, were still with the hounds at the finish, but all of those who started shared in the fame and were listed in the official account. All, bar one, were men—the exception was Sarah, Duchess of Richmond.[20] The description of the Grand Chase was carefully kept and treasured and later was framed in oak and placed on public display.[21]

The duke and duchess stayed at Fox Hall in Charlton so much that their letters were addressed to them there rather than to Goodwood House.[22] It was during her time there that the duchess came to know the maids of Charlton, Singleton, West Dean, and Chilgrove. In the summer, when the hunting had finished for the year, cricket was central to their entertainment and social life, but one cannot play cricket without a team. Thus, the duke would select teams from the local players and arrange matches against other gentlemen who would also select a team. In time, his interest gravitated to Slindon, a village just southeast of Goodwood House, where Richard, Adam, and John Newland, three outstanding cricketing brothers, played. The duke became Slindon's patron and employed several of the Slindon players at Goodwood or in his service in London. In the 1740s, under this patronage and guidance, the Slindon team became one of the best in England, and the match they played at the Artillery Ground in London against "eleven pick'd Gentlemen" in 1742 was also described as "the best Match that ever was play'd."[23] Even before it commenced, it was described as "the greatest Match at Cricket that has been play'd for many Years. . . . 'Tis expected there will be the greatest Number of People that ever was known on the like Occasion."[24] The boast of "the greatest match and the biggest crowd" had a history and had been used from at least

1742 and was linked to the Duke of Richmond's team. Whoever claimed these accolades for the women's match on Gosden Common was also taking aim at the Duke of Richmond's Slindon team.

The duchess had been conspicuously involved in cricket long before we learn of her involvement with the women cricketers: she had arranged matches for men's sides,[25] sponsored men's matches,[26] and even acted as patron for three men's matches between Sussex and Surrey—an involvement unknown for any other woman of the eighteenth century.[27] It is unsurprising, therefore, that she encouraged (and almost certainly patronized) the local villages' women cricketers. Charlton, Singleton, West Dean, and Chilgrove were neighbors, and it would have been much more convenient to play the match locally—the Artillery Ground was over sixty miles away. They must have played with and against each other many times to have earned the plaudit "they play very well." Precisely why the match was played in London is unknown, but the hand of Sarah, Duchess of Richmond, is almost certainly behind it, and the greatest likelihood is that it was arranged as a kind of recognition for the women. They should also play at this special venue, just as other West Sussex (men's) village teams did. Slindon had played there on four days of the previous week and were scheduled to play a five-a-side match there on the day after the women's match. That makes three consecutive matches involving West Sussex village teams—it was almost a West Sussex cricket festival. It is possible that a sizable contingent of men and women cricketers and their families, supporters, and managers from West Sussex traveled together and supported each other in this "festival," both logistically and with encouragement on and off the field, support the women would need. It would have been impossible for the women to travel to London and compete on the same day. Moreover, after the afternoon match, they could not have begun the journey home, so two nights' accommodation had to be arranged in advance.

To make life simpler for everyone, the Charlton-Singleton team was known as the "Women of the Dales," and the West Dean–Chilgrove team was known as the "Women of the Hills." The Women of the Dales wore blue ribbons to identify themselves, and the Women of the Hills wore orange.[28]

The match began at two p.m. on Monday, 13 July 1747, but when play was underway some spectators refused to be restricted to their side of the ropes and went into the playing area, creating an obvious nuisance that led to arguments and confrontation. In this heated atmosphere, some of the players "were very much frighted, and others hurt," and so play had to be abandoned for the day. The women deserve enormous credit for going back the next morning at nine a.m. to finish the match. In addition, to satisfy the paying spectators, they played a second match against each other in the afternoon, thus having to extend their stay by another day. They probably had little choice, though. It was said that "several large bets" had been staked on the outcome, at least one of which would have been staked by the Duke or Duchess of Richmond, or both.

The crowd disorder may have reflected the general dissatisfaction at the cost of admission, which was sixpence and required a crowd of 3,200 to cover costs. For other matches admission had cost two pence. It seems that a deal had been struck by the Duke and Duchess of Richmond for the expenses of the women's teams to be paid, which required George Smith, who ran the Artillery Ground, to raise £80 in admission charges.[29]

Sadly, no results of these women's matches have been found, and no similar matches seem to have been arranged for women's teams at the Artillery Ground. There is no other record in the eighteenth century of two women's teams playing a match so far from home or one that that consumed so much time. We can see the hand of Sarah Duchess of Richmond behind it, and can we see her behind the letter describing the women's cricket matches as the best ever?

Cricket is a complex game, and in the eighteenth century it was played in a bewildering number of variations. The classic version has always been eleven-a-side with two batters and two bowlers at a time, but the men sometimes played with smaller or larger teams and even with different numbers on each side. They also played single-wicket matches with a multitude of team sizes, single-innings matches, double-innings matches, and even three-innings matches. George Buckley listed twenty-six different versions of the game played by men in the eighteenth century.[30] Until 1825 women played the classic eleven-a-side game, as well as six-a-side, ten-a-side, and single-wicket matches. As noted above, there was mention of a match between eleven women and twenty-two men, but that was probably never played.[31]

Cricket was always a country game, but because of its subtleties it always appealed to gentlemen, lords, and even princes who played alongside country players, though seldom emulating them. Much the same can probably be said of gentlewomen, ladies, duchesses, and princesses, but the latter probably played on the grounds of their houses and not on public display, so we know very little of them. Sarah Lennox, the Duchess of Richmond's youngest daughter, played cricket,[32] as did the Princesses Charlotte[33] and Amelia,[34] George III's oldest and youngest daughters, respectively. They played in imitation of the country people. This willingness to allow the social distance to dissolve, at least for the length of the match, between themselves and those much lower on the social ladder was noticed by Jean-Bernard, Abbé le Blanc when he came to live in Britain for a few years in the 1740s. Although his observations were unrelated to cricket, he wrote: "The English ladies also . . . amuse themselves in the country with their women; and are often reduc'd to the necessity of dancing with them, for want of knowing how to spend their leisure time"[35] Moreover, "at Paris the . . . Ladies-women are frequently the apes of their mistresses in dress. At London 'tis just the reverse: masters dress like their valets, and duchesses copy after their chamber-maids."[36] On the cricket field the Duke of Richmond, the Duke of Dorset, the Earl of Tankerville, and Frederick, Prince of Wales, not only played cricket with their gardeners and valets but were captained by them.[37]

Over the following decades, aristocratic women continued to be involved in cricket. In August 1777 we hear of it somewhat obliquely in an advertisement for a *Lottery Magazine* that contained "a view [i.e., artistic rendering] of the CRICKET-MATCH played at Sevenoaks, by the Countess of Derby, and other Ladies of Quality."[38] This view seems to have been lost, but there is a watercolor by "T.H." in the MCC Museum at Lord's Cricket Ground entitled *Cricket Match Played by the Countess of Derby and Other Ladies at the Oaks, Surrey, 1779* (fig. 26). The conflation of these images includes dates that do not agree (1777 must be correct, based on the newspaper accounts) and other inconsistencies as well. First, the match was not played at Sevenoaks, Kent, but at the Oaks in Surrey, the home of the Earl and Countess of Derby. It seems to have been played shortly after a men's match—Chertsey vs. Coulsdon (two Surrey villages)— also at the Oaks, which was attended by earls, dukes, and lords in abundance, and also by "the Countesses of Carlisle, Essex, Eglinton, and Derby."[39] Perhaps all these countesses and ladies of distinction played in the Countess of Derby's match; we know that Elizabeth Anne Burrell played because she was the top scorer in both innings; she later married the Duke of Hamilton, who, the newspaper gossips tell us, fell in love with her while she was playing in that match.[40]

THE TEAM PLAYERS   189

FIGURE 26. *Cricket Match Played by the Countess of Derby and Other Ladies at the Oaks, Surrey*, T.H., watercolor, 1779. (Marylebone Cricket Club Museum, Lord's Cricket Ground, London)

T.H.'s image has assumed an importance in women's cricket history that it almost certainly does not deserve. Phillis Cunnington and Alan Mansfield took it at face value and used it to illustrate women's dress when playing cricket in the eighteenth century.[41] Although the image appears in many cricket books, has any game of cricket ever looked like this, with all the fielders standing in small, static groups chatting, all on the legside, and four at square leg or fine leg? Note that the bowler rolls the ball along the ground and no officials are present.[42] In 1777 balls were bowled underarm, on the run, and from a height so that they bounced; bowlers never rolled the ball along the ground.[43] In *The Cricketers of My Time* (1832), John Nyren wrote that in the 1770s "the bowling was all fast."[44] We also have to ask: Would it even have been possible to play cricket wearing those high-flying hats? We are all hungry for images and want to know what things looked like, but most of the illustrations of eighteenth-century sporting events were drawn by people who were not eyewitnesses and were thus created from their imaginations. Was T.H. at the countess's cricket match? It was said to have been "played in private"[45] in the grounds of the Oaks, and the countess expressed astonishment that Charles James Fox even knew that it had taken place: "In the name of wonder (answered the Countess) how came you to know any thing of my cricket-match?"[46]

Judging from his watercolor, it seems likely T.H. had never seen a women's cricket match of any kind and had produced his watercolor after seeing John

FIGURE 27. *Miss Wicket and Miss Trigger,* John Collett, mezzotint, 1778. Note the sensible headwear on the girl in the background (left) getting ready to catch a high ball. (Yale Center for British Art, Paul Mellon Fund)

Collett's mezzotint *Miss Wicket and Miss Trigger* (1778), which carries the legend: "Miss Trigger you see is an excellent shot, And forty five notches Miss Wicket has just got" (fig. 27).[47] Miss Wicket's hat seems to be the inspiration for T.H., though Collett is at pains to show that she didn't wear it when playing, for he shows another player catching a ball behind her. The player in the background appears to be a girl, but she shows textbook skill in catching a high ball—she is getting under it, her eyes on it, with elbows in and hands ready, just below eyelevel, to catch the ball. She seems to be wearing a beribboned but serviceable cap, and she is the only reliable image of a female cricketer in action that we have from the eighteenth century.

The chronology seems to be that the countess's match was played in 1777, Collett's *Miss Wicket* was printed in 1778, and T.H. produced his image in 1779 after seeing Collett's image. He accurately dated his own watercolor, which was produced two years after the match. T.H.'s assumption that the women all played in those hats may have come from another of Collett's images, *Miss Tipapin Going for All Nine*, in which Miss Tipapin does wear such a hat while playing skittles at her local tavern.[48] *Miss Tipapin* was published in 1779.

Collett makes the overall theme of *Miss Trigger and Wicket* explicit, for Miss Trigger has her left foot on a piece of paper that reads "Effeminacy." Words acquire different shades of meaning at different times in history, so it might be more accurately translated today as "femininity." The message is partly that Miss Trigger is trampling on, or has lost, her femininity (as Collet shows by her sturdy and unadorned clothing), but Miss Wicket has not, as we can see from *her* dress. Even though she is playing a *manly* game—Collett tell us through Miss Wicket's cross-legged pose that she *is* doing something manly—she does so elegantly. In their analysis of cricket art, Robin Simon and Allistair Smart comment on Collett's image: "There is a more concealed joke in Miss Wicket and Miss Trigger, for Miss Wicket is shown in a cross-legged pose—leaning on her bat— of a kind unthinkable for eighteenth-century ladies but common in portraits of men."[49]

In discussing the significance of this pose and its importance to men, Simon and Smart point out that David Martin painted *John Campbell of South Hall* (1771) holding a cricket bat, his posture very similar to Miss Wicket's, and argue that this posture can be found in many portraits of fashionable men in the eighteenth century and derived from Classical antiquity. As examples they cite the figure of Mercury in the Uffizi in Florence and the marble figure *Fawn with Pipes* in the Villa Borghese in Rome. Collett's paradox is that Miss Wicket, though engaged in a manly activity (cricket), is still feminine. But Miss Trigger tramples on her gender when she takes up another manly activity (shooting). However, I note here that "manly" and "manliness" are also words whose meanings have varied through time. Cricket was very frequently referred to as being a "manly" game, but that usage does not seem to have meant "masculine." In *The Crickters of My Time*, Nyren gives a contemporary interpretation of "manly" as it relates to a cricketer: "He must be cool-tempered and, in the best sense of the term, manly; for he must be able to endure fatigue and make light of pain, since, like all athletic sports, cricket is not unattended with danger, resulting from inattention or inexperience. . . . He must be active in all his faculties: he must be active in mind to prepare for every advantage, and active in eye and limb to avail himself of those advantages."[50] Other contemporary writers and commentators on women cricketers in the eighteenth century follow the lead of Collett and an anonymous newspaper writer in 1745 and see no contradiction in women playing the manly game of cricket, and playing it well.

Could women cricketers even be an example to men? The Duke of Dorset seems to have thought so. His open letter, published after his death but written soon after the Countess of Derby's match in 1777, makes so many bold statements about women, and women cricketers in particular, that it needs to be printed in full.[51]

A Letter written by the late Duke of Dorset, to a Circle of Ladies, his intimate Friends, describing a Cricket Match played at the Oaks, in Surry, by some of the first Female Characters in the Island; accompanied with a Drawing* of the Scene, by his Grace's own Pencil.

* *The drawing is unfortunately lost.*

LADIES,

WHILE you are eagerly pursuing the round of court-pleasures, and cutting out new figures for fashion, permit me to add to your entertainments a novelty of no less singularity than those which of late so amply diverted your little society. Divest yourselves, then, for a moment, of too much importance; cast aside your needles, and attend to my essay.

Though the gentlemen have long assumed to themselves the sole prerogative of being cricket-players, yet the ladies have lately given in a specimen, that they know how to handle the ball and the bat with the best of us, and can knock down a wicket even as well as Lord Tankerville himself.

The inclosed drawing, which I thought proper to make for your information, is a true representation of a cricket-match played lately in private between the Countess of Derby and some other ladies of quality and fashion, at the Oaks, in Surry, the rural and enchanting retreat of her ladyship.

I shall not particularize the dress of the ladies on this occasion, as the drawing will fully describe it; nor shall I pass any censures on their usurping a game which custom, that cruel tyrant, has hitherto confined to the opposite sex

What is human life but a game of cricket? and, if so, why should not the ladies play at it as well as we? Beauty is the bat, and men are the ball which are buffeted about just as the ladies skill directs them. An expert female will long hold the ball in play, and carefully keep it from the wicket; for when the wicket is once knocked down, the game of matrimony begins, and that of love ends.

Methinks I hear some little macaroni youth, some trifling apology for the figure of a man, exclaiming with the greatest vehemence, How can the ladies hurt their delicate hands, and even bring them to blisters, with holding a nasty filthy bat? How can their sweet, delicate fingers, bear the jarrings attending the catching of a dirty ball? Are they not afraid lest the ball should misplace an ivory tooth, or extinguish the fire of an eye which has long been considered as a blazing meteor in the horizon of beauty, and which has brought many a roving, obdurate, and flinty heart, to a true sense of its duty? Are not the soft charms of music, accompanied with the melody of female voice, and the delight of their conversation, more irresistible than all the masculine sports they can usurp? And is there not reason to believe, that if cricket should become the favourite game of the ladies, they will next learn fencing, and kill half of us in duels.

Mind not, my dear ladies, the impertinent interrogatories of silly Coxcombs, or the dreadful apprehensions of demi-men. Let your sex go on, and assert their right to every pursuit that does not debase the mind. Go on, and attach yourselves to the athletic, and, by that, convince your neighbours the French, that you despise their washes, their paint, and their pormatums; and that you are now determined to convince all Europe, how worthy you are of being considered the wives of plain, generous, and native Englishmen.

His mocking of "demi-men" and "Macaroni youths" makes for uncomfortable reading in the twenty-first century, but then he patronizes women as well as praising them and only just falls short of insulting the French. The letter contains some memorable phrases nevertheless: "What is human life but a game of cricket?" and "Let your sex go on, and assert your right to every pursuit that does not debase the mind. Go on, and attach yourselves to the athletic." Once again, in the Duke of Dorset's open letter to women, we find praise of the quality of women cricketers' play: "They know how to handle a bat and ball with the best of us" and "can knock down a wicket even as well as Lord Tankerville himself." (Lord Tankerville was a noted fielder.) Is it significant that the duke equated women cricketers with married women and not maids? And despite quibbles we might have about the letter's content and meaning, this early endorsement of women cricketers by a lord of the realm is remarkable.

The Countess of Derby's cricket match was wrongly described, initially, as taking place at Sevenoaks in Kent, but the error is perhaps understandable, for the Duke of Dorset lived in Knole House at Sevenoaks, and it was commonly rumored that aristocratic and other women played cricket there, among whom was the Countess of Derby (with whom he was said to be having an affair); la Baccelli,[52] the principal ballerina at the King's Theatre, Haymarket, London; and Nancy Parsons,[53] who had previously been mistress to the Prime Minister Augustus FitzRoy, the 3rd Duke of Grafton. There seems little doubt that women did play cricket there—the financial accounts concerning la Baccelli at Knole show an expenditure of eight shillings and sixpence on "Batts and Stumps."[54] There is no record, however, that women ever played *matches* there.

These examples of women, aristocratic and otherwise, who were drawn into the orbit of aristocratic men bring a new element into our understanding of women's cricket in the eighteenth century, but they should not deflect our attention from the single example, above, of Sarah, Duchess of Richmond, helping the village women in West Sussex to improve their play. As far as the record shows, other women cricketers did it without such help.

15

CRICKETERS OF ALL AGES AND SIZES

Women's intertown, intervillage, and even interparish cricket matches continued throughout the eighteenth century and even led to an intercounty match in the early nineteenth century, but the records thus far reveal that women only played cricket in the south of England—in Essex, Hampshire, Middlesex, Surrey, Sussex, and Wiltshire, with an occasional reference from Norfolk and Leicestershire. The game had not penetrated the whole of Britain, even when played by men; the *Bath and Bristol Chronicle* wrote that "the manly exercise of cricket" was unknown in Gloucestershire up to 1769.[1]

Nevertheless, in the eight counties listed above, the representative matches in which women played one another for their parish, village, town, or county were significant events. For the players they presented entirely different challenges from those they faced when playing for fun. Players on a representative team have been selected, and the players carry their community's reputation and prestige with them onto the field of play. These players have a particular status as well as responsibility far beyond their own enjoyment; they represent others who will wish them well and hope that they are successful—and often even expect it. What each individual does will be closely watched and remembered.

On Harting Hill in June 1768, eleven women from Harting, a parish in West Sussex, played eleven from Rogate, a neighboring parish. The home team won by fifteen notches, and the match "afforded great diversion to a large body of spectators."[2] The players "performed their several parts with great alacrity and courage."[3] This rural area was sparsely populated, on the South Downs, so a large body of spectators must have contained many who had traveled some distance to get to the match. Nevertheless, a return match

{195}

was called for and was played on Rogate Common, where the home team won by a very narrow margin—two notches. The rematch attracted "near 2000 spectators," a prodigious crowd for such a rural area.[4] Since women's cricket had been played in this area for over twenty years, it was not the novelty that drew the crowd; it was the rivalry and the quality of the competition. It was one of those compelling matches that was "exceedingly contested on both sides" and where the result is in doubt right to the end, yet it was played with "great cheerfulness and agility on both sides." The large crowd must have gone home well satisfied at seeing a memorable match. With the result now standing at one each, it was decided that the teams would play two more.

The third match was also played on Rogate Common and "near 3,000 spectators" turned up. This time Harting overwhelmed Rogate by 77 notches. In their surge to victory the Harting players urged each other on as jockeys urged on their horses, while the Rogate players had to content themselves with playing solidly with "hearts of oak." Yet they were determined to attack the opposition in the fourth match five days later. No record of the fourth match has been found, but the reports of the first three matches give us insights into the enthusiasm and competitive spirit of women's cricket in West Sussex in the 1760s.

These matches were officiated by men, one of whom was "a principal in the Hambledon Club, who was so delighted with the activity that he made them a very genteel offer if they would play on Broad-halfpenny Common, which they likewise agreed to."[5] Slindon was no longer the powerhouse of (men's) cricket; the Duke of Richmond had died in 1750, and the Duchess followed him twelve months later. By the 1760s the influential center of (men's) cricket had moved over the county border to Hampshire and the Hambledon Club, which was based on Broadhalfpenny Down. It was a mark of the status of the women cricketers from Harting and Rogate that one of the Hambledon principals officiated at their matches. It was also a clear endorsement of their standard of play that he invited them to play on the Hambledon Club's ground. What a commentary on the confidence and spirit of the women that they so quickly accepted it.

We may never know who this "Hambledon principal" was who was "so delighted" with the women's play, but he must have been very senior in the club's organization to make such an offer without having to check with someone else first. And he would have needed a reason to be officiating at Rogate in the first place. The most likely candidate, and perhaps the only candidate to satisfy both criteria, is John Small. He was born in Empshott, Hampshire, in 1735, but his family moved to Petersfield when he was six and he stayed there all his life.[6] Petersfield was Rogate's nearest town and only about three and a half to four miles away. On the cricket pitches around Petersfield, Rogate, and Harting John Small acquired his own cricketing skills, and acquire them he certainly did. He may have played for the Hambledon Club in 1755, and he has even been described as one of the Hambledon Club's "fathers."[7] He certainly became one of their stars.[8] He developed into a great player and thinker about the game, and he also made bats and balls in his workshop in Petersfield. (The matches on Rogate Common were almost certainly played with them.)[9] The women cricketers of Harting and Rogate would have known John Small's haberdashery shop on the north side of the square in Petersfield; they would also have known Ann, his wife. The following is addressed to their son Jack, also a good cricketer but not in his father's class:

> They say, Jack, you were born with a bat in your hand. I can believe the tale, for I am sure you inherited the craft from both father and mother. She, I think, took as much delight and interest in the game as he. Many's the time I have seen that worthy woman (every way deserving of so kind and excellent a husband) come galloping up the ground at a grand match, where he was to play (for, you know, she always accompanied him to those high solemnities); and no player even could show more interest in the progress of the game than she, and certainly no one, as was natural, felt so much pride in her husband's fine playing.[10]

The report of the first match between the women of Harting and Rogate stated that the match was played "for a considerable sum," but no other source mentions it or tells us if any bets or money was at stake in their other matches. No mention is made of anyone who might have staked such a sum or who might have acted as patron to either team, but cricket at that time was played for money, and betting was commonplace. Nevertheless, all the evidence points to money being a much smaller factor in women's cricket than in men's. Five hundred pounds was supposed to be at stake in the "whimsical match" talked about between twenty-two gentlemen and eleven women in 1772, but it was never a serious proposition, and the match was almost certainly never played.[11] "Great betts" were depending in 1775 on a six-a-side married vs. single match on Moulsey Hurst, but we have been left with no details on how much money "great" indicated.[12]

In 1793 the Bury women cricketers challenged "any village in their own country, for any sum,"[13] but the match between Marchwood and the New Forest in 1795 was played for five shillings a head, a practice employed by men's teams, who played for much larger sums—five guineas a head in Derby in 1785[14] and one guinea a head at Stowmarket, Suffolk, in 1780.[15] Playing for large stakes or big bets was very unusual for women cricketers, who more often seem to have played for fun, prestige, or local pride. Perhaps the best example of that is a match in Leicestershire in 1792, when a team of eleven girls from Rotherby played eleven girls from Hoby. These small parishes were neighbors on either side of the River Wreak, and Hoby had fewer than sixty houses in it; Rotherby had about ten! After "astonishing feats of skill and activity," the "fair maidens" of Rotherby won, due mainly to the skill of their bowlers: "The bowlers of the conquering party were immediately placed in a form of triumphal car, preceded by music and flying streamers, and thus conducted home by the youths of Rotherby, amidst the acclamations of a numerous group of pleased spectators."[16] Such an experience would never be forgotten by the players.

Money, however, played a major role in a match between a team of eleven women from Hampshire and eleven from Surrey; the match was made by two unnamed noblemen who staked five hundred guineas each on its outcome.[17] This was the first women's match that we know of in which the players represented their counties. It had originally been scheduled and advertised to be played on Clapham Common, Surrey, on Monday, 30 September 1811 (fig. 28). For some unknown reason (described as "some unforeseen misunderstanding"[18]), it was rescheduled and took place two days later on a field that belonged to a Mr. Strong at the back of Newington Green near Islington, North London. I wonder how many of the women on either side knew that it was to Newington Green that Mary Wollstonecraft moved her school for girls in 1788? It appears that it was the Hampshire team and its patron who issued the initial challenge, and perhaps each side eventually thought the match should be played on neutral territory. However, the change of venue must have posed some significant problems for everyone. In readiness for the match both teams seem to have been staying at the Duke of York Inn on Great Surrey Street. When the match was rescheduled, their stay was

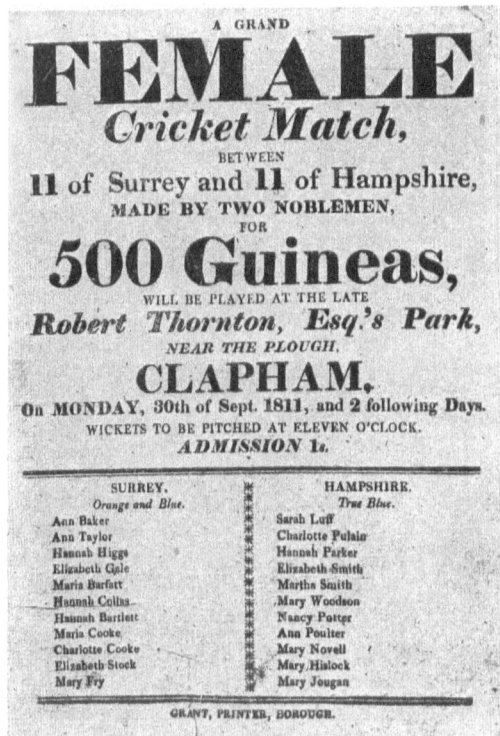

FIGURE 28. "A Grand Female Cricket Match," poster, 1811. Reproduced in Horace G. Hutchinson, ed., *Cricket* (1903), facing 152.

extended by two days, and on Wednesday morning they had to move about five miles, traveling in carriages across Blackfriars Bridge to the Angel Inn, Islington, which was to be their new base.

The Hampshire team was made up of hop-pickers who had labored in the sun throughout September, and one eyewitness described them as "being not only seasoned to the sun, but in fact nearly an Æthiopian color and complexion."[19] The Surrey team was of "fairer hue." Some supporters of both teams seem to have gathered at the Angel Inn, and at the allotted time the teams and their supporters walked together as a "great concourse" to Newington Green. The teams were distinguished by colored ribbons—one account says that Hampshire's were royal purple, but others described them as "true blue";[20] all agree that the Surrey colors were orange and blue.[21] The Hampshire team pinned their colors to their bonnets in the shape of the Prince of Wales's feathers, and perhaps the Surrey did the same with their orange and blue ribbons. Fewer than seven months had passed since the Regency had officially begun, and the Prince of Wales was central to everyone's thoughts.

FIGURE 29. *The Grand Female Cricket Match*, unknown artist, engraving, 1811.

The teams were "dressed in loose trowsers, with short fringed petticoats descending only to the knees, and fine light flannel waistcoats, with sashes round the waist. Their limbs and shapes were elegant, reminding us of the brave Lacademonian women, on the one side the Surry [Surrey], and the Amazons on the other the Hampshire."[22]

Once again, the women of ancient Sparta sprang into the minds of those watching these early women athletes. A primitive drawing appeared at the end of October purporting to show the match, but the loose trousers, short-fringed and knee-length petticoats, and light waistcoats do not appear (fig. 29). The writer and the artist were obviously not watching the same match. But there are some oddities about this image: the wickets seem to be leaning backwards, and they look like backs of chairs. No wickets ever looked like that.

Thomas Rowlandson also produced an image of the match that became part of his *Rural Sports* series—*Cricket Match Extraordinary at Ball's Pond* (fig. 30). It shares several compositional features with the anonymous primitive drawing: the two batters are running between the wickets (the only two images showing this in any eighteenth-century art); the ball is in the air in the top right-hand quarter of the image and a fielder is running to catch it; and a large tent dominates the background. Rowlandson, however, gives the scene his usual element of farce. One woman is shown tripped up by a stray dog, and another falls over with her skirt up above her waist. Is this an eye-witness account? It seems very unlikely, for there is a rather glaring error—Rowlandson shows the wickets as having two stumps, a style that went out of use in the 1770s, over forty years earlier. The loose trousers and light flannel waistcoats aren't in evidence either. Thomas Rowlandson does not seem to have been at this match. Both images show the women to be much alike, with one player hardly distinguishable from another, but the reality was rather different. In addition to one team looking nearly like "Æthiopians," the players ranged in age from fourteen to sixty. The teams were unchanged from when they were first announced:

Hampshire	Surrey
Sarah Luff	Ann Baker
Charlotte Pulain	Ann Taylor
Hannah Parker	Maria Barfatt or Barfitt
Elizabeth Smith	Hannah Higgs
Martha Smith	Elizabeth Gale
Mary Woodson	Hannah Collas or Cottar
Nancy Porter or Potter	Hannah Bartlett
Ann Poulters or Poulter or Porter	Maria Cooke
Mary Novell or Nevil	Charlotte Cooke
Mary Hislock or Histock	Elizabeth Stock
Mary Jougan	Mary Fry

The oldest was Anne Baker, who was sixty and said to be the best runner and bowler on the Surrey side. She and the older players traveled to the ground in long cloaks, while the young women wore shawls that they changed as soon as they got there: "The amateurs on the ground prognosticated a conflict not likely to be terminated in one or two days, and excited a degree of curiosity and interest never equaled on such an occasion." Wickets were pitched at eleven a.m., and play started as soon as the teams and their supporters got there. Already "the concourse of people ... was immense" and had "clogged all the surrounding roads to get there."[23]

The weather was kind when Hampshire batted first and put on 81 runs (one player got 41) before being run out, but by the time Surrey went into bat the weather had deteriorated, and they had scored only seven before play

FIGURE 30. *Rural Sports or a Cricket Match Extraordinary*, Thomas Rowlandson, colored engraving, 1811.

was stopped for the day. Commentators reported that "some very excellent play and much skill was displayed,"[24] and the crowd would have gone home satisfied with a good day's play. On the second day (Thursday), however, the weather was worse, and rain stopped play, but in what little play there was, Surrey lost no more wickets. At this stage the betting was 5 to 1 on Hampshire.

The last day attracted a huge crowd: "An unusual assemblage of vehicles of all descriptions surrounded the ground by eleven o'clock; tandems, dog-carts, hackney-coaches, &c. formed a complete ring; several handsome females, dressed in azure blue mantles, graced those vehicles." Play continued until three in the afternoon, when Hampshire dismissed the last Surrey player and so won the match by two wickets. As it the afternoon was still young and the match had been a close one, the teams decided to play a single-wicket match, in which Hampshire was again successful.

It had been a huge success, and one report commented on the players' "health, spirit, and apparent coolness mixed with a pensive and determined aspect, unprecedented in the female sex in modern times in England."[25] The praise could hardly have been higher, but this was to be the last women's intercounty match for more than a century.

In addition to the intertown, village, parish, or county matches, there was another kind of representative cricket match; contests *within* a community, when the married women played those who were single. In September 1765 such a match was played at Upham in Hampshire and was reported in five and a half lines in the *Salisbury Journal*.[26] Within a few days this small item was copied and read in newspapers seventy-five miles away, and within two weeks, over 550 miles away (see table 4). Newspaper readers all over England and Scotland learned that the women at Upham played not for money but for a large plumb cake, a barrel of ale, and a regale of tea. The usual practice in married vs. single matches was for the winners to be served by the losers after the match; in this case the married women won, and that evening the whole village joined them for a ball. This was an annual event for which there are reports in 1768 and 1769, but it was probably played long after this.

Although good crowds attended women's cricket matches in the south of England, far more people knew about women cricketers from reading the newspapers than ever went to see them play. In areas of Britain where cricket

TABLE 4. Newspapers copying item about married versus single women's cricket match

NEWSPAPER	DATE OF PUBLICATION	DISTANCE FROM UPHAM, HANTS
The Salisbury Journal	23 Sep. 1765	32 miles
Lloyd's Evening Post	23–25 Sept. 1765	75 miles
The London Evening Post	24–26 Sept. 1765	75 miles
Pope's Bath Chronicle	26 Sept. 1765	76 miles
The Public Advertiser	26 Sept. 1765	75 miles
The Gazetteer, and New Daily Advertiser	26 Sept. 1765	75 miles
Jackson's Oxford Journal	28 Sept. 1765	61 miles
Ipswich Journal	28 Sept. 1765	164 miles
The Caledonian Mercury	30 Sept. 1765	426 miles
The Leedes Intelligencer	1 Oct. 1765	230 miles
The Derby Mercury	4 Oct. 1765	163 miles
The Aberdeen Journal	7 Oct. 1765	557 miles

was unknown, perhaps the item's very novelty explains why so many newspaper editors were keen to copy it. The mind of the eighteenth-century newspaper editor is sometimes difficult to fathom; the item in a Sussex newspaper in 1756 that described a single-wicket match between Sarah Chase from Boxgrove and Mary Coote from Chichester, on Long Down in Sussex, for five guineas a side remained uncopied even though they were described as "the two most famous Women in the Kingdom."[27]

The married vs. single format for cricket had first been played by men in 1749 at Sturry, Kent, but it became particularly popular among women all over the south of England in the second half of the eighteenth century; similar matches were played on Moulsey Hurst, Surrey, in 1775;[28] on Elstone Downs, Wiltshire, in 1777;[29] on Felley Green, near Chobham, Surrey, in 1788 (when they played best-of-three single-innings matches);[30] and on Bury Common, Sussex, in 1793. In this last game Sarah Norcross, one of the unmarried team, scored 107 runs, the highest run total so far discovered for a woman in the eighteenth century.[31]

The format's popularity continued into the nineteenth century. One match at Marchwood, Hampshire, in 1819 reportedly attracting two thousand spectators "of all ranks,"[32] some of whom were of "first respectability and fashion" and who were "Highly gratified at witnessing" the players' "skill and activity."[33] The married women wore white with orange ribbons around their waists and in their caps; the single women's ribbons were blue. The crowd had probably been attracted by the novelty of the match, for no women's cricket had been played there for twenty-four years, and one report described their pleasure at seeing the "dexterity, neat appearance, and, above all, the modest demeanour of the fair cricketers."[34]

Its novelty, however, was a problem. In the nineteenth century, when women's cricket moved into places where it was previously unknown, there was no natural body to support it. "What will women do next?" wrote one newspaper.[35] Another refused to take it seriously at all: "The matrons found a *bat* more difficult to manage than a *husband*, and . . . it was observed that the ladies on both sides were much vexed when *caught out*."[36] Unlike the women from the Sussex villages in the eighteenth century for whom playing cricket carried no social stigma, the women who wanted to play cricket in the nineteenth century, in places where it was previously unknown, knew that they were defying an increasing body of public opinion lining up against them.

Nevertheless, women's married vs. single matches continued in the nineteenth century. We have found records of them on the Lavant Level, near Chichester, Sussex, though they seemed to be mixed teams since there are two "misses" in the dames' team, and two dames in the misses' team. The newspaper report of this match provides us with the first full scorecard on record, and we can see the quality of the Howard family: Dame G. Howard was top scorer and took six wickets in the match, while Dame H. Howard was bowled by Miss E. Howard in both innings. Dame H. Howard struck back and bowled Miss E. Howard in the second inning. There was also a Miss Howard, with no initial, on the misses' side. Three thousand spectators were said to have attended, and before the start a band of musicians led out the players, all of whom were dressed in white and wearing white caps. The married women wore blue sashes, shoulder-knots, and top-knots; the single women's sashes and shoulder- and top-knots were pink. The day concluded with "tea and coffee, with a dance on the green."[37] Thus, the married vs. single matches continued to be the focus of community fun and amusement and brought people together rather than set them against each other.

By the second decade of the nineteenth century, however, social pressures were increasingly against them, and fewer women played. It was not always easy to find enough players for an eleven-a-side match. This led to two most unusual matches in Hampshire in 1822, for they were a mix of the married vs. singles formula and an intervillage match. On a wet Wednesday in August, an eleven-a-side team of married women from Cheriton played a combined team of eleven single women from their own village combined with women from Beauworth, a nearby hamlet. They played the match on Ganders Down [Gander Down], east of Winchester, a spot more or less equidistant from the two communities. The players were of "all ages and sizes";[38] the single women wore pink ribbons, and the married women wore blue. A double-innings match had been arranged that attracted a thousand spectators despite the weather being poor and the grass wet. The combined team of unmarried women won comfortably. When the match was over, girls ran for prizes, but it must have been difficult for them on the wet grass, though these were chalk downs and would have drained quickly.

Most intervillage matches were played on a home-and-away basis, but this was difficult to do with a mixed team. Nevertheless, a return match of sorts was arranged for the following Wednesday, but the teams were differently mixed; it was better to reconfigure the teams than not play at all. Bad weather prevented the match going ahead, so it was rescheduled for the following Monday, 9 September, on Milberry Down [Mulbury], almost certainly just behind the inn there. It was the home ground for the players from Beauworth, but the combination of teams was different, and this time the single women of Cheriton played the married women of Beauworth and Kilmeston combined, so it wasn't really a return match at all. It was a good excuse, nevertheless, to play another game of cricket and for the best cricketers to display their skill. It was also a good excuse for the cricket-loving crowd to turn out again. They "literally crammed and covered" the roads leading to the ground. Of the players, Miss Ruth Stonen and Miss Budd were singled out for praise: "There [sic] scientific play and manly exertions . . . have seldom been exceeded by many of the bolder sex! one scored 41 runs, and the other 17, and such bowling was never seen."[39]

Another newspaper commentated that the match was won "in a style which would have reflected credit on an equal number of the other sex. The agility and good management of these ladies were highly conspicuous. . . . The bowling of one was truly scientific; and so confident are these novel cricketers of their ability at the game, that one of them has undertaken to play an experienced hand of the Alresford (men's) Club."[40] This last report is reminiscent of the match between the maids of Bramley and Hambleton more than seventy-five years earlier. As the decades passed and men developed their cricketing skills, some women were doing so, too, and this is the first reference to a woman (presumably either Miss Ruth Stonen or Miss Budd) undertaking to play a man. A single-wicket match must have been envisaged, and Alresford's "experienced hand" may have been James Francis, who had been playing for them for at least nine years, but no record has been found of their match.[41] Nevertheless, it suggests that the talk of the players being so good that the bolder sex had seldom been better was not mere talk. This is also the first time that women cricketers had been specifically praised for their "manly exertions" without any hint of irony or condescension.

Understandably, the unmarried women of Cheriton who had been on the winning side twice were anxious to keep on playing: "Elate with their success, the damsels of Cheriton have thrown down the gauntlet to any eleven in all Hampshire. We have received slight intimations that, no further off than Marchwood, in the New Forest, there are females of cricketing celebrity, who, if the festivities of harvest home, and the lateness of the season did not prevent them, would fearlessly take up the challenge."[42] Once again, there is no record that the challenge was taken up.

Despite the praise heaped on them, the young women cricketers from Cheriton and the surrounding villages were likely to be made fun of; one newspaper reporter ignored the crowd that "literally crammed and covered" the roads and preferred to write that the match was "stared at by all the *ganders* and *geese* on the common."[43] The article continued: "Surely, when the fair sex wield the *cricket bat,* they ought to wear the *breeches.*"

Cricket was never static, and there were often innovations, if only in the prizes on offer. In the married vs. single match in Norfolk in 1823, the players wore "jackets and trowsers, decorated with blue ribband."[44] Jackets and trousers sound similar to the dress worn by the two county teams at Newington Green twelve years earlier, but on this occasion each member of the winning team won a pair of gloves.

Cricket still fitted into the annual rural cycle in Hampshire, but that rural past was disappearing fast as a new, urbanized, industrial world was emerging. We see this in a new type of event in Kent in 1823—a new twist to the old tradition. Ten married women played ten single women, all employees at the Buckland Paper Mills near Dover. This parallels the smock race at Tenterden in 1828 when women ran for a smock along a street with the smock blowing from a lamppost rather than from the branches of an old tree; an attempt to adapt an old rural tradition to an urban and more industrial world.

Meanwhile, attitudes continued to harden against women in any sport, and in 1833 the following report was printed in a Nottingham newspaper: "A correspondent informs us, that last week, at Sileby feast, the women so far forgot themselves as to enter upon a game of cricket, and by their deportment, as well as their frequent applications to the tankard, they rendered themselves objects such as no husband, brother, parent, or lover could contemplate with any degree of satisfaction."[45] This was now a world in which women cricketers were reported not for themselves but in terms of the satisfaction, or lack of it, that their husband, brothers, parents, or lovers might experience from them playing. Although women continued to play, it was against a rising tide of male disapproval and ridicule.

In 1850 a match between two combined women's village teams in Hampshire was the subject of this damning report: "*Female Cricketers*—Eleven women of Lyndhurst and Minestead [Minstead] played other women of Poulner and Picket Post, on Thursday, when the latter were victorious. The scene was a disgusting one, and altogether discreditable to the district."[46] This was now Victorian England, and this sort of critical attitude was to become more and more common, as was a kind of cultural amnesia. In 1860, in answer to the question "When was there a regular cricket match of women in England?" the answer only mentioned the match between the women of Hampshire and Surrey at Newington Green in 1811, thus passing over all the matches of the previous sixty-six years. The writer continued:

> Cricket is not a lady's game; it has been termed a "manly exercise," and is so; but there are womanly exercises too; but bats, balls, and wickets, and scouting, long stop, short stop, point, middle wicket, bowling, batting, long field, &c., have nothing to do with lady like exercises. A woman should only bowl at her husband's heart, "catch him out" when he plays wildly, act as "short stop" to his follies, give no chance to "long stop," "strike" at his failings, never allow him to make a desperate "run;" so treat him that he makes a respectable "innings" in the notch of time; and ever respect his "bail," when it is in danger; but never bowl sharply at him; never take a bat in hand; never cause him to be "stumped," but through life plays a friendly and comfortable game, so that there shall be no annoyance to the loser, and all honour to the winner.[47]

In short, a woman's only role was to play the supporting role to her husband. This was precisely the male attitude that Virginia Woolf took aim at eighty years later in *Three Guineas*.[48] In her assessment, the male-dominated society of Victorian England began in the home with the control and domination of women by their fathers and husbands. The impulse stemmed from a "dark place," an infantile fixation that led them to infantilize the women in their households as the necessary first step to keeping their own dominant place in society. It was an attitude supported and encouraged by the law, the church, education, business, and even sport. The latter, in this male view, was connected to unchastity. This was a major change in tone from the reports of cricket in the eighteenth century.

Nevertheless, in Victorian England women continued to play against a background of male disapproval in which they were often ridiculed and made fun of. In 1867 women were due to play a cricket match at the Antelope Grounds at Southampton and were practicing daily to get ready for it.[49] The

Rev. Mark Cooper, "who had some control over the ground," prohibited its use, and the players had to look for an alternative venue.[50] Almost everything was against them, including the weather; it rained continuously, pelting down pitilessly. Undaunted, or perhaps even vitalized by the reverend's action, the women looked for another venue, which they found at Abbott's Park, Portswood, even though they could not get started start until four o'clock in the afternoon.[51] Some reports were merciless: "The women, together with the thoughtless and ill-judged persons who had induced them to make worse fools of themselves, found admittance to Abbott's Park, Portswood. . . . We hope never again to hear of such doings in Hampshire, or any other county."[52] Another report of the same match argued that cricket wasn't a woman's game anyway; it was "too rough and masculine, and too dangerous—As a mere exhibition of twenty-two women engaged in violent maneuvers, it can serve no other purpose than that of gratifying unhealthy curiosity."[53] After the match, to finally put women cricketers in their place, a correspondent who signed himself "Nemo" wrote to the *Portsmouth Times* to pass on a lesson from history. To do so he makes no mention of more than fifty other women's cricket matches. Nemo wrote of a cricket match "full 100 years since," in which "one gentleman" played a team of "eleven ladies," and "obtained an easy victory over his eleven fair competitors."[54]

No record can be found of this match or any other even remotely similar.

16

THE FIGHTERS

Prizefighting emerged as a popular spectacle in the second half of the seventeenth century in and around the venues where bear and bullbaiting took place, usually in the rough end of the town. In 1667 Samuel Pepys went to a "bear garden" south of the River Thames to see two men fight:

> The house was so full there was no getting in there, so forced to go through an alehouse into the pit, where the bears are baited; and upon a stool did see them fight, which they did very furiously, a butcher and a waterman. The former had the better all along, till by and by the latter dropped his sword out of his hand, and the butcher, whether not seeing his sword dropped I know not, but did give him a cut over the wrist, so as he was disabled to fight any longer. But, Lord! to see how in a minute the whole stage was full of watermen to revenge the foul play, and the butchers to defend their fellow, though most blamed him; and there they all fell to it to knocking down and cutting many on each side. It was pleasant to see, but that I stood in the pit, and feared that in the tumult I might get some hurt.[1]

In prizefighting, so-called because the participants competed for a prized (i.e., money), the combatants met on a stage inside designated venues and faced each other with a wide variety of weapons: swords, smallswords, backswords, broadswords, daggers, cudgels, and fists. Bouts were also staged in large tents to take prizefighting out of the towns to various country fairs.

In 1710, forty-three years after Pepys's expedition to the bear garden, Zacharias Conrad von Uffenbach, a German visitor, was taken to another somewhat disorderly bear garden west of the City of London at Hockley-in-the-Hole. There he saw a prizefight in which men fought with swords and daggers; when reporting it in one of his letters, he commented that "women sometimes fight in their shifts," although he had not seen it.² On this same trip he went to see another fight, and as he watched, a woman behind him told everyone that *she* was a fighter and that two years earlier she "had fought another female in this place without stays and in nothing but a shift." According to her, "They had both fought stoutly and drawn blood." Such women's fights were a common occurrence, he was told.³

Although the bear garden at Hockley-in-the-Hole was also known as His Majesty's Bear Garden, its grand title could not disguise the fact that it was a disreputable place. But by 1719 the fighter James Figg (see chapter 6 for more on the Figgs) was well established and had acquired sufficient stature and ambition that he was able to change the future of prizefighting. He had arrived in London from Thame, Oxfordshire, and had fought in all the London venues but became more or less based at the Boarded House in Marylebone-Fields. He also opened the Tiled Booth at the September Southwark Fair and began to separate prizefighting from the sports of bear and bull baiting. In this process he also became a successful promoter, and the Boarded House became a rival to His Majesty's Bear Garden.

In June 1722 the following challenge appeared in a London newspaper:

I, Elizabeth Wilkinson, of Clerkenwell, having had some words with Hannah Hyfield, and requiring satisfaction, do invite her to meet me upon the stage, and box me for *three guineas;* each woman holding *half a crown* in each hand, and the first woman that drops the money to lose the battle.

ANSWER: I, Hannah Hyfield, of Newgate market, hearing of the resoluteness of Elizabeth Wilkinson, will not fail, *God willing,* to give her more blows than words, desiring home blows and from her no favour; she may expect a good thumping.⁴

"The stage" was almost certainly at the Boarded House, and this was a novel fist fight, typical of James Fig's emphasis. Later historians have tried to explain the half-crowns clutched in the women's hands as a way of stopping them scratching each other, but that is highly unlikely; the coin-holding was probably a variation of boxing, which was still evolving as a sport and still twenty years away from having its first published rules.

Elizabeth Wilkinson is central to the story of women's prizefighting in the eighteenth century. Within a few weeks of her fight with Hannah Hyfield, she found herself a widow when her husband, Robert Wilkinson, who was a prizefighter at His Majesty's Bear Garden in Hockley-in-the-Hole, was hanged at Tyburn as a murderer.[5] This was the last time that Elizabeth Wilkinson challenged another fighter; for the many future fights in which she was involved, she was in the dominant position—others challenged her.

In 1723 the following notice appeared:

> At the Boarded House in Marylebone Fields, to-morrow being Thursday, the 8th day of August, will be performed an extraordinary Match at Boxing, between Joanna Heyfield, of Newgate Market, basket-woman, and the City Championess, for Ten Pounds Note. There has not been such a battle for these 20 years past, and as these two Heroines are as brave and as bold as the ancient Amazons, the spectators may expect abundance of Diversion and Satisfaction from these Female Combatants.
>
> They will mount at the usual hour, and the Company will be diverted with Cudgel-playing till they mount.[6]

It is almost certain that the "City Championess" was Elizabeth Wilkinson, and if the above notice is to be believed, women had engaged in high-profile fights in London as early as 1703.

The year 1724 marked a turning point for prizefighting when James Figg took over as the sole proprietor of the Boarded House in London, which he began advertising as Figg's New Amphitheater. There he continued the process of separating prizefighting from the uncouth aspects of the bear-baiting venues, determined to gentrify its appeal. His advertisement in 1724 for his New Amphitheater, concluded with the assurance: "N.B. That at the above Place all Care is taken for the Reception of Gentlemen, whereby they are secur'd from the Insults of the Mob, in throwing Stones, or such like; none being admitted but those of good Appearance, &c."[7] Amphitheaters are expensive to run and require a constant flow of paying customers; thus, Figg needed to offer new and exciting contests to lure spectators. In August 1725 he advertised a mixed bout in which the well-known prizefighter James Stokes and his wife would face another mixed pair: "Sutton, the Champion of Kent, and a courageous *female heroine*" were to fight "Stokes and his much admir'd consort of London" in a sword and quarterstaff event. His "much admir'd" wife was the former Elizabeth Wilkinson.

The event was driven by monetary rewards based on how much punishment each fighter could inflict on the opposition: "40 l. [£40] was to be given to the male or female who gave most cuts with the sword, and 20 l. [£20] for most blows at quarterstaff, besides the collection in the box."[8] It is not easy, however, to work out how the event was structured. It seems to have been a four-bout contest: James Stokes vs. Sutton, swords; Elizabeth Stokes vs. the female heroine, swords; James Stokes vs. Sutton, quarterstaffs; Elizabeth Stokes vs. the female heroine, quarterstaffs. Although the women competed in the same event as the men for the money, they did not fight face-to-face in the contests. "The box" refers to the money thrown onto the stage by satisfied customers, which was collected up and stored in a box.

We do not have an eyewitness account of this mixed encounter, but Mrs. Stokes was obviously good box office, for later that season she appeared at Figg's Amphitheater again:

> We hear that that the Gentlemen of Ireland have been long picking out an Hibernian heroine to match Mrs. Stokes, the bold and famous championess; there is now one arrived here, who, by her make and stature, seems mighty enough to eat her up: however, Mrs. Stokes, being true English blood (and remembering some late reflections that were cast on her husband by some of that country *volk*), is resolved to see her out *vi at armis* [by force and arms]. This being like to prove a notable and diverting engagement, it is not doubted but abundance of gentlemen will crowd to Mr. Figg's amphitheatre, on Wednesday, 24th instant, on purpose to see this uncommon performance.[9]

In this scenario, Mrs. Stokes was cast in the defender of her husband's honor, a new twist to an old story that was designed to attract curious spectators. However, this fight was almost certainly arranged by Figg, who used the supposed quarrel between the men as a pretext for an equally supposed grudge match. Meanwhile, James Stokes continued plying his trade at His Majesty's Bear Garden at Hockley-in-the-Hole.

In this third decade of the eighteenth century, prizefighting was a fast-moving story. Although Figg was the sole proprietor of his amphitheater, he still had a landlord, Mr. Bouch. In November 1726 Figg and Bouch faced each other in court over how freely Figg could do what he wanted with his amphitheater. Meanwhile, Elizabeth and James Stokes had decided that their days at Figg's and His Majesty's Bear Garden were over, and they opened their own amphitheater a couple of miles from Figg's, on Islington Road near Clerkenwell, not far from His Majesty's Bear Garden. They opened it the autumn of 1726, having decided that instead of Figg profiting from Elizabeth Stokes's appearances in his amphitheater, they could use her appearances to make money for themselves. Also, in opening a new amphitheater so close to His Majesty's Bear Garden where he had so often appeared, James Stokes might persuade his fans to follow him, particularly the gentlemen for whom the older establishment was just too rough. It was a business decision.

By the autumn of 1726 Figg was faced with losing his hold on his amphitheater in a dispute with his landlord, while James and Elizabeth Stokes had the prospect of losing their main competition almost as soon as they arrived on the scene. However, Figg won his case, and he and the Stokeses began a period in which London had two permanent prizefighting venues, which had to find ways of attracting and keeping their own spectators and supporters while trying to tempt the opposition's.

Despite the rivalry, Figg and the Stokeses worked with each other to develop an audience for prizefighting and to keep interest in it alive. They both advertised widely and competed with the London theaters for audiences. Figg's and the Stokeses' advertisements often appeared one above the other in the newspapers and alongside the theater notices. For the next ten years or so, the Stokeses' amphitheater usually operated from May to the end of September (sometimes a little earlier or a little later) and was open one day a week. The Stokeses' amphitheater staged events on Mondays. Figg's held his events on Wednesdays and had a longer season, but there were variations, such as special openings on St. George's Day.

James Figg's amphitheater held more people and was firmly established as the number one prizefighting venue in London. He began calling it his "Great Room" to emphasize the fact. He was also the sport's biggest star, whose fame reached far beyond the prizefighting world. In October 1725 a mock-heroic poem was written in praise of Figg and the fight he had with Sutton, and it was printed in the *London Journal* within a few days of the fight. It proclaimed him the "great Figg" and "Sole Monarch acknowledg'd," and described just how good a showman James Figg was in addition to his skill as a fighter.[10] Elizabeth and James Stokes had taken on a very significant challenge.

Central to the success of both amphitheaters was their advertising. This took the form of challenges printed in the newspapers, each one followed by a response that was partly an acceptance of the challenge and partly a counter challenge.

In October 1726 the *Weekly Journal* published the following:

> At Mr. STOKES's Amphitheatre, in Islington Road, near Sadler's Wells, on Monday next, being the 3d of October, will be perform'd a trial of skill by the following Championesses.
>
> Whereas I Mary Welch, from the Kingdom of Ireland, being taught, and knowing the noble science of defence, and thought to be the only female of this kind in Europe, understanding there is one in this Kingdom, who has exercised on the publick stage several times, which is Mrs. Stokes, who is stiled the famous Championess of England; I do hereby invite her to meet me, and exercise the usual weapons practis'd on the stage, at her own amphitheatre, doubting not, but to let her and the worthy spectators see, that my judgment and courage is beyond hers.
>
> I Elizabeth Stokes, of the famous City of London, being well known by the name of the Invincible City Championess for my abilities and judgment in the above-said science; having never engaged with any of my own sex but I always came off with victory and applause, shall make no apology for accepting the challenge of this Irish Heroine, not doubting but to maintain the reputation I have hitherto establish'd, and shew my country, that the contest of it's honour, is not ill entrusted in the present battle with their Championess, Elizabeth Stokes.
>
> Note, The doors will be open'd at two, and the Championesses mount at four.
>
> N.B. They fight in close jackets, short petticoats, coming just below the knee, Holland drawers, white stockings, and pumps.[11]

It was skillfully crafted. In essence it was to be an England vs. Ireland fight, with both fighters carrying the title "championess"; one also claimed to be championess of Europe, while the other styled herself as the undefeated "Invincible City Championess." Both acknowledge and accept the other's status, which was an essential part of the formula: no one wants to see a one-sided fight. Indeed Elizabeth Stokes calls her opponent an "Irish Heroine." Both also flatter the audience, and both project confidence in their own success. At the end, a third voice appears: the objective voice of the amphitheater's management describes the dress that the fighters would wear and specifies what time the doors would open.

No reporter attended Stokes's Amphitheater, so we have no report of the fight.

The words "at her own amphitheatre" in Mary Welch's challenge reveal the step Elizabeth Stokes had taken; the amphitheater on the Islington Road was *hers*. Not entirely, maybe, but hers nevertheless; it was a big step for a stage fighter, but she was not the only woman who could claim to have "her own" amphitheater. In Southwark, south of the river, Mrs. Lee ran her Great Booth in Blue Maid Alley, near the gates of Marshalsea Prison, at which some of the prize ring's biggest names fought. We do not know if she ever hosted any women fighters, however.[12]

Elizabeth Stokes fought Mary Welch again, nine months later, in another double event: Robert Barker and Mary Welch vs. James Stokes and Elizabeth Stokes:

> In Islington Road, on Monday, being the 17th of July, 1727, will be performed a trial of skill by the following combatants:
>
> We, Robert Barker and Mary Welsh, from Ireland, having often *contaminated* our swords in the *abdominous corporations* of such antagonists as have had the insolence to dispute our skill, do find ourselves once more necessitated to challenge, defy, and invite Mister Stokes, and his bold Amazonian *virago*, to meet us on stage; where we hope to give a satisfaction to the *honourable Lord* of our nation, who has laid a wager of twenty guineas onour heads. They that give the most cuts to have the whole money, and the benefit of the house. And if swords, daggers, quarter-staff, *fury, rage,* and resolution will prevail, our friends shall not meet with a disappointment.
>
> We, James and Elizabeth Stokes, of the city of London, having already gained an universal approbation by our ability of body, dexterous hands, and courageous hearts, need not *preambulate* on this occasion, but rather choose to exercise the sword to their sorrow, and corroborate the general opinion of the town, than to follow the custom of our *repartee* antagonists.

This will be the last time of Mrs. Stokes performing on the stage. There will be a door on purpose for the reception of the gentlemen, where coaches may drive up to it, and the company come in without being crowded.

Attendance will be given at three, and the combatants mount at six. They all fight in the same dresses as before.[13]

This is one of the few references to the bets that were laid—twenty guineas put up by an "honourable Lord" on James and Elizabeth Stokes on their own stage, plus the takings of the house. This was not, however, Mrs. Stokes's last performance on the stage.

A year later, she had taken on the title of "European Championess":

Whereas, I, Ann Field, of Stoke Newington; ass-driver, well known for my abilities in boxing in my own defence wherever it happens in my way, having been affronted by Mrs. Stokes, styled the European championess, do fairly invite her to a fair trial of her best skill in boxing for ten pounds, fair rise and fall; and question not but to give her such proofs of my judgement that shall oblige her to acknowledge *me* Championess of the Stage, to the entire satisfaction of all my friends.

I, Elizabeth Stokes, of the city of London, have not fought in this way since I fought the famous boxing woman of Billingsgate 29 minutes, and gained a complete victory (which is six years ago); but as the famous Stoke Newington ass woman dares me fight her for ten pounds, I do assure her I will not fail meeting her for the said sum, and doubt not that the blows which I shall present her with will be more difficult for her to digest than she ever gave her asses....

N.B.—Attendance will be given at one, and the encounter to be given at four precisely. There will be the diversion of cudgel-playing as usual.[14]

This format of public challenge and counter challenge had always been used in the prize ring, although it was mocked by those who thought it overbombastic and hackneyed.[15] Yet Figg and the Stokeses developed it into a kind of art form. So similar are the advertisements for Figg's and Stokes' amphitheaters that it is tempting to think that they were all written by the same person; but there cannot be anydoubt that the text of each individual challenge and counterchallenge advertisement *was* written by one person, was agreed upon by the two fighters before publication, and followed an accepted format.

Yet they cannot be relied on to give us a historical record of what happened. For example, are we to take from the text of this last challenge (dated 1728) that that Elizabeth Stokes's earlier fight with Mary Welch (advertised in 1726) never took place? Or the bout against the Hibernian Heroine in 1724? They do, nevertheless, provide some useful insights, such as the description of "boxing in my self defence," which was demonstrably not what she did and may have been inserted for the benefit of the magistrates who wanted to be reassured that these fights were harmless entertainment—demonstrations of the science of defense rather than angry confrontations or grudge matches likely to incite crowd or even lead to street violence.

The last two advertisements tell us that in addition to fighting with swords, knives, and quarterstaffs, Elizabeth Stokes fought with her fists. Boxing, or fist fighting, had always been a part of prizefighting, albeit a minor part, but boxing was beginning to emerge as a sport in its own right. It was not boxing as the Marquess of Queensberry's rules laid out in 1867, or even as it was known after 1743 when Jack Broughton's rules "for the better regulation" of fights in his New Amphitheater were more generally accepted. Still, there were well-known rules at the time. When fighters went down, they were allowed to get up fairly before the fighting started again, and no kicking or gouging was allowed. Reports, or even results, of the bouts in Figg's and the Stokeses' amphitheaters are very few and lack much of the detail we would like to see. We do, however, have a report of a women's prizefight with knives and daggers, held in His Majesty's Bear Garden in February 1728; it was written by César de Saussure, and is worth quoting in full:

> The day I went to see the gladiators fight I witnessed an extraordinary combat, two women being the champions. As soon as they appeared on the stage they made the spectators a profound reverence; they then saluted each other and engaged in a lively and amusing conversation. They boasted that they had a great amount of courage, strength, and intrepidity. One of them regretted she was not born a man, else she would have made her fortune by her powers; the other declared she beat her husband every morning to keep her hand in, etc. Both these women were very scantily clothed, and wore little bodices and very

short petticoats of white linen. One of these amazons was a stout Irishwoman, strong and lithe to look at, the other was a small Englishwoman, full of fire and very agile. The first was decked with blue ribbons on the head, waist, and right arm; the second wore red ribbons. Their weapons were a sort of two-handed sword, three or three and a half feet in length; the guard was covered, and the blade was about three inches wide and not sharp only about half a foot of it was, but then that part cut like a razor. The spectators made numerous bets, and some peers who were there some very large wagers. On either side of the two amazons a man stood by, holding a long staff, ready to separate them should blood flow. After a time the combat became very animated, and was conducted with force and vigour with the broad side of the weapons, for points there were none. The Irishwoman presently received a great cut across her forehead, and that put a stop to the first part of the combat. The Englishwoman's backers threw her shillings and half-crowns and applauded her. During this time the wounded woman's forehead was sewn up, this being done on the stage; a plaster was applied to it, and she drank a good big glass of spirits to revive her courage, and the fight began again, each combatant holding a dagger in her left hand to ward off the blows. The Irish-woman was wounded a second time, and her adversary again received coins and plaudits from her admirers. The wound was sewn up, and for the third time the battle recommenced, the women holding wicker shields as defensive weapons. This third combat was fought for some time without result, but the poor Irishwoman was destined to be the loser, for she received a long and deep wound all across her neck and throat. The surgeon sewed it up, but she was too badly hurt to fight any more, and it was time, for the combatants were dripping with perspiration, and the Irishwoman also with blood. A few coins were thrown to her to console her, but the victor made a good day's work out of the combat. Fortunately it is very rarely one hears of women *gladiators*.[16]

The world of the prizefighter was not for the faint-hearted.

In the absence of a strong archival evidence, we are left to wonder how rare women's prizefights were. In June 1730 the *Daily Journal* published the following:

Mr Stokes and his Wife being last Wednesday at Mr. Figg's, in order to receive some Money that was due from Mr. Gill, Mr. Mac Colley, and Mr. Sutton, which they refused to pay, and Mr. Stokes being challeng'd, fought at Staff, and Mrs. Stokes was likewise challeng'd, there having lately arrived in Town four Women on purpose to fight her, but she not intending to make a Practice of Fighting, dares the said four Women to come to her Seat of Valour on the above Day [Monday, 22 June 1730], before the Champions mount, and will fight them Bout and Bout till she and they are defeated.

The Doors will be opened at Three, and the Champions mount at Five.[17]

That four women had arrived in London with the express purpose of fighting Elizabeth Stokes suggests that women fighters were not all that rare. In 1730 there were more women fighters in London than ever before. Even before Monday 22 June arrived, Elizabeth Stokes had arranged to fight yet another woman:

Not Perform'd this Season

At Mr. STOKES's AMPHITHEATRE,

In Islington Road, this Day, the 16th Instant, will be a Trial of Skill in the Judgment of the Sword, between the two following Heroines, viz.

I Sarah Barret, from Whitehaven in the County of Cumberland, Mistress of the Science of Defence, who, in above 40 Battles, have distinguished the Power of my Sex, and shone like a Star of the first Magnitude in the Opinion of the Publick; having defeated the famous Mrs. Mary Barker, and improv'd a former Quarrel with Mrs. Elizabeth Stokes to such a Height, that only Blood can make us Friends, hereby invite her at the Time and Place above, to fight me with the usual Weapons of the Stage, or disown her Title to the Sword, in which (like a Woman!) I believe myself to have the Pre-eminence, and cannot be flatter'd Success should fail, when sweet Revenge to Mischief leads the Way, &c.

ANNE BARRET.

I Elizabeth Stokes, too much Mistress of my Sword to apprehend Danger in the above Challenge, assure my Northern Opponent, I shall use my utmost Endeavours to eclipse her Starry Character, and by Deeds, exceeding Words, shew Mankind, I am an Orb above my Sex; and that Britannia shall to Ages boast, London has robb'd Arabia of its Ensign, the Phœnix only lodging in my Jemmy's Breast, &c.

ELIZ. STOKES

Note, Mr Thomas Barret, Husband of the above-named Sarah, having challenged Mr. James Stokes in like manner, the Men are engaged in Bouts alternately, each on Behalf of his Wife; a Cause precarious! but, in this Age, meritorious.

The Passage for Gentlemen will be render'd commodious, and no Entertainment be wanting to yield desired Satisfaction.

The Doors will be open'd at Three, and the Heroes and Heroines mount at Six.[18]

From a challenge issued four weeks later, we can conclude that Elizabeth Stokes won the above fight, but there are surprises in the original challenge. The whole challenge and reply seem straightforward enough (once we have recovered from the surprise of reading that a woman who starts a challenge with, "I Sarah Barret," would sign herself "Anne") until the note that follows it, which changes the whole nature of it. Although billed as a fight between the two women, it was in fact to be a mixed battle rather like the one five years earlier at Figg's Amphitheater, where the men and women fought alternately but with cumulative scoring.

The language of this challenge and counter challenge is unusually overblown, even by the standards of the day, and it contains more than the usual array of literary references: *Success should fail, when sweet Revenge to Mischief leads the Way;* and *Britannia shall to Ages boast, London has robb'd Arabia of its Ensign, the Phœnix only lodging in my Jemmy's Breast*, were not the typical style of challenge to a fight, but the Stokeses had already made a decision to target theater audiences, and the advertisements for their amphitheater had become more like those for a playhouse, as in the "Tragi-comi-pastoral Farce, of one Act":

By COMMAND,

At Mr. STOKES's AMPHITHEATRE,

In Islington Road, on Tuesday *the 9th of* June,

THE Publick will be entertained in an extraordinary Manner, with a tragic-comi-pastoral Farce, of one Act, call'd

The RIVAL COMBATANTS:

OR,

THE BEST MAN MASTER.

> Under the Character of a Boxing Match, in which the two greatest Proficients of the Age are concern'd, VIZ. THOMAS ALLEN, (vulgarly call'd Pipes) and John Gretton, of St. Anne's, Westminster, Cabinet maker; Men of Proof, and hitherto as equally famous; insomuch that neither of them need Encomiums to set off their Abilities, and Words in their Praise would be wholly lost.[19]

Sarah and Thomas Barret fought on 16 June at the Stokes's Amphitheater and lost, but it must have been a successful crowd-pleaser, for they appeared eight days later in Figg's great room (24 June). This was most unusual, for a few weeks between matches were usually allowed for wounds and injuries to heal. Moreover, they appeared again in the Stokes's Amphitheater three weeks after the second match (13 July).

Meanwhile, on 22 June Elizabeth Stokes fought the four women who had come to London specifically to test her, "Bout and Bout till she or they [were] defeated," but no names are given. Two days later (24 June) Thomas and Sarah Barrat [sic] fought at Figg's great room against William Gill and Mary Garvin from Coventry, who had "imbib'd the Documents of as Celebrated a Master as any in Europe, from her Cradle." They acknowledged that they had lost against the Stokeses but claimed that they did "as well as possible" considering their state of fatigue from the "Toil of a tedious Journey" from "Terra Incognita," having just arrived in London "after several Years abroad."[20] Whatever the reason for the secrecy, and wherever they had been, Sarah and Thomas Barret seem to have been traveling prizefighters whose life required them to be on the road for years at a time (probably in Europe).

The second fight between the Stokeses and the Barrets took place on 13 July, and the published challenge made it clear from the outset that this was to be yet another mixed fight with the male and female combatants fighting alternately—"between Two complete Masters of the Science of Defence, and their accomplish'd Wives."[21] This highly intense period of public fighting continued one week later (20 July) when yet another double event took place, and this time the Stokes's opponents were Joseph Paddon, from Exeter, and an unnamed woman who gave her initials as M.G. (This was probably Mary Garvin, who had fought against Sarah Barret three weeks earlier.) This time it was to be "A Trial of Skill between two Masters of the Science of Defence, and two Women, whose Genius renders them the Admiration of both Sexes."[22] Once again the challenge and counter challenge are couched in flowery language and allusions to the theatre: "Let Paddon live a Julius of the Stage, or make Stokes, like him, lament the Fail of honest Brutus." Mary Garvin might have been one of the four women who had gone to London to challenge Elizabeth Stokes, and the note at the end of the challenge suggests that she was the last of the four to meet Mrs. Stokes. Another might have been Sarah Barret, who had also fought alongside Felix Maguire, plus another fighter whose name has been lost.[23] Mary Garvin, who partnered Joseph Paddon, had previously been linked with Edward Sutton, but let us hope she was not one of the women whom Sutton injured six weeks later. He was arrested and locked up in the Surrey county jail "for desperately wounding several women in the Mint with his sword, and in particular one woman, who received a dangerous wound in her thigh."[24] The incident provoked the observation: "Strange! That so great a Hero should at last stoop to draw his puissant sword upon feeble women!"[25] Strange indeed, but also strange perhaps that the writer to the *Grub Street Journal* should call women feeble when one thinks of the exploits of Elizabeth Stokes, Hannah Hyfield, Joanna Heyfield, Mary Welch, Ann Field, Sarah Barret, Mary Garvin, Mary Barker, and the many other women prizefighters who operated in and around London, for whom the word *feeble* could never be used.

We know that the prizefighters came to London from Ireland and all parts of Britain and that they traveled all around Britain and probably in Europe as well. In 1729 in Bristol, a local woman prizefighter, Moll Buck, fought a traveling London prizefighter before she moved south to Bedminster: "Monday next, at the Green Dragon, upon St. Michael's Hill, is to be a compleat Boxing Bout by Moll Buck, of this City, and Mary Baker [Mary Barker?], from London, for seven guineas. The latter has fought many prizes at Sword and Staff, and she designs to perform the same at Bedminster one day next week."[26] Chronicling the activities of so many women prizefighters in 1730 and the years leading up to it might lead one to the think that this was its heyday with years of future activity ahead of it, but prizefighting was nearing its end. James Figg died unexpectedly of "lethargy" in 1734, and the fortunes of the old prize ring began to ebb away. Figg had given up fencing a few years before he died, and he was always the trend-setter. Elizabeth Stokes was, in her own way, the James Figg of women's prizefighting, and she, too, had decided to give it up. In June 1730 she said that she was "not intending to make a Practice of Fighting," though, of course, she had said that before. After fighting the four women challengers who had come to London to meet her, and after fighting on her stage on the Islington Road on 20 July 1730, Elizabeth Stokes disappeared from the record after a career as a prizefighter that lasted at least eight years.

Elizabeth Stokes was a fighter that other fighters admired; her adversaries called her "bold," "celebrated," "famous," "victorious," and "an impregnable fortress," and they commented on her resoluteness. Joseph Paddon tells us that she was "train'd from her Cradle to the Toils of War." She wasn't reticent about her own ability either, and said of herself that she was "invincible," had "always come off with victory," and that she was an "Orb above her Sex."

We do not know Elizabeth Stokes's maiden name, but perhaps we can imagine her being born of parents who were fighters at His Majesty's Bear Garden at the end of the seventeenth or beginning of the eighteenth century. Perhaps she had grown up to love fighting—a girl in the early years of Queen Anne loving to fight and longing for her chance to mount the prizefighting stage.

Without James Figg's amphitheater and without Elizabeth Stokes's celebrity, prizefighting in London struggled to draw crowds. James Stokes resorted to going down-market again, and in the 1731 season he staged bull- and bear-baits, added ass- and badger-baits, and advertised himself as an animal trainer.[27] The public appetite for sword and knife fighting was on the decline, and once it began, its slide was irreversible. Curiously, however, prizefighting still had a future, and it was shaped by a young athlete who had appeared at Stokes's Amphitheater in October 1730, just two months after winning Doggett's Coat and Badge by six lengths (a boat race on the River Thames against five other apprentice watermen). Jack Broughton was brought up in the old-school and could fight with sword, staff, or fists, but he specialized in fist fighting. When he opened his own amphitheater in 1743, just behind Figg's old location, he promoted fist fighting over the other disciplines and became a highly respected teacher of it. The sport was still called prizefighting, but (confusingly perhaps) it was done without the swords and staffs. In August 1743 Broughton published seven rules to govern fist fighting on his stage, the sport's first written rules. Fist fighting, or pugilism, quickly became a national craze, out of which boxing emerged, although this early version included throws as well as blows.

Pugilism quickly became a national phenomenon, and Britons became very proud of it. Not only did it become a national sport, it also penetrated into everyday life as a sort of spontaneous form of dispute management. If a disagreement arose, those involved were expected to fight it out according to rules that everyone seemed to know and were enforced by passers-by if the adversaries' friends were not forthcoming.[28] It was a sport, however, that failed to attract women who persevered with it. They fought, of course, and there are many records of them, but they were mainly fights that followed an argument, drunken brawls, or street fights.

Women boxers were not entirely absent though. In July 1768 a most unusual even took place at Spaw [Spa] Fields in Islington: "Two Women against two Taylors, for a Guinea," which the women won, beating the tailors "in a severe Manner."[29] Two weeks earlier, however, two women had fought there for "a new Shift" valued at a half-guinea, and the winner was Bruising Peg "who beat her Antagonist in a terrible manner."[30] Nothing else is known of Bruising Peg, but the newspaper report was picked up again ninety-five years later, and she continued to be referenced for the next sixty years.[31] Perhaps we should look to Paul Creswick for an explanation. In 1890 he published a fictional account of Bruising Peg (a.k.a. Margaret Molloy) in the form of a journal. His account was an invention, although Margaret Molly was real enough.[32]

Fist fighting had always been a part of prizefighting, and women had always engaged in it. Some, like the "boxing woman of Billingsgate," excelled at it, but for most of the women prizefighters in the first third of the eighteenth century, including Elizabeth Stokes, swordplay was their forté. Perhaps it was the throws, the cross-buttocks, and flying mares that took the new style of pugilism away from them. Such throws were easy to execute whilst wearing breeches but not when wearing skirts, petticoats (even short ones), and drawers. Another factor contributed to women losing their position in the pugilistic firmament: after 1750, when Broughton's Amphitheater closed, London lost its last indoor arena for prizefighting, and these enclosed arenas had provided some security to women fighters, a security that was not to be found when fighting moved outside into the streets, fields, and fairgrounds.[33]

No fighter came along to fill the gap left by Elizabeth Stokes, but women fighters never disappeared completely, and some were probably brought up in a fighting environment, just as was Elizabeth Stokes. Pierce Egan tells of

Grace Maddox, who acted as second for her pugilist brother, George.[34] In 1776 Grace Maddox seconded her brother at Tothill Fields, and

> upon its [the fight's] conclusion, [she] tossed up her hat in defiance, and offered to fight any man present. GEORGE has often declared since, that he never had a better SECOND—and GRACE has been frequently heard to explain, whenever her brother had been defeated, "that she was *certain sure,* if she had the handling of him, that it would not have happened so unfortunate!" and which gave rise to the following *crambonian* effusion, which was handed out about the period:—
>
> "MADDOX, the pride of the *milling* race,—
> Secur'd his conquests with a GRACE—
> But once neglected, changed the case,
> GEORGE ne'er had lost, had he said,—GRACE!"

Although none were able to build a fighting career, some women did fight. In 1793 two women fought for forty-five minutes at Chelmsford, Essex, at the end of which one of them was "so dreadfully beat" only her husband encouraged her on.[35] Others developed considerable skill as was evident in a fight in June 1795 when

> [a] well-fought pugilistic contest took place in a field near the New-road, between two heroic females, for two guineas a side—Mary Ann Fielding, of Whitechapel, who was seconded by Jackson,[36] and a noted Jewess, of Wentworth-street, seconded by Mendoza,[37] two of their own sex being bottle-holders. Every thing having been properly arranged, the combatants set to, and for some time each displayed great intrepidity and astonishingly well-concerted manœuvres in the art of boxing. Fielding fought with great coolness and singularity of temper, and by well-directed hits knocked down her adversary upward of 70 times. After the battle had lasted one hour and 20 minutes, with much alternate dexterity, Fielding was declared conqueror.[38]

Have any two fighters ever had two such distinguished seconds?!

17

THE EQUESTRIANS

On 20 May 1758, Samuel Johnson's *Idler*, carried the following:

Ταμείον αρετῆςγενναία γυνη

The lady who had undertaken to ride on one horse a thousand miles in a thousand hours, has completed her journey in little more than two-thirds of the time stipulated, and was conducted through the last mile with triumphal honours. Acclamation shouted before her, and all the flowers of the spring were scattered in her way.

Every heart ought to rejoice when true merit is distinguished with publick notice. I am far from wishing either to the amazon or her horse any diminution of happiness or fame, and cannot but lament that they were not more amply and suitably rewarded....

Since the spirit of antiquity so much prevails amongst us, that even on this great occasion we have given flowers instead of money, let us at least complete our imitation of the ancients, and endeavour to transmit to posterity the memory of that virtue, which we consider as superior to pecuniary recompense. Let an equestrian statue of this heroine be erected, near the starting-post on the heath of Newmarket, to fill kindred souls with emulation, and tell the granddaughters of our grand-daughters what an English maiden has once performed.[1]

The lady was Miss Pond, and she completed the wager in twenty-eight days and almost certainly rode sidesaddle.[2] As had others before him, Dr. Johnson invoked the ghosts of antiquity and the Amazons.

Before the internal combustion engine, electricity, or steam power, people relied on leg power to travel from place to place, or on horses, asses, donkeys, and other beasts of burden that carried them on their backs or pulled them in a variety of carts and carriages. Almost everyone, of every class, was familiar with these essential beasts of transport, for they were also central to enjoyment and sport. Royalty rode them to hunts, and kings and queens around the world were portrayed on horseback to emphasize, or even increase, their status.

Sometimes women rode horseback from necessity: in 1566, when Mary Stuart was six months pregnant, she rode twenty miles overnight with a panicked Darnley flogging both his and her horses; two years later she rode "ninety-two miles across the country without stopping or alighting" to flee from the Battle of Langside.[3]

Between 1688 and 1712 Celia Fiennes traveled through much of England riding sidesaddle on horseback and compiling her journal, and in 1758 Samuel Johnson told his readers that women could also ride for a wager. How good their performances were is difficult to know, as we are rarely told anything about the horse or what assistance either rider or horse might have received. Nevertheless, riding was a common part of women's lives regardless of their place in society, although the quality of their mounts would differ greatly. Some women riders were also all-round athletes and wanted to demonstrate their abilities by competing against others. In 1701 Susan Butterfield issued the challenge described in full in chapter 5: "To leap a horse, or ride a horse, or run on foot, or holloa with any woman in England of my age."[4] The challenge was annual and given on Dame Butterfield's Feast (to mark her birthday in late April) and each year it varied somewhat. The *Percy Anecdotes* give details of one year "at the beginning of the last century" when she challenged "any woman in England seven years younger, but not a day older, because I won't undervalue myself, being now seventy-four years of age."[5] *How* women rode, however, was extremely important; if they had any pretensions to gentility—in short, if they wished to be considered a lady—they rode sidesaddle. Only country women or those who did not care about what people thought of them rode astride like men.

In 1724 an advertisement for a fifteen-pound "Ladies Plate" at Rippon, Yorkshire, gave them a choice: it was "to be run for by Women, to ride aside or astride, as they please," but how a women rode told its own story.[6] For example, in June 1746, after the Battle of Culloden, Charles Stuart's army fled, pursued by the Duke of Cumberland and Howard's Old Buffs.[7] At the

FIGURE 31. *Mrs. Thornton*, J. Wheble, stipple engraving, 1805. From *Sporting Magazine*, vol. 25, January 1805, p. 171.

beginning of June, when the duke's troops were assembled at Fort Augusta in the Scottish Highlands, he gave his soldiers a break. He offered prizes for them and their wives to race for on Galloway ponies that they had taken from the rebels. They raced the ponies without saddles, and the soldiers' wives were described as "riding with their Limbs on each side of the Horse like the Men."[8] Eight women started, and they resulted in "three of the finest Heats ever seen." For soldier's wives to ride *astride*, like men, was to be expected (wed to enlisted men, the wives traveled and camped with troops), but even then, it was unusual enough to be worth reporting.

Women, however, who might have attracted the comment "She's no lady" for other reasons, could ride sidesaddle to reverse the gossip, for riding like a lady and doing it well made its own point. A completely different point was made by those women who could ride sidesaddle as well as men could ride astride. Lady Lade was an example of this, but the outstanding example was Alicia Thornton, who was probably born in Norfolk in 1782 (fig. 31). Known as Mrs. Thornton by 1804, she lived with Col. Thomas Thornton as his wife at Thornville Royal, previously known as Allerton Park (now Allerton Castle) when it was owned by Frederick, Duke of York.[9] Colonel Thornton was forty-seven, Alicia was twenty-two.

In the summer of 1804 Mrs. Thornton went riding with her brother-in-law, William Flint; she rode a favorite mare called Vinagrillo, and he rode a brown hunter called Thornville.[10] She repeatedly beat him in friendly gallops, but he said he could beat her in a proper race,[11] knowing that Vinagrillo was reported to be about twenty years old.[12] Friendly banter turned into a serious challenge, and it was agreed that they would race each other for five hundred guineas on Saturday, 25 August 1804, the last day of the York August meeting at Knavesmire. The race was over a four-mile course, and as before, Alicia Thornton rode Vinagrillo and Flint rode Thornville. As Vinagrillo was a mare, the match was seen by the public as a battle of the sexes:[13] "Mrs Thornton to ride her weight against Mr Flint's," though there is no record of what those weights were. "Such a Match, in which a Lady rides against a Gentleman, is unprecedented in the annals of the Turf," wrote the *York Herald*.[14] And on the day of the race "thousands from every part of the country thronged the ground"; "never did we witness such an assemblage of people—100,000 at least"; "betting greatly in her favour"; "at least £200,000 depending in bets";[15] and "shouts of the 'PETTICOAT FOR EVER' resounded from one end of the course to the other."[16] The 6th Light Dragoons were employed to keep the course clear.

Alicia Thornton led for the first three miles, but then Vinagrillo went lame. Flint passed her and went on to win. At the start, Vinagrillo was 5 and 6 to 4 on, and during the race, 2 to 1 on Mr. Flint: "Thus ended the most interesting race ever run at Knavesmire" in one second under ten minutes.[17]

Three days earlier, during a trial gallop, her saddle-girths had given way and her saddle slid round causing her to fall heavily. So after her defeat in the race, she had more than one reason to call it a day. Alicia Thornton had lost, but *how* she lost was considered almost as good as victory. Newspapers wrote, "Never, surely did a lady ride in better style,"[18] and "the spirit she displayed, and the good humour with which she has borne her defeat have greatly diminished the joy of many of the winners" (i.e., those who had bet on Mr. Flint).[19] An etching of the race by Charles Williams tells a different story: the "speech bubbles" above the image express disappointment from people who lost their money; one is only interested in what she wore: "As you say those Trowsers are a great dissapointment [*sic*]" (i.e., denying them a view of her ankles).[20]

Nevertheless, prints were produced and circulated, and within a week theater goers at the Royal Amphitheater (Astley's) would witness *York Races; or, The Female Jockey* in which her skills and horsemanship were portrayed in a "Theatrical Representation of the late Extraordinary Match for which purpose the whole stage will be arranged as Knavesmire Race Course." "The applause with which it was received surpasses every thing of the kind ever heard before." New songs and recitatives were hastily written, and it was scheduled to be performed "this and every night for some time to come."[21] Indeed, Alicia Thornton's act of challenging a man to a physical contest was seen as a kind of victory, and newspapers and magazines ran pieces about the physical prowess of women. The *Evening Mail* and others retold the story of Miss Pond and her one thousand miles in one thousand hours,[22] and Pierce Egan told the story of Lady Dareall (Harriet Hawthorne) who had "strong animal spirits, great muscular strength, and rude health[;] she preferred partaking of the field sports of her father, to the lessons of the French governess and dancing-master . . . and who would take the most desperate leaps, and clear a five-barred gate with the keenest fox-hunter in the county. She was always in at the death; was reckoned the best shot within a hundred mile." Egan concluded: "From hence we may date the era of women venturing their pretty necks in a fox-chase, shooting flying [game], and becoming female charioteers, to rival the celebrity of the fair huntress, who was at the head of the *haut-ton*, with all these dashing ladies; and we had *Dareall riding-hats, Dareall boots* and *spurs,* and *Dareall saddles!*"[23]

Alicia Thornton, however, did not wish to be remembered for her temerity in challenging and competing against a man. She believed she was a better rider than any man and wanted to prove it. Six days after losing her wager, she wrote to the *York Herald* complaining that during their contest Mr. Flint had not offered her even the basic courtesies. He had not shaken her hand (as they would have done before a boxing match, she said), had shouted instructions to her at the start, and had taken up a position that preventing her from using her whip-hand (they must have been riding very close). She concludes her letter with a challenge to run the same match, with the same terms, and over the same course, the following year.

Her exploits were known all over England, and it was soon known that Mr. Flint had refused her return challenge, which could be construed as conceding the argument and thus the superiority to Thornton.[24] Although

Mr. Bromford took on the challenge on Mr. Flint's behalf, he later withdrew, leaving Alicia Thornton to "walk over" the course, and so win the wager which was for £3,000 and "4 hogsheads of Cote Rotie."[25] It was a victory of sorts, but it still did not demonstrate her superiority as a rider, and so Alicia Thornton challenged Francis Buckle, who was not only a professional (male) jockey but had won eleven "classics": the Derby three times (1792, 1794, and 1802); the Oaks six times (1797, 1798, 1799, 1802, 1803, 1805); and the St. Leger twice (1800 and 1804). Alicia Thornton, therefore, had challenged the best jockey in England. Nor was he an aging jockey past his prime; in the years after his race against Mrs. Thornton he went on to win sixteen more classics. Francis Buckle's total of twenty-seven wins in classic races would not be exceeded for the next 150 years; he was one of the greatest jockeys in history and was at the peak of his powers.[26]

They raced on Saturday 24 August 1805, on the last day of the York August meeting. The crowd was smaller than the previous year but was still reported to be thirty thousand.[27] The race was to be over two miles. Alicia Thornton (9 stone 6 lbs [132 lbs or 59.9 kg]) rode Louisa and Francis Buckle (13 stone 6 lbs [188 lbs or 85.3 kg]) rode Allegro, for a cup valued at seven hundred guineas (approximately £63,450 in 2022)[28]: "At half-past-three they started: Mrs. Thornton took the lead, which she kept for some time; Mr. Buckle then put in trial his jockeyship, and passed the Lady, which he kept for only a few lengths, when Mrs. Thornton, by the most excellent, we may truly say—*horsemanship*—pushed forwards, and came-in in a style far superior to anything of the kind we ever witnessed, gaining her Race by half a-neck."[29]

Alicia Thornton was granted celebrity status: portraits and images of her in action appeared in the print shops in London and York (fig. 32), and magazines ran stories about her exploits and her life. She slipped into the stuff of legend. It has been pointed out, however, that Alicia Thornton had a four-stone advantage [56 lbs., 25.4 kg] and won by only a neck; without such a weight advantage, she might not have crossed the finish line first.[30] But to offset her weight advantage Alicia Thornton rode sidesaddle in both races, making her victory truly extraordinary. Her actions in 1805 reveal her motivation. Had her aim been notoriety or even fame, she need not have continued after her defeat in 1804 when she received extraordinary publicity and recognition. Had she only wanted money, she would have stopped after winning her wager against Mr. Bromford in 1805: at this point she had lost

FIGURE 32. *Alicia Thornton Defeating Francis Buckle by Half a Neck, 1805,* unknown artist, engraving. From Pierce Egan, *Book of Sports, and Mirror of Life* (1832)

five hundred guineas but won three thousand pounds. But she continued the high-risk chain of challenges, counterchallenges, and races after these events because she wanted more: she wanted to publicly demonstrate that she was a better jockey than any man.

Alicia Thornton demonstrated great skill and fitness, but she also showed great determination, persistence, self-confidence, and courage. In racing Francis Buckle, she took a great risk. In wanting to publicly defeat the best male jockey in Britain, she committed herself to doing something that had never been done before.

18

WOMEN ATHLETES

Summary

The Athletes

No woman was referred to as being "athletic" until 1826, but the adjective was not commonly ascribed to men, either. Nevertheless, from our perspective in the twenty-first century, it seems a fitting way to describe women who ran long distances repeatedly, fought for a living on the public stage, or played cricket in front of thousands—women who challenged others and were said to be as good, if not better, than the men. They were of almost any age—girls, maidens, married women, older women, and even pregnant women. Many were local, but some traveled long distances to compete, and we occasionally read of Roma and Black runners. In the early decades covered in this study, many women athletes would have been country girls and women, but as the towns grew at the end of the eighteenth century and the beginning of the nineteenth, a new population of urban runners and game-players developed. These competitors often prepared well: chapter 13 describes one tennis player who spent hours on the court from five a.m. in preparation for a big match. Aristocratic women and even royal princesses played cricket, and chapter 14 tells of one duchess who was a patron of cricket and actively encouraged the local women in West Sussex to play and almost certainly arranged a match for them in London.

Few of the races (and fewer still of the fights, cricket matches, and tennis matches) were spontaneous affairs. Most were organized well in advance and offered prizes and money rewards, involved well-advertised entry procedures, and often attracted significant crowds.

Women's sports in early modern Britain did not just mirror men's, and the women who took part were not just female versions of the male athletes. The women who walked, ran, played on teams, and rode had to face and overcome attitudes and challenges that were unknown to men. Women were on display and were watched and judged in ways that men were not. While men could take off a jacket or even a shirt and be thought merely practical—not so the women. Every item of clothing that a woman took off was scrutinized, and her motives for doing so were questioned: Was she immodest? Was she immoral? In addition, women in most cases would have had to ask permission from a father or a husband to compete, a restriction that would not have been imposed on those same fathers or husbands. Women who took part in sports in the early modern world performed an act of self-assertion, sometimes even defiance, that was of a different order from that experienced by men. Central to the women's sporting experience was what they wore.

From the standpoint of the women and girls who raced for smocks or ran in wagers or played cricket or football, their performances, which were always in public, would have been significant events in their lives. We hear almost nothing of them from their own pens or through their own eyes, for these women left behind few such records. Only by examining the fragments from other people's records do we know they lived at all. We can imagine, however, a young woman deciding to race, either with or without her family's blessing—or maybe even against their wishes—and envision her resolution, bordering on bravery, to face the public gaze as she decides what strategy to use to defeat the others. Such moments were moments to savor in their lives; rare moments in lives that were otherwise under someone else's control. Similarly, cricketers would face that moment when they stood their ground alone, bat in hand, waiting for the bowler to attack, with every eye on them: teammates, opponents, and spectators alike. In those moments their lives had an immediacy, a significance, even an importance, missing at other times. The risks were great, failure and even ridicule perhaps, but the satisfactions could be enormous. The bowlers of the Rothby team in 1792 who were paraded by the youths of the village in "a sort of triumphal car, preceded by music and flying streamers . . . amidst the acclamation of a numerous group of pleased spectators," would probably remember those moments all their lives. And some women achieved very considerable reputations; Sarah Chase and Mary Coote were described in 1756 as "the two most famous Women in the Kingdom," with all the satisfaction that such a reputation would bring, and yet without a printed description of one of their cricket matches, they would be entirely forgotten. Their sporting efforts and successes, and those of the many other women runners and team players, are their only monument.

Dress and Undress in Women's Sport

During the centuries covered in this study, women's clothing was commonly a matter of layering. During the summer fewer layers would be worn, and in sport fewer still. So before they started to race or play a team game, men and women would shed some clothes. We hear of women running in their petticoats in Ireland in 1714[1] and also on Hackney Marshes in 1728.[2] But when the women "stripped to their Shifts and Under Petticoats" to race on Barnet Common in 1752, they were accused of "exposing themselves very indecently";[3] when the maids "stripped" for a match of running in Kent in 1769, they were accused of being "disorderly and lewd" for "presuming to expose themselves." Offended observers asked the justices of the peace to apprehend them and take them into custody.[4] Men were never accused of exposing themselves when they stripping to race, and what they wore was rarely mentioned.

What women wore to race and play, however, was a regular topic, and foreigners wrote about it even when they hadn't seen it for themselves: "The womenfolk run for a prize in petticoats and low-necked shifts" (1710);[5] "Women and girls, scantily clothed, run races, the smock being the prize" (1728).[6] Neither of the men who wrote these reports had seen what they described, but they were intrigued by what they had heard. Some men (who also had not seen the women race) could be extremely hostile, not so much to the fact that they raced but to what they wore or did not wear. In 1681 a Presbyterian minister was so shocked at hearing about women racing in Lancashire that he wrote: "Oh unparaleld [sic] insolence." He claimed that the runners were "stark naked only their privatys covered with a rag." But how can we interpret that description when we know that he wasn't even sure whether there were three or four runners?

Local parsons could always be relied on to look critically at women runners, even if they were not serious runners but were simply joining in to have a bit of fun. In 1800 at Stowey, Somerset, a parson wrote: "A little before dusk there was a large Cavalcade marching up Castle Hill for another[7] race downwards. We stood on one side but this was so terrible a race. Petticoats tucked up to the knees and stays open, or taken off, that I began to think it became almost indecent. I don't think I shall stand by to countenance such exhibitions in future for I hate to see the female character let down."[8] Once again, we see a man determined to protect women from themselves, but his concern seems almost entirely about what they wore, how they wore it, and what they took off.

This monograph covers the period of ten reigns plus the Interregnum and the Cromwellian commonwealth, all of which encompasses two centuries of political, religious, social, agricultural, industrial, and economic change. The nation moved from a predominantly agricultural society to an industrial one, accompanied by the growth of large new towns and new patterns of life. It is inevitable that across such a time span, society's attitudes would change in a multitude of ways, not least in England and Wales, where in the eighteenth century John Wesley and others traveled extensively and preached an Evangelical revival that was to have a deep and lasting influence.

The hostility to women racing, fired by religious fervor and moralizing, came to a bizarre head in 1809 when a group of men launched a prosecution of the organizers of rural sports in Plaistow, a hamlet in Essex, for conspiracy and riot. At the center of the prosecution was the women's smock race. The prosecution put it to the jury that the circumstances of worshiping their God in the way their forefathers had taught them should not subject the accusers to violence and insult. Part of that violence and insult, the prosecution claimed, stemmed from the way the women had "exhibited themselves on the race course" and had run naked, which was "disgraceful and abominable." To deepen their degradation, the prosecutors claimed, the women runners had been lashed with whips "to urge them on." No witness could be found, however, to substantiate either the nakedness or the whipping.

The counsel for the prosecution made his position clear: "I rather think that a smock race would be the last of amusements he would recommend to the females of his household, if he at all regarded their morals; because, in my opinion, and I am sure it is the opinion of every moral man, that nothing tends more to break down the moral tendency of the mind of that sex, than such disgraceful exhibitions."[9] In defense of the runners, one witness said that the women had run "in their natural and ordinary dress."

The counsel for the defense then admonished those who brought the prosecution:

> The women were not naked but attired as they are used to be, when engaged in the labours of the field. I hope the saints of *Plaistow* are not so hot-blooded that the appearance of women so habited can excite their passions, or so shamefaced that it can shock their modesty. If they are, they must lock themselves up during the harvest months, or their virtue might be exposed to such continued attacks as all their sanctity will not enable them to withstand.
> ... The Jury Immediately found all the defendants—*Not Guilty*.[10]

But women *did* sometimes run naked and had done since at least 1725. In August 1808 three young women "not incommoded with clothes or modesty" ran for a "Holland Shift" on Tothill Fields, Westminster.[11] This report seems to be a description of the women running without any clothes, and doing so brazenly, but there is a degree of ambiguity about it; does "not incommoded with clothes" mean without *any* clothes? It is identical to a report from 1735, seventy-four years earlier, in which the six women who ran for a Holland smock in Moorfields were also said to be "not incommoded with Cloaths or Modesty."[12]

The first known reference to women running naked appeared in late October 1725 when the two young damsels who intended to run their four-mile wager *in puris naturalibus* were overruled.[13] Were these damsels indecent, disorderly, lewd, disgraceful, and abominable? Maybe, but maybe not. It is curious that on the occasions when women *did* run naked the comments made about them are far less critical and judgmental than those occasions when they stripped to their undergarments. In 1725 it was merely reported that the women were "over-ruled" with no hint of criticism. In 1735 at Moorfields the comment "not incommoded with Cloaths or Modesty" is hardly a criticism at all, and around the same date, when the women ran naked on Stepney Fields, in the East End of London, it was merely reported that "for Decencey's Sake" they would have to be dressed in the future. Even the serving maid who in 1740 ran "quite naked from her Master's House to Essex-Bridge, and back again, for a Callimanco Gown" was simply described as "impudent." Perhaps the reporters recognized that these were serious athletic undertakings and that the women had stripped naked, as the men did, to engage in the most testing wagers. The men had been doing it for generations.

Although a few women stripped naked to race, the majority simply took off a layer or two of their clothes. However, from early in the eighteenth century a few women did solve the problem of what to wear by turning to alternative, more functional clothing for sport. In the seventeenth and eighteenth centuries women who took part in sports introduced drawers, waistcoats, jackets, and trousers to allow them freedom to move without restriction as well as to provide support and protection that their everyday dress did not provide. Sometimes, for appearance's sake, over their drawers or trousers they might wear petticoats to the knee (prizefighting) or just below it (cricket), or skirts over their trousers (horseracing).

A ballad of 1682 tells of four virgins who took part in a two-mile race in Yorkshire and wore "half-shirts & Drawers"; either by chance or by design each runner wore different colored drawers. Women's history commonly argues that women needed the rational dress movement and Emelia Bloomer's costume of the mid-nineteenth century to pave the way for women to wear suitable clothing for sport,[14] but women had discovered the usefulness of drawers more than two hundred years before that, and they became a favorite among sportswomen over the next 150 years: see, for example, the runners on Barnet Common, London (1725), Epsom Downs (1731), Stepney Fields (1735), and Walworth Common (1744).[15] The prizefighters Elizabeth Stokes and Mary Welsh also wore "Holland drawers" at Stokes's Amphitheater in 1726 and 1727 and wore "short petticoats, coming just below the knee" over them.[16] Drawers served much the same purpose in the seventeenth and eighteenth centuries as did bloomers in the nineteenth and early twentieth centuries.

Another innovation was the tight-fitted waistcoat (i.e., vest in the United States). In 1725 and 1735 the women at Barnet and Stepney Fields were required to wear white waistcoats when next they ran. Waistcoats allowed the arms to be free, but their tight fit provided a measure of bust support for the runners. Elizabeth Stokes's and Mary Welsh's "close jackets" were perhaps a version of this. The equestrian Mrs. Thornton also wore a jacket in her horserace against Francis Buckle in 1805. In 1728 César de Saussure described two prizefighters as "very scantily clothed"; they "wore little bodices and very short petticoats of white linen."[17] The bodice may have served the same function as waistcoats.

Cricket produced new challenges because the matches took so long to play, but "fine light flannel waistcoats" were worn by the Hampshire and Surrey players in 1811,[18] and jackets were worn by the players at Hockwold cum Wilton, Norfolk, in 1823.[19] Trousers made their appearance in cricket in the Hampshire vs. Surrey match in 1811, but they had already been worn in 1805 by a woman engaged in a sport when Mrs. Thornton wore them under her "long nankeen-coloured skirts."[20] Trousers were also worn in Hockwold cum Wilton in 1823.

The tradition of white clothing being worn during cricket matches reaches back to the mid-eighteenth century. In 1745 the maids of Bramley and Hambledon wore white, and that has remained the color of choice ever since. White had an advantage because it was thought that it reflected the sun on hot sunny days; thus, *both* teams wore white, and the teams identified themselves with different colored ribbons (see table 5). Analyzing women's cricket matches up to 1825 shows that when the color of clothing was mentioned, it was always white. We are told that the women cricketers wore "light uniforms" at Southampton in 1786, and they were "dressed in white" in 1795.[21] On Marchwood Marsh in 1819 they were "dressed in white gowns,"[22] and they wore "white dresses" on Lavant Levels, Chichester, in 1821.[23]

The first mention of any sort of hat is in 1811, when reference is made to the players "bonnets";[24] their "caps" were referred to in 1819[25] and 1821.[26] Collett's detail of the young cricket player behind *Miss Wicket* (1770) shows the girl wearing a cap, but not of the peaked variety. The images of women wearing large, impractical hats while playing are likely to be the artists' inventions.

Clothing should not be judged purely from the standpoint of functionality. Women playing cricket attracted a lot of attention, and the matches lasted for several hours. The players placed importance on how they looked. Since white dresses were probably universally worn, they found other ways of distinguishing themselves and their teams. They wore colored ribbons in their hair, on caps and bonnets, on their shoulders, and around their waists. Sometimes the ribbons were fashioned into sashes, shoulder-knots, or topknots, and in one case, into the Prince of Wales's feathers.

The prizefighters wore ribbons too. Saussure described one fighter in 1728 as "decked with blue ribbons on the head, waist, and right arm," while her opponent wore red ribbons.[27]

Regarding footwear, shoes are seldom mentioned. They would have been necessary in cricket and prizefighting for protection, but it seems likely that women usually raced barefoot, as shown in Collett's image of a

TABLE 5. Cricket team colors

1745	Bramley: Blue ribbons on their heads	Hambledon: Red ribbons on their heads
1747	Women of the Hills: Orange ribbons	Women of the Dales: Blue ribbons
1795	Marchwood: Green ribbons	New Forest: Blue ribbons
1811	Hampshire: True-blue/Royal-purple pinned in their bonnets in the shape of the Prince of Wales' plume	Surrey: Blue surmounted with orange
1819	Marchwood (singles): Blue ribbons round their waists and blue bows in their caps	Marchwood (marrieds): Orange-colored ribbons round their waists and orange bows in their caps
1821	Chichester lasses: Sashes, shoulder-knots, and topknots in pink	Chichester dames: Sashes, shoulder-knots, and topknots in blue
1822	Cheriton and Beauworth singles: Pink ribbons	Cheriton marrieds: Blue ribbons
1823	Hockwold cum Wilton singles: Blue ribbands*	Hockwold cum Wilton marrieds

* The report is incomplete; it gives the colors as "blue ribbands" but does not say which team wore them.

smock race in 1770. Even the long-distance runners who ran on the roads probably ran barefoot.

The Rewards

When women and girls ran for smocks and shifts in the early modern era, their efforts transformed the garment from a humble item of clothing into a trophy to be proud of, and they became symbols of achievement and the winner's athleticism. The roots of the smock race in the old rural custom of riding skimmington had given it a special status; while the smock or shift was carried on a pole or flew overhead like a flag, the normal rules were suspended and women were free to show their strength, competitiveness, and fortitude. The idea of reversing the normal rules of behavior led the people of Tollesbury, Essex, to try a novel, double reversal in 1755: the *men* ran for a "Holland Shift," and the women ran a best-of-three race for "a Pair of Buckskin Breeches," but it seems never to have been repeated.[28]

The symbolic smock did not only radiate its power for skimmington rides or smock races. In 1751 "A Full-trimmed Holland Shift" was *danced* for in Southwark, with the women having to pay sixpence to enter,[29] and in 1768 two women *fought* for a "new Shift" in Islington.[30] Unlike the women who raced for smocks, however, the women fighters made their living from their athletic ability. They needed not only skills and courage to fight on public stages but also a public image that could draw a crowd. They were in a kind of partnership with the managers of the amphitheaters. This was a business, and for it to be successful, publicity was almost as important as fighting. The women fighters had to develop a swagger and braggadocio to be successful, not all of which should be taken at face value. The tennis players were professionals, too, but tennis in England was a game for the social elite, and cricket, though popular with all strata of society (and allowed challenges to be made and money to change hands) was never a money-making prospect for women. The poor women (and girls) a century later who made their living with long-distance walks needed money; they had no one to support them except their own families, and they had to rely on the public's generosity as they went—and they often labored in vain. Almost certainly poorly nourished, they demonstrated some remarkable powers of endurance and fortitude.

Often against the odds, many early modern women and girls performed their sport in public, to a high level of skill, and in front of large crowds. With the passage of time their exploits have been almost entirely forgotten, as Samuel Johnson in 1758 suspected they would. It has been my task to expand his wish about Miss Pond's exploits and to "tell the grand-daughters of our grand-daughters" how British women and girls participated and excelled in sports. Perhaps this volume will go some way to fill the gap left by Mr. Johnson's wished-for (but unmade) statue over 250 years ago.

APPENDIX

Understanding Distances, Money, Wagers, and Betting

Distance

In Britain in the seventeenth and eighteenth centuries, distances were measured in feet, yards, rod, and miles; the relationships between them are listed below. For convenience, metric equivalents are listed alongside them in parentheses but would not have been known in Britain at the time.

    3 feet = 1 yard (0.91 m)
    5 and a half yards = 1 rod (5.03 m)
    1,760 yards = 1 mile (1609.4 m)

Distances quoted in this text may be understood and expanded by reference to the following:

    820 feet (249.94 m)
    30 rod = 165 yards (150.88 m)
    40 rod = 220 yards = one-eighth of a mile (201.17 m)
    80 rod = 440 yards (402.34 m)
    Quarter mile = 440 yards (402.34 m)
    Half mile = 880 yards (804.67 m)
    One mile (1.61 k)
    One and a half miles (2.41 k)
    Two miles (3.22 k)
    Four miles (6.44 k)
    Four and three-quarters miles (7.64 k)

Money

British money was denominated in pounds, shillings, and pence, known as L.S.D. Every schoolchild was told these initials referred to the Latin terms Libra, Sestertius, and Denarius, held over from Roman England, but which have evolved into pounds, shillings, and pence in everyday usage.

In the seventeenth century ten pounds might be written in numerals (10 l or 10*l*), but by the eighteenth century it was much more useful to put the L sign *before* the number, and so it would have been written as L10 or £10.

The abbreviation for shillings (s) always came *after* the number, as in 10s or 10/- (meaning 10 shillings and no pence).

The abbreviation for pence (d) always came *after* the number, as in 6d or 6^d. Sixpence was half a shilling, and there were twenty shillings to a pound, so 6d was one-fortieth of a pound. A small silver coin was circulated as a sixpenny piece.

A *shilling* was a silver coin. There were 20 shillings in a pound (20s = £1) and twelve pence in a shilling (12d =1s, or 1/-). Sometimes sums of money greater than a pound would be expressed in shillings: for example, fifty shillings (or £2. 10s).

A *crown* was a large silver coin that was valued at five shillings (5/-).

Two shillings and sixpence, known colloquially as *two and six* (2/6), was also known as *half a crown* and circulated as a silver coin.

A *sovereign* was a gold coin worth £1.

A *guinea* was a gold coin worth 21 shillings (£1. 1s).

For ease of understanding, values mentioned in this text are listed below as they relate to one pound, but the way they are expressed as percentages of a pound (as shown within the parentheses) would never have been used in the seventeenth or eighteenth centuries:

Five guineas, £5. 5s (£5.25)
Four guineas, £4. 4s (£4.20)
One guinea, £1. 1s (£1.05)
One pound, £1
Eighteen shillings, 18s or 18/- (£0.90)
Fifteen shillings, 15s or 15/- (£0.75)

Five shillings, 5s or 5/- (£0.25)

Two shillings and sixpence, 2s 6d or 2/6- (£0.125)

Gambling

Wagers. Men often ran races for wagers, but—so far as the record indicates—women rarely did. Two people would wager, say, that Smith would defeat Jones over a one-mile course and would stake one guinea each on the outcome. The wager would then be described as *one guinea-side*. The wagering parties would then deposit their guineas with a mutually agreed upon third party (the stakeholder) until the race ended and both sides agreed that the victory was fair and that the distance run was indeed a mile. The stakeholder would pay the winning bettor after each party verified the terms of the wager.

Another type of wager involved running against time instead of against another runner. This type of race was usually referred to as a *match against time*. In this instance, one person would wager that he or she (or a chosen runner) could run a specified distance—say one mile (e.g., from the tavern door to the church door)—within a specified time. The two parties to the wager would deposit their stake money with a stakeholder as before, but there were, of course, added complications—most importantly that both parties agreed to how the time would be measured, and by whom.

It was always possible that principals in a wager would appoint someone to run on their behalf, and there is ample evidence of that happening for men but not for women.

In a match against time, it was the *time* that was measured and not the runner. In the example above, a timekeeper would stand at the finishing line and call "Time" precisely one hour after the start. If the runner had already touched the church door by then, the wager was won; if not, it was lost—and the converse for those who had wagered against it being done. When times were announced for runners, they were usually estimated, though there may have been occasions in which a watch was *started* when the runner reached the finish to measure how much time had elapsed before the call of "Time." Similarly, a watch could be started at the call to see how much time passed before the runner arrived.

Betting. Onlookers could also bet on the outcome of a race, independently of the runners or those engaged in the wager, and the principals could bet on it as well. There were no central bookmakers to offer odds, so bets were laid by individuals with other individuals, and when women ran races at horse meets, it was almost inevitable that betting on them went on unreported. In those instances, however, the runners would usually not know about it and so would be uninfluenced by it.

Most horserace courses had a *betting post* where people who wanted to lay a bet gathered to meet others of a similar mind. Among them would be so-called *Knowing Ones,* who claimed to know the form of all the horses and who would suggest odds. In this gambling-mad age, one regularly hears of the Knowing Ones being taken in completely.

NOTES

Introduction

1. *Athletic News*, 12 December 1921.
2. *Illustrated Police News*, 22 December 1921.
3. *Derby Daily Telegraph*, 6 August 1928.
4. *Mail* (Adelaide), 4 August 1928.
5. *Maitland Daily Mercury*, 8 August 1928.
6. *Liverpool Echo*, 28 August 1928.
7. *Idler*, No. 6, Saturday, 20 May 1758.

1. In Hera's Footsteps

1. Ken Dowden, *Death of the Maiden: Girls' Initiation Rites in Greek Mythology* (London: Routledge, 1989).
2. Judith M. Barringer, "Atalanta as Model: The Hunter and the Hunted," *Classical Antiquity* 15, no. 1 (April 1996): 48–76.
3. See, for example, a letter from Thomas Hill to Charles Lennox, 2nd Duke of Richmond [1734]: "But who do you think this Atalanta is?," in Earl of March, *A Duke and His Friends*, vol. 1 (London: Hutchinson & Co., 1911) 290–91.
4. They raced or were chased by symbolic "bears." There is a fine line between racing and chasing, as we see later in the paper chases and hares and hounds games of the nineteenth century that evolved into cross-country running.
5. Dolores Mirón, "The Heraia at Olympia: Gender and Peace," *American Journal of Ancient History*, New Series, vol. 3–4 (2007): 7–38.
6. Isabelle Clark, "The Games of Hera: Myth and Ritual," in *The Sacred and the Feminine in Ancient Greece*, eds. Sue Blundell and Margaret Williamson (London: Routledge, 1998).
7. Catherine Morgan, "The Origins of Pan-Hellenism," in *Greek Sanctuaries: New Perspectives*, eds. Nanno Matinatos and Robin Hägg (London: Routledge, 1993), 16–20; and Paul Christesen, "Whence 776? The Origin of the Date of the First Olympiad," *International Journal of the History of Sport* 26, no. 2 (2009): 161–82.
8. Antonis Kotsonas, "Sanctuaries, Temples and Altars in Early Iron Age: A Chronological and Regional Accounting," in *Regional Stories: Towards a New Perception of the Early Greek*

{247}

World, eds. A. M. Ainian, A. Alexandidou, and X. Charalambidou (Volos: University of Thessaly Press, 2017), 55–66; Jennifer Larson, *Ancient Greek Cults* (New York: Routledge, 2007), 35–36; and Catherine Morgan, *Athletes and Oracles* (Cambridge: Cambridge University Press, 1990), 42.
9. Dowden, *Death of the Maiden*, 2.
10. Heather L. Reid, "La parthenoseroica: Flavia Thalassiae i valori dell'atletica femminile," paper presented at Essere Sempre Il Migliore: Concorsi e Gare Nella Napoli Antica, Naples, 15–17 May 2019.
11. E. Norman Gardiner, *Athletics of the Ancient World* (Oxford: Clarendon Press, 1930), 128.
12. Newlyn Walkup, "Eratosthenes and the Mystery of the Stade: How Long Is a Stade?" *Convergence*, August 2010.
13. Stephen G. Miller, *Ancient Greek Athletics* (New Haven, CT: Yale University Press, 2004), 89.
14. Mirón, "Heraia at Olympia," 8.
15. Nigel Spivey, *The Ancient Olympic Games* (Oxford: Oxford University Press, 2004), 208–37.
16. Pausanias, *Description of Greece*, 5.16.2–7.
17. Mirón, "Heraia at Olympia," 10.
18. Mark Golden, *Sport and Society in Ancient Greece* (Cambridge: Cambridge University Press, 1998), 130–31; Judith Swaddling, *The Ancient Olympic Games* (London: British Museum Press, 1999), 43.
19. David Gilman Romano, "The Ancient Stadium: Athletes and Arete," *Ancient World* 7 (1983): 1–2; Golden, *Sport and Society in Ancient Greece*, 131.
20. In Greek mythology, Herakles was the half-human son of the god Zeus and was the founder of the Olympic Games.
21. Matthew Dillon, "Did Parthenoi Attend the Olympic Games? Girls and Women Competing, Spectating, and Carrying Out Cult Roles at Greek Religious Festivals," *Hermes* 128, no. 4 (2000): 457–80.
22. Plutarch, *The Parallel Lives: The Life of Lycurgus*.
23. Euripides, *Andromache*.
24. Pausanias, *Description of Greece*, 5.16.2–3.
25. Formerly in the Barberini Collection in Rome and acquired by the Vatican Museum in 1772.
26. The figure was acquired in 1876.
27. Richard Hamilton, "Alkman and the Athenian Arkteia," *Hesperia* (1989): 449–72.
28. Allen B. West, "Notes on Achaean Prosopography and Chronology," *Classical Philology* 23. no. 3 (July 1928): 258–69.
29. Luigi Moretti, *Iscrizioni Agonistiche Greche* (Rome: A. Signorelli, 1953), 63; West, "Notes on Achaean Prosopography."
30. C. Suetonius Tranquilus, *The Lives of the Twelve Caesars—The Life of Domitian*, 4, 1, 347; Heather Reid, "La parthenoseroica."
31. This is the so-called *Coronation of the Winner*, Villa Romana del Casale, Sicily.
32. Red-figured pottery water jar showing a female tumbler, 340–330 BCE, British Museum, acquired in 1814 from Peregine Edward Towneley; red-figure belly amphora, women swimming, c. 520 BCE, the Louvre, Paris; Moretti, *Iscrizioni Agonistiche Greche*, 63.
33. Dowden, *Death of the Maiden*.
34. Adrienne Mayor, *The Amazons: Lives and Legends of Warrior Women across the Ancient World* (Princeton, NJ: Princeton University Press, 2014).

35. Alison A. MacIntosh, Ron Pinhasi, and Jay T. Stock, "Prehistoric Women's Manual Labor Exceeded that of Athletes through the First 5,500 years of Farming in Central Europe," *Science Advances* 3, no. 11 (29 November 2017); Alison Macintosh, University of Cambridge, Research News, https://www.cam.ac.uk/research/news/from-athletes-to-couch-potatoes-humans-through-6000-years-of-farming, November 2017.
36. MacIntosh, Pinhasi, and Stock, "Prehistoric Women's Manual Labor."
37. Ibid.
38. Archibald Ballantyne, *Voltaire's Visit to England, 1726–1729* (London: John Murray, 1919) 31; [Jean-Bernard] Abbé le Blanc, *Letters on the English and French Nations* (London: J. Brindley, R. Francklin, and J. Hodges, 1747), 2:141.
39. Walter Endrei and Lásló Zolnay, *Fun and Games in Old Europe* (Budapest: Corvina Kiadó, 1986), 85–86.
40. Guillaume Depping, *Wonders of Bodily Strength and Skill, in all Ages and all Countries*, trans. Charles Russell (New York: Charles Scribner & Co., 1871), 134–39.
41. Endrei and Zolnay, *Fun and Games in Old Europe*, 85–86.
42. Richard Trexler, *Public Life in Renaissance Florence* (Ithaca, NY: Cornell University Press, 1980).
43. Deanna Shemek, *Ladies Errant: Wayward Women and Social Order in Early Modern Italy* (Durham, NC: Duke University Press, 1998), 23–25; Endrei and Zolnay, *Fun and Games in Old Europe*, 137–38.
44. Endrei and Zolnay, *Fun and Games in Old Europe*, 177.
45. Joseph Strutt, *Glig-Gamena Angel-Deod. Or, the Sports and Pastimes of the People of England* (London: J. White, 1801), 94; Julian Marshall, *The Annals of Tennis* (London: The Field Office, 1878), 42.
46. Kathleen Ann González, *A Beautiful Woman in Venice* (Venice, Italy: Supernova, 2015).
47. Peter Radford, "The Olympic Games in the Long Eighteenth Century," *Journal for Eighteenth-Century Studies* 35, no. 2 (2012): 161–84.
48. James I, *The King's Majesty's Declaration to his Subjects, Concerning Lawful Sports to be used* (London: printed by Bonham Norton, 1618), reproduced in Andrew Lang, *Social England Illustrated: A Collection of Seventeenth-Century Tracts* (New York: Cooper Square Publishers, 1964), 309–14.
49. Hocktide is the second week after Easter and a traditional time for some sports and games.
50. John Trussell, "To My Noble Friend Mr. Robert Dover, on his Annuall Assemblies upon Cotswold," is the second poem in Mat[hewe] Walbancke, *Annalia Dubrensia. Upon the Yeerly Celebration of Mr Robert Dovers Olimpick Games Upon Cotswold-Hills* (London: Printed for Robert Raworth, 1636). The work carries no page numbers.
51. The Lords Assembled in Parliament, *An Additionall ORDINANCE OF THE LORDS and COMMONS Assembled in Parliament: Concerning the dayes of Recreation, allowed unto Schollars, Apprentices and other Servants* (London: Printed for John Wright, 1647).
52. David Cram, Jeffrey L. Forgeng, and Dorothy Johnston, eds., *Francis Willughby's Book of Games: A Seventeenth-Century Treatise on Sports, Games and Pastimes* (Aldershot, Hants.: Ashgate Publishing, 2003). Originally compiled 1662–72.
53. White Kennett, *Parochial Antiquities Attempted in the History of Ambroseden, Bicester and other Adjacent Parts in the Counties of Oxford and Bucks* (Oxford: At the Theatre, 1695).
54. Radford, "Olympic Games in the Long Eighteenth Century," 178.

55. Colin Blakemore and Sheila Jennett, eds., *The Oxford Companion to the Human Body* (Oxford: Oxford University Press, 2001), 305–6, 370–71.
56. *Romeo and Juliet*, I, 1; *Love's Labour's Lost*, I, 1; *As You Like It*, II, 4; *Henry IV, Part II*, II, 4.
57. [John Shirley] J.S., *The Accomplished Ladies Rich Closet of Rarities: or the Ingenious Gentlewoman and Servant Maids Delightful Companion*, 2nd ed. (London: Printed by W.W. for Nicholas Boddington, 1687), 200–201.
58. James Beattie, *Dissertations Moral and Critical* (London: Printed for W. Strahan and T. Cadell, 1783), 125–26.
59. *Gentleman's Magazine*, vol. 54, Part the First, 1784, pp. 25–26.

2. Women Runners in Britain

1. Stuart Sherman, *Telling Time: Clocks, Diaries, and English Diurnal Form, 1660–1785* (Chicago: University of Chicago Press, 1996), 174.
2. *Derby Mercury*, 20 December 1733.
3. *Sporting Magazine*, March 1794, p. 302.
4. John Gay, *The Shepherd's Week, Pastoral IV, Thursday; or the Spell* (London: Ferd. Burleigh, 1714).
5. James Ward, *The Smock-Race, at Finglas* (London: Jacob Tonson, 1714).
6. William Somervile, *Hobbinol, or the Rural Games. A Burlesque Poem* (Edinburgh: Printed for J. Stagg, [1740]); ibid., canto I, line 229.
7. Radford, "Olympic Games in the Long Eighteenth Century"; *Spectator* 161, Tuesday, 4 September [1711], 290–93.
8. Budgell, Addison's cousin, wrote several issues of the *Spectator*, although its usual editors were Joseph Addison and Richard Steele. See also Kennett, *Parochial Antiquities*, 2:309.
9. Oliver Goldsmith, *The Vicar of Wakefield* (London: F. Newbery, 1766), ch. 10.
10. [Richard Graves], *The Spiritual Quixote: or, the Summer's Ramble of Mr. Geoffrey Wildgoose* (London: J. Dodsley, 1773).
11. Ibid., ch. 10, book 2.
12. Frances Burney, *Evelina, or The History of a Young Lady's Entrance into the World* (London: T. Lowndes, 1778).
13. Doody's comments are in the Penguin Books edition of *Evelina* (1994), 494–95.
14. Betty Rizzo, "Equivocations of Gender and Rank: Eighteenth-Century Sporting Women," *Eighteenth-Century Life* 26, no. 1(2002): 73, 74.
15. Earl R. Anderson, "Footnotes More Pedestrian than Sublime: A Historical Background for the Foot-race in *Evelina* and *Humphry Clinker*," *Eighteenth-Century Studies* 14, no. 1 (1980): 56–68.
16. Arthur Sherbo, "Addenda to 'Footnotes More Pedestrian than Sublime,'" *Eighteenth-Century Studies* 14, no. 3 (1981): 313–16.
17. Tobias Smollett, *The Adventures of Ferdinand Count Fathom* (Dublin: R. Main, 1753), ch.50.
18. Published by Thos. Tegg, 29 September 1811. The *Rural Sports* series also included *A Milling Match, A Cricket Match Extraordinary, An Old Mole Catcher in Full Scent, Coney Hunting*, and *Balloon Hunting*. A seventh title, *A Pleasant Way of Making Hay*, seems to have been added in 1814.
19. Allen Guttmann, *Women's Sports: A History* (New York: Columbia University Press, 1991), 72–73.

20. Published as the Act directs, 1770. Printed for Robt Sayer, No. 53 in Fleet Street and Jhn Smith, No. 35 in Cheapside, London.
21. Patricia Crown, "Sporting with Clothes: John Collet's Prints in the 1770s," *Eighteenth-Century Life* 26, no. 1 (Winter 2002): 119–35; David Alexander, "Prints after John Collet: Their Publishing History and a Chronological Checklist," ibid., 136–46.
22. William Somervile, *Hobbinol, or The Rural Games*, 4th ed., etchings by Anthony Walker (London: G. Hawkins, 1757), facing 70.
23. William Hogarth, *Southwark Fair*, 1733, oil on canvas, Cincinnati Art Museum, Cincinnati, OH; anon., *Fairlop Fair*, c. 1815, engraving published by T. Tegg, 7 July 1815; William Redmore Bigg, *The Village Fair*, oil on canvas, Upton House, Warwickshire. Attribution on the latter is not certain; it may also be by Luke Clennell.
24. Henry Alken, *A Horn Fair*, reproduced in John Armitage, *Man at Play: Nine Centuries of Pleasure Making* (London: Frederick Warne, 1977), 106.
25. William Somervile, *Hobbinol, or The Rural Games*, illustrations by Charlton Nesbitt and John Thurston (London: William Bulmer and Co., for R. Ackermann, 1813), 66.
26. Anon., reproduced in George Clinch, *Marylebone and St. Pancras: Their History, Celebrities, Buildings, and Institutions* (London: Truslove and Shirley, 1890).
27. Anon., reproduced in Dennis Brailsford, *A Taste for Diversions: Sport in Georgian England* (Cambridge: Lutterworth Press, 1999) 150.
28. Collet, *An Holland Smock to be run for*, 1770, in the author's collection.
29. A single-stick match was known as a broadsword match in some parts of England.
30. Charles II, *Articles ordered by his Majestie to be observed by all persons that put in horses to run for the Plate, the new Round-heate at Newmarkett . . .* , reproduced in *Newmarket: Its Sport and Personalities,* by Frank Siltzer (London: Cassell and Co., 1923).
31. *Jackson's Oxford Journal*, 10 June 1775.

3. "Of Good Conversation"

1. Thomas Digges (1603–87) was the oldest of eleven children of Sir Dudley Digges and Lady Mary Kemp.
2. Sir Dudley was awarded a BA at University College, Oxford, in 1601.
3. James Brome, Travels over England, Scotland, and Wales, 2nd ed., "With Large Additions" (London: printed for Rob. Gosling, 1707), 283.
4. The plural of "rod" is sometimes "rods" but is more usually given as "rod."
5. Radford, "Olympic Games in the Long Eighteenth Century," 161–84.
6. Walbancke, *Annalia Dubrensia*. It concludes with a poem by Robert Dover and includes poems by thirty-one or thirty-two others. There are two poems by "John Trussell," whom Edward Vyvyan believes to be different people (see Vyvyan, *Cotswold Games, Annalia Dubrensia* [Cheltenham: Williams & Son, 1878], viii), but Christopher Whitfield argues they are by the same person (see Whitfield, *Robert Dover and the Cotswold Games: Annalia Dubrensia* [Evesham: Journal Press, 1962], 171).
7. Whitfield, *Robert Dover and the Cotswold Games*, 40–43.
8. Richard Brome, *A Joviall Crew; or The Merry Beggars*, act 2, scene 2, Richard Brome online, accessed August 23, 2022, https://www.dhi.ac.uk/brome/.
9. Trussell, *To My Noble Friend Mr. Robert Dover*, [6]. Hocktide is the second week after Easter.

10. R.N. [R. Newburgh?], *To My Kinde Friend, Master Robert Dover, upon his Cotswold meetings*, in Walbancke, *Annalia Dubrensia*, [60]; Thomas Randall, *An Eglogve on the Palilia and Noble Assemblies Revived on Cotswold Hills, by Mr. Robert Dover*, ibid., [17]; Michaell Drayton, *To My Noble Friend Mr. Robert Dover, on his brave annual Assemblies vpon Cotswold*, ibid., [4].
11. In 1639 the estate passed to Thomas Digges; in 1687 he bequeathed it to Leonard Digges; in 1718 it passed to John Digges. On John Digges's death in 1720, the estate went to his brother Col. Thomas Digges, the brother of Sir Henry Digges's great-grandson. In 1724 it passed out of the family to James Colebrooke, and on his death in 1752, it passed to his son Robert. In 1774 it passed to Robert Heron.
12. The amounts are calculated as of 2021: see Measuring Worth online, accessed 21 October 2021, https://www.measuringworth.com/calculators/ukcompare/. GDP stands for Gross Domestic Product.
13. *Kentish Post and Canterbury News-Letter*, 4–8 June 1726.
14. Ibid., 29 May–2 June 1731.
15. Ibid., 17–20 July 1751.
16. Ibid., 17–21 July 1756.
17. Edward Hasted, *The History and Topographical Survey of the County of Kent*, 2nd ed., vol. 6 (Canterbury: W. Bristow, 1798), 263–92.
18. *Daily Advertiser*, Tuesday, 23 April 1751.
19. Hasted, *History and Topographical Survey of the County of Kent*, 266.
20. *Kentish Post and Canterbury News-Letter*, 22–25 June 1743.
21. E.g., *Kentish Gazette*, Saturday 2–6 July 1768, and 19–23 June 1773. See also Brome, *Travels over England, Scotland, and Wales*, 282.
22. For goal running, see *Evening Telegraph and Post* [Dundee], 29 May 1937; and a film clip of a 1951 game at British Pathé online, accessed July 26, 2022, https://www.britishpathe.com/video/goal-running/query/goal+running.
23. *Kentish Gazette*, 8–11 June 1768.
24. Ibid., 2–6 July 1768.
25. Ibid., 22–26 July 1769.
26. Ibid., 26–30 June 1770.
27. Ibid., 19–22 July 1769.
28. Ibid., 23–26 June 1770.
29. Ibid., 12–16 June 1773.
30. Ibid., 15–19 July, and 19–22 July 1769.
31. *Kentish Post, or Canterbury News-Letter*, 17–20 July 1751.
32. *Kentish Gazette*, 8–11 June 1768.
33. Ibid., 2–5 August 1769.
34. Hasted, *History and Topographical Survey of the County of Kent*, 265.
35. *Kentish Post, or, Canterbury News-Letter*, 4–8 June 1726.
36. Ibid., 9–13 May 1730.
37. Ibid., 17–21 July 1756.
38. Ibid., 17–21 June 1749.
39. Ibid., 17–20 July 1751.
40. *Kentish Gazette*, 18–21 May 1774.
41. Ibid., 18–22 May 1776.
42. Ibid., 2 May 1788.
43. Ibid., 20 May 1788.

4. Running for Shifts and Smocks

1. Until 1752 the legal year in England began on 25 March; thus, February 1659 would be February 1660 by our reckoning.
2. *The Diary of Samuel Pepys*, accessed 27 January 2022, https://www.pepysdiary.com/diary/1660/02/. Theophila Turner was also known The[e].
3. Extract from the *Caledonian Mercury of 1660–61*, in *Scots Magazine, and Edinburgh Literary Miscellany*, October 1815, p. 762.
4. The hundred-pound cheese was equivalent to 110 pounds Imperial, Anet Scottish Running, accessed 31 November 2021, http://www.anentscottishrunning.com/early-days-unusual-races/.
5. Robert Chambers, *Domestic Annals of Scotland from the Reformation to the Revolution* (Edinburgh: W. & R. Chambers, 1859), 273.
6. Robert Brand, *Observations on the Popular Antiquities of Great Britain* (London: Henry G. Bohn, 1849), 2:70–72.
7. Quoted in *Scots Magazine and Edinburgh Literary Miscellany* 67 (October 1815), 762.
8. See Prof Craig Sharp, Anent Scottish Running, accessed 27 July 2022, http://www.anentscottishrunning.com/early-days-unusual-races/.
9. A creel is a willow (osier) basket.
10. Dr. Alexander Carlyle, "The Parish of Inveresk," in Sir John Sinclair, *The Statistical Account of Scotland* (Edinburgh: William Creech, 1795), 19, 16.
11. Ibid, 17.
12. Ibid, 19–20.
13. Ibid.
14. Ibid.
15. John Raithby, ed., *An Act against deceitfull disorderly and excessive Gameing* (1664), in *Statutes of the Realm: Volume 5: 1628–80* (London: G. Eyre and A. Strahan, 1819), 523.
16. *Diary of Samuel Pepys*, Sunday, 14 April 1667, accessed August 23, 2022, https://www.pepysdiary.com/diary/1667/04/14/.
17. William Blundell, "The Cavalier, A Country song eopleng the harmeless mirth of Lancashyre in peaceable tymes," in Nicholas Blundell, *The Great Diurnal of Nicholas Blundell, of Little Crosby, Lancashire*, vol.1, 1702–11, ed. J. J. Bagley (Liverpool: Record Society of Lancashire and Cheshire, [1968]), appendix H (1709), 322–23.
18. Anon., *The Virgin race; Or, York-shires Glory* (London: Printed for I[ohn]. Wright, I[ohn]. Clark, W[illiam]. Thackeray, and T[homas]. Passinger, 1682?). The text of the ballad is reproduced at the English Broadside Ballad Archive online (EBBA 31483), accessed 23 August 2022, https://ebba.english.ucsb.edu/ballad/31483/xml.
19. Oliver Heywood, *His Autobiography, Diaries, Anecdote and Event Books*, ed. J. Horsfall Turner (Brighouse: A. B. Bayes, 1881), 2:284 (Thursday, 1 September 1681); 2:281 (Wednesday, 1 June 1681); 2:295 (Tuesday, 15 to Thursday, 17 August 1682); 2:270–71 (Saturday, 1 May 1680).
20. *London Gazette*, 18–22 June 1696.
21. J. Goulstone, *Smock Racing* (Erith, Kent: Published by the author, 2005), 9.
22. *Post Boy*, 4–7 June 1698.
23. John Stow, *A survay of London, contayning the originall, antiquity, increase, moderne estate, and description of that citie* (London: J. Wolfe, 1598).
24. James I, *The King's Majesty' Declaration to His Subjects, Concerning Lawful Sports to be Used* (London: Bonham Norton and John Bill, 1618).

25. Shack[erley] Marmyon, "To Mr. Robert Dover, Upon His Annuall Sports at Cotswold," in Walbancke, *Annalia Dubrensia*.
26. A distaff was a stick on which women and girls wound flax or wool for hand-spinning (i.e., without a spinning wheel). Using the distaff was "women's work" and came to symbolize women generally.
27. *Diary of Samuel Pepys*, Monday, 6 June 1667.
28. Henri Misson, *Memoires et Observations Faites par un Voyageur en Angleterre* (La Haye: Henri van Bulderen, 1698), 70.
29. William Combe, with etchings by Thomas Rowlandson, *The Second Tour of Doctor Syntax in Search of Consolation* (London: R. Ackermann, 1820).
30. Thomas Hardy, *The Mayor of Casterbridge* (London: Smith Elder & Co., 1886), ch. 39.
31. Samuel Butler, *Hudibras* (London: Printed by T.N. for John Martyn and Henry Herringman, 1674).
32. Williams, Thomas Platter's Travels in England 1599, 182.

5. "A Prince's Wine and Biskets"

1. John Ashton, *Social Life in the Reign of Queen Anne, Taken from Original Sources* (London: Chatto & Windus, 1897), 243.
2. *Flying Postman*, 22 April 1699.
3. *London Post*, 23–25 April 1701. To "hollow" (or "halloo") meant to hunt with hounds.
4. *The Courier*, 21 November 1829.
5. *Post Boy*, 24–26 April 1718.
6. Frank Siltzer, *Newmarket, Its Sport and Personalities* (London: Cassell and Co., 1923), 48–49.
7. Ashton, *Social Life in the Reign of Queen Anne* (1882), 144; *Sheffield Weekly Telegraph*, 25 July 1885.
8. *Newcastle Courant*, 15–18 October 1712.
9. *Evening Post*, 30 April 1720.
10. *Post Boy*, 28–30 March 1700.
11. *Annals of Sporting* 10, no. 57 (September 1826): 166.
12. Guildford (Surrey), Woodstock (Oxfordshire), Port-Meadow (Oxford), Bourne (Lincolnshire), Odsey (Hertfordshire), Wantage (Oxfordshire), March Common (Isle of Ely), Arundel (Sussex), Sleaford (Lincolnshire), Lilly Hoo (Hertfordshire), and Sunderland (Co. Durham).
13. Finchley (Middlesex), Windsor (Berkshire), *Daily Courant*, 19 April 1720, and Enfield (Middlesex), *Daily Courant*, 29 June 1724.
14. Henrietta, Countess of Suffolk, *Letters to and From Henrietta, Countess of Suffolk*, vol. 1 (London: John Murray, 1824), 98.
15. *Post-Man: and the Historical Account, &c.*, 19–22 August 1710.
16. Ibid.
17. Ibid., 9–12 September 1710; *Daily Courant*, 28 May 1712; 24 August 1713; 23 June 1714; *Post-Man: and the Historical Account, &c.*, 18–24 August 1715; *Daily Courant*, 30 July 1716.
18. *Post-Man: and the Historical Account, &c.*, 27–29 July 1704.
19. *Daily Courant*, 28 August 1713.
20. *Stamford Mercury*, 28 June 1716.
21. *Daily Courant*, 19 April 1720.

22. *Daily Courant*, 29 July 1724.
23. *Post-Man, and the Historical Account, &c.*, 25–27 June 1719. A backsword was a sword with one sharp edge, but to enable safe practice of the necessary skills, a hard wooden stick of the same dimensions was used. These competitions with sticks became so popular that they became a major entertainment, but it was still called back-swording. See Egerton Castle, *Schools and Masters of Fence* (London: Bell & Sons, 1885), 209.
24. In this context "clocks" means a pattern worked in silk on the outer side of the stocking, at and above the ankle.
25. *Daily Post*, 6 August 1724.
26. *Newcastle Courant*, 9–11 February 1712.
27. *Daily Post*, 1 August 1721.
28. Ibid., 29 August 1721.
29. E.H. Cordeaux and D.H. Merry, "Port Meadow Races," *Oxoniensia* 13 (1948): 55–65.
30. *Weekly Journal*, 9 September 1721.
31. *Evening Post*, 20 September 1722.
32. Sarcenet is a fine, soft silk fabric of Italian origin.
33. *Weekly Journal or British Gazetteer*, 29 September 1716.
34. "Couronné d'une belle paire de Cornes." The translation of "une belle" as "ample" comes from the English translation of Misson's *Travels* in 1719; see *M. Misson's Memoirs and Observations in His Travels over England*, trans. Mr. Ozell (London: D. Browne, and others, 1719).
35. Daniel Defoe [A Gentleman], *A Tour Thro' the Whole Island of Great Britain* (London: G. Strahan, W. Mears, R. Francklin, S. Chapman, R. Stagg, and J. Graves, 1724).
36. William Combe, *Doctor Syntax's Three Tours; in Search of the Picturesque, Consolation and a Wife*, with illustrations by Thomas Rowlandson (London: R. Ackerman's Repository of Arts, 1812), second tour.
37. [Francis] Grose, *Lexicon Balatronicum: A Dictionary of Buckish Slang, Universal Wit, and Pickpocket Eloquence* (London: C. Chappel, 1811).
38. It continued ". . . a servant's prison, and a horse's hell." Williams, *Thomas Platter's Travels in England 1599*, 182.

6. Visitors Write Home

1. Voltaire, *Lettres Philosophique* (1730), in *Oeuvres Complètes de Voltaire*, ed. Louis Moland (Paris: Garnier, 1877–85), vol. 22; Ballantyne, *Voltaire's Visit to England*, 31.
2. Abbé le Blanc, *Letters on the English and French Nations*, 2:141.
3. Ibid., 1:298.
4. César de Suassure, *A Foreign View of England in the Reign of George I and George II: The Letters of Monsieur César de Suassure to his Family*, trans. and ed. Madame Van Muyden, (London: John Murray, 1902), 293.
5. *Mist's Weekly Journal*, 23 October 1725; *St. James's Evening-Post*, 23 October 1725; *Ipswich-Journal, or, The Weekly-Mercury*, 23–30 October 1725; and *Caledonian Mercury*, 1 November 1725.
6. *Read's Weekly Journal, or, British-Gazetteer*, 2 August 1735; *Ipswich Gazette*, 2 August 1735; *Derby Mercury*, 7 August 1735; and *Caledonian Mercury*, 8 August 1735.
7. *Caledonian Mercury*, 21 August 1735.
8. *Daily Advertiser*, 16 September 1740.

9. *Penny London Morning Advertiser*, 24 June 1748.
10. *Newcastle Courant*, 2–9 July 1748.
11. This work is now known as his *Book of Games*.
12. Cram, Forgeng, and Johnston, *Francis Willughby's Book of Games*, 165.
13. Stephen Glover, and Thomas Noble, *The History, Gazetteer, and Directory of the County of Derby . . .* (London: Longman and Co., 1839), 314.
14. J. P. Hore, *The History of Newmarket, and the Annals of the Turf*, vol.2 (London, A. H. Baily and Co., 1886). 301.
15. Philip Bliss, *Reliquiae Hearnianae. Vol II: The Remains of Thomas Hearne M.A., of Edmund Hall, Being Extracts from His Ms Diaries, Collected with a Few Notes, by Philip Bliss* (London: John Russell Smith, 1869), 112.
16. Erasmus Philipps, *Manuscript Diary*, 19 September 1720, quoted by Old Blue, in *Sporting Life*, 30 September 1903.
17. *The Craftsman; or, Say's Weekly Journal*, 18 September 1790; *Adams's Weekly Courant*, 21 September 1790.
18. *Jackson's Oxford Journal*, 20 December 1787; *Ipswich Journal*, 22 December 1787.
19. Quoted in John Harland and T. T. Wilkinson, *Lancashire Legends* (London: George Routledge and Sons, 1873), 159.
20. Charles-Lewis de Pollnitz, *The Memoirs of Charles-Lewis, baron de Pollnitz: Being the Observations he Made in his Late Travels . . .*, vol. 2 (London: Daniel Browne, 1739), 470 (letter 54, 4 May 1733).
21. *Sporting Magazine*, November 1792, p. 103.
22. *A Jovial Crew*, Richard Brome online, accessed 23 August 2022, https://www.dhi.ac.uk/brome/viewTranscripts.jsp?type=BOTH&play=JC&act=2.
23. Suffolk, *Letters to and from Henrietta, Countess of Suffolk*, 1:98–99.
24. See the three young women who ran "not incommoded with clothes or modesty, three times round a given space in Tothill-fields, for a Holland shift and half-a-guinea," *British Press*, 2 September 1808.
25. *Daily Post*, 19 September 1730.
26. The surname is variously spelled "Fig" and "Figg." Captain Godfrey always refers to James as "Fig"; see John Godfrey, *A Treatise Upon the Useful Science of Defence* (London: T. Gardner, 1741). "Figg" was the more common spelling. See also *Ipswich-Journal, or, The Weekly-Mercury*, 10 October 1730.
27. The Sign of the City of Oxford was behind Oxford Street near its junction with Tottenham Court Road, near what is Hanway Street today.
28. E.g., "the Noble Science of Self Defence"; *Post-Man*, 8 July 1718; *Daily Post*, 10 September 1729; *Daily Journal*, 3 May 1726.
29. *Mist's Weekly Journal*, 20 November 1725; *Annual Register or a View of the History, Politics, and Literature for the Year 1794* (London: F. C. & J. Rivington, 1808), 1095–96.
30. Ballantyne, *Voltaire's Visit to England*, 30.
31. *Ipswich-Journal, or, The Weekly-Mercury*, 16–23 July 1726.
32. *Daily Journal*, 4 October 1733; *Weekly Miscellany*, 6 October 1733.
33. *Daily Advertiser*, 11 October 1733; *Country Journal: or the Craftsman*, 6 October 1733.
34. Earl of March, *A Duke and His Friends*, 290–91.
35. Cambric is a fine woven linen or cotton cloth often treated to be glossy and stiff. A tucker is a piece of outer clothing that covered a woman's neck and shoulders.

36. *Penny London Post*, 8 October 1733.
37. During rest periods male runners and walkers in competition were known to have their feet and ankles rubbed with a dry cloth or their legs rubbed with vinegar. They also often changed their clothes. Nothing is known about women, but we may suppose they did much the same. See Peter Radford, *The Celebrated Captain Barclay: Sport, Money, and Fame in Regency Britain* (London: Headline Book Publishing, 2001).
38. *Oracle*, 20 May 1749.
39. *Derby Mercury*, 12–19 May 1749.
40. *Daily Post*, 5 June 1729; *Newcastle Courant*, 16 August 1735.
41. *Newcastle Courant*, 2–9 July 1748.
42. *Northampton Mercury*, 15 June 1747.
43. *Newcastle Courant*, 19 July 1746.
44. Crowley, Sir Ambrose (1658–1713) of Greenwich, Kent, History of Parliament online, accessed 23 August 2022, http://www.historyofparliamentonline.org/volume/1690-1715/member/crowley-sir-ambrose-1658-1713.
45. "Winlaton, A Brief History," Winlaton and District Local History Society, accessed 23 August 2022, http://www.winlatonlocalhistorysociety.org.uk/index.asp?pageid=719600.
46. Letter from L. F. Longstaffe to the *Northern Evening Mail*, 11 August 1883.
47. *Caledonian Mercury*, 14 November 1726.
48. *Ipswich-Journal, or, The Weekly-Mercury*, 8 September 1733; *Derby Mercury*, 13 September 1733.
49. *County Journal: or The Craftsman*, 15 September 1733, refers to him as "Captain Litular."
50. *Caledonian Mercury*, 21 January 1731.
51. The Marlborough to Bristol road. Four to five thousand attended. *Gloucester Journal*, 9 November 1736.
52. *Ipswich-Journal, or, The Weekly-Mercury*, 5 October 1728.
53. *Daily Post*, 5 June 1729.
54. *London Evening-Post*, 30 April–3 May 1737.
55. *Kentish Post, or Canterbury News-Letter*, 23–27 July 1748.
56. Ibid., 4–8 June 1726.
57. Not to be confused with a match of running, a team game with twelve to twenty-four players side.
58. The text of the letter can be found in Elizabeth Carter, *Memoirs of the Life of Mrs. Elizabeth Carter* (London: F. C. and J. Rivington, 1808), 92, and clues to its date can be found in Carter, *A Series of Letters between Mrs. Elizabeth Carter and Miss Catherine Talbot from the Year 1741 to 1770*, vol. 1, ed. Montague Pennington (London: F. C. and J. Rivington, 1809), 157.
59. Kerri Andrews, *Wanderers—A History of Women Walking* (London: Reaktion Books, 2020), 41.
60. Ibid., 12.

7. Paying the Ultimate Price

1. *Daily Advertiser*, 4 August 1755.
2. James Woodforde, *The Diary of a Country Parson, 1758–1781*, vol. 1, ed. J. Beresford (London: Humphrey Milford, Oxford University Press, 1924), 90.
3. *Salisbury Journal*, 30 September 1765.

4. *Faulkner's Dublin Journal*, 16 June 1753.
5. *Salisbury Journal*, 30 September 1765.
6. William Pick, *The Turf Register, and Sportsman & Breeder's Stud-Book*, vol. 1 (Selby, Yorkshire: Printed by A. Bartholoman, 1803), 8–9.
7. Ibid, 50–51.
8. Ibid, 59.
9. Woodforde, *Diary of a Country Parson*, 318 (2 April 1788).
10. Peter Radford, "Escaping the Phillippedes Connection: Death, Injury and Illness in Eighteenth-Century Sport in Britain," in *Sport and Health in History*, ed. Thierry Terret (Sankt Augustin: Academia Verlag, 1999), 87–100.
11. *Country Journal: or the Craftsman*, 22 December 1733.
12. Glanffrwd, *Plwyf Llanwyno: Yr Hen Amser, Yr Hen Bobl, A'r Hen Droion* (Pontypridd: Argraffwyd Gan David J. Hopkin, 1888). Portions translated into English by Peter Radford are at Athlos online, accessed 23 August 2022, https://athlos.co.uk/books/the-parish-of-llanwyno-extracts/.
13. *London Chronicle, or Universal Advertiser*, 3–5 March 1757; *Derby Mercury*, 4 March 1757.
14. *Public Advertiser*, 6 September 1771.
15. G. H. Wilson, *Wonderful Characters: Comprising Memoirs and Anecdotes of the Most Remarkable Persons of Every Age and Nation* (London: J. Barr and Co., 1842), 51.
16. Samuel Auguste David Tissot (1728–97). His text, *Avis au eople sur sa santé, ou, Traité des maladies les plus fréquentes* (1763) appeared in English as *Advice to the people in general, with regard to their health . . .*, trans. J. Kirkpatrick (London: Printed for T. Becket and P. A. de Hondt, 1765), 31.
17. *Caledonian Mercury*, 24 September 1724.
18. Ibid., 19 October 1724.
19. Sir John Sinclair, *The Code of Health and Longevity*, vol. 2 (Edinburgh: Arch. Constable, 1807), appendix, 104.
20. Ibid., 106.
21. *Gloucester Journal*, 20 August 1904, quoting *Gloucester Journal*, 20 June 1750.
22. See, for example, the *St. James's Evening Post*, 17 August 1745.
23. G. B. Buckley, *Fresh Light on Eighteenth-Century Cricket* (Birmingham: Cotterell & Co., 1935).
24. *London Evening Post*, 8–10 July 1746.
25. *Lloyd's Evening Post*, 13–15 October 1773.
26. *Ipswich Journal*, 2 October 1773.
27. Thomas Lowe was a well-known tenor who, in his forties, decided to go into management and took the lease of Marylebone Gardens. In that venue he engaged other singers and produced crowd-pleasing entertainments. On this day in 1767 it ended with a fireworks display. He also sang what can only be called advertising songs—one that was popular in 1766 was in praise of "sparkling champagne" (*Dublin Courier*, 18 June 1766). See also Warwick Wroth, *The London Pleasure Gardens of the Eighteenth Century* (London: Macmillan, 1896), 101–3.
28. *St. James's Chronicle or the British Evening Post*, 15–18 August 1767.
29. *Covent-Garden Journal*, 23 May 1752.
30. *Public Advertiser*, 22 September 1774.
31. *Reading Mercury and Oxford Gazette*, 21 June 1773.

32. Ibid., 27 June 1774.
33. *Daily Advertiser*, 17 September 1756.
34. *Hampshire Chronicle, or Winchester, Southampton, and Portsmouth Mercury*, 18 July 1774.
35. *Salisbury Journal*, 15 July 1765.
36. *Monthly Miscellany, or Gentleman and Lady's Complete Magazine*, vol. 1(1775): 26; see also Pierce Egan, *Sporting Anecdotes, Original and Selected* (London: Albion Press, 1804), 321.

8. Exhilaration and Athleticism

1. *Leeds Intelligencer*, 22 May 1781.
2. Christopher Hibbert, *George IV, Prince of Wales, 1762–1811* (London: Longman, 1972), 109.
3. John Burgess, *Diary and Letters*, quoted in Emma Griffin, *England's Revelry: A History of Popular Sports and Pastimes 1660–1830* (Oxford: Oxford University Press, 2005), 53.
4. *Morning Post and Daily Advertiser*, 15 August 1789.
5. *Oracle, or, Bell's New World*, 15 August 1789.
6. John Van Der Kiste, *George III's Children* (Thrupp, Stoud: Sutton Publishing, 1992), 15–16.
7. Morris Marples, *Six Royal Sisters: Daughters of George III* (London: Michael Joseph, 1969), 13.
8. *London Courant, and Westminster Chronicle*, 26 October 1780; *Jackson's Oxford Journal*, 28 October 1780; and others.
9. *A History of the County of Middlesex*, vol. 2 (London: Victoria County History, 1911), 283–92.
10. C. J. Longman and Col. H. Walrond, *Archery* (London: Longmans & Co., 1894), ch. 12.
11. *Morning Post and Daily Advertiser*, 14 August 1789. "Jingling" was a game played in a restricted area, in which a man (in this case John Baker), wore a cap with bells on it, and ten others, blindfold, tried to catch him. The game lasted half an hour, and John Baker won it.
12. *Morning Post and Daily Advertiser*, 15 August 1789.
13. *Public Advertiser*, 15 August 1789.
14. Raymond Flower, *The Old Ship: A Prospect of Brighton* (Beckenham, Kent: Croom Helm Ltd., 1986), 61–63.
15. A hogshead contained fifty-four gallons (Imperial), so 8,640 pints of beer.
16. *Morning Post and Daily Advertiser*, 14 August 1789.
17. *Public Advertiser*, 20 August 1791.
18. W. Hylton Dyer Longstaffe, *The History and Antiquities of the Parish of Darlington in the Bishoprick* (London: J. Henry Parker, 1854), 310.
19. *St. James's Chronicle*, 18–21 July 1778.
20. *Reading Mercury, Oxford Gazette and General Advertiser*, 9 May 1796.
21. *Sporting Magazine*, June 1794, pp. 174–75.
22. *Reading Mercury, Oxford Gazette and General Advertiser*, 20 June 1796.
23. *Sporting Magazine*, May 1797, pp. 97–98.
24. *Jackson's Oxford Journal*, 30 April 1791.
25. *Sporting Magazine*, April 1799, pp. 25–26.
26. *Reading Mercury*, 1 May 1780.
27. *Morning Post, and Daily Advertiser*, 16 August 1788.
28. *World*, 23 August 1787.

29. *Edinburgh Advertiser*, 12–16 April 1776.
30. *Public Advertiser*, 11 April 1776.
31. *World*, 31 August 1791.
32. *Morning Post, and Daily Advertiser*, 2 September 1791.
33. *Morning Herald, and Daily Advertiser*, 14 August 1781.
34. *Norfolk Chronicle, or the Norwich Gazette*, 10 June 1786.
35. The ambassador wanted "between two and three hundred thousand guineas"; see letter from Thomas Jefferson to John Jay, 23 May 1786, accessed 30 October 2021, https://founders.archives.gov/documents/Jefferson/01-09-02-0465.
36. Thomas Hughes, *The Scouring of the White Horse* (Cambridge: Macmillan & Co. 1859), 92–93; *Reading Mercury and Oxford Gazette*, 1 May 1780.
37. *Sporting Magazine*, June 1798, pp. 164–65; and *Reading Mercury and Oxford Gazette*, 1 May 1780.
38. *Sporting Magazine*, August 1799.
39. *Cumberland Pacquet, and Ware's Whitehaven Advertiser*, 3 September 1782.
40. *Country Journal: or the Craftsman*, 22 December 1733.
41. *Longitude Found: The Story of Harrison's Clocks*, Royal Museums Greenwich online, accessed 23 August 2022, https://www.rmg.co.uk/stories/topics/harrisons-clocks-longitude-problem.
42. Peter Radford and A. J. Ward-Smith, "British Running Performances in the Long Eighteenth Century," *Journal of Sports Sciences* 21 (2003): 429–38.
43. A. E. Kennelly, "An Approximate Law of Fatigue in the Speeds of Racing Animals," *Proceedings of the American Academy of Arts and Sciences* 42 (1906): 275–331.
44. Peter Radford, "The Time a Land Forgot," *Observer*, 2 May 2004.
45. Peter Radford, "Performance Trends of British Male Elite Runners since 1700," in *Pedestrianism*, ed. Dave Day (Crewe, Cheshire: Manchester Metropolitan University Sport and Leisure History, 2014), 1–33.
46. Andrew Huxtable, ed., *A Statistical History of UK Track and Field Athletics* (London: National Union of Track and Field Statisticians, 1990), 52; Eric L. Cowe, *Early Women's Athletics: Statistics and History*, vol. 1 (Keighley, W. Yorkshire: Self-published, 1999).

9. The Power to Endure

1. *Star*, 13 October 1801.
2. Ibid.
3. *Morning Chronicle*, 23 July 1802.
4. Richard Turnbull, *Reviving the Heart: The Story of the Eighteenth-Century Revival* (Oxford: Lion Hudson, 2012), 13.
5. *Sporting Magazine*, July 1810, pp. 166–71, 209–14, 261–65.
6. Ibid., October 1810, pp. 18–25.
7. The "King's Serjeant" was counsel for the defense.
8. *Sporting Magazine*, October 1810, p. 19.
9. Ibid., September 1810, pp. 211–12.
10. *Kentish Chronicle*, 15 July 1808.
11. *Town and Country Magazine*, December 1773; *London Chronicle*, 14–17 June 1788; *Morning Post and Daily Advertiser*, 30 August 1788; Wilson, *Wonderful Characters*, 49–51.

12. *Morning Post and Daily Advertiser*, 6 and 11 September 1790.
13. *Morning Chronicle*, 12 October 1815; *St. James's Chronicle*, 12–14 October 1815; *Kentish Chronicle*, 13 October 1815; *Liverpool Mercury*, 13 October 1815; *Carlisle Journal*, 21 October 1815; *Northampton Mercury*, 21 October 1815; *Tyne Mercury; or Northumberland, Durham and Cumberland Gazette*, 24 October 1815.
14. *Monthly Miscellany, or Gentleman and Lady's Complete Magazine*, vol. 1 (1774): 26.
15. Edward Hall, *Miss Weeton: Journal of a Governess*, vol. 1, 1807–11 (London: Oxford University Press, 1938), 168.
16. Dorothy Wordsworth, *Journals*, vol. 2, ed. William Knight (London: Macmillan, 1904), 157.
17. *Westminster Journal and Old British Spy*, 31 January–7 February 1807.
18. Kennelly, "Approximate Law of Fatigue."
19. *London Chronicle*, 31 January–2 February 1807.
20. Radford, *Celebrated Captain Barclay*.
21. *National Register*, 21 April 1811.
22. Carolly Erickson, *Our Tempestuous Day: A History of Regency England* (London: Robson Books, 1996), 106–7.
23. Anon. [William Oxberry], *Pancratia, or a History of Pugilism. Containing a Full Account of Every Battle of Note from the Time of Broughton and Slack, down to the Present Day* (London: W. Hildyard, 1812).
24. Pierce Egan [One of The Fancy], *Boxiana; or Sketches of Ancient and Modern Pugilism; from the Days of the Renowned Broughton and Slack to the Heroes of the Present Milling Æra!* (London: G. Smeeton, 1812).
25. Walter Thom [Author of the History of Aberdeen], *Pedestrianism; or an Account of the Performances of Celebrated Pedestrians during the Last and Present Century* (Aberdeen: D. Chalmers and Co., 1813).
26. Egan, *Boxiana*, 181.
27. *Sportsman's Magazine; or Chronicle of Games and Pastimes*, February 1824, pp. 50–52
28. Edward Wedlake Brayley and Francis Philip Stephanoff, *Popular Pastimes, Being a Selection of Picturesque Representations of the Customs & Amusements of Great Britain, in Ancient and Modern Times* (London: Sherwood, Neely, and Jones, 1816), 121.
29. Ibid.
30. *Staffordshire Advertiser*, 9 July 1814.
31. George Wilson, *A Sketch of the Life of George Wilson, the Blackheath Pedestrian; Who Undertook to Walk One Thousand Miles in Twenty Days!* (London: Printed for the author by Hay and Turner, 1815), 49–94.
32. E.g., John Ashton, *The History of Gambling in England* (London: Duckworth & Co., 1898).
33. Wilson, *Sketch of the Life*, 20.
34. Anon., *Memoirs of the Life and Exploits of George Wilson, The Celebrated Pedestrian* (London: Dean & Munday [1815]), 19.
35. *Courier*, 25 September 1815; *National Register*, 1 October 1815.
36. *Courier*, 11 December 1815.
37. *Star*, 29 August 1817.
38. *Edinburgh Advertiser*, 7 November 1817.
39. *Morning Advertiser*, 20 September 1823.
40. William Lennox, *Pictures of Sporting Life and Character*, vol. I (London: Hurst and Blackett, 1860), 114, quoting the *Leamington Spa Courier*, May 1820, but otherwise undated.

41. Ibid.
42. *Annals of Sporting*, October 1822, p. 256.
43. *Patriot, or Carlisle and Cumberland Advertiser*, 29 November 1817.
44. *Annals of Sporting*, August 1823, p. 123.
45. *Leeds Intelligencer*, 21 August 1823; *Annals of Sporting*, August 1823, p. 207.
46. *Morning Advertiser*, 27 August 1823.
47. *Annals of Sporting*, October 1823, p. 277.
48. *Bell's Weekly Dispatch*, 5 January 1823.
49. *Caledonian Mercury*, 13 November 1823.

10. Moral Meddling, Cant, and Sheer Humbug

1. Birnie, a Scot, was police magistrate at Bow Street.
2. "Robin Redbreasts" was a nickname given to the Bow Street Runners because of the scarlet waistcoats they wore under their gray greatcoats.
3. "Lifting operatives" were pickpockets.
4. *Morning Advertiser*, 23 August 1828.
5. Pierce Egan, *The Finish to the Adventures of Tom, Jerry, and Logic, in their Pursuits through Life in and out of London. Illustrations by Robert Cruikshank* (London: J. S. Virtue, undated [1828]). See J. C. Reid, *Bucks and Bruisers: Pierce Egan and Regency England* (London: Routledge & Kegan Paul, 1971).
6. *Sussex Advertiser*, 10 April 1826.
7. *Salisbury and Winchester Journal*, 8 May 1826.
8. *Bell's Life in London and Sporting Chronicle*, 14 May 1826.
9. *Sun*, 6 May 1826.
10. *Belfast Commercial Chronicle*, 13 May 1826.
11. *Annals of Sporting*, September 1826, pp. 305–6.
12. Ibid., 306.
13. Ibid.
14. Ibid., 307.
15. Ibid.
16. *Morning Advertiser*, 23 August 1833.
17. *Banbury Guardian, and General Advertiser*, Thursday, 28 December 1843.
18. *Nottingham Review and General Advertiser for the Midland Counties*, 4 June 1830.
19. *Illustrated London News*, 25 November 1843.
20. John Mayhall, *The Annals of York, Leeds, Bradford, Halifax, Doncaster, Barnsley, Wakefield, Dewsbury, Huddersfield, Heighley, and Other Places in the County of York* (Leeds: Joseph Johnson, 1860), 501.
21. Ibid.
22. *Kentish Chronicle*, 6 April 1830.
23. Ibid., 13 April 1830.
24. E.g., *Kentish Gazette*, 3 January 1865.
25. *Daily Herald*, 21 May 1945.
26. Peter Radford, "Robert Dover's Olimpick Games," *Journal of Olympic History* 22, no. 2 (2014): 40–49.
27. G. D. Bourne, "Inaugural Address," *Transactions of the Bristol and Gloucestershire Archæological Society* 9, no. 12 (1884–85).

28. These included Vyvyan, *Cotswold Games;* G. M. Stratton, "Reminiscences of the Dover's Hill Sports," in *Evesham Journal Notes & Queries, 1906–8,* ed. E. A. B. Barnard (Evesham, UK: n.p., 1911), 166–69; C. R. Ashbee, *The Last Records of a Cotswold Community: The Weston Subedge Field Account Book* (Chipping Campden: Essex House Press, 1904); and Whitfield, *Robert Dover and the Cotswold Games,* 78–80.
29. C. J. Bearman, "The Ending of the Cotswold Games," *Transactions of the Bristol and Gloucestershire Archaeological Society* 114 (1996): 131–41.
30. Ibid.

11. The Runners

1. Brayley, Stephanoff, *Popular Pastimes,* 26. This section of the text is headed "Skimmington," but Stephanoff's image that accompanies it is labeled *The Shrew.*
2. Grose, *Lexicon Balatronicum.*
3. Alessandro Arcangeli, "Exercise for Women," in *Sport and Physical Exercise in Early Modern Culture,* eds. Rebekka von Mallinckrodt and Angela Schattner (London: Routledge, 2016), 147–63.
4. Things did become disorderly in 1791. See *Jackson's Oxford Journal,* 30 April 1791.
5. E.g., *Annals of Sporting,* August 1822.
6. *Post-Man, and the Historical Account, &c.,* 25–27 June 1719.
7. *Daily Journal,* 15 May 1732.
8. *Pope's Bath Chronicle,* 12 July 1764.
9. *Trewman's Exeter Flying Post,* 3 July 1806.
10. Longstaffe, *History and Antiquities of the Parish of Darlington,* 310.
11. *Morning Herald, and Daily Advertiser,* 14 August 1781.
12. *Morning Post,* 4 October 1808.
13. *Sun,* 13 September 1802.
14. *Sporting Magazine, or, Monthly Calendar,* May 1797, p. 97.
15. *St. James's Chronicle,* 14–16 March 1805.
16. *Morning Advertiser,* 9 June 1806.
17. *Kentish Gazette,* 22 May 1807.
18. *Salisbury and Winchester Journal,* Monday, 8 August 1808.
19. Grose, *Lexicon Balatronicum.*
20. As it did in 1667 when Pepys's four young maids ran against each other on a bowling green "with much pleasure." Pepys, *Diary,* 14 April 1667.
21. *Star,* 13 October 1801.
22. *Morning Chronicle,* 23 July 1802.
23. *Morning Herald,* 14 August 1781.
24. *Lloyd's Evening Post,* 13–15 October 1773.
25. *Norfolk Chronicle,* 10 June 1786.
26. *Caledonian Mercury,* 14 November 1726.
27. Duchess Maria of Württemberg was Maria Wirtemberska, 1768–1854; see *Caledonian Mercury,* 6 October 1798.
28. Elizabeth Ham, *Elizabeth Ham by Herself,* ed. Eric Gill (London: Faber & Faber [1945]), 46.
29. *Sporting Magazine,* June 1798, pp. 164–65.
30. *Morning Post,* 21 July 1821.
31. *Cambridge Chronicle and Journal,* 20 July 1821.

32. See Darby's wife (1711) in Nicholas Blundell, *The Great Diurnal of Nicholas Blundell*, vol. 1: 1702–11, ed. J. J. Bagley (Liverpool: Record Society of Lancashire and Cheshire, [1968]), 33; and Robert Burns's Racer Jess in "The Holy Fair" (1775).

12. Women Tennis Players, Team Players, Fighters, and Jockeys

1. Alfred Bedford, "Women at Cricket," *Cricketer* 8, no. 10 (July 9 1927): 301; Nancy Joy, *Maiden Over: A Short History of Women's Cricket and a Diary of the 1948–49 Test Tour to Australia* (London: Sporting Handbooks Limited, 1950); Rachel Heyhoe Flint and Netta Rheinberg, *Fair Play: The Story of Women's Cricket* (London: Angus & Robertson, 1976); Kathleen E. McCrone, *Playing the Game: Sport and the Physical Emancipation of English Women, 1870–1914* (Lexington: University Press of Kentucky, 1988); Catriona M. Parratt, *More than Mere Amusement: Working-Class Women's Leisure in England, 1750–1914* (Boston: Northeastern University Press, 2001); Betty Rizzo, "Equivocations of Gender and Rank: Eighteenth-Century Sporting Women," *Eighteenth Century Life* 26, no. 1 (Winter 2002): 70–93; Isabelle Duncan, *Skirting the Boundary. A History of Women's Cricket* (London: Robson Press, 2013); and Rafaelle Nicholson, *Ladies and Lords: A History of Women's Cricket in Britain* (Oxford: Peter Lang, 2019).
2. Malissa Smith, *A History of Women's Boxing* (Lanham, MD: Rowman & Littlefield, 2014); L. A. Jennings, *She's a Knockout: A History of Women's Fighting Sports* (Lanham, MD: Rowman & Littlefield, 2015).
3. Paul Creswick, ed., *Bruising Peg: Pages from the Journal of Margaret Molloy, 1768–9* (London: Downey & Co., 1898). Newspapers did make reference to Bruising Peg in 1768 (see *Public Advertiser*, 22 June 1768), but little is known of her. See also Anna Freeman, *The Fair Fight* (London: Weidenfeld & Nicolson, 2014).
4. See Jennings, *She's a Knockout*, 21–24.
5. *Daily Advertiser*, 26 August 1742.
6. Timothy J. McCann, ed., *Sussex Cricket in the Eighteenth Century* (Lewes, East Sussex: Sussex Record Society, 2004), lviii–lix.
7. In St. Michael's churchyard in Coventry a grave carries the following inscription: "To the memory of Mr John Parkes, a native of this city. He was a man of mild disposition, a gladiator by profession; who after having fought 350 battles, in the principal parts of Europe, with honour and applause, at length quitted the stage, sheathed his sword, and with Christian resignation, submitted to the Grand Victor, in the 52nd year of his age. Anno 1733." See also Castle, *Schools and Masters of Fence*, 205.
8. *Daily Post*, 16 June 1730.
9. *Daily Advertiser*, 11 July 1747.
10. Ibid., 15 July 1747.
11. *Reading Mercury, and Oxford Gazette*, Monday, 6 July 1772.
12. *Sporting Magazine*, June 1793, p. 180.
13. *Lincoln, Rutland, and Stamford Mercury*, 21 June 1793; *Ipswich Journal*, 22 June 1793; *Hampshire Chronicle, and Portsmouth and Chichester Journal*, 24 June 1793; and *Derby Mercury*, 27 June 1793.
14. *Times*, 20 June 1793.
15. *Annals of Sporting*, October 1822, p. 253.
16. *Weekly Journal, or, The British Gazetteer*, 1 October 1726.

17. *Daily Post*, 7 July 1728.
18. Ibid., 16 June 1730.
19. Charles Williams, *The Boxing Baroness*, etching published by S. W. Fores, 1819, which appeared in the *Bon Ton* magazine, March 1819.
20. "The Truth about Lady Barrymore, the Boxing Baroness," All Things Georgian (blog), accessed August 25, 2022, https://georgianera.wordpress.com/2015/03/03/the-truth-about-lady-barrymore-the-boxing-baroness.

13. The Tennis Players

1. Strutt, *Glig-Gamena Angel-Deod*, 94; J. M. Heathcote, C. G. Heathcote, E. O. P.-Bouverie, and A. C. Ainger, *Tennis: Lawn Tennis: Rackets: Fives* (London: Longman's, Green, 1890), 15; Marshall, *Annals of Tennis*, 5.
2. *Gazetteer and New Daily Advertiser*, 21 May 1767; *Ipswich Journal*, 23 May 1767; *Derby Mercury*, 29 May 1767.
3. *Jackson's Oxford Journal*, 27 February 1768; *Caledonian Mercury*, 2 March 1768.
4. E.g., 19 May, 5:03 a.m.; 20 May, 5:02 a.m.; 21 May, 5:00 a.m.; 22 May, 4:59 a.m.; 23 May, 4:58 a.m.
5. *Derby Mercury*, 14 August 1752.
6. Scale drawing of St. James's Street Tennis Court, Royal Institute of British Architects (1700; copy, 1829), accessed 30 October 2021, https://www.ribapix.com/Measured-drawing-of-james-street-covered-tennis-court-near-Haymarket-London-plan-and-interior-elevation_RIBA68593.html.
7. *Newcastle Courant*, 19–26 December 1741; *Derby Mercury*, 14 August 1752.
8. Slack vs. Stevenson, June 1760; Maggs vs. Stevenson, July 1761.
9. A tiger vs. two bull dogs, December 1761.
10. *Gazetteer and New Daily Advertiser*, 14 March 1767
11. *Derby Mercury*, 17 April 1767.
12. *Derby Mercury*, 17 April 1767; *London Evening-Post*, 9 April 1767; *Stamford Mercury*, 16 April 1767.
13. *Public Advertiser*, 11 April 1767; *Lloyd's Evening Post*, 17–20 April 1767.
14. Ibid.
15. *London Evening-Post*, 28–30 April 1767.
16. Ibid.
17. *Derby Mercury*, 1 May 1767.
18. Rizzo, "Equivocations of Gender and Rank," 70–93.
19. *Daily Advertiser*, 17 July 1767.
20. *St. James's Chronicle or British Evening Post*, 23–25 February 1768.
21. *Jackson's Oxford Journal*, 27 February 1768.
22. *Caledonian Mercury*, 12 March 1768.
23. *Derby Mercury*, 8 May; 24 April; 1 May 1767.
24. *Jackson's Oxford Journal*, 2 May 1767.
25. Ibid., 14 May 1763.
26. Jeremy Potter, *Tennis and Oxford* (Oxford: Oxford Unicorn Press, 1994), 82–83.
27. David Best and Brian Rich, *Disturb'd with Chaces* (Oxford: Ronaldson Publications, 2009), 13.

28. Louis-Claude Bruyset de Manevieux, *Treatise on the Royal Game of Tennis* (1783), trans. Richard Travers (Romsey, Victoria, Australia: Historical Publications, 2004), 80.
29. Marshall, *Annals of Tennis*, 42.
30. De Manevieux, *Treatise*, 80.
31. Ibid.
32. *Public Advertiser*, 25 February 1768.
33. *St. James Chronicle or British Evening Post*, 23–25 February 1768; *Public Advertiser*, 25 February 1768; *Jackson's Oxford Journal*, 27 February 1768; *Caledonian Mercury*, 2 March 1768.
34. *St. James's Chronicle*, 23 February 1768.
35. *Jackson's Oxford Journal*, 27 February 1768.
36. *Caledonian Mercury*, 2 March 1768.
37. *Virginia Gazette*, 12 May 1768.
38. *Public Advertiser*, 11 April 1767.
39. *Stamford Mercury*, 16 April 1767.
40. *Gazetteer and New Daily Advertiser*, 7 March 1768.
41. Marshall, *Annals of Tennis*, 42.
42. Louis-Claude Bruyset de Manevieux was born in Lyon in 1738 and was shot by firing squad in 1793 during the French Revolution (de Manevieux, *Treatise*. xi). He described himself as "an amateur" of tennis but "not of the first rank." M. De Man***eux [Louis-Claude Bruyset de Manevieux], *Traité sur la connoissance du royal jeu de paume* (Neuchatel: n.p., 1783), j, 160–63. Translations from the French edition of de Manevieux's *Traité* are mine.
43. Ibid., 165.
44. De Manevieux, *Treatise*, 81; Peter Radford, "Women as Athletes in Early Modern Britain," *Early Modern Women: An Interdisciplinary Journal* 10, no.2 (Spring 2016): 42–64.
45. De Manevieux, *Treatise*, 165.
46. Ibid., 80.
47. *Caledonian Mercury*, 4 March 1790.
48. Ibid.
49. Sarah Gristwood, *Perdita: Royal Mistress, Writer, Romantic* (London: Bantam Press, 2005), 176–77.
50. Joseph Foster, *Alumni Oxoniensis: The Members of the University of Oxford, 1715–1886 A.D.* (Oxford: Parker and Co., [1888]), 115.
51. Radford, *Celebrated Captain Barclay*, 22.
52. *Dublin Evening Post*, 8 April 1790.

14. The Team Players

1. Thomas Crosfield, *The Diary of Thomas Crosfield*, ed. Frederick S. Boas (London: Oxford University Press, 1935), 63.
2. Blundell, *Great Diurnal*, vol. 2, 1712–19, ed. J. J. Bagley (Liverpool: Record Society of Lancashire and Cheshire, n.d.), 134.
3. *London Magazine, or, Gentleman's Monthly Intelligencer*, vol. 2, 1733, p. 637.
4. Sir Philip Sidney, "A Dialogue Betweene Two Shepherds," in *The Complete Poems of Sir Philip Sidney*, ed. Alexander B. Grosart (London: Robson & Sons, 1873), 207–11.
5. Cram, Forgeng, and Johnston, *Francis Willughby's Book of Games*.

6. *Ipswich Journal*, Saturday, 23 February 1740.
7. *Scots Magazine*, 1 July 1744, price one shilling.
8. Scriblerus Maximus [James Love], *Cricket: An Heroic Poem* (London: For W. Bickerton at the *Gazette*, [1744]).
9. Neville Cardus, foreword to Joy, *Short History of Women's Cricket*, 9–10.
10. Three generations earlier would have been 1677; see Alan Tomlinson, *Dictionary of Sport Sciences* (Oxford: Oxford University Press, 2010), 489.
11. *Derby Mercury*, 9–16 August 1745.
12. *Newcastle Courant*, 10 August 1745.
13. *Stamford Mercury*, 15 August 1745.
14. *Sussex Weekly Advertiser, or Lewes Journal*, 13 July 1747.
15. Earl of March, *A Duke and His Friends*, 34–35.
16. Ibid., 191–92.
17. Earl of March [Charles Henry Gordon-Lennox Richmond], *Records of the Old Charlton Hunt* (London: Elkin Mathews, 1910).
18. Ibid., 107.
19. Ibid., 6.
20. George Dacre Wolfertstan, *A New and Revised Guide Book, with Map, to Midhurst, and Neighbourhood, Giving a Full Account of the Ruins at Cowdray, the Charlton Hunt, etc.* (Self-published, 1884), 98–99.
21. John Marshall, *The Duke Who Was Cricket* (London: Frederick Muller, 1961), 93–96.
22. Earl of March, *Records of the Old Charlton Hunt*, 1.
23. *London Evening Post*, 4–7 September 1742.
24. *Daily Advertiser*, 30 August 1742.
25. McCann, *Sussex Cricket in the Eighteenth Century*, 19.
26. Ibid., 12.
27. Ibid., 34–35.
28. *Daily Advertiser*, 15 July 1747.
29. *General Advertiser*, 11 July 1747.
30. Buckley, *Fresh Light on Eighteenth-Century Cricket*, 242–43.
31. *Salisbury and Winchester Journal*, 14 August 1775; *Sussex Advertiser*, 11 August 1823; *Sussex Weekly Advertiser or Lewes Journal*, 18 August 1756; *Reading Mercury, and Oxford Gazette*, 6 July 1772.
32. C. R. Leslie and Tom Taylor, *The Life and Times of Joshua Reynolds*, vol. 1 (London: John Murray, 1865), 247.
33. Van der Kiste, *George III's Children*, 15–16.
34. Marples, *Six Royal Sisters*, 13.
35. Abbé le Blanc, *Letters on the English and French Nations*, 1:265.
36. Ibid, 18.
37. David Underdown, *Start of Play: Cricket and Culture in Eighteenth-Century England* (London: Allen Lane, 2000), 142–44.
38. *Drewry's Derby Mercury*, 22 August 1777.
39. *St. James's Chronicle*, 12 June 1777.
40. *Morning Post and Daily Advertiser*, 22 January 1778.
41. Phillis Cunnington and Alan Mansfield, *English Costume for Sports and Recreation: From the Sixteenth to the Nineteenth Centuries* (New York: Barnes & Noble, Inc., 1969).

42. "Square-leg" and "fine-leg" are names given to specific fielders' positions alongside, and behind the batter.
43. Nyren, *John Nyren's The Cricketers of My Time* (1998 ed.), 125–27.
44. Ibid., 57.
45. *Morning Post and Daily Advertiser*, 22 January 1778.
46. *Stamford Mercury*, 18 September 1777.
47. John Collett, *Miss Wicket and Miss Trigger*, mezzotint, from the original picture in the possession of Carington Bowles, printed and sold by Carington Bowes, London, 1778. Forty-five notches would have been the highest recorded score by any woman cricketer up to that date.
48. John Collett, *Miss Tipapin Going For All Nine*, mezzotint, from the original picture in the possession of Carington Bowles, printed and sold by Carington Bowes, London, 1779.
49. Robin Simon and Alistair Smart, *The Art of Cricket* (London: Secker & Warburg, 1983), 24, 20.
50. Nyren, *John Nyren's The Cricketers of My Time* (1998 ed.), 115.
51. *Sporting Magazine*, April 1803, pp. 13–14.
52. Giovanna Francesca Antonia Zanerini (1753–1801), who was known as Giovanna Baccelli.
53. Underdown, *Start of Play*, 146–48.
54. Simon and Smart, *Art of Cricket*, 24.

15. Cricketers of All Ages and Sizes

1. *Bath and Bristol Chronicle*, 1 June 1769.
2. *Gazetteer and New Daily Advertiser*, 15 June 1768.
3. *Reading Mercury, Oxford Gazette, Newbury Herald, and Berks County Paper*, 13 April 1895.
4. H. T. Waghorne, *Cricket Scores, Notes, &c. From 1730–1773* (Edinburgh: William Blackwood and Sons, 1899), 64.
5. Ibid., 64–65.
6. John Goulstone, *Hambledon: The Men and the Myths* (Cambridge: Roger Heavens, 2001), 42.
7. E. V. Lucas, ed., *The Hambledon Men, Being a New Edition of John Nyren's "Young Cricketer's Tutor,"* (Oxford: Clarendon Press, 1907), 101–2.
8. Ashley Mote, *The Glory Days of Cricket: The Extraordinary Story of Broadhalfpenny Down* (London: Robson Books, 1997), 92–99.
9. Hugh Barty-King, *Quilt Winders and Pod Shavers: The History of Cricket Bat and Ball Manufacture* (London: Macdonald and Jane's Publishers, 1979), 30–33.
10. Lucas, *Hambledon Men*, 82.
11. *Reading Mercury, and Oxford Gazette*, 6 July 1772.
12. *Salisbury and Winchester Journal*, 14 August 1775.
13. *Stamford Mercury*, 21 June 1793. The *Sporting Magazine* reported that the challenge was any village in their own *county* (June 1793, p. 180), whilst *The Times* reported it as being to *All England* (20 June 1793).
14. *Leicester Journal*, 13 August 1785.
15. *Ipswich Journal*, 2 September 1780.
16. *Kentish Gazette*, 4 December 1792.

17. *Morning Post*, 5 October 1811.
18. *Hampshire Telegraph and Sussex Chronicle; or, Portsmouth and Chichester Advertiser*, 14 October 1811.
19. *Cheltenham Chronicle, and Gloucestershire General Advertiser*, 10 October 1811.
20. *Hampshire Telegraph and Sussex Chronicle; or, Portsmouth and Chichester Advertiser*, 14 October 1811.
21. *Morning Post*, 5 October 1811.
22. *Cheltenham Chronicle, and Gloucestershire General Advertiser*, 10 October 1811.
23. Ibid.
24. *Morning Post*, 5 October 1811.
25. *Cheltenham Chronicle, and Gloucestershire General Advertiser*, 10 October 1811.
26. *Salisbury Journal*, 23 September 1765.
27. *Sussex Weekly Advertiser, or Lewes Journal*, 18 August 1756.
28. *Salisbury and Winchester Journal*, 14 August 1775.
29. *Bath Chronicle*, 16 October 1777.
30. *Reading Mercury and Oxford Gazette*, 21 July 1788.
31. *Sporting Magazine*, vol. 9, January 1797, p. 202.
32. *Royal Cornwall Gazette, Falmouth Packet, and Plymouth Journal*, 14 August 1819.
33. *British Press*, 2 August 1819.
34. *Hampshire Chronicle and Courier*, 6 August 1821.
35. *Carlisle Patriot*, 14 August 1819.
36. *Suffolk Chronicle; or Weekly General Advertiser & County Express*, 18 September 1819.
37. *The Fancy*, vol.1, no. 10 (1821): 240.
38. *Morning Post*, Tuesday, 3 September 1822.
39. *Annals of Sporting*, October 1822, p. 253.
40. *Salisbury and Winchester Journal*, 9 September 1822.
41. Buckley, *Fresh Light on Pre-Victorian Cricket*, 68, 112; and *Hampshire Chronicle and Courier*, Monday, 2 September 1822.
42. *Annals of Sporting*, October 1822, p. 253.
43. *Cumberland Pacquet, and Ware's Whitehaven Advertiser*, Monday, 9 September 1822.
44. *Morning Post*, 12 June 1823.
45. *Nottingham Review and General Advertiser for the Midland Counties*, 4 October 1833.
46. *Dorset County Chronicle, and Somersetshire Gazette*, 8 August 1850.
47. *Cambridge Independent Press*, 22 September 1860.
48. Virginia Woolf, *Three Guineas* (London: Hogarth Press, 1938), 235–55, 265.
49. *Daily News*, 22 August 1867.
50. *Hampshire Telegraph*, 24 August 1867.
51. *Hampshire Advertiser*, 31 August 1867; *Hampshire Chronicle*, 31 August 1867.
52. *Hampshire Advertiser*, 31 August 1867.
53. *Northern Standard, Monaghan, Cavan, and Tyrone Advertiser*, 31 August 1867.
54. *Portsmouth Times and Naval Gazette*, 7 September 1867.

16. The Fighters

1. Pepys, *Diary*, Monday, 27 May 1667, accessed 30 October 2021, https://www.pepysdiary.com/diary/1667/05/27/.

2. J. E. B. Mayor, ed., *Cambridge under Queen Anne: Illustrated by Memoir of Ambrose Bonwicke and Diaries of Francis Burman and Zacharias Conrad von Uffenbach* (London: G. Bell & Sons, 1911), 363–64.
3. Zacharias Conrad von Uffenbach, *London in 1710, from the travels of Zacharias Conrad von Uffenbach*, eds. W. H. Quarrell and Margaret Mare (London: Faber & Faber, [1934]), 90–93.
4. Quoted from "a diurnal print, in the month of June, 1722," by the *Stamford Mercury*, 3 January 1800; within a few days repeated by the *Sussex Weekly Advertiser*, 6 January 1800, and the *Chester Courant*, 7 January 1800. The *Liverpool Mercury*, 8 June 1832, quotes the same item and gives its source as "from the *London Journal* of June 1722." No earlier copy of the item has been found.
5. [Arthur L. Hayward], *The Lives of the Most Remarkable Criminals, etc.*, vol. 2 (London: Printed and sold by John Applebee, 1732), 139–43.
6. Clinch, *Marylebone and St. Pancras*, 41.
7. *Daily Post*, 4 August 1724.
8. James Peller Malcolm, *Anecdotes of the Manners and Customs of London During the Eighteenth Century*, vol. 2 (London: Longman, Hurst, Rees, and Orme, 1810), 164–65.
9. *Mist's Weekly Journal*, 20 November 1725.
10. *London Journal*, 30 October 1725.
11. *Weekly Journal, or The British Gazetteer*, 1 October 1726.
12. Ibid., 28 January 1727.
13. Malcolm, *Anecdotes of the Manners and Customs*, 2:170–71.
14. *Daily Post*, 7 July 1728.
15. *Grub Street Journal*, 27 May 1731.
16. Suassure, *Foreign View of England*, 277–82.
17. Gill, Mac Colley, and Sutton were all prizefighters who fought at Figg's Amphitheatre. See *Daily Journal*, 29 June 1730, and 22 June 1730.
18. *Daily Post*, 16 June 1730.
19. Ibid., 27 May 1730.
20. *Daily Journal*, 24 June 1730.
21. Ibid., 13 July 1730.
22. Ibid., 20 July 1730.
23. George Perkins Marsh, *Lectures on the English Language* (New York: C. Scribner's and Sons, 1885), 70.
24. *Daily Journal*, 27 August 1730.
25. *Grub Street Journal*, 27 August 1730.
26. *Farley's Bristol Newspaper*, 31 May 1729.
27. *Daily Journal*, 18 September 1731.
28. See, for example, James Boswell, entry for Monday, 13 June 1763, in *Boswell's London Journal: 1762–1763* (London: Wm Heinemann Ltd., 1950), 270.
29. *Public Advertiser*, 6 July 1768.
30. Ibid., 28 June 1768.
31. *Clerkenwell News: and General Advertiser*, 27 May 1863.
32. Creswick, *Bruising Peg*.
33. Dennis Brailsford, *Bareknuckles: A Social History of Prize-Fighting* (Cambridge: Lutterworth Press, 1988), 10–14.

34. Egan, *Boxiana*, 206–7.
35. Anon. [William Oxberry?], *Pancratia, Or, a History of Pugilism* (London: Printed by W. Hildyard, 1812), 113 [wrongly printed as 116].
36. John Jackson was champion of the prize ring from 1795 and was later known as "Gentleman" Jackson.
37. Daniel Mendoza was champion of the prize ring 1792–95.
38. Anon., *Pancratia*, 120.

17. The Equestrians

1. The Greek translates: "A noble woman is a treasury of virtue." Thanks to J. L. Ainsworth for the translation. See *Idler*, No. 6, Saturday, 20 May 1758.
2. *Annals of Sporting*, August 1822, pp. 98–99; *Times*, 21 July 1809.
3. Letter dictated by Mary Queen of Scots to Elizabeth, 15 March 1566 (SP 52/12 f77v), National Archives online, accessed 30 October 2021, https://www.nationalarchives.gov.uk/education/resources/elizabeth-monarchy/letter-dictated-by-mary-queen-of-scots/; William Turnbull, *Letters of Mary Stuart, Queen of Scotland* (London: Charles Dolman, 1845), 163–64.
4. *London Post*, 23–25 April 1701.
5. Reuben Percy and Sholto Percy, *The Percy Anecdotes* (London: Frederick Warne and Co., 1868), 855.
6. *Newcastle Courant*, 18 July 1724.
7. Royal East Kent, 3rd Foot Regiment.
8. *Derby Mercury*, 4–11 July 1746.
9. Royal Collection Trust online, accessed 30 October 2021, https://www.rct.uk/collection/400997/laetitia-lady-lade-d-1825. There is some doubt about whether Alicia Thornton was actually married to Col. Thomas Thornton. See Andrew Ward, *Horse-Racing's Strangest Races* (London: Robson Books, 2000); and Pierce Egan, *Book of Sports, and Mirror of Life: Embracing the Turf, the Chase, the Ring, and the Stage* (London: Thomas Tegg, 1832), 133. However, she signed herself "Alicia Thornton" in her letter to the *York Herald* (1804), so that is how I will refer to her. She was born Alicia Meynell or perhaps Alicia Massingham.
10. William Flint was her sister's husband. Thornville was later renamed Black Strap.
11. Pierce Egan, *Sporting Anecdotes, Original and Selected* (London: Sherwood, Neely & Jones 1820), 159.
12. Tim Cox, "Portrait of Alicia Thornton," *Autumn Newsletter* (2016), National Horseracing Museum, Newmarket.
13. Egan, *Book of Sports*, 129–35.
14. *York Herald and County Advertiser*, 11 August 1804.
15. Ibid., 25 August 1804.
16. Egan, *Book of Sports*, 131.
17. Nevill, *Light Come, Light Go*, 416–17.
18. *Chester Chronicle*, 31 August 1804.
19. *Morning Post*, 28 August 1804.
20. See *Knavesmire Jockeyship or too far North for the knowing ones*, British Museum Registration Number 1935,0522.8.147, accessed 25 August 2022, https://www.britishmuseum.org/collection/object/P_1935-0522-8-147.

21. *Morning Post*, 1 September 1804.
22. *Evening Mail*, 24 August 1804.
23. Egan, *Sporting Anecdotes*, 209–20.
24. Things are seldom as simple as they appear, and it seems that Colonel Thornton had not paid his betting dues when Alicia lost, claiming that it was a "nominal thing," intended to attract people to the racecourse. See Nevill, *Light Come, Light Go*, 416; and John Stevens, *Knavesmire: York's Great Racecourse and its Stories* (London: Pelham Books, 1984), 73–80.
25. I.e., 210 Imperial gallons (252 US gallons; 954.8 litres).
26. Egan, *Sporting Anecdotes*, 197–99.
27. *Sporting Magazine*, vol. 25, January 1805, p. 171.
28. Measuring worth, Purchasing Power of British Pounds, accessed 3 September 2022, https://www.measuringworth.com/.
29. *Courier*, Monday 26 August 1805.
30. Ward, *Horse-Racing's Strangest Races*, 3–5.

18. Women Athletes

1. John Gay, *The Fan. A Poem. In Three Books. To which is added, The Smock-Race at Finglas* (London: J. Tonson, 1714).
2. *Ipswich Journal*, 5 October 1728.
3. *Covent-Garden Journal*, 23 May 1752.
4. *Kentish Gazette*, 19–22 July 1769.
5. Cordeaux and Merry, "Port Meadow Races," 55–65. He also described what the men wore when they raced, though he did not see them either.
6. Suassure, *Foreign View of England*, 293.
7. Earlier in the day girls had raced for ribbons.
8. William Holland, *Paupers and Pig Killers: The Diary of William Holland, a Somerset Parson 1799–1818* (Gloucester: Alan Sutton Publishing, 1984), 35.
9. *Sporting Magazine*, July 1810, p. 169.
10. Ibid., October 1810, pp. 19, 25.
11. *British Press*, 2 September 1808.
12. *Read's Weekly Journal, or, British-Gazetteer*, 2 August 1735.
13. *St. James's Evening-Post*, 23 October 1725.
14. See McCrone, *Playing the Game*, 216–46; Guttmann, *Women's Sport*, 90.
15. *St. James's Evening Post*, 23 October 1725; *Daily Advertiser*, 18 June 1731; *Daily Post-Boy*, 16 August 1735; *Penny London Morning Advertiser*, 8–11 June 1744.
16. *Weekly Journal, or The British Gazetteer*, 1 October 1726; Malcolm, *Anecdotes of the Manners and Customs of London*, 170–71.
17. Saussure, *Foreign View of England*, 277–82.
18. *Cheltenham Chronicle, and Gloucestershire General Advertiser*, 10 October 1811.
19. *Morning Post*, 12 June 1823.
20. See the speech bubble in Charles Williams's engraving *Knavesmire Jockeyship*, British Museum Registration Number 1935,0522.8.147.
21. *Hampshire Chronicle, and Portsmouth and Chichester Journal*, 26 June 1786.
22. *Royal Cornwall Gazette, Falmouth Packet, and Plymouth Journal*, 14 August 1819.
23. *Hampshire Chronicle and Courier*, 6 August 1821.

24. *Hampshire Telegraph and Sussex Chronicle; or, Portsmouth and Chichester Advertiser*, 14 October 1811.
25. *Royal Cornwall Gazette, Falmouth Packet, and Plymouth Journal*, 14 August 1819.
26. *Hampshire Chronicle and Courier*, 6 August 1821.
27. Saussure, *Foreign View of England*, 277–82.
28. *Ipswich Journal*, 22 March 1755.
29. *Daily Advertiser*, 9 August 1751.
30. *Public Advertiser*, 28 June 1768.

BIBLIOGRAPHY

Primary Sources

Letters, Diaries, Ballads, Poems, and Plays

Abbé le Blanc, Jean-Bernard. *Letters on the English and French Nations*. 2 vols. London: J. Brindley, R. Francklin, C. Davis, and J. Hodges, 1747.

Anon. "Stool-ball, or the Easter Diversion." *London Magazine, or, Gentleman's Monthly Intelligencer*, vol. 2, 1733.

Anon. *The Virgin race; Or, York-shires Glory*. London: Printed for I[ohn]. Wright, I[ohn]. Clark, W[illiam] Thackeray, and T[homas] Passinger, [1682].

Ballantyne, Archibald. *Voltaire's Visit to England, 1726–1729*. London: John Murray, 1919.

Bliss, Philip. *Reliquiae Hearnianae*. Vol. 2: *The Remains of Thomas Hearne M.A., of Edmund Hall, Being Extracts from His Ms Diaries, Collected with a Few Notes*. London: John Russell Smith, 1869.

Blundell, Nicholas. *The Great Diurnal of Nicholas Blundell*. Vol. 1: 1702–11. Edited by J. J. Bagley. Liverpool: Record Society of Lancashire and Cheshire, [1968].

Blundell, Nicholas. *The Great Diurnal of Nicholas Blundell*. Vol. 2: 1712–19. Edited by J. J. Bagley. Liverpool: Record Society of Lancashire and Cheshire [1970].

Boswell, James. *Boswell's London Journal: 1762–1763*. London: Wm Heinemann, 1950.

Butler, Samuel. *Hudibras*. London: Printed by T.N. for John Martyn and Henry Herringman, 1674.

Carter, Elizabeth. *Memoirs of the Life of Mrs. Elizabeth Carter*. Edited by Montague Pennington. London: F. C. and J. Rivington, 1808.

Carter, Elizabeth. *A Series of Letters between Mrs. Elizabeth Carter and Miss Catherine Talbot from the Year 1741 to 1770*. Vol. 1. Edited by Montague Pennington. London: F. C. and J. Rivington, 1809.

Combe, William, with illustrations by Thomas Rowlandson. *Doctor Syntax's Three Tours; in Search of the Picturesque, Consolation and a Wife*. London: R. Ackerman's Repository of Arts, 1812.

Combe, William, with etchings by Thomas Rowlandson. *The Second Tour of Doctor Syntax in Search of Consolation*. London: R. Ackermann, 1820.

Crosfield, Thomas. *The Diary of Thomas Crosfield*. Edited by Frederick S. Boas. London: Oxford University Press, 1935.

Gay, John. *The Fan. A Poem. In Three Books. To which is added, The Smock-Race at Finglas*. London: J. Tonson, 1714.

Gay, John. *The Shepherd's Week, Pastoral IV, Thursday; or the Spell*. London: Ferd. Burleigh, 1714.

Grose, [Francis]. *Lexicon Balatronicum: A Dictionary of Buckish Slang, Universal Wit, and Pickpocket Eloquence*. London: C. Chappel, 1811.

Ham, Elizabeth. *Elizabeth Ham by Herself*. Edited by Eric Gill. London: Faber & Faber [1945].

Heywood, Oliver. *His Autobiography, Diaries, Anecdote and Event Books*. Vol. 2. Edited by J. Horsfall Turner. Brighouse: A. B. Bayes, 1881.

Holland, William. *Paupers and Pig Killers: The Diary of William Holland, a Somerset Parson, 1799–1818*. Gloucester: Alan Sutton Publishing, 1984.

Pepys, Samuel. *The Diary of Samuel Pepys*. https://www.pepysdiary.com.

Pollnitz, Charles-Lewis de. *The Memoirs of Charles-Lewis, baron de Pollnitz: Being the Observations he Made in his Late Travels from Prussia thro' Germany, Italy, France, Flanders, Holland, England, etc., in letters to a Friend*. Vol. 2. London: Daniel Browne, 1739.

Scriblerus Maximus [James Love]. *Cricket. An Heroic Poem*. London: For W. Bickerton at the Gazette, [1744].

Sidney, Sir Philip. *A Dialogue Betweene Two Shepherds*. In *The Complete Poems of Sir Philip Sidney*, edited by Alexander B. Grosart. London: Robson & Sons, 1873.

Somervile, William. *Hobbinol, or The Rural Games*. Illustrations by Charlton Nesbitt and John Thurston. London: William Bulmer and Co., for R. Ackermann, 1813.

Somervile, William. *Hobbinol, or The Rural Games. A Burlesque Poem*. Edinburgh: Printed for J. Stagg [1740].

Somervile, William. *Hobbinol, or The Rural Games*. 4th ed. Etchings by Anthony Walker. London: G. Hawkins, 1757.

Suassure, César de. *A Foreign View of England in the Reign of George I and George II: The Letters of Monsieur César de Suassure to His Family*. Translated and edited by Madame Van Muyden. London: John Murray, 1902.

Suffolk, Henrietta. *Letters to and from Henrietta, Countess of Suffolk, and Her Second Husband, The Hon. George Berkley: From 1712 to 1767*. Vol. 1. London: John Murray, 1824.

Turnbull, William. *Letters of Mary Stuart, Queen of Scotland*. London: Charles Dolman, 1845.

Uffenbach, Zacharias Conrad von. *London in 1710, from the travels of Zacharias Conrad von Uffenbach*. Edited by W. H. Quarrell and Margaret Mare. London: Faber & Faber [1934].

Voltaire. *Lettres Philosophique* [1730]. In *Oeuvres Complètes de Voltair*, edited by Louis Moland, vol. 22. Paris: Garnier, 1877–85.

Ward, James. *The Smock-Race, at Finglas*. London: Jacob Tonson, 1714.

Woodforde, James. *The Diary of a Country Parson, 1758–1781*. Vol. 1. Edited by J. Beresford. London: Oxford University Press, 1924.

Wordsworth, Dorothy. *Journals*. Vol. 2. Edited by William Knight. London: Macmillan, 1904.

Books

Anon. *Memoirs of the Life and Exploits of George Wilson, The Celebrated Pedestrian*. London: Dean & Munday [1815].

Anon.[William Oxberry?]. *Pancratia, or a History of Pugilism. Containing a Full Account of Every Battle of Note from the Time of Broughton and Slack, down to the Present Day*. London: W. Hildyard, 1812.

Bruyset de Manevieux, Louis-Claude. *Treatise on the Royal Game of Tennis* [1783]. Translated by Richard Travers. Romsey, Victoria, Australia: Historical Publications, 2004.

Brayley, Edward Wedlake, and Francis Philip Stephanoff. *Popular Pastimes, Being a Selection of Picturesque Representations of the Customs & Amusements of Great Britain, in Ancient and Modern Times*. London: Sherwood, Neely, and Jones, 1816.

Brome, James. *Travels over England, Scotland, and Wales*. 2nd ed., "With Large Additions." London: printed for Rob. Gosling, 1707.

Burney, Frances. *Evelina, or The History of a Young Lady's Entrance into the World*. London: T. Lowndes, 1778.

Burney, Frances. *Evelina, or The History of a Young Lady's Entrance into the World*. Edited by Margaret Anne Doody. London: Penguin, 1994.

Charles I. *The King's Majesty's Declaration to His Subjects, Concerning Lawful Sports to be Used*. London: Robert Barker, 1633. Reissue of James I, *The King's Majesty's Declaration to His Subjects, Concerning Lawful Sports to be Used*. London: Bonham Norton and John Bill, 1618.

Charles II. *Articles ordered by his Majestie to be observed by all persons that put in horses to run for the Plate, the new Round-heate at Newmarkett, set out the 16th day of October [1664], in the 17th year of our Soveraign Lord King Charles II. Which Plate is to be rid for yearly, the seconde Thursday in October, for ever*. Reprinted in *Newmarket: Its Sport and Personalities*, by Frank Siltzer. London: Cassell and Co., 1923.

Cram, David, Jeffrey L Forgeng, and Dorothy Johnston, eds. *Francis Willughby's Book of Games: A Seventeenth-Century Treatise on Sports, Games and Pastimes*. Aldershot, Hants.: Ashgate Publishing, 2003 [1662–72].

Defoe, Daniel [A Gentleman]. *A Tour Thro' the Whole Island of Great Britain*. London: G. Strahan, W. Mears, R. Francklin, S. Chapman, R. Stagg, and J. Graves, 1724.

Egan, Pierce. *Book of Sports, and Mirror of Life: Embracing the Turf, the Chase, the Ring, and the Stage*. London: Thomas Tegg, 1832.

Egan, Pierce [One of the Fancy]. *Boxiana; or Sketches of Ancient and Modern Pugilism; from the Days of the Renowned Broughton and Slack to the Heroes of the Present Milling Æra!* London: G. Smeeton, 1812.

Egan, Pierce. *The Finish to the Adventures of Tom, Jerry, and Logic, in their Pursuits through Life in and out of London*. Illustrations by Robert Cruikshank. London: J. S. Virtue, undated [1828].

Egan, Pierce [An Amateur Sportsman]. *Sporting Anecdotes, Original and Select: Including Characteristic Sketches of Eminent Persons Who Have Appeared on the Turf*. London: Albion Press, 1804.

Egan, Pierce. *Sporting Anecdotes, Original and Selected: Including Numerous Characteristic Portraits of Persons in Every Walk of Life*. London: Sherwood, Jones, and Co., 1825.

Glover, Stephen, and Thomas Noble. *The History, Gazetteer, and Directory of the County of Derby Drawn Up from Actual Observation, and from the Best Authorities; Containing a Variety of Geological, Mineralogical, Commercial, and Statistical Information*. London: Longman and Co., 1839.

Godfrey, John. *A Treatise Upon the Useful Science of Defence*. London: Printed by T. Gardner, 1741.

Goldsmith, Oliver. *The Vicar of Wakefield*. London: F. Newbery, 1766.

[Graves, Richard]. *The Spiritual Quixote: or, the Summer's Ramble of Mr. Geoffrey Wildgoose*. London: J. Dodsley, 1773.

Hasted, Edward. *The History and Topographical Survey of the County of Kent*. 2nd ed., vol 6. Canterbury: Printed by W. Bristow, 1798.

[Hayward, Arthur L.]. *The Lives of the Most Remarkable Criminals, etc*. Vol. 2. London: Printed and sold by John Applebee, 1732.

Hibbert, Christopher. *George IV, Prince of Wales, 1762–1811*. London: Longman, 1972.
James I of England. *The King's Majesty's Declaration to his Subjects, Concerning Lawful Sports to be used*. London: Printed by Bonham Norton, 1618. In *Social England Illustrated: A Collection of Seventeenth-Century Tracts*, edited by Andrew Lang. New York: Cooper Square Publishers, 1964.
Johnson, Samuel. *A Dictionary of the English Language*. London: J. and P. Knapton, 1755.
Kennett, White. *Parochial Antiquities Attempted in the History of Ambroseden, Bicester and other Adjacent Parts in the Counties of Oxford and Bucks*. Oxford: At the Theatre, 1695. New ed., vol 2. Oxford: Clarendon Press, 1818.
Lords Assembled in Parliament. *An Additionall ORDINANCE OF THE LORDS and COMMONS Assembled in Parliament: Concerning the dayes of Recreation, allowed unto Schollars, Apprentices and other Servants*. London: Printed for John Wright, 1647.
Malcolm, James Peller. *Anecdotes of the Manners and Customs of London during the Eighteenth Century*. Vol. 2. London: Longman, Hurst, Rees, and Orme, 1810.
Misson, Henri. *Memoires et Observations Faites par un Voyageur en Angleterre*. La Haye: Henri van Bulderen, 1698.
Misson, Henri. *M. Misson's Memoirs and Observations in His Travels over England*. Translated by Mr. Ozell. London: D. Browne, and others, 1719.
Pausanias. *Description of Greece*. Perseus Digital Library. Accessed 28 August 2022.
Pick, William. *The Turf Register, and Sportsman & Breeder's Stud-Book*. Vol. 1. Selby, Yorkshire: Printed by A. Bartholoman, 1803.
Plutarch. *The Parallel Lives: The Life of Lycurgus*. Perseus Digital Library. Accessed 28 August 2022.
Raithby, John, ed. *An Act against deceitfull disorderly and excessive Gameing* [1664]. In *Statutes of the Realm*. Vol. 5: 1628–80. London: G. Eyre and A. Strahan, 1819.
[Shirley, John] J.S. *The Accomplished Ladies Rich Closet of Rarities: or the Ingenious Gentlewoman and Servant Maids Delightful Companion*. 2nd ed. London: Printed by W.W. for Nicholas Boddington, 1687.
Sinclair, Sir John. *The Statistical Account of Scotland*. 21 vols. Edinburgh: William Creech, 1791–99.
Sinclair, Sir John. *The Code of Health and Longevity*. Vol. 2. Edinburgh: Arch. Constable, 1807.
Smollett, Tobias [Author of Roderick Random.] *The Adventures of Ferdinand Count Fathom*. Dublin: R. Main, 1753.
Stow, John. *A survay of London, contayning the originall, antiquity, increase, moderne estate, and description of that citie*. London: J. Wolfe, 1598.
Strutt, Joseph. *Glig-Gamena Angel-Deod. Or, the Sports and Pastimes of the People of England*. London: J. White, 1801.
Thom, Walter [Author of the History of Aberdeen]. *Pedestrianism: Or an Account of the Performances of Celebrated Pedestrians during the Last and Present Century*. Aberdeen: D. Chalmers and Co., 1813.
Tissot, Samuel Auguste David. *Advice to the people in general, with regard to their health: but more particularly calculated for those, who, by their distance from regular physicians, or other very experienced practitioners, are the most unlikely to be seasonably provided with the best advice and assistance* [1763]. Translated by J. Kirkpatrick. London: Printed for T. Becket and P. A. de Hondt, 1765.
Tranquillus, C. Suetonius. *The Lives of the Twelve Caesars—The Life of Domitian*. Accessed 7 October 2022. https://www.gutenberg.org/files/6400/6400-h/6400-h.htm.

Tusser, Thomas. *Redivivus being part of Mr. Thomas Tusser's Five hundred points of husbandrie: To which are added notes and observations explaining many obsolete terms*. London: Printed by J. Morphew, 1710.

Waghorne, H. T. *Cricket Scores, Notes, &c., from 1730–1773*. Edinburgh: William Blackwood and Sons, 1899.

Walbancke, Mat[hewe]. *Annalia Dubrensia. Upon the Yeerly Celebration of Mr Robert Dovers Olimpick Games Upon Cotswold-Hills*. London: Printed by Robert Raworth, 1636.

Wilson, George. *A Sketch of the Life of George Wilson, the Blackheath Pedestrian: Who Undertook to Walk One Thousand Miles in Twenty Days!* London: Printed for the author by Hay and Turner, 1815.

Wilson, G. H. *Wonderful Characters*. London: J. Barr and Co., 1842.

Newspapers and Other Periodicals

Aberdeen Journal, 7 October 1765.
Adams's Weekly Courant, 21 September 1790.
Annual Register or a View of the History, Politics, and Literature for the Year 1794 (London: F.C. & J. Rivington, 1808).
Annals of Sporting, August 1822; October 1822; August 1823; October 1823; September 1826; January 1827, July 1827.
Athletic News, 12 December 1921.
Atlas, 22 November 1829.
Banbury Guardian, and General Advertiser, 28 December 1843.
Bath and Bristol Chronicle, 1 June 1769.
Bath Chronicle (see also *Pope's Bath Chronicle*), 16 October 1777.
Belfast Commercial Chronicle, 13 May 1826.
Bell's Life in London and Sporting Chronicle, 14 May 1826.
Bell's Weekly Dispatch, 5 January 1823.
Bristol Mercury, Monday 28 May 1827.
British Press, 2 September 1808; 2 August 1819.
Caledonian Mercury, 24 September 1724; 19 October 1724; 1 November 1725; 14 November 1726; 21 January 1731; 8 August 1735; 21 August 1735; 30 September 1765; 2 March 1768; 12 March 1768; 4 March 1790; 24 August 1792; 6 October 1798; 13 November 1823.
Cambridge Chronicle and Journal, 20 July 1821.
Cambridge Independent Press, 22 September 1860.
Carlisle Journal, 21 October 1815.
Carlisle Patriot, 14 August 1819.
Cheltenham Chronicle, and Gloucestershire General Advertiser, 10 October 1811.
Chester Chronicle, 31 August 1804.
Chester Courant, 7 January 1800.
Clerkenwell New and General Advertiser, 27 May 1863.
Country Journal, or the Craftsman, 15 September 1733; 6 October 1733; 22 December 1733.
Covent-Garden Journal, 23 May 1752.
Courier, 11 December 1815; 21 November 1829.
Craftsman; or, Saye's Weekly Journal, 18 September 1790.
Cumberland Pacquet, and Ware's Whitehaven Advertiser, 3 September 1782; 3 September 1822.

Daily Advertiser, 18 June 1731; 11 October 1733; 16 September 1740; 26 August 1742; 30 August 1742; 11 July 1747; 15 July 1747; 23 April 1751; 4 August 1755; 17 September 1756; 17 July 1767.

Daily Courant, 28 May 1712; 24 August 1713; 28 August 1713; 23 June 1714; 30 July 1716; 19 April 1720; 29 June 1724; 29 July 1724.

Daily Herald, 21 May 1945.

Daily Journal, 3 May 1726; 22 June 1730; 29 June 1730; 13 July 1730; 27 August 1730; 18 September 1731; 15 May 1732; 4 October 1733.

Daily News, 22 August 1867.

Daily Post, 1 August 1721; 29 August 1721; 4 August 1724; 6 August 1724; 7 July 1728; 5 June 1729; 10 September 1729; 27 May 1730; 16 June 1730; 19 September 1730.

Daily Post-Boy, 16 August 1735.

Derby Daily Telegraph, 6 August 1928.

Derby Mercury, 13 September 1733; 20 December 1733; 7 August 1735; 9–16 August 1745; 4–11 July 1746; 12–19 May 1749; 5–12 July 1751; 14 August 1752; 4 March 1757; 4 October 1765; 17 April 1767; 24 April 1767; 1 May 1767; 8 May 1767; 29 May 1767; 27 June 1793.

Dorset County Chronicle, and Somersetshire Gazette, 8 August 1850.

Drewry's Derby Mercury, 22 August 1777; 28 February–7 March 1782.

Dublin Courier, 18 June 1766.

Dublin Evening Post, 8 April 1790.

Edinburgh Advertiser, 12–16 April 1776; 7 November 1817.

Evening Mail, 24 August 1804.

Evening Post, 30 April 1720; 20 September 1722.

Evening Telegraph and Post [Dundee], 29 May 1937.

Fancy, 1, no. 10 [August] 1821.

Farley's Bristol Newspaper, 31 May 1729.

Faulkner's Dublin Journal, 16 June 1753.

Flying Postman, 22 April 1699.

Gazetteer and New Daily Advertiser, 26 September 1765; 14 March 1767; 21 May 1767; 7 March 1768; 15 June 1768.

General Advertiser, 11 July 1747.

Gentleman's Magazine, vol. 54, Part the First, 1784.

Gloucester Journal, 9 November 1736; 20 August 1904.

Grub Street Journal, 27 August 1730; 27 May 1731; 11 October 1733.

Hampshire Advertiser, 31 August 1867.

Hampshire Chronicle and Courier, 6 August 1821; 2 September 1822.

Hampshire Chronicle, and Portsmouth and Chichester Journal, 24 June 1793.

Hampshire Chronicle & Southampton Courier, 14 December 1829.

Hampshire Chronicle; Southampton and Isle of Wight Courier, 31 August 1867.

Hampshire Chronicle, or Winchester, Southampton, and Portsmouth Mercury, 18 July 1774.

Hampshire Telegraph, 24 August 1867; 14 October 1811.

Hampshire Telegraph and Sussex Chronicle; or, Portsmouth and Chichester Advertiser, 14 October 1811.

Idler, No. 6, 20 May 1758.

Illustrated London News, 25 November 1843.

Illustrated Police News, 22 December 1921.

Ipswich Gazette, 2 August 1735.

Ipswich Journal, 28 September 1765; 23 May 1767; 2 October 1773; 2 September 1780; 22 December 1787; 22 June 1793.

Ipswich-Journal, or, Weekly-Mercury, 23–30 October 1725; 16–23 July 1726; 5 October 1728; 8 September 1733; 10 October 1730.

Jackson's Oxford Journal, 14 May 1763; 28 September 1765; 2 May 1767; 27 February 1768; 20 December 1787; 28 October 1780; 30 April 1791.

Kentish Chronicle, 15 July 1808; 13 October 1815; 6 April 1830; 13 April 1830.

Kentish Gazette, 8–11 June 1768; 2–6 July 1768; 15–19 July 1769; 19–22 July 1769; 22–26 July 1769; 2–5 August 1769; 23–26 June 1770; 26–30 June 1770; 12–16 June 1773; 18–21 May 1774; 18–22 May 1776; 2 May 1788; 20 May 1788; 4 December 1792; 22 May 1807; 3 January 1865.

Kentish Post, or Canterbury News-Letter, 4–8 June 1726; 9–13 May 1730; 29 May-2 June 1731; 22–25 June 1743; 23–27 July 1748; 17–21 June 1749; 17–20 July 1751; 17–21 July 1756.

Leedes Intelligencer, 1 October 1765.

Leeds Intelligencer, 22 May 1781; 21 August 1823.

Leicester Journal, 13 August 1785.

Liverpool Echo, 28 August 1928.

Lloyd's Evening Post, 23–25 September 1765; 17–20 April 1767; 13–15 October 1773.

Lincoln, Rutland, and Stamford Mercury, 21 June 1793.

Liverpool Mercury, 13 October 1815; 8 June 1832.

London Chronicle, 14–17 June 1788; 31 January–2 February 1807.

London Chronicle, or Universal Advertiser, 3–5 March 1757.

London Courant, and Westminster Chronicle, 26 October 1780.

London Evening-Post, 30 April-3 May 1737; 25–28 June 1737; 4–7 September 1742; 8–10 July 1746; 24–26 Sept 1765; 28–30 April 1767.

London Gazette, 18–22 June 1696.

London Journal, 30 October 1725.

London Magazine, or, Gentleman's Monthly Intelligencer, vol. 2, 1733.

London Packet, 5–7 November 1827.

London Post, 23–25 April 1701.

Mail (Adelaide, Australia), 4 August 1928.

Maitland Daily Mercury, 8 August 1928.

Mist's Weekly Journal, 23 October 1725; 20 November 1725.

Monthly Miscellany, or Gentleman and Lady's Complete Magazine, vol. 1, 1774.

Morning Advertiser, 9 June 1806; 27 August 1823; 20 September 1823; 23 August 1828.

Morning Chronicle, 23 July 1802; 12 October 1815.

Morning Herald, and Daily Advertiser, 14 August 1781.

Morning Post, 28 August 1804; 4 October 1808; 5 October 1811; 21 July 1821; 3 September 1822; 12 June 1823; 26 November 1827.

Morning Post & Daily Advertiser, 22 January 1778; 16 August 1788; 30 August 1788; 14 August 1789; 15 August 1789; 6 September 1790; 11 September 1790; 2 September 1791.

Morning Post, Nottingham Review, and General Advertiser for the Midland Counties, 21 May 1830; 4 June 1830.

National Register, 1811.

Newcastle Courant, 9–11 February 1712; 15–18 October 1712; 18 July 1/24; 21 August 1731; 16 August 1735; 19–26 December 1741; 10 August 1745; 19 July 1746; 2–9 July 1748; 20 September 1828.

Norfolk Chronicle, or the Norwich Gazette, 10 June 1786; 17 October 182.
Northampton Mercury, 15 June 1747; 21 October 1815.
Northern Evening Mail, 11 August 1883.
Northern Standard, Monaghan, Cavan, and Tyrone Advertiser, 31 August 1867.
Nottingham Review and General Advertiser for the Midland Counties, 4 October 1833.
Oracle, 20 May 1749.
Oracle, Bell's New World, 15 August 1789.
Patriot, or Carlisle and Cumberland Advertiser, 29 November 1817.
Penny London Morning Advertiser, 8–11 June 1744; 24 June 1748.
Penny London Post, 8 October 1733.
Pope's Bath Chronicle (see also *Bath Chronicle*), 12 July 1764; 26 September 1765.
Portsmouth Times and Naval Gazette, 7 September 1867.
Post Boy, 4–7 June 1698; 28–30 March 1700; 24–26 April 1718.
Post Man, 27–29 July 1704; 19–22 August 1710; 9–12 September 1710; 18–24 August 1715; 8 July 1718; 25–27 June 1719.
Public Advertiser, 26 September 1765; 11 April 1767; 25 February 1768; 6 September 1771; 22 September 1774; 11 April 1776; 5 August 1789; 20 August 1791.
Reading Mercury, and Oxford Gazette, 6 July 1772; 27 June 1774; 1 May 1780; 21 July 1788.
Reading Mercury, Oxford Gazette, and General Advertiser, 9 May 1796; 20 June 1796.
Reading Mercury, Oxford Gazette, Newbury Herald, and Berks County Paper, 13 April 1895.
Read's Weekly Journal, or, British-Gazetteer, 2 August 1735.
Royal Cornwall Gazette, Falmouth Packet & Plymouth Journal, 14 August 1819.
Salisbury Journal, 15 July 1765; 23 September 1765; 30 September 1765.
Salisbury and Winchester Journal, 14 August 1775; 8 August 1808; 9 September 1822; 8 May 1826.
Scots Magazine, and Edinburgh Literary Miscellany, 1 July 1744; 1 October 1815.
Sheffield Weekly Telegraph, 25 July 1885.
Spectator, no. 161, 4 September 1711.
Sporting Magazine, November 1792; June 1793; March 1794; June 1794; January 1797; May 1797; June 1798; April 1799; August 1799; April 1803; January 1805; July 1810; September 1810; October 1810.
Sportsman's Magazine; or Chronicle of Games and Pastimes, February 1824.
Staffordshire Advertiser, 9 July 1814.
Stamford Mercury, 28 June 1716; 15 August 1745; 16 April 1767; 18 September 1777; 21 June 1793; 3 January 1800.
Star, 13 October 1801; 28 May 1806; 29 August 1817.
St James's Chronicle, or British Evening Post, 15–18 August 1767; 23–25 February 1768; 12- 14 June 1777; 18–21 July 1778; 14–16 March 1805; 12–14 October 1815.
St James's Evening-Post, 23 October 1725; 17 August 1745.
Suffolk Chronicle; or Weekly General Advertiser & County Express, 18 September 1819.
Sun, 13 September 1802; 6 May 1826; 27 January 1827.
Sussex Advertiser, 11 August 1823; 10 April 1826; 16 November 1829.
Sussex Weekly Advertiser, 13 July 1747; 18 August 1756; 6 January 1800.
Times, 20 June 1793; 20 June 1793; 21 July 1809.
Tipperary Free Press, 28 March 1827.
Town and Country Magazine, December 1773.
Trewman's Exeter Flying Post, 3 July 1806.

Tyne Mercury; or Northumberland, Durham, and Cumberland Gazette, 24 October 1815.
Virginia Gazette, 12 May 1768.
Weekly Journal, or, British Gazetteer, 29 September 1716; 9 September 1721; 1 October 1726; 28 January 1727.
Weekly Miscellany, 6 October 1733.
Westminster Journal and Old British Spy, 31 January–7 February 1807.
World, 23 August 1787; 31 August 1791.
York Herald and County Advertiser, 11 August 1804; 25 August 1804.

Secondary Sources

Alexander, David. "Prints after John Collet: Their Publishing History and a Chronological Checklist." *Eighteenth-Century Life* 26, no. 1 (Winter 2002): 136–46.

Anderson, Earl R. "Footnotes More Pedestrian than Sublime: A Historical Background for the Foot-race in Evelina and Humphry Clinker." *Eighteenth-Century Studies* 14, no. 1 (1980): 56–68.

Andrews, Kerri. *Wanderers—A History of Women Walking* (London: Reaktion Books, 2020).

Arcangeli, Alessandro. "Exercise for Women." In *Sport and Physical Exercise in Early Modern Culture,* edited by Rebekka von Mallinckrodt and Angela Schattner, 147–63. London: Routledge, 2016.

Armitage, John. *Man at Play: Nine Centuries of Pleasure Making* (London: Frederick Warne, 1977).

Ashbee, C. R. *The Last Records of a Cotswold Community: The Weston Subedge Field Account Book.* Chipping Campden: Essex House Press, 1904.

Ashton, John. *The History of Gambling in England.* London: Duckworth & Co., 1898.

Ashton, John. *Social Life in the Reign of Queen Anne, Taken from Original Sources.* London: Chatto & Windus, 1897.

Barringer, Judith M. "Atalanta as Model: The Hunter and the Hunted." *Classical Antiquity* 15, no. 1 (April 1996): 48–76.

Barty-King, Hugh. *Quilt Winders and Pod Shavers: The History of Cricket Bat and Ball Manufacture.* London: Macdonald and Jane's Publishers, 1979.

Bearman, C. J. "The Ending of the Cotswold Games." *Transactions of the Bristol and Gloucestershire Archaeological Society* 114 (1996): 131–41.

Bedford, Alfred. "Women at Cricket." *The Cricketer* 8, no. 10 (9 July 1927).

Best, David, and Brian Rich. *Disturb'd with Chaces.* Oxford: Ronaldson Publications, 2009.

Blakemore, Colin, and Sheila Jennett, eds. *The Oxford Companion to the Human Body.* Oxford: Oxford University Press, 2001.

Blundell, Sue, and Margaret Williamson, eds. *The Sacred and the Feminine in Ancient Greece.* London: Routledge, 1998.

Bourne, G. D. "Inaugural Address." In *Transactions of the Bristol and Gloucestershire Archæological Society* 9, no. 12 (1884–85).

Brailsford, Dennis. *Bareknuckles: A Social History of Prize-Fighting.* Cambridge: Lutterworth Press, 1988.

Brailsford, Dennis. *A Taste for Diversions: Sport in Georgian England.* Cambridge: Lutterworth Press, 1999.

Brand, Robert. *Observations on the Popular Antiquities of Great Britain.* Vol. 2. London: Henry G. Bohn, 1849.

Buckley, G. B. *Fresh Light on Eighteenth-Century Cricket*. Birmingham: Cotterell & Co., 1935.
Buckley, G. B. *Fresh Light on Pre-Victorian Cricket*. Birmingham: Cotterell & Co., 1937.
Castle, Egerton. *Schools and Masters of Fence*. London: Bell & Sons, 1885.
Chambers, Robert. *Domestic Annals of Scotland from the Reformation to the Revolution*. Edinburgh: W. & R. Chambers, 1859.
Christesen, Paul. "Whence 776? The Origin of the Date of the First Olympiad." *International Journal of the History of Sport* 26, no. 2 (2009): 161–82.
Clark, Isabelle. "The Gams of Hera: Myth and Ritual." In *The Sacred and the Feminine in Ancient Greece*, edited by Sue Blundell and Margaret Williamson. London: Routledge, 1998.
Clinch, George. *Marylebone and St. Pancras: Their History, Celebrities, Buildings, and Institutions*. London: Truslove & Shirley, 1890.
Cordeaux, E. H., and D. H. Merry. "Port Meadow Races." *Oxoniensia* 13(1948).
Cowe, Eric L. *Early Women's Athletics: Statistics and History*. Vol. 1. Keighley, Yorkshire: Self-published, 1999.
Cox, Tim. "Portrait of Alicia Thornton." Autumn newsletter of the National Horseracing Museum, Newmarket, 2016.
Creswick, Paul, ed. *Bruising Peg: Pages from the Journal of Margaret Molloy, 1768–9*. London: Downey & Co., 1898.
Crown, Patricia. "Sporting with Clothes: John Collet's Prints in the 1770s." *Eighteenth-Century Life* 26, no. 1 (Winter 2002): 119–35.
Cunnington, Phillis, and Alan Mansfield. *English Costume for Sports and Recreation: From the Sixteenth to the Nineteenth Centuries*. New York: Barnes & Noble, 1969.
Depping, Guillaume. *Wonders of Bodily Strength and Skill, in all Ages and all Countries*. Translated by Charles Russell. New York: Charles Scribner, 1871.
Dillon, Matthew. "Did Parthenoi Attend the Olympic Games? Girls and Women Competing, Spectating, and Carrying out Cult Roles at Greek Religious Festivals." *Hermes* 128, no. 4 (2000): 457–80.
Dowden, Ken. *Death of the Maiden: Girls' Initiation Rites in Greek Mythology*. London: Routledge, 1989.
Duncan, Isabelle. *Skirting the Boundary: A History of Women's Cricket*. London: Robson Press, 2013.
Endrei, Walter, and Lásló Zolnay. *Fun and Games in Old Europe*. Budapest: Corvina Kiadó, 1986.
Erickson, Carolly. *Our Tempestuous Day: A History of Regency England*. London: Robson Books, 1996.
Flint, Rachel Heyhoe, and Netta Rheinberg. *Fair Play: The Story of Women's Cricket*. London: Angus & Robertson, 1976.
Flower, Raymond. *The Old Ship: A Prospect of Brighton*. Beckenham, Kent: Croom Helm Ltd., 1986.
Foster, Joseph. *Alumni Oxoniensis: The Members of the University of Oxford, 1715–1886 A.D*. Oxford: Parker and Co. [1888].
Freeman, Anna. *The Fair Fight*. London: Weidenfeld & Nicolson, 2014.
Gardiner, E. Norman. *Athletics of the Ancient World*. Oxford: Clarendon Press, 1930.
Glanffrwd. *Plwyf Llanwyno: Yr Hen Amser, Yr Hen Bobl, A'r Hen Droion*. Pontypridd: Argraffwyd Gan David J. Hopkin, 1888. Portions translated into English by Peter Radford, at Athlos online, accessed 23 August 2022, https://athlos.co.uk/books/the-parish-of-llanwyno-extracts/.

Golden, Mark. *Sport and Society in Ancient Greece*. Cambridge: Cambridge University Press, 1998.
González, Kathleen Ann. *A Beautiful Woman in Venice*. Venice: Supernova, 2015.
Goulstone, John. *Hambledon: The Men and the Myths*. Cambridge: Roger Heavens, 2001.
Goulstone, John. *Smock Racing*. Erith, Kent: Published by the author, 2005.
Griffin, Emma. *England's Revelry: A History of Popular Sports and Pastimes, 1660–1830*. Oxford: Oxford University Press, 2005.
Gristwood, Sarah. *Perdita: Royal Mistress, Writer, Romantic*. London: Bantam Press, 2005.
Guttmann, Allen. *Women's Sport: A History*. New York: Columbia University Press, 1991.
Hall, Edward. *Miss Weeton: Journal of a Governess*. Vol. 1: 1807–11. London: Oxford University Press, 1938.
Hamilton, Richard. "Alkman and the Athenian Arkteia." *Hesperia* 58 (1989): 449–72.
Hardy, Thomas. *The Mayor of Casterbridge*. London: Smith Elder & Co., 1886.
Harland, John, and T. T. Wilkinson. *Lancashire Legends*. London: George Routledge and Sons, 1873.
Heathcote, J. M., C. G. Heathcote, E. O. P.-Bouverie, and A. C. Ainger. *Tennis: Lawn Tennis: Rackets: Fives*. London: Longman's, Green, 1890.
Hore, J. P. *The History of Newmarket, and the Annals of the Turf*. Vol. 2. London: A. H. Baily and Co., 1886.
Hughes, Thomas. *The Scouring of the White Horse*. Cambridge: Macmillan & Co. 1859.
Hutchinson, Horace G., ed. *Cricket*. London: G. Newnes, 1903.
Huxtable, Andrew, ed. *A Statistical History of UK Track and Field Athletics*. London: National Union of Track and Field Statisticians, 1990.
Jennings, L. A. *She's a Knockout: A History of Women's Fighting Sports*. Lanham, MD: Rowman & Littlefield, 2015.
Joy, Nancy. *Maiden Over: A Short History of Women's Cricket and a Diary of the 1948–49 Test Tour to Australia*. London: Sporting Handbooks Limited, 1950.
Kennelly, A. E. "An Approximate Law of Fatigue in the Speeds of Racing Animals." *Proceedings of the American Academy of Arts and Sciences* 42 (1906): 275–331.
Kotsonas, Antonis. "Sanctuaries, Temples, and Altars in Early Iron Age: A Chronological and Regional Accounting." In *Regional Stories: Towards a New Perception of the Early Greek World*, edited by A. M. Ainian, A. Alexandidou, and X. Charalambidou, 55–66. Volos: University of Thessaly Press, 2017.
Larson, Jennifer. *Ancient Greek Cults*. New York: Routledge, 2007.
Lennox, William. *Pictures of Sporting Life and Character*. Vol. 1. London: Hurst and Blackett, 1860.
Leslie, C. R., and Tom Taylor. *The Life and Times of Joshua Reynolds*. Vol. 1. London: John Murray, 1865.
Longman, C. J., and Col. H. Walrond. *Archery*. London: Longmans & Co, 1894.
Longstaffe, W. Hylton Dyer. *The History and Antiquities of the Parish of Darlington in the Bishoprick*. London: J. Henry Parker, 1854.
Lucas E. V., ed. *The Hambledon Men, Being a New Edition of John Nyren's "Young Cricketer's Tutor," Together with a Collection of Other Matter Drawn from Various Sources, All Bearing Upon the Greatest Batsmen and Bowlers before Round-Arm Came In*. Oxford: Clarendon Press, 1907.
Macintosh, Alison A., Ron Pinhasi, and Jay T. Stock. "Prehistoric Women's Manual Labour Exceeded that of Athletes through the First 5500 years of Farming in Central Europe." *Science Advances* 3, no. 11 (November 2017). https://www.science.org/doi/10.1126/sciadv.aao3893.

Mallinckrodt, Rebekka von. "Attractive or Repugnant? Foot Races in Eighteenth-Century Germany and Britain." In *The Allure of Sports in Western Culture,* edited by John Zilcosky and Marlo A. Burks. Toronto: University of Toronto Press, 2019.
March, Earl of [Charles Henry Gordon-Lennox Richmond]. *A Duke and His Friends: The Life and Letters of the Second Duke of Richmond.* London: Hutchinson & Co., 1911.
March, Earl of [Charles Henry Gordon-Lennox Richmond]. *Records of the Old Charlton Hunt.* London: Elkin Mathews, 1910.
Marples, Morris. *Six Royal Sisters: Daughters of George III.* London: Michael Joseph, 1969.
Marsh, George Perkins. *Lectures on the English Language.* New York: C. Scribner's and Sons, 1885.
Marshall, John. *The Duke Who Was Cricket.* London: Frederick Muller, 1961.
Marshall, Julian. *The Annals of Tennis.* London: The Field Office, 1878.
Matinatos, Nanno, and Robin Hägg, eds. *Greek Sanctuaries: New Perspectives.* London: Routledge, 1993.
Mayhall, John. *The Annals of York, Leeds, Bradford, Halifax, Doncaster, Barnsley, Wakefield, Dewsbury, Huddersfield, Heighley, and Other Places in the County of York.* Leeds: Joseph Johnson, 1860.
Mayor, Adrienne. *The Amazons: Lives and Legends of Warrior Women across the Ancient World.* Princeton, NJ: Princeton University Press, 2014.
Mayor, J. E. B., ed. *Cambridge under Queen Anne: Illustrated by Memoir of Ambrose Bonwicke and Diaries of Francis Burman and Zacharias Conrad von Uffenbach.* London: G. Bell & Sons, 1911.
McCann, Timothy J., ed. *Sussex Cricket in the Eighteenth Century.* Lewes, East Sussex: Sussex Record Society, 2004.
McCrone, Kathleen E. *Playing the Game: Sport and the Physical Emancipation of English Women, 1870–1914.* Lexington: University Press of Kentucky, 1988.
Miller, Stephen G. *Ancient Greek Athletics.* New Haven, CT: Yale University Press, 2004.
Mirón, Dolores. "The Heraia at Olympia: Gender and Peace." *American Journal of Ancient History,* New Series, vol. 3–4 (2007): 7–38.
Moretti, Luigi. *Iscrizioni Agonistiche Greche.* Rome: A. Signorelli, 1953.
Morgan, Catherine. "The Origins of Pan-Hellenism." In *Greek Sanctuaries: New Perspectives,* edited by Nanno Matinatos and Robin Hägg, 16–20. London: Routledge, 1993.
Morgan, Catherine. *Athletes and Oracles.* Cambridge: Cambridge University Press, 1990.
Mote, Ashley. *The Glory Days of Cricket: The Extraordinary Story of Broadhalfpenny Down.* London: Robson Books, 1997.
Nevill, Ralph. *Light Come, Light Go: Gambling, Gamesters, Wagers, the Turf.* London: Macmillan, 1909.
Nicholson, Rafaelle. *Ladies and Lords: A History of Women's Cricket in Britain.* Oxford: Peter Lang, 2019.
Nyren, John. *John Nyren's The Cricketers of My Time: The Original Version.* Edited by Ashley Mote. London: Robson Books, 1998.
Osborne, Carol A., and Fiona Skillen. *Women in Sports History.* London: Routledge, 2011.
Parratt, Catriona M. *More than Mere Amusement: Working-Class Women's Leisure in England, 1750–1914.* Boston: Northeastern University Press, 2001.
Percy, Reuben, and Sholto Percy. *The Percy Anecdotes.* London: Frederick Warne and Co., 1868.
Potter, Jeremy. *Tennis and Oxford.* Oxford: Oxford Unicorn Press, 1994.
Radford, Peter. *The Celebrated Captain Barclay: Sport, Money, and Fame in Regency Britain.* London: Headline Book Publishing, 2001.

Radford, Peter. "Escaping the Phillippedes Connection: Death, Injury, and Illness in Eighteenth-Century Sport in Britain." In *Sport and Health in History*, edited by Thierry Terret. Sankt Augustin: Academia Verlag, 1999.
Radford, Peter. "The Olympic Games in the Long Eighteenth Century." *Journal for Eighteenth-Century Studies* 35, no. 2 (2012): 161–84.
Radford, Peter. "Performance Trends of British Male Elite Runners Since 1700." In *Pedestrianism*, edited by Dave Day. Crewe, Cheshire: Manchester Metropolitan University Sport and Leisure History, 2014.
Radford, Peter. "Robert Dover's Olimpick Games." *Journal of Olympic History* 22, no. 2 (2014).
Radford, Peter. "The Time a Land Forgot." *The Observer*, 2 May 2004.
Radford, Peter. "Women as Athletes in Early Modern Britain." *Early Modern Women: An Interdisciplinary Journal* 10, no.2 (Spring 2016): 42–64.
Radford, Peter, and A. J. Ward-Smith. "British Running Performances in the Long Eighteenth Century." *Journal of Sports Sciences* 21 (2003): 429–38.
Reid, Heather L. "La parthenoseroica: Flavia Thalassiae i valori dell'atletica femminile." Paper presented at Essere Sempre Il Migliore, Concorsi e Gare Nella Napoli Antica, Naples, 15–17 May 2019.
Reid, J. C. *Bucks and Bruisers: Pierce Egan and Regency England*. London: Routledge & Kegan Paul, 1971.
Rizzo, Betty. "Equivocations of Gender and Rank: Eighteenth-Century Sporting Women." *Eighteenth-Century Life* 26, no. 1 (Winter 2002): 70–94.
Romano, David Gilman. "The Ancient Stadium: Athletes and Arete." *Ancient World* 7, no. 1(1983): 9–16.
Shemek, Deanna. *Ladies Errant: Wayward Women and Social Order in Early Modern Italy*. Durham, NC: Duke University Press, 1998.
Sherbo, Arthur. "Addenda to 'Footnotes More Pedestrian than Sublime.'" *Eighteenth-Century Studies* 14, no. 3 (1981): 313–16.
Sherman, Stuart. *Telling Time: Clocks, Diaries, and English Diurnal Form, 1660–1785*. Chicago: University of Chicago Press, 1996.
Siltzer, Frank. *Newmarket: Its Sport and Personalities*. London: Cassell and Co., 1923.
Simon, Robin, and Alistair Smart. *The Art of Cricket*. London: Secker & Warburg, 1983.
Smith, Malissa. *A History of Women's Boxing*. Lanham, MD: Rowman & Littlefield, 2014.
Spivey, Nigel. *The Ancient Olympic Games*. Oxford: Oxford University Press, 2004.
Stevens, John. *Knavesmire: York's Great Racecourse and Its Stories*. London: Pelham Books, 1984.
Stratton, G. M. Reminiscences of the Dover's Hill Sports." In *Evesham Journal Notes & Queries, 1906–8*, edited by E. A. B. Barnard, 166–69. Evesham, UK: n.p., 1911.
Swaddling, Judith. *The Ancient Olympic Games*. London: British Museum Press, 1999.
Tomlinson, Alan. *Dictionary of Sport Sciences*. Oxford: Oxford University Press, 2010.
Trexler, Richard. *Public Life in Renaissance Florence*. Ithaca, NY: Cornell University Press, 1980.
Turnbull, Richard. *Reviving the Heart: The Story of the Eighteenth-Century Revival*. Oxford: Lion Hudson, 2012.
Underdown, David. *Start of Play: Cricket and Culture in Eighteenth-Century England*. London: Allen Lane, 2000.
Van der Kiste, John. *George III's Children*. Stroud, UK: Sutton Publishing, 1992.
Victoria County History. *A History of the County of Middlesex*. Vol. 2. London: 1911.
Vyvyan, Edward R. *Cotswold Games, Annalia Dubrensia*. Cheltenham: Williams & Son, 1878.

Walkup, Newlyn. "Eratosthenes and the Mystery of the Stade: How Long is a Stade?" *Convergence,* August 2010.

Ward, Andrew. *Horse-Racing's Strangest Races.* London: Robson Books, 2000.

West, Allen B. "Notes on Achaean Prosopography and Chronology." *Classical Philology* 23, no.3 (July 1928): 258–69.

Whitfield, Christopher. *Robert Dover and the Cotswold Games: Annalia Dubrensia.* Evesham, UK: Henry Sotheran, 1962.

Williams, Jean. *A Contemporary History of Women's Sport: Part One, Sporting Women, 1850–1960.* London: Routledge, 2014.

Wilson, G. H. *Wonderful Characters: Comprising Memoirs and Anecdotes of the Most Remarkable Persons of Every Age and Nation.* London: J. Barr and Co., 1842.

Wolfertstan, George Dacre. *A New and Revised Guide Book, with Map, to Midhurst, and Neighbourhood, Giving a Full Account of the Ruins at Cowdray, the Charlton Hunt, etc.* Published by the author, 1884.

Woolf, Virginia. *Three Guineas.* London: Hogarth Press, 1938.

Wroth, Warwick. *The London Pleasure Gardens of the Eighteenth Century.* London: Macmillan, 1896.

Zilcosky, John, and Marlo A. Burks, eds. *The Allure of Sports in Western Culture.* Toronto: University of Toronto Press, 2019.

INDEX

Page numbers in italics refer figures.

Acton, Middlesex, 72–73, 74, 79–80
Adamites, 85
age, 46, 68, 90, 94, 97, 102, 107–8, 112, 121, 122, 127, 134, 136, 137, 144–45, 151, 161, 174, 201, 228
Alken, Henry Thomas, 33, 35, 79
Alresford, Essex, 206
Amazons, 12, 64–65, 200, 212, 216, 219, 227
Amelia, Princess, 188
Annalia Dubrensia, 18, 43, 62, 251n6
Anne, Queen, 68, 70, 224
Arcangeli, Alessandro, 152
archery, 18, 108–9
Artillery Ground, Finsbury, London, 99, 165–66, 181–87
Arundel, Sussex, 74, 254n12
ass racing. *See* jackass racing
Atalanta: later references to, 14, 130, 151, 246; myth and legend of, 5–6
Augusta, Princess, 108

Baccelli, la (Giovanna Zanerini), 194
backsword, 72, 73, 87, 210, 255n23
ballads, 24, 60, 239
Barclay Allardice, Robert (1732–1797), 122

Barclay Allardice, Captain Robert (1779–1854), 126, 132, 135, 147
barefooted, 14, 28, 58, 84, 85, 144, 161, 240–41
Barnes Common, Surrey, 121, 158
Barnet Common, Hertfordshire, 82, 84, 86, 101, 236, 239
Barry, Richard, Earl of Barrymore, 175–76
Basford, Nottinghamshire, 147
Bath, Somerset, 178
Battersea, Surrey, 114
bear-baiting, 210–11, 212–14, 218, 224
Beauworth, Hampshire, 205–6, 241
Belmore, Hampshire, 138
best-of-three, 26, 36–39, 86–87, 89–90, 93, 96–97, 102, 104, 107, 113, 115, 129, 154–55, 204, 241
Bethnal Green, London, 97
Berkshire, 61, 74, 90, 102, 112–13, 115, 138, 146
betting, 18, 30–31, 58–59, 69, 75, 82–83, 84, 90, 133, 155, 162, 173–74, 197–98, 202, 230, 246, 272
Bewick, Thomas, 33–34
Bible: King James version, 21; William Tyndale's translation, 20–21

{289}

Blackheath, Middlesex, 132–33
Blanc, Jean-Bernard, Abbé le, 14, 81, 188
Blanker-Koen, Fanny, 3
Blencogo, Cumberland, 103, 124
blockade of British trade, 121, 124
bloomers, 161, 239
Bodmin, Cornwall, 120, 157–58
bonnets. *See* clothing
Boughton Green, Northamptonshire, 90
Bourne, Lincolnshire, 74
Bow Street Runners, 113, 121, 140, 262n2
boxing, 3, 87, 109, 127, 164, 167, 211, 217–18, 224–26, 242
Bramley, Surrey, 180–82
Brentford, Middlesex, 61, 94, 158
Brighton, Sussex, 105–11, 159–60
Bristol, 89–90, 133, 223
Brome, James, 42–45, 47–48
Brome, Richard, 85
Buckinghamshire, 61, 138
Buckland, Kent, 207
Buckle, Francis, 232–33
bull-baiting, 210–11, 224
Bunel, Louise-Bonne, 170–74, 176
Burney, Frances, *Evelina*, 30–32
Burrell, Elizabeth Anne, 188
Bury Green, Sussex, 204
Bushey Heath, Hertfordshire, 101
Butler, Samuel, 64–65, 77
Butterfield, Susan (Dame, Lady), 67–68, 75, 228

Cambridgeshire, 74, 146
Capell, Elizabeth, Countess of Essex, 188
caps. *See* clothing
Carlisle, Countess of (Isabella Howard), 188
Carlisle, Cumberland, 97, 146
Carter, Elizabeth, 94–95
Castle Carey, Somerset, 96
Castle Douglas, Kirkcudbrightshire, 137–38

challenges, 68–69, 87, 137, 166, 198, 206–7, 211–18, 220–23, 228, 231–32
Chapel Row, Berkshire, 138
Chaple Heath, Buckinghamshire, 138
charivari. *See* skimmington ride
Charles I, King, 19, 41, 55
Charles II, King, 19, 37, 44, 55, 57, 84
Charlotte, Princess Royal, 108–9, 188
Charlotte, Queen, 108, 159
Charlton, Sussex, 182–86
Charlton Congress, 183–85
Chartism, 139
Chelsea, London, 87–88, 96, 135
chemise. *See* smock
Cheshire, 74, 83, 84, 86
Chichester, Sussex, 204–5, 240, 241
Chilgrove, Sussex, 182–86
Chilham, Kent, 40–45, 54, 148
church festivals: Christmas, 19; Easter, 19, 69, 115, 177; Hocktide, 43, 249n49; Michaelmas, 70; Shrovetide, 177–78; Whitsuntide, 18–19, 46, 112, 115–16, 124, 157
Church of England, 30, 43
civil war (English), 19, 44, 55, 59, 62, 65
Clapham Common, 69, 71, 74
class, 57–59, 121–22, 135, 142, 151
Clifton, York, 144
clothing, 236–41; bloomers, 161, 239; bonnets, 160, 199, 240–41; caps, 168, 204–5, 240–41; drawers, 49, 60, 82, 161, 174–75, 215, 225, 239; hats, 15, 53, 73, 75, 107–8, 114–15, 139, 153, 189–89, 226, 240; jackets, 110, 127, 172, 207, 215, 239–40; layering, 236; petticoats, 73–75, 76, 93, 101, 175, 200, 236–37, 239; ribbons, 24, 89, 96, 153, 162, 199, 200, 204–5, 207, 219, 240–41; shoes, 73, 82, 89, 240; stockings, 73–74, 82, 89, 117, 144, 215; trousers, 110, 174, 200–201, 207, 230, 239–40; undergarments, 238; waistcoats, 82, 161, 200–201, 239

cock-fighting, 36, 58, 68
Collett, John, 32–33, *33*, 35–39, 53, 142, 167–68, 189–91, *190*, 240
Cornwall, 61, 120, 157
cricket, 70, 82, 108, 109, 163–64, 180–209
Cromwell, Oliver, 19, 44, 55, 60–61, 64
crowds, 50, 90, 106–10, 204, 207
Cruikshank, Robert, 33, 141–42
cudgeling, 29, 36, 53, 70, 76, 92, 101, 129, 151
Cumberland, 103, 114, 117, 124, 146, 167
curling, 94, 179

dancing, 18, 29, 44, 59, 62, 92, 129, 132, 141, 173, 188, 205, 231, 242
Dareall, Lady, 231
Darlington, County Durham, 112
Datchet Common, Berkshire, 90, 153
Defoe, Daniel, 75–76
Deptford, Surrey, 103
Derby, 182, 198
Derby, Countess of (Elizabeth Stanley), 167, 188–89, 192, 194
Derbyshire, 83
Devon, 61
Devonshire, 121, 143
Didrikson, Mildred "Babe," 3
Digges, Sir Dudley, 4, 40–44, *41*, 50–52, 54, 148, 150, 156, 162, 252n11
dogs, 32, 37, 53, 58, 64, 97, 99, 185, 200–201, 202
Dorset, 61, 159
Dorset, Duke of (John Sackville), 188, 192
Dover, Robert, *Olimpick Games*, 18, 24, 30, 42–43, 55, 115, 148–49
drawers. *See* clothing
dress. *See* clothing
Durdham Downs, Bristol, 89–90
Durham, County, 74, 90–92, 112

Ealing Common, 73–74
Earl's Court, London, 96

Easter Monday. *See* church festivals
Eccles Wake, 77, 153
Edinburgh, 56–58, 135, 137
Egan, Pierce, 127–28, 141–42, 225, 231–33
Eglinton, Countess of (Jean [Jane] Lindsay), 188
Elizabeth I, Queen, 17, 65–66
Elstone Downs, Wiltshire, 204
Ely, Isle of, 74
Enfield, Middlesex, 74
Epping Forest, 71, 74
Epsom Downs, 74
Essex, 61, 67, 117, 121–22, 195, 206, 241
Essex, Countess of (Elizabeth Capell), 188
ethnicity: Black, 37, 87–88, 93, 94, 148, 151, 234; Roma, 28, 93, 151, 234
Evelina (Burney), 30–32
Exeter, 143, 222

fairs, horn, 75, 79, 80, 152
fatality, 97
Felley Green, Surrey, 204
fencing, 87, 109, 193, 223
Fiennes, Celia, 228
Fig(g), James (prize-fighter), 87–88, 211–23
Fig(g), John (publican), 87–88
Figg's amphitheatre, 87–88, 212–15
fighters. *See* boxing; prize-fighters
Finchley Common, 74, 101
Finglas, Ireland, 27–28, 74, 77
Fire of London (1666), 58
Flint, Rachel Heyhoe, 3
football, 1–3, 17, 29, 59, 108, 177–79, 235
Fordenbridge, Oxfordshire, 138
foreign visitors to England, observations of: Jean-Bernard, Abbé le Blanc (1737–44), 14, 81, 188; Thomas Platter (1499), 66, 78; Karl Ludwig von Pollnitz (1733), 85; César de Saussure (1725–30), 81, 218–19; Zacharias Conrad von Uffenbach (1710), 73, 81, 210; Voltaire (1726), 13–14, 81, 89

Fox-hunting, 92
Frederick, Duke of York, 108–12, 159, 175–76
Frederick Louis, Prince of Wales, 88, 188
French Revolution, 107, 120, 174, 266n42

Galen, 20
gambling. *See* betting
Gander Down, Hampshire, 205
Gawsworth Park, Cheshire, 74, 86
George I, King, 74
George II, King, 92–93; as Prince of Wales, 74, 92
George III, King, 105, 108, 115, 127, 160
George IV, King, 160; as Prince of Wales, 104–10
Gibb, Roberta "Bobbi," 3
Godmanchester, Cambridgeshire, 146
golf, 17, 59
Gosden Common, Guildford, Surrey, 180–82
Grandchamp, Gail, 3
Gray's Inn Road, London, 138
Gray's Meadow, Oxford, 102
Greenwich, 13–14, 75, 81, 89, 153
Greig, Dale, 3
Grose, Francis, 77, 154
Guildford, Surrey, 74, 180–81
gurning (a grinning competition), 114, 116–17, 140

Hackney Marshes, 73–74, 93, 97
Hall Garth, County Durham, 90–92
Hambledon, Surrey, 180–82
Hambledon Club (Hampshire), 196
Hammersmith, 73
Hampshire, 102, 138, 146, 195, 198, 203, 206
Hampton Court, 74, 92
Hardy, Thomas, 63
Harting Hill, Sussex, 195–96
hats. *See* clothing
health, 29, 58, 91, 92, 94–95, 177, 202, 231
Hendon, Middlesex, 115–16, 139–41

Hera, 7–9; temple of, 7–8, 10–11
Heraian Games, 5–10
Hertfordshire, 61, 74, 101, 114–15
Hobbinol (Somervile), 28–29, 33–35
Hoby, Leicestershire, 198
Hockley-in-the-Hole, London, 210
Hogarth, William, 34, 75–76
Holland (fabric), 61, 154, 215. *See also* smock
Holland smock. *See* smock: Holland
horn fair, 75, 79–80, 152
horse racing, 3, 68, 100, 115; astride, 228–29; side-saddle, 228–29, 232
Hounslow Heath, 69
Houston, Hampshire, 138
Howard, Isabella, Countess of Carlisle, 188
Hudibras (Butler), 30, 63–65, 75, 76, 77
Hungerford, Wiltshire, 89, 138
hunting, 67, 99, 108, 184–85
Huntingtonshire, 97
Hurstpierpoint, Sussex, 74
Hyde Park, London, 85

Ireland, Irish competitors, 61, 74, 93, 97, 102, 167

jackass racing, 100, 105, 107, 111–12, 114, 116, 151
jackets. *See* clothing
James I (of England), 18, 21
jingling, 109, 259n11
Johnson, Dr. Samuel, 3–4, 42, 227–28, 242

Kent, 61, 93–95, 113, 117, 134, 135, 141, 150, 188–90
Kersal Moor, 60–61
Keswick, Cumberland, 114, 117
Kilmeston, Hampshire, 206
King, Billie Jean, 3
King's Book of Sports (Charles I, 1633), 18, 19, 62
King's Book of Sports (James I, 1618), 18

Kingsbury, Middlesex, 146
Knossos, Palace at, Crete, 11
Knutsford, Staffordshire, 146
Kusner, Hathy, 3

Lacadæmon, *See* Sparta
Lade, Lady Laetitia, 229
Lambeth Wells, 70, 74
Lancashire, 59–60, 85, 124, 176
law enforcement: bailiffs, 132–33; constables, 49–50, 91, 101, 122; courts, 121–22, 191, 213; magistrates, 114–15, 140, 157, 218; police office, 113; sheriffs, 110, 145–47. *See also* Bow Street Runners
Layerthorpe, Yorkshire, 145
Lee, Mrs. (proprietor of prize-fight venue), 216
Leeds, Yorkshire, 104, 147
Leicestershire, 195, 198, 207
Lennox, Sarah, Duchess of Richmond, 182–86, 183, 194
Lennox, Sarah (daughter of Duchess of Richmond), 188
Lilly Hoo, Hertfordshire, 74
Lincolnshire, 74, 146
Lindsay, Jean (Jane), Countess of Eglinton, 188
Little Crosby, Lancashire, 176
London, 61, 93, 99, 100, 102, 103, 104, 116, 124, 125, 126, 127, 129, 133, 134, 136, 139, 146, 161, 169, 171, 176, 181–86, 188, 198, 210–24, 238, 239
long-distance runners, 99, 241
long-distance walkers, 94–95, 99, 124–26, 133, 135, 242
Long Down, Sussex, 204
Long Marston, Yorkshire, 92, 159

Maiden Castle, Dorset, 159
Maidstone, Kent, 134, 135
Mall, the, London, 85, 89–90

manliness, 51, 109, 116, 148, 181, 191–92, 195, 206, 208–9
Mansfield, Nottinghamshire, 135, 146
March Common, Isle of Ely, 74
Marchwood, Hampshire, 198, 204
Margate, Kent, 153, 154
Margo, handball player, 15
married versus single matches: cricket, 198, 203–6, 207; curling, 179; running, 94
Mary Stuart (Queen of Scots), 17, 169, 228
massage. *See* rubbing
Masson, Mme, 174–76
Maypoles, 18, 55, 60
medical opinion, 2, 20–22
Merrie England, 61, 139, 155
Methodists, 30, 104, 115, 121, 124
Meynell, Alicia. *See* Thornton, Mrs.
Middlesex, 61, 74, 100, 115, 146, 195
midsummer day, 47, 115
Milford Green, Staffordshire, 132
Mill Green, Essex, 117
Misson, Henri, 63, 75
Moorfields, London, 82, 238
Morris dancing, 18, 104
Mortlake, Surrey, 121
Moulsey Hurst, Surrey, 198, 204
Mulberrry Down, Hampshire, 206

naked runners: female, 82–83, 121–22, 132, 237–38; male, 83–86
Nesbitt, Charles, 34, 35
Newcastle-upon-Tyne, 73–74, 83, 90, 103, 124, 132, 146
New Forest, 198, 206, 241
Newington Green, Middlesex, 198–99, 207, 208
Newmarket, 4, 68, 84, 227
Norfolk, 195, 207, 229, 240
Northamptonshire, 90
Nottinghamshire, 135, 146
nudity. *See* naked runners
Nyren, John, 189, 191

Oaks, the, Kent, 188–89, 192
Odsey, Hertfordshire, 74
officials' roles: clerk of the course, 36; committee, 138; "distance" official, 36; judges, 138
Old Wives Lees, 25, 41, 45–47, 51, 53–54, 148, 156
Olympia, 5–8, 11, 14, 42, 151
Olympic Games, 1–2, 11, 42, 81, 115–16, 151. *See also* Dover, Robert
organisers, 101; entrance official, 52; master of the ring, 29; stewards, 138: umpires, 48, 113, 114
Oxford, Oxfordshire, 73–74, 102, 112, 114, 138, 176

Pall Mall, London, 89
Parry, Joseph, 33, 153
Parsons, Nancy, 194
Parthenos/oi, 5–11, 247n4
Pausanias, 6–9, 13, 42
Pepys, Samuel, 55, 58–59, 63, 210
petticoats. *See* clothing
Piercy, Violet, 3
Pinkeys Green, Berkshire, 112–13, 153
Plaistow, Essex, 121–22, 237
Platter, Thomas, 66, 78
Pollnitz, Karl Ludwig von, 85
Pond, Miss, 3, 227
prison bars/prisoner's base, 47–49, 70, 86, 115
prize-fighters, 163–68; Mary Barker, 220; Sarah (Anne) Barret, 167, 220–23; Moll Buck, 223; Ann Field, 167, 217; Mary Garvin, 222; Joanna Heyfield, 212; Hannah Hyfield, 211; Elizabeth Stokes, 87, 164, 211–24; Mary Welch, 167, 215, 218; Elizabeth Wilkinson, 211–12
prize-fighting, 210, 211, 212–22, 223–25, 239
Puritanism (and anti-Puritanism), 43–44, 55, 60, 83

Queensferry, Scotland, 137

radicalism, 134, 139
Ranelagh Gardens, London, 146
Reform Bill (1832), 139
ribbons. *See* clothing
Richmond, Charles, Duke of, 89, 183–88, 196
Richmond, Sarah, Duchess of, 182–86, *183*, 194
Rogate, Sussex, 195–96
Romanization of Greek sport, 11
Rotherby, Leicestershire, 198
Rotherfield Peppard, Oxfordshire, 114
Rowlandson, Thomas, 32–33, 35, 63, 77–78, 142, 167–68, 200–202
Royal British Bowmen, 109
Royal Kentish Bowmen, 109
Royal Society, 19, 83
Royal Tennis Court, St. James's Street, Leicester Square, *170*, 170–71
Royal Toxophilite Society, 109
rubbing, 78, 87, 90, 257n37
running races: distances, 6–9, 45, 47, 52–53, 62, 70, 71, 82, 86–89, 90, 93, 118, 125–26, 130, 133–36, 143, 146, 150, 154–55, 242; entrance fees, 52, 91, 93; falling over, 22, 28, 32, 35, 82, 130–32, 160, 201; fatalities, 97; finances, 24, 44, 52, 73, 92; times reported of, 82, 84, 97, 117–19, 138

sack race, jumping in sacks, 36, 115
Sackville, John, 3rd Duke of Dorset, 188, 192
Sandbed, Dumfriesshire, 135
Saussure, César de, 81, 218–19
Scotland and Scottish competitors, 56, 94, 135, 137–38, 145, 179
Sevenoaks, Kent, 188, 194
Shakespeare, William, 17, 21; *As You Like It*, 21; *Henry IV Part II*, 21; *Love's Labour's Lost*, 21; *Romeo and Juliet*, 21; *The Winter's Tale*, 62

Sheldwich Lees, 41, 45–47
shoes. *See* barefooted; clothing
Shorncliffe, Kent, 113
Shropshire, 99, 121, 158
Sileby, Leicestershire, 207
single-stick. *See* cudgeling
Singleton, Sussex, 182–85, 186
skimmington ride, 4, 63, 72, 75–80, 152
skittles, 108
Sleaford, Lincolnshire, 74
Small, John, 197
smock: carried on a pole, 34, 64, 77, 152, 153; decorated with ribbons, 89, 115, 158; displayed overhead, 27, 34, 35, 36, 37, 241; Holland, 30, 33, 36, 36, 61, 70, 73, 82, 87, 89, 90, 93, 97, 101, 102, 112, 114, 116, 117, 121, *131*, 153, 160; lace, 71; laced, 28, 71, 153; linen, 112; ornamented, 158; as prize, 28, 30, 48, 61, 89, 92, 101, 115, 158; regional use of word, 61; trimmed, 112, 242; symbolic importance of, 65, 77–80, 116, 152, 154; as underwear, 61, 160; value of, 36, 51–52, 61, 69, 71–73, 82, 90, 92–93, 99, 102–3, 104, 153, 155–57
smock racing/running, attitudes to, 29–30, 34, 61, 69, 74, 92, 152
Snaefell, Isle of Man, 125
Sneinton, Nottinghamshire, 145–46
Snowdonia, Wales, 125
social class. *See* class
Somerset, 61, 96, 236–37
Somervile, William, *Hobinol*, 28–29, 33–35
Southampton, Hampshire, 208–9
Southwark, 69, 94, 211, 216, 242
Sparta, 9, 14, 81, 84, 200
Spilsby, Lincolnshire, 146
stade, 6–11, 42
stadium, 11, 41–42
Staffordshire, 82, 132, 146
St James's, London, 89, 94
St James's Park, London, 85, 90

Stanley, Elizabeth, Countess of Derby, 167, 188–89, 192, 194
Stephanoff, Philip Francis, 33, 78–79, 130–31, 142
Stepney, London, 82, 135
stockings. *See* clothing
Stockton, County Durham, 90, 92
Stockwell Green, Surrey, 112
Stoke Newington, Middlesex, 167, 217
Stokes, Elizabeth, 87, 164, 211–24
Stokes's Amphitheatre, 87, 214–24
stool-ball, 106–7, 176
Stowey, Somerset, 236–37
Stowmarket, Suffolk, 198
Suffolk, 110, 136, 166, 198
Sunderland, County Durham, 74
Surrey, 61, 70, 74, 103, 112, 114, 115, 121, 195, 198
Sussex, 74, 106–10, 122, 195, 204
Swansea, Wales, 176
sweats. *See* training
Switzer, Kathrine, 3
Syntax, Dr., 76–78

Tarleton, Banastre, 175
tennis, 169–76
Tenterden, Kent, 141
Thornton, Mrs. (Alicia), 229–33, 239–40, 271n9, 272n24
Thurston, John, 33, 35
Tissot, Samuel, 98
Tollesbury, Essex, 241
Tompkins, Edmund, 170–72
Tothill Fields, London, 153–54, 226, 238
Tottenham Court Road, London, 35, 113, 126
training, 99–100, 150
transvestite, 93
trousers. *See* clothing
Trussell, John, 43–44
Tynron, Dumfriesshire, 179

Uffenbach, Zacharias Conrad von, 73, 81, 210
Uffington, Oxfordshire, 115, 153
underwear, 101, 160, 236, 240
Upham, Hampshire, 203

vests. *See* clothing: waistcoats
Voltaire, 13–14, 81, 89

wagers: cricket, 166, 204; dancing, 59; prize-fighting, 216; riding, 227, 231–32; running, 69, 75, 82, 117, 126, 157, 161–62, 238; walking, 95, 103, 127, 133–34, 135–36
waistcoats. *See* clothing
Wales and Welsh competitors, 96, 103, 114, 125, 177
Walker, Anthony, 33
Walworth Common, 82, 239
Wandsworth, Surrey, 138
Wanstead Heath, 71
Wantage Down, Oxon, 69, 74
Ward, James, 77
Warwick, Warwickshire, 134
Watford, Hertfordshire, 114–15
"weaker vessel," 20–21
West Dean, Sussex, 182–86
Westminster, 41, 70, 103, 222, 238

Westmorland, 135
Whigs, 105–7, 121
Whitehaven, Cumberland, 167
Whitworth Moor, Lancashire, 85
Wilkes, John, 100–101
Willughby, Francis, 83, 179
William, Prince, Duke of Clarence, 105, 108–10
Wilson, George, 122–23, 132–33
Wiltshire, 195, 204
Wimbledon Common, 74
Winchester, Hampshire, 146, 148, 205
Windsor, Berkshire, 74, 93, 115, 146
Wisbech, Cambridgeshire, 146, 160
Woodstock Park, 69–70, 74, 84
Woolf, Virginia, 208
Wordsworth, Dorothy, 125–26
wrestling, 5, 7, 9, 62, 72, 73, 87, 109, 140
Wrotham, Kent, 117–19

Yattendon, Berkshire, 102
Yaxley, Cambridgeshire, 74
York, Yorkshire, 60, 92, 104, 124, 144, 146, 230–33

Zanerini, Giovanna (la Baccelli), 194

Peculiar Bodies: Stories and Histories

Melville's Other Lives: Bodies on Trial in "The Piazza Tales"
CHRISTOPHER STEN

Lame Captains and Left-Handed Admirals: Amputee Officers in Nelson's Navy
TERESA MICHALS

Beyond the Moulin Rouge: The Life and Legacy of La Goulue
WILL VISCONTI

Sapphic Crossings: Cross-Dressing Women in Eighteenth-Century British Literature
ULA LUKSZO KLEIN

Sight Correction: Vision and Blindness in Eighteenth-Century Britain
CHRIS MOUNSEY

www.ingramcontent.com/pod-product-compliance
Lightning Source LLC
Chambersburg PA
CBHW030609230426
43661CB00053B/1901